The Complete
Baseball Handbook

The Complete Baseball Handbook

Strategies and Techniques for Winning

WALTER ALSTON

and Don Weiskopf

Allyn and Bacon, Inc.
Boston • London • Sydney • Toronto

Library of Congress Catalog Card Number: 78–178185

ISBN: 0-205-03387-3

Seventh printing . . . February, 1976

Dedicated to the young baseball players of
America, including my grandson, Robin Ogle,
with the hope that the instruction and knowledge in this book will further their progress.

Contents

Foreword

WALTER F. O'MALLEY
Chairman of the Board,
Los Angeles Dodgers

I am delighted that Walt Alston has decided to put his vast knowledge of the game of baseball into printed form.

This is a book, expertly told and absorbingly written, which will interest youngsters and budding professional ballplayers for many generations to come.

One of the greatest charms of baseball is that, over the years, the game has not changed greatly. It is better played today than it was a century or a half century ago, and it will be better played a half century and a century in the future. But, the game will be basically the same in 2070 as it is today.

When Walt Alston talks of managerial strategy, playing techniques or the handling of professional ballplayers, he talks not only for the baseball buff of today but the stars, the managers and the fans of tomorrow.

Walt Alston's qualifications to author such a book need no recital by me. No manager in the game today has been associated with the same club for a longer period of years. If it were not for the rules which insist on formal contracts, Alston and the Dodgers could have worked over the years on a verbal agreement. When he emerged from the minors to pilot the Dodgers of 1954, the press and fans chorused: "Who?" They stopped asking the question the following year, when he managed the 1955 Dodgers to a come-from-behind seventh-game World Series win over the Yankees for the Dodgers' first World Championship.

He is the only man in baseball who has led teams to pennants on both the Atlantic and Pacific coasts. He has compiled a record which compares favorably with the achievements of the greatest managers of the game's history. He takes his place with John McGraw, Connie Mack, Joe McCarthy, Bill McKechnie and Casey Stengel, and other legendary leaders of baseball's past.

Managers are measured by their league pennants and World Series triumphs but those of us who are a little closer to the situation know that some of Walt's non-pennant years were among his best campaigns. Seasons given over to rebuilding brought out his ability to teach the game. When the Dodgers of 1962 lost a long lead and a play-off to the Giants, Walt Alston faced the press and assumed the blame. When triumphs, such as the 1963 four-game sweep of the New York Yankees, came his way, Walt humbly passed the credit to the men who had pitched and batted and fielded so brilliantly throughout the series. It was not won by the manager, he told the press.

I have enjoyed the many years Walt Alston has served as the manager of the Dodgers. I believe *he* has thoroughly enjoyed them too. It has been a relationship of accord unique in our highly competitive game.

I wouldn't know how to get into an argument with Walt Alston, but then I am not an umpire!

WALTER F. O'MALLEY
Chairman of the Board,
Los Angeles Dodgers

Acknowledgments

To the many major league players for their excellent demonstrations of the basic techniques of baseball and their candid commentary on how they play their positions.

Special thanks should go to Pete Rose and Tom Seaver, whose question-answer dialogues appear in the batting and pitching chapters, respectively, and to the following managers, coaches, scouts and players who made significant contributions: Ted Williams, Wally Moses, Henry Aaron, Maury Wills, Sandy Koufax, Jim Brewer, Jeff Torborg, Tom Haller, Bill Singer, Johnny Bench, Jim LeFebvre, Wes Parker, Ron Perranoski, Billy Grabarkewitz, Manny Mota, Glenn Beckert, Don Kessinger, Bob Barton, Nelson Briles, Don Money, Bobby Knoop, Jim Fregosi, Jim Northrup, Brooks Robinson, Bill Mazeroski, Bill Russell, Bill Avila, Willie Mays, John Vukovich and many others.

To the members of my coaching staff: Red Adams, Danny Ozark, Jim Gilliam, Roy Hartsfield and Dixie Walker, for the instructional contributions they made in the writing of the book.

To Walter F. O'Malley, chairman of the Dodgers' Board of Directors, for writing the Foreword to this text and with whom I have had a long and satisfying association; his son, Peter O'Malley, president of the Dodgers; Al Campanis, Director of Player Personnel; and Buzzy Bavasi, former general manager of the Dodgers.

To Arthur E. "Red" Patterson, vice-president, Public Relations, and his assistant, Fred Claire, for their valuable and generous assistance in support of this publication.

To Bowie Kuhn, commissioner of baseball; Charles S. Feeney, president of the National League; and Joseph E. Cronin, president of the American League, for their cooperation in behalf of the book.

To C. C. Johnson Spink, publisher of *The Sporting News,* for permission to reproduce the numbering system in scoring; and Peter J. McGovern, president of Little League Baseball, Inc., for the layouts of the Little League baseball field and the regulation size diamond.

To Lela, my wife, and to Emmons and Lenora Alston, my parents; my in-laws, daughter Doris and her husband Harry Ogle; my sister Dorothy (Mrs. Kenneth Tolley) and my grandchildren, Robin and Kimberly, all of whom have been a source of inspiration down through the years.

To Johnny Mauer, my old basketball coach at Miami University, perhaps the greatest influence on my life in athletics.

To the many coaches across the nation who made important contributions to the organization chapters on the college, high school and youth league levels, particularly Bobby Winkles, Arizona State University; Pete Beiden, Fresno State College; Dr. Calvin Boyes, Sacramento State College; and Jim Enos, Bella Vista High School (Sacramento); to Dr. Arthur A. Esslinger, member of the Board of Directors, Little League Baseball, Inc.; and Brent Marchetti, Director of Recreation and Parks, City of Yuma, Arizona, and his staff.

To Bill Buhler, head trainer of the Dodgers; Dr. Robert Bauman, head trainer, St. Louis Cardinals; E. E. Holkesvick, president, Exer-Genie, Inc., and Wayne Hironaka, American Physical Fitness Institute, for their authoritative assistance in the conditioning chapter.

To John Griffith, publisher of *Athletic Journal,* for the use of his sequence-speed camera, and to contributing photographers: to Sam Houston, Don Hale, Don Ploke and Fred Kaplan.

Some of the game action photographs used in this book are reproduced by courtesy of the Associated Press, *Los Angeles Times, Los Angeles Herald-Examiner* and the Los Angeles Dodgers.

To Mrs. Annegrete Weiskopf, for her long hours of dedicated service in typing the lengthy manuscript and handling a variety of important assignments; to Dave Drennan, whose outstanding printing work in the photo lab was responsible for many of the photos; and to Ray Morrison for his clerical assistance.

Sincere thanks to Russell Mead for his fine editorial work, to Wayne Barcomb, director of the college division, and to the entire production staff of Allyn and Bacon, Inc. Without their close cooperation, this publication could not be the book it is.

And to my good friend Don Weiskopf of Sacramento for his excellent assistance in planning, writing and editing this publication. Don is the author of many books and articles on sports and was responsible for taking the majority of the photographs in this book.

WALTER ALSTON
Oxford, Ohio

The Complete
Baseball Handbook

Batting /1/

For a long time, I have felt that too many hitters were swinging for the fences. I based this assumption on the fact that pitchers today are better coached than ever before and possess better control. In addition, they have come up with a half-dozen different pitches. They throw a couple of different speeds on their curve ball, and they throw sliders. They turn the ball over on the sinker, screwball or the change of pace. And they have a couple of speeds on the fast ball.

Hitting, therefore, becomes an element of timing. The longer the swing, the longer the stride, the harder it is to time the pitch. True, the Mayses, Aarons and Mantles are blessed with exceptional talent. They will always hit with power. They have the knack of good timing, even with their full swing. These players will consistently get their quota of base hits, but how about the average hitter?

For the average ballplayer, though, the fellow who has trouble hitting .270 or .280, to combat this kind of pitching, he should: 1) shorten the stride, and 2) shorten the stroke. A good, quick swing is the secret to good hitting. By shortening the stride and stroke of the bat, he can compensate for the off-speed pitches and get better contact and better wood on the ball than he can if he wraps the bat around his head and takes a long swing and a long lunging stride.

Effective Hitting

The basic point a hitter must concentrate on most is *contact*. More than anything else, he must put the bat on the ball. Once a pitcher has two strikes on the hitter, it is time to adjust and concentrate on mak-

> *Be quick with the hands. Get that bat moving fast once you decide to pull the trigger.*
> TED WILLIAMS

ing contact. This might mean changing the position of the feet or the grip on the bat.

The good hitter is the one who is aggressive (Fig. 1–2). I like to see a batter up at the plate who will attack the ball, one who is always going into the ball. I am not saying that he should lunge into the ball. Rather, I prefer him to take a casual stride into the pitch. I speak of a casual stride simply because a casual stride allows him to keep his body back. If his body gets out in front too fast, he will have a difficult time adjusting to the pitch. Consequently, he will lose power in his swing. He will begin to get "fisted," or he will hit the ball on the end of the bat. A casual stride will allow him to glide into the swing, resulting in a smooth stride, rather than jump into it.

Fig. 1–2. AN AGGRESSIVE HITTER is able to get his bat out in front quickly and hit the ball with authority.

A hitter should try to hit the ball where it is pitched. If it is outside, go to the opposite field, and if it is inside, pull it to your power field.
STAN MUSIAL

A lot of hitters in baseball are uppercut swingers, and they wonder why they hit so many fly balls. Now, for the fellow who has the home run power, the ability to consistently drive the ball out of the park, this swing is all right on low pitches. But, if he happens to be one of those fellows who will not hit one out of 20 right on the button, then percentage-wise, he is defeating himself. Therefore, a hitter must be knowledgeable enough to know what his capabilities are and what he should not do.

Quickness with the hands and wrists is a most important phase of hitting. The ability to be quick with the hands, wrists and arms will determine just how good a hitter he is going to be. If a hitter can learn how to be fast with his hands and wrists, he will be able to wait longer for the pitch.

How can a hitter become quicker with his hands and his wrists? To get more bat speed, he has to develop more strength. While push-ups, squeezing balls and chin-ups are all good exercises, I think the best way of all is for a hitter to get a bat eight or ten ounces heavier than the one he uses in the game and swing it—and keep on swinging it!

Then, there are hitting authorities such as Ted Williams who say that, "It's in the hips! You have to put your hips into it."

By letting the front hip open up, the hitter will gain more room for his hands to come through, particularly for the tight pitch. In so doing, he will transfer his weight forward. This is what he wants—like the golfer who transfers his weight.

Lately, there has been a tendency for the hitter to go back to a heavier bat with a thicker handle, and maybe choke up on it—especially the average hitters we are talking about. Five or six years ago, I favored the thin-handled, whip-like bat, one which was longer and lighter, but today I favor a little shorter bat with better wood. With a little heavier bat, a hitter is more likely to get some wood on the ball, even if he gets jammed on the fists (Fig. 1–3).

The only way to become a good hitter is to swing the bat constantly, not just when taking the few swings in batting practice. It is the desire to hit and the willingness to practice that makes the great hitters. While not every boy can become a great hitter, every player can improve through instruction and practice.

Perhaps the two most important rules in batting are *keeping the bat level*—a level swing, and *timing*—hitting the ball where it is pitched. Successful hitting involves hitting outside pitches to the opposite

A level swing provides the greatest hitting arc—to hit the ball where it is pitched.
HARRY WALKER

Fig. 1–3. GRIP OF THE BAT. While many good hitters, such as Billy Williams (left), prefer holding the bat down at the end, batting champions like Matty Alou (right) find they have greater bat control choking up on the bat a few inches. The bottom hand is firm, while the top hand is loose.

field. Inside pitches, of course, should be pulled. Only constant work at the plate, swinging at every type of pitch, will give a hitter timing.

What is the proper swing? Perhaps the most discussed topic on hitting is the proper hitting swing, particularly the correct hitting arc. For years, the majority of baseball authorities, among them such former hitters as Stan Musial, Rogers Hornsby and Ernie Banks, stressed the importance of the level swing. Of course, this theory is still dominant among batting instructors today.

However, there are a growing number of hitting instructors who are now emphasizing the "slightly downward swing," the chop swing in which the hitter shortens up and swings down slightly. Matty Alou, Tony Oliva and Maury Wills are among the hitters who have found this type of swing effective for them (Fig. 1–9).

"The reason why we tell our hitters to swing down slightly," says Dick Sisler, former batting coach of the St. Louis Cardinals, "is to more or less go to the extreme to make them level off. I think that if a hitter will level off on a high pitch, he will hit the ball on a line more."

Then, there is Ted Williams, who prefers to stress "the slightly upward swing." Ted, who was one of the game's truly great hitters with the Boston Red Sox, believes that "a hitter can generate more power this way than he can swinging down on the pitch."

The type of swing depends on the hitter himself and, of course, where the ball is pitched. Each hitter must develop his own style to meet his physical abilities, such as power and speed. On the low ball, the batter has to come up; otherwise, he will hit the ball on the ground. On the high pitch, he has to take a slightly downward stroke at the ball.

Most home run hitters have a slight uppercut, which is all right for a player with good power; but for the majority of hitters, I stress the level swing and have them put more weight forward to prevent uppercutting.

Spray hitters, those who hit to all fields, should use a heavier bat, choke up and try to make contact. They will find that the ball will come off the bat more sharply than if they use a lighter bat.

Generally, I like to see our hitters stress line drives at all times. True, a batter will hit a percentage of the balls on the ground, and he will hit a percentage of fly balls. However, by concentrating on going to the line drive, I feel that he is more apt to make good contact consistently.

Select a bat you can control

The weight of the bat is very important. Each player must decide for himself what type of bat is right for him. He should find one that feels good in his hands, neither too heavy nor too light. The bat has to feel comfortable to *him*.

There is no certain size bat for any particular individual. A coach should fit the bat to the individual, taking into consideration the size of his hands and his physical abilities. It should be more or less a feel. A hitter should pick up a bat and balance it and determine whether he likes the feel of the handle, whether or not it feels good in his hands. Its weight should also be considered.

"A hitter should use a heavier bat with a thicker handle," advised Joe DiMaggio. "The more wood, the more chance he has of hitting the ball. I used a heavier bat because I thought I could control it better."

"When the bat is a little too light, though, a hitter is bound to overswing," continued Joe. "When I used a bat that was too light, I had a tendency to swing too hard."

Many hitters have found success with the lighter and thinner bats, with the weight out on the hitting area. The idea behind this is to swing the bat faster and more quickly, thus getting more velocity into the swing.

College and professional hitters generally use 34–36-inch bats, while in ounces, they normally employ bats from 32 to 36 ounces. On the high school level, most hitters use 32–36-inch bats, 30 to 36 ounces in weight. Little Leaguers generally prefer bats 29 to 33 inches in length and 28 to 30 ounces in weight.

For the majority of hitters, a heavier bat choked up for balance is more effective than a light bat swung from the end.

Assume a comfortable stance

A player should move his feet around until he finds a stance that feels good. The best stance is the most comfortable one. The feet are spread enough to be comfortable and on balance. Above all, the batter must be on balance at all times while in the box (Fig. 1–4).

Basically, I like to start a young hitter out with both of his feet even, not closed, not open, and we adjust from there. The most balanced position is one with the feet shoulder-width apart, with the front foot turned a little toward the pitcher. The weight is distributed equally on the balls of the feet.

The head must be stationary and fairly still. It has to move a little, but very little. It is like a good golf swing. Both eyes should be facing the pitcher and the ball. A hitter should move his eyes to watch the ball, *but never move his head.*

The hips and shoulders must be kept *level,* with the front hip and shoulder pointing at the pitcher. If a player maintains level hips and shoulders while swinging, he will very likely take a level swing, keeping his hands about chest-high and above the toes of his rear foot. He should tuck the chin in close to the front shoulder to keep his head from pulling away as he swings. Some hitters believe they see the ball better when they keep their eyes level as they watch the ball.

The hitter should assume a slight bend in the knees. This will help him to relax. He must keep his hips under him. If his hips and butt stick out too far, he will be on his heels, rather than the balls of the feet. He can move more quickly and maintain better control of his body if he starts in a relaxed position, rather than a tense one. I do not like to see hitters bent over too much. This is what makes them stiff.

If they are a little slow with the bat, maybe they should open up. If they cannot handle the outside pitch, many hitters hit from a closed stance and get closer to the plate. Then, they pull away as the pitch is on its way. Again, it comes down to the individual involved.

A closed stance is effective against pitchers who throw a lot of breaking pitches. This enables a hitter to hang in there a little better. I find no fault with the closed stance if the hitter can get his hips out of the way. The original stance is not that important—how the batter finishes is what counts.

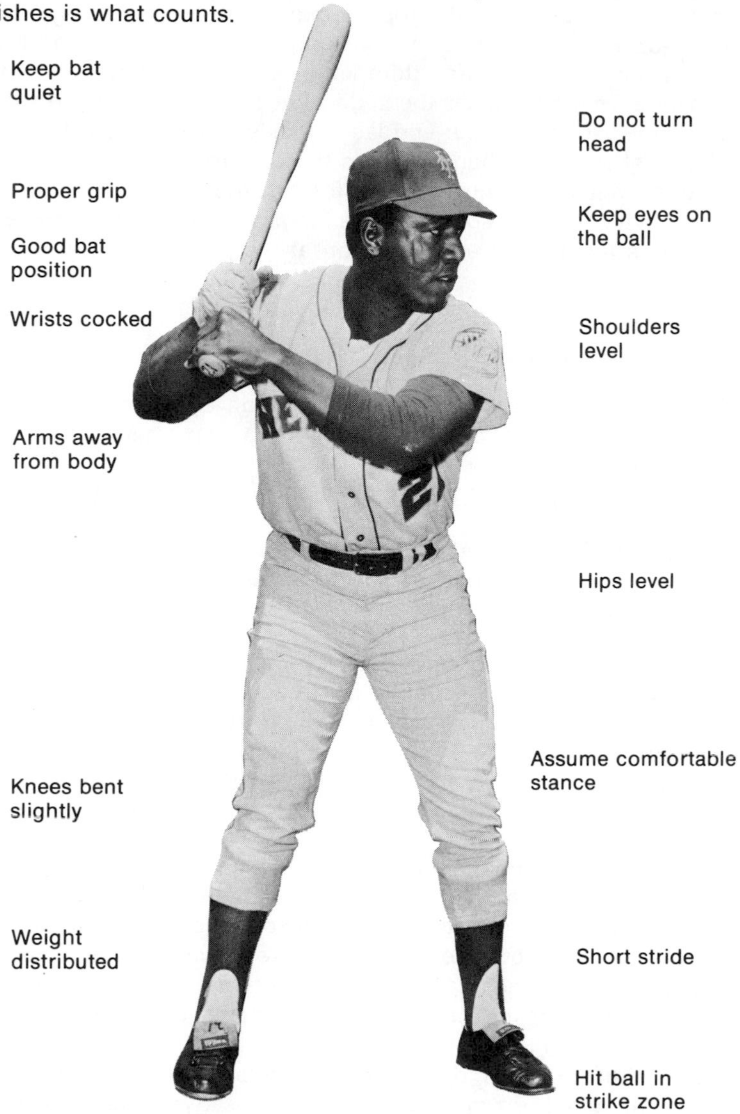

Keep bat
quiet

Do not turn
head

Proper grip

Keep eyes on
the ball

Good bat
position

Wrists cocked

Shoulders
level

Arms away
from body

Hips level

Knees bent
slightly

Assume comfortable
stance

Weight
distributed

Short stride

Hit ball in
strike zone

Fig. 1–4. THE CORRECT POSITION AND STANCE AT HOME PLATE (Cleon Jones).

"I had an open stance," said Wally Moses, one of baseball's finest hitting coaches, "but when I would stride, I closed it up. We all have to close our stances when we start our swing, with the bat back. Hitters swing from pretty close to the same place as they begin their swings."

Grip The grip of the batter should be comfortable and firm but not tense and tight. The hitter should grip the bat where he can swing it best (Fig. 1–3). He can do this by "shaking hands" with the bat. Most hitters align the second and third knuckles with a flat surface of the two hands. This grip places the middle knuckle of the top hand somewhere between the middle and last knuckle of the bottom hand for better wrist snap. The hands should be close together.

A loose, relaxed grip is essential for quickness and power. A tight grip has a tendency to tighten up the forearm muscles and the biceps.

While assuming a relaxed position at the plate, the hitter should have:

a firm grip with his bottom hand

a loose grip with his top hand.

Then, as he throws the bat at the ball on the swing, he should tighten up his grip. So, he must remember to relax until he is ready to actually swing. He keeps his grip loose, but as he starts swinging, the hands and wrists should tighten, providing maximum power at the right time.

A hitter will find his bat is better balanced if he chokes up a little. By choking up on the bat, he will have better control of the bat—and a higher batting average.

Holding the hands The hitter should hold his bat in the "ready" position which is comfortable to him. I urge my players to hold their hands about chest-high because that is where the high pitch is going to be. If the ball is above their hands, they are urged to take it. If it is below their hands, they should "jump" on it. This gives a young player a better idea of the strike zone.

Most hitters will hold their hands approximately letter-high, and just slightly in back of their back leg. True, there are hitters like Carl Yastrzemski and Brooks Robinson who keep their hands quite high, higher than usual, but they have to come down to swing. When a player places his hands up high, he is not perfectly relaxed. He cannot be. However, as the ball approaches the plate he moves his hands to the proper position.

Many hitters like to hold the bat at an angle about halfway between an upright and horizontal position. The disadvantage of using a strictly upright bat is that the swing has to be made in a big circle before the hitter can bring the power end of the bat into the same plane as the ball.

How the bat should be held depends on the hitter. What I do not like to see, though, is a hitter wrapping it around his head and back toward the pitcher—the bat has to come all the way around and flatten out before it makes contact. This is a long swing and a long stroke, and unquestionably can take something away from the timing.

Before the start of the swing, I like to see a little movement of the hands, rather than see them kept dead still. I call it a little "cocking" action, with the hands coming up just slightly. As the batter gets ready for the pitch, the hands move slightly up, rather than down and then up.

By holding the bat straight up or slightly toward the pitcher, the hitter will have a longer stroke but a hard throwing pitcher might be able to get his fast ball past him, especially when it is inside and high. Thus, the batsman may have to adjust into a flatter position, although this will give him a shorter distance to bring the bat into the plane of the ball. He can wait a little longer, but he will give up some power.

The most common fault of hitters is to commit their stride too soon. As a result, off-speed pitches cause timing problems. I would urge them to wait awhile longer on their stride but to be quick with their hands. With proper timing, they can handle the pitch with the fat part of the bat, and they will have a good line shot.

Position in the box

The majority of hitters prefer a position somewhere even with the plate, and they can adjust from there. By being even with the plate, the hitter has only to cover balls that are coming over the plate— right at the plate, where he is going to hit them.

Some fellows think it is better to stand in the back of the box, giving them more time to look at the pitch. One disadvantage, however, in being in the extreme end of the box is that breaking stuff will break even bigger back there. In other words, the ball gets the full sweep of its break toward the plate there. The farther away a hitter stands from the plate on a curve ball, the bigger break he has to take care of while covering the plate.

"Many of the major league hitters hit from the back of the box, close to the catcher," observed Moses. "I like a hitter who is more even with the plate."

"I think the hitter is better off hitting a curve ball as it is breaking in, rather than after it breaks. Therefore, the sooner he can catch it, the better off he will be, before it breaks bigger," said Johnny Sain, a great pitching coach and exponent of the breaking ball.

"Most of the young hitters have a tendency to crowd the plate," according to Williams. "That, to me, is the hardest way of all to hit. If I crowd the plate, my hands and arms extend over to the inside corner of the plate, and in order for me to hit it, I have to get my bat out well in front of the plate. Because I am so close to the plate, I have to hit the ball well out in front of the plate, allowing me less time to hit the ball squarely on the meat of the bat. In short, I am hitting the ball roughly at $58\frac{1}{2}$ feet from the pitcher's mound."

"Now, in order to become a good hitter, the quicker you can be, the more time you give yourself," continued Williams. "So, in order to get more time and be fooled less, simply move away from the plate, approximately 10 inches to a foot. With my hands in the same position, and with this position in the box, I don't have to worry about that inside pitch anymore, because I am not crowding the plate. Therefore, now, I will be able to hit the ball over the plate again.

"By moving away from the plate, I have now lost some length of stroke and a little power. So, in order to increase your length of stroke and have sufficient power and still keep my position in the box, all I have to do is to turn around a little bit and assume a more closed stance.

"Now, I have the same length of stroke which is a full swing, and I am hitting the ball 60 feet from the pitcher, but there is one very important other thing that I have gained. I will be hitting the ball at right angles in the similar direction the ball is pitched on."

"So, don't crowd the plate," says Ted. "Turn toward the pitcher with your front shoulder down and in. Step toward the pitcher so that your momentum and weight is going right back toward the pitcher. This enables you to keep your head down so that you are looking at the pitch all the time."

"When you get too close to the plate," says Williams, "you have a tendency to open up—because you know you have to be quick. You know you have to be quick so you start throwing your head out. You start committing yourself too soon. You are not waiting like you should."

Of course, a hitter has to be close enough to the plate to control the outside part of the plate. He must be close enough to hit any ball that is over the plate. By touching the outside corner with his bat, the batter can tell whether he is close enough to the plate. Batters who do not have adequate plate coverage are vulnerable to the pitch on the outside corner.

For a sinker ball pitcher, who tries to make a hitter top the ball, by moving up toward the pitcher, the hitter has a tendency to catch the ball a little before it makes its complete break and goes down.

If he stands around the top of the plate, he probably will stride toward the pitcher, even open up a little and still cover the whole plate. If he stands back away from the plate, he must stride so that he can control the outside corner of the entire plate. The important points about any stance is that *the hitter must have full coverage of the plate,* and *the stance and stride must go together.*

Know the strike zone   An important aspect of hitting is knowledge of the strike zone. A baseball, thrown with great speed and plenty of stuff on it, is tough enough to hit even when it is in the strike zone. When the hitter makes the mistake of going after bad pitches, out of the strike zone, he makes his job much more difficult. The strike zone is a pitch that covers the width of the plate, above the knees, and slightly under the armpits.

"The more critical you are in learning the strike zone," asserted Williams, "the easier it will be for you to develop into a good hitter. This is because you will be hitting more times when ahead of the pitcher. You will have him more in the hole, rather than yourself."

"When you start hitting balls two or three inches outside, two or three inches inside, and two or three inches high," he continued, "you will find that you will increase your strike zone for the pitcher to shoot at. You are going to find that you will have more difficulty getting good balls to hit."

Wait on the pitch

The good hitter is a waiter. He gets that last, extra look. The better he is at watching the pitch as it comes toward him, the longer he can wait before swinging. Hitters with good wrists and hands can wait until the last split-second and then whip the bat forward with power as well as authority.

Patience is one of the best qualities a hitter can have. In order to hit the ball well, a hitter must wait until it gets to the plate and then rip into it. *Take a real good look at the pitch, and then hit it!*

The hitter should try to keep from watching the body motion or eccentric moves by pitchers. If he follows their pumps or motions too much, he may get attracted to something else other than the ball, such as a high leg kick or a jerky shoulder movement.

To be a good waiter, the hitter must have quick reflexes, quick hands and wrists, excellent eye and muscle coordination.

The Hitting Swing

A level, natural swing is the quality possessed by all batting champions. The young hitter, particularly, should just go for the line drive and let the home runs take care of themselves. He should always try to meet the ball solidly, and not try to overswing (Fig. 1–7).

By making good contact, a batter always has a chance for a hit. The shorter and more compact the swing is, the better chance a hitter has for contact. This is the secret of hitting.

There are many theories, past and present, as to what is the proper hitting swing. Every batting instructor has his own approach to hitting technique. Perhaps the most widely used principle is "Take a level, natural swing," and top batters at all levels of play have been using this principle with great success from the time baseball began.

Indeed, the success of such big league batting champions as Stan Musial, Ted Williams, Henry Aaron, Pete Rose and Tony Oliva can be attributed to a level, free swing (Fig. 1–5).

The good swing is as nearly level as it can possibly be. Naturally, the type of swing depends on where the ball is pitched. On the low pitch the hitter does come up on his swing. He has to come up. In

Throwing a fast ball by Henry Aaron is like trying to sneak the sun by a rooster.
                                                            CURT SIMMONS

Fig. 1–5. A CLASSIC SWING. Henry Aaron demonstrates one of the greatest batting swings in the history of baseball. Aaron's quick hands and wrists enable him to hit the ball out in front of the plate. He prefers a short stride because it keeps his body balanced and gives him split-second timing.

fact, most hitters uppercut slightly. It is perfectly natural to swing up on a low pitch. However, if he uppercuts pitches across his letters or high pitches, he will have a lot of trouble. These are the pitches he must swing slightly down on, particularly with a hard infield and if the hitter has good speed afoot. It is somewhat of a chopping swing.

"It is not just one part of the swing that enables the batter to hit the ball with authority," observed Harmon Killebrew, one of baseball's finest hitters. "It is everything! You have to put everything together—the shoulders and arms, the hips, and the wrists and hands." (Fig. 1–14)

The secret is to put it all together, to coordinate all the parts of the hitting swing into perfect unison, which requires perfect timing. *Timing is the key to the hitting game.*

On the low pitch, the hitter must bend his knees a little to get down after the ball. This gets his whole body down and his bat has to get down on that angle.

As the hitting swing starts, the weight is shifted from the back foot and ends on the front foot after contact.

The hitter must not bend his rear leg too much, or he will have a tendency to uppercut. Of course, when hitting a curve ball he has to

Fig. 1–5. (Continued) "Just concentrate on hitting the ball where it is pitched," says Aaron. "If you hit it good, it'll go. So, just meet it squarely. If it is outside, hit it to right field (right-handed batter). Don't try to pull an outside pitch!"

bend his knees slightly. If he is too stiff in the legs, he will definitely have curve ball problems.

The front shoulder has a tendency to affect the hitter a good deal. Too many hitters let their front shoulder pull out just a fraction too early. This causes them to pull their body away just enough to get the ball on the end of the bat rather than on the good part of it. Of course, the shoulder has to give eventually if it is going to go around, but if the hitter makes that move just a fraction too early, he will draw the bat away from the ball. Again, the hitter should tuck his chin in close to the front shoulder to keep the shoulder from pulling out too early.

The head of the bat should be whipped or snapped into the plane of the baseball. Keeping his arms away from him, the hitter should have both of his arms extended as he hits and completes his follow-through on the ball. He should meet the ball squarely in front of the plate.

Whip the bat

As he swings his bat, he pushes off with his rear foot so his hips will come around against a firm front stride. The ball is met with the power end of the bat, in front of the plate, just before he breaks his wrists.

Above all, *the batter should not swing too hard!* If he does, he will

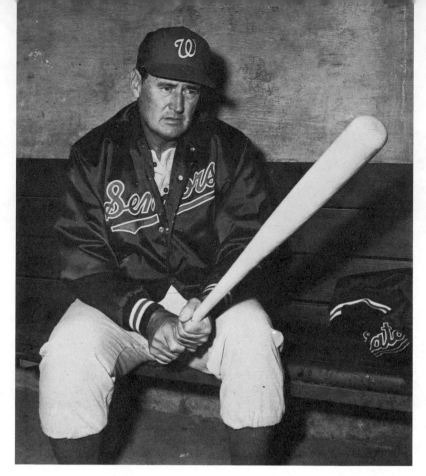

Fig. 1–6. A GOOD GRIP. "Pick up the bat as you would an axe," says Ted Williams, member of baseball's Hall of Fame. "Form a simple 'V' off the handle and make sure you have good feel in your fingers."

very likely pull his front shoulder away; and since the head and eyes are connected to the shoulders, they, too, will be pulled out of focus. When his head goes out, his front shoulder usually goes out with it. All this excess power will cause lunging and overstriding. Off-speed pitches, in particular, will have the hitter in serious trouble.

Keep a strong front arm

A hitter has to use his front arm correctly. The front arm more or less guides his swing, and then the top hand does a little snapping. Unfortunately, many hitters fail to use the front arm properly, one reason being that they are weak in the triceps muscle, which is responsible for "whipping the front arm out." Therefore, a hitter must build up those muscles which will give him this bat speed: the muscles in the back of the arm. The triceps muscle is the one he should build up. This is the arm which throws the bat out at the ball (Fig. 1–14).

Unfortunately, quite a few hitters get their top hand in too quickly and begin rolling their wrist when the ball is fairly even with them. Some batters use their top hand too much but fail to use the front arm enough of the time.

A hitter should hit the ball before he breaks his wrists. When he swings the bat, the head of his bat is what turns his wrist over. He, himself, does not actually turn them over; the bat does it.

Henry Aaron, one of baseball's greatest hitters, actually "throws the head of the bat into the ball." (Fig. 1–5) When he hits the ball, it really jumps. *He does not swing the bat. He "throws the bat"!*

The really good hitters have the knack of getting the fat part of the bat on the ball. They are able to whip the big end of the bat with explosive drive.

The quick bat

Roberto Clemente, of the Pittsburgh Pirates, is a prime example of a quick bat. Even if the ball is outside, he "pops those wrists" and reaches out and gets the fat part of the bat on the ball. A lot of hitters would hit the ball on the end of the bat.

If the ball is a little inside, the hands come across in front of the body, in order to drag the bat across to get the fat part on it. The arms are extended more on the outside pitch.

The Dodgers have always placed considerable emphasis on using a variety of methods to move the runners around. We insist on a lot of little fundamentals, such as hitting the ball to the opposite field, hitting the ball where it is pitched and the hit and run. I like to see the ball hit to all fields. This is why we devote so much time to these fundamentals during spring training.

Dodger Hitting Styles

Through the years, the Dodgers have had many types of outstanding hitters, each of whom had his own individual abilities and qualities. For versatility and all-round prowess at the plate, I will always remember the fine hitters we had on the 1956 and 1959 pennant winners, such as Carl Furillo, Duke Snider, Wally Moon, Junior Gilliam and Gil Hodges.

Basically a high ball hitter, Furillo was good at swinging down on the ball, rather than trying to uppercut the high pitch. Carl was a better high ball hitter than he was a low ball hitter, and he could go to the opposite field with the best of them.

Moon would swing up slightly on the low pitch. He was a fellow who could adapt himself to any ball park. When we moved into the Coliseum, Wally was one of the few players who took advantage of our short left field screen. Although he was a left-handed hitter, Moon would go for the inside pitch and hit it to left field.

Essentially, Snider was a pull hitter, although he could and did hit long balls to left and right center field. They were his power alleys. Duke was a natural hitter. He did not have to worry too much about any faults. When he first came up, though, he had trouble with his strike zone, but through experience he became much better. Snider was an aggressive hitter. He had the power and the good swing.

Never a power hitter, Gilliam was smart enough to know that he could not hit the ball out of the park. So, Jimmy went for the finer points of making contact and hitting the ball where it was pitched and advancing base runners.

With a runner on second and nobody out, I would rather see Gilliam up at the plate than anybody I had. I knew that somehow he would get this man to third base. Jim could really handle the bat and was able to move the ball around. If the third baseman played too

| D | C | B | A |

Fig. 1–7. LINE DRIVE HITTER WITH POWER. Like Henry Aaron, the level hitting swing of Tony Oliva provides a potent combination of line drives with power.

deep at third base, he would lay a bunt down the third base line. Gilliam was one of the smartest players in game situations that I ever managed—and he was very difficult to strike out.

Swinging down on the ball

To obtain a level swing, more hitters are using a theory popularized by Joe Gordon, former great second baseman and manager: the technique of "tommyhawking" the ball—swinging slightly down on the ball. Joe believes that hitters who have a tendency to loft high flies do so because they uppercut the ball. To compensate, Joe insists that they chop down on the high pitch. This lowers the front shoulder and results in a level swing.

The hitter should keep his top hand on top so his wrist will not be below the front wrist at the point of contact. He should then follow-through on his swing by breaking his top wrist over the front wrist.

When the hitter is swinging down at the ball, what he is trying to do is to keep the head of the bat above the ball at all times. Basically, it makes him a line drive hitter.

Maury Wills, like Matty and Jesus Alou, has a tendency to swing down on the ball. These hitters know that if they hit a ball on the ground, they have a pretty good chance of getting on base. They try to give the swing a little more top hand (Fig. 1–9).

"Most of the good hitters in baseball swing slightly down and into the high pitch," stated Gordon, "and down and then up on the low pitch, picking it up, as would be done in tennis. In fact, hitting the high pitch is like a tennis serve," continued the former Yankee second baseman. "The racket comes down into the ball. On a high pitch, the bat should be swung overhand and into the pitch. On contact, the batter must throw the top hand over, or he will finish uppercutting the ball. The correct stroke is just slightly downward, like a tennis backhand."

When coaches advise a hitter to come down on the pitch, they are speaking mostly about the letter-high pitch. There is a tendency to pop up the high pitch. By hitting down on the ball, he is less likely to pop up on it.

"The reason why we tell our hitters to do this," explained Sisler, "is to more or less go to the extreme to make them level off. I think that if a hitter will level off on a high pitch, he will hit the ball on a line more. Naturally, he cannot uppercut the high pitch."

"When I came out of the American League into the National League," said Dixie Walker, our batting instructor with the Dodgers, "I was a dead low ball hitter, and I had a difficult time hitting anything around the letters. As the pitch was made, I would take a long stride and drop down beneath the ball and come up on it. I found myself hitting a lot of fly balls if I hit it at all.

"So, I worked on this problem during pepper games, and I had my teammates pitch me high. I found that by standing more upright and as the pitch was thrown and I realized that it was high, I would raise my arms and get it coming down more. I was able to get the flight of the bat down more on a flat trajectory. After a while, I learned to hit the high pitch, and today, I still teach this technique."

Harry Walker, Dixie's brother, who has gained considerable success as a batting coach in addition to his managerial role, put it this way: "It is not so much teaching a hitter to swing down. Rather, you just try to keep him from uppercutting the ball. You try to give the bat and the ball a chance to meet."

"If you are uppercutting the ball, you have a tendency to pop it up or miss it," advised Walker. "Whereas if the bat is level, you will start with a downstroke and level off before you get into the hitting area. This means that you keep the bat level for about two feet, a foot and a half to two feet, in a swing that you will be able to give the bat a chance to make contact. When you are uppercutting the ball too much, then the bat and the ball have a very small area to make contact and hit it solidly."

"I never liked to swing actually down," said Gilliam. "Of course, if the ball is letter-high, you have to swing down, but it's more of a level, downward swing, not a chopping swing."

Taking a rather short stride

I like the short stride because it keeps the hitter's body balanced and enables him to have split-second timing. In addition, the short stride allows him to check a swing if the pitch is bad (Fig. 1–5).

The player who takes a short step controls his forward motion. He is not only properly balanced, but he is able to focus his eyes better on the ball. He can wait longer on the ball, and then he can adjust to the pitch.

The purpose of the stride is to force and keep the weight on the rear foot until the swing is started. The body weight must never be ahead of the swing. Motion pictures show that a batter hits the ball a slight fraction of a second after the stride.

We find that batters who stride longer are getting ready too quickly; this causes them to become lunge hitters. Usually, the player who takes a long stride is a lunge hitter. Consequently, he goes out too quickly to meet the ball, and the only thing he is using to hit is his arms. Essentially, if he can stay back and wait and take a short stride, he will have the compact swing necessary for successful hitting.

I have always advocated a shorter stride, but I do not think there is much we can do with the overstriders. Willie Mays and other outstanding hitters overstride, but it should be noticed that when their front foot moves forward, the rear foot and body weight stay back. They do not take these with them, which would take away their entire swing and command of the bat.

If a player finds he has to overstride and cannot cut his stride down, he should try to hold his bat back until the pitcher gets the ball on the way. If he does not commit his bat with his front foot, he can take a big stride, as long as he does not start his bat with his foot.

The hitter who takes a long stride and tends to uppercut the ball should be encouraged to drag his back foot to shove his weight forward to keep his stroke level. There have been many hitters who have been able to overcome the long stride by doing that.

By taking a short stride, the hitter can more or less just shift his weight from the back to the front foot. He should hit off the back foot onto the front foot. The front foot that he hits into is firm.

By pushing off his rear foot vigorously, a hitter has a better chance of maintaining a level swing. By sagging his rear leg against a firm front leg, the right-handed swinger will very likely develop an uppercut swing because his right shoulder will be lower than his left.

The casual stride

We like a hitter to take a short, "casual stride," simply because it allows him to keep his body back. The "casual stride" is not a lunge.

It is more of a lifting or shifting of the weight from both feet to a little more on the back foot. In doing so, the front or striding foot is more or less free to just take the "casual stride" into the pitch.

A common fault among high school and college players is to stride too far. They want to hit the ball a long way, so they try to lunge into the ball.

If the hitter's body gets out in front ahead of the swing, his hands will have a difficult time in catching up. He will begin to get "fisted," and he will wonder why. The reason is simple: if his body gets out in front too fast, his hands will have a tough time to catch up.

Look at a hitter from the side: if his head and shoulders lunge forward a foot or so, good timing will be difficult to achieve. The good hitter, by pivoting both his hips and his body, can get just as much power as the fellow who lunges at the ball.

The casual stride enables the hitter to stride forward with his front foot but not let his body go forward. The weight of the body is kept back, and the bat is back. Although he has taken the same length of stride, he has held his body back, and his bat is back, cocked and ready to meet the ball when it comes. He is on balance, as he is throughout the entire swing.

If a hitter has a tendency to lunge forward and the pitch happens to be a change of pace, or if the ball is a bit inside, he will have committed himself too quickly. If it is a fast pitch, inside, all he can do is hit the ball foul or on the fists. And if it is a change-up, he has already committed himself and he will not have the power left to hit the ball.

The stride is not nearly as important as where the hitter keeps his bat. I have always stated: "I do not care whether you step in the bucket or toward the plate, or straight toward the pitcher, just as long as you keep that bat back, cocked, and your front shoulder in. Your front foot should be able to go where it wants to."

Rotating the hips

Along with the wrists and arms, batting power comes from rotating the hips. According to many hitting experts, the action of the hips is more responsible for a powerful swing than the role of the wrists and hands (Fig. 1–10).

The hips, in being able to get out of the way and let the momentum and power of the body come forward into the swing, is one of the most important points in hitting. The batter who hits from a closed stance and locked hips must try to open up, in order to get his hips out of the way.

Ted Williams asserts emphatically: "It's in the hips. You have to put your hips into it!" He asks the question, "How much do the wrists and hands move right up to the point of contact? High-speed pictures indicate that they move hardly at all! The power is generated in the hips, like in golf."

I would have to agree with Ted. I have talked to a golf pro, and he had the same idea. A hitter pivots his hips to get drive and a powerful swing. As for the wrists and hands, they do not lap or turn over until after contact.

Good wrists and hands are essential because they "pop the ball" well, but on contact with the ball the hands are still fairly straight and the wrist turn-over occurs afterward, like a follow-through which provides the extra pop. So, it all comes back to the power of the hips. *A hitter has to put his hips into it!*

The hips help turn the shoulders when swinging the bat. They bring the hips and shoulders around together. The back hip is whipped around as the front hip is thrown out of the way.

For good hip rotation, the rear foot must turn as though it were facing toward the pitcher. As it turns, it forces the front hip to open up. When the back foot turns, there is no way that a hitter can stop the front hip from opening.

Why must the hips open up? The reason is to give the hitter room for his hands to come through and to bring the hands in for the tight pitch. In so doing, he is transferring his weight forward—and this is what he should do. It is like the golfer who transfers his weight, and he ties it altogether at that one little split-second so that he gets the full benefit of his weight, his hand and wrist action all tied into one.

The hitter has to hit against a firm front side, a closed front hip. He actually opens up before he swings, but he should start his swing against a firm front hip to bring the belt buckle around. The hands do this. If he throws the bat, this pulls him in behind the ball. He pivots on that back foot, with a relaxed bent knee. He pushes vigorously forward with his back foot.

Good hip rotation is what produces bat speed. Paul Waner, like his brother, a great hitter with the Pittsburgh Pirates, called it "the quick belly button." When he referred to "the quick belly button," he meant speed in the rotation of the hips. But what helps the batter with that speed is the manner in which the bat is thrown out. It makes him quick in the hips, which means a quick pivot.

Quickness with the hands and wrists

Being able to be quick with the hands and wrists is one of the most important phases of hitting (Fig. 1–8). "The quicker they are as the ball comes to the plate," explained Williams, "the longer you can wait to judge the pitcher, and the less you will be fooled."

Once the hitter decides to pull the trigger, he must get his bat moving quickly. Everything—shoulders, hips, hands and wrists—is brought through smoothly, unleashing his full power on the ball. The wrist snap is the final accelerator after the hips, shoulders, forearms and hands have laid the bat on the ball.

For years, many baseball authorities were erroneously stating that the hitter breaks his wrists when the bat is across the plate. Wally

Fig. 1–8. POWERFUL ARM AND WRIST ACTION. The front arm of Ernie Banks is straight and provides power into the swing. The wrists stay cocked until the hands reach the center of the body, then snap with explosive power.

Moses, in refuting this theory, said that "a hitter should hit the ball before he breaks his wrists." This means that the head of the bat is what turns the wrists over. Again, *the ball should be met in front of the plate, just before the hitter breaks his wrists.*

Quite a few hitters, incorrectly, will bring their top hand in too quickly and begin rolling their wrist when the ball is fairly even with them. Instead, a hitter should hit the ball before he breaks his wrists.

"As you swing, your hips start moving," said Williams, "and as your hips start opening up, your hands come through, following your hips."

"As you hit the ball, your wrists have not broken as yet," continued Ted. "As you make contact with the ball, and you are hitting the ball, your wrists start breaking—not before, just as you hit it, and then the follow-through."

Just at impact, and slightly after, the hitter's wrists start breaking, and then comes the smooth follow-through. The wrists break just after contact with the ball, to give the swing that extra punch that sends the ball well on its way.

The hitter who has good wrists and quick reflexes can learn to wait. The man with the best reflexes, like Musial or Williams, Banks or Aaron, can wait the longest.

As the stride takes place, the hitter's hands and the bat should move backward away from the stride, with the wrists still cocked while awaiting the pitch. When the bat is at a right angle with the hitter's shoulders, he can be certain his wrists are cocked, provided his front arm is kept almost straight. The hitter should be sure his wrists do not break or uncock until after impact is made on the ball. When the swing begins, the wrists should stay cocked until his hands reach the center of his body.

The swing should come down and across the plate, leveling out as it meets the ball. Then the hitter's wrists should roll over as the ball is met well out in front of the plate.

Along with good hip rotation, the more quickly a young player can develop the whipping of his hands and wrists into his swing, the sooner he will become a good hitter. Whenever he is in the batting cage, he should pay heed to his coach who continually calls out: *"Use those wrists!"*

Follow-through

After the hips and wrists have whipped through and hit the ball, a complete follow-through is necessary. A complete follow-through provides power to the swing and gives distance to the hits. The body follows through in the direction the ball is hit, and the bat continues under its own momentum to the rear of the body. The wrists snap and roll over. The arms swing to the rear. The hitter should be in perfect balance, with the body facing the direction of the ball just hit (Fig. 1–15).

A batter should never stop or "chop off" his swing. When he completes his swing, his bat should be at the middle of his back. The rear hip follows through. The belt buckle comes around and faces left field on an inside pitch, center on a pitch down the middle and right on an outside pitch. The weight comes forward, causing the back foot to pivot, or for some hitters, to lift on contact with the pitch.

While some hitters have their rear foot off the ground, the lifting comes only after they have made contact with the ball, and not before. To obtain a controlled stride, it is essential to maintain a firm rear foot. This is necessary because a hitter generates his power in his push forward as he throws the bat at the ball.

Proper mental approach

One of the best things any hitter can do when he is up at the plate is to concentrate on the pitcher and try to imagine that every pitch is coming into the strike zone and he is going to put the bat on the ball. He must have confidence in himself, *a positive feeling that he can do it!* He has to have a mental attitude which says, "I know I can do it."

Above all, a hitter has to be as relaxed as possible. He cannot react quickly enough or take a smooth swing if his muscles are tight. He should not get set too soon. He should wait until the pitcher is "ready" to pitch before he gets into his ready position. If the battery is getting their signals, the hitter would be wise to relax by putting the bat on his shoulder.

Fig. 1–9. THE SLAP OR CHOP SWING. A growing number of hitters like Matty Alou have found success at the plate by shortening up and swinging down slightly. As the number of ball diamonds with artificial playing surfaces increases, more hitters will be striving to hit sharp ground balls through the holes of the infield.

The batter has to stay up there and cover the plate. If he is up there and he is letting his muscles control his mind, and he tends to get all nervous and keyed up, he simply will not do the job. Under pressure, the player who remains in his groove is the one who will do well.

When a hitter is hitting well, he walks up there, and if he sees a good pitch, he rips into it! He does not think anything about it. However, when he is struggling a little bit and trying to get back in the groove, there might be some doubt in his mind. Maybe he is giving the pitcher too much credit.

"The biggest thing in becoming a good hitter," according to Bobby Bragan, a former big league manager and coach, "is *courage*. The good hitters, mostly, can hit to both fields, and the only way you can hit to the opposite field is to step into the ball. And it takes a little courage to step into that ball when it is thrown as hard as it is by most major league pitchers."

Relaxation is most essential in becoming a good hitter. Actually, concentration and relaxation go together in hitting a baseball. By concentrating on what he is doing, a player can remove tension and fear from his mind, and substitute the all-important vehicles to success—a confident mind and a relaxed body.

A ballplayer must keep his chin high and erect because there are going to be days when he will go "0-for-4" or "get knocked out of the box." The ballplayer who refuses to be beaten is tough to beat.

The batter must stay in there and go after the ball all the time. If he is alert, he can always get out of the way. The only thing he should be thinking about is what that pitcher is going to throw.

"In hitting, the element of fear has to be eliminated," said Charlie Lau. "A hitter has to go out on his front foot and get that ball. Subconsciously, a hitter doesn't realize that he is pulling away from the ball. A lot of hitters are rocking back away from the ball, and they don't know it. Instead, he must go out on his front foot and attack that ball!"

One good way to help a hitter to overcome fear at the plate is to throw him tennis balls instead of baseballs in batting practice. He will gain confidence when he realizes he is able to move effectively away from pitches inside him, over his head, behind him or occasionally even hitting him. Of course, wearing a helmet which provides good overall protection of the head should help in overcoming fear.

A coach can help a player get away from pitched balls so they will not hurt him badly. For example, a hitter might make an inward roll while keeping his eye on the ball. He must learn to ride the blow on his shoulder, his hips and even the top of the helmet. On the inside, tight pitch, for example, he should move his front shoulder away from the pitches. If it hits him, it will not hurt him badly.

Hitters who plant themselves solidly at the plate and take that big stride are more apt to be hit than the fellow who is light on his feet, who can twist and turn. Quick reflexes are important in getting away from a close pitch.

Hitting the ball where it is pitched

The batters who have hit for average—Stan Musial, Matty Alou, Tommy Davis, Pete Rose, Roberto Clemente and Tony Oliva—hit to all fields; they try to hit the ball where it is pitched. They know how to punch the ball and push it toward left field, how to slap the ball through infield gaps, bunt for hits and go to the opposite field. They even beat the ball into the ground and beat it out for base hits. *They go into the ball.* That is why they are high in the averages.

A   B

C   D

Fig. 1–10. RIGHT-HANDED POWER HITTER. Along with the wrists and arms, batting power comes from rotating the hips. The hips help turn the shoulders when swinging the bat. Bring the hips and shoulders around together. The back hip is whipped around as the front hip is thrown out of the way (Johnny Bench).

Interestingly enough, the success of each of these outstanding hitters can be attributed to his ability to hit the ball where it is pitched. When they are hitting the outside pitch to the opposite field, they are waiting on the ball the way they should be. They go right with the pitch, and most of these hitters find they will get their home runs anyway.

"I am not a pull hitter," said switch-hitting Roy White of the Yankees. "I like to spray the ball. I hit the ball where it is pitched. I have been able to poke the outside pitch safely. They do not jam me very often because I choke up on the bat. Right-handed, I try to slice the ball to right field. If there is a big hole, I will try to go for it."

"As I wait for the pitch, I try to remind myself that I want to hit the ball back at the pitcher," explained Tommy Davis, who was a fine hitter for the Dodgers. "If the pitch is down the pipe, I will step straight ahead. If the pitch is over the inside part of the plate, I usually step away from the plate with my front foot and pull it into left field. However, if the ball is away from me, on the outside corner, I have found it effective to step toward the plate with my front foot and hit it into the opposite field."

Pulling the ball

In order to pull the ball, a hitter must use strong wrist action and get out in front of the ball. This means his bat should meet the ball before it reaches him.

The pull hitter should time his swing to hit the ball before it comes even with his body. Hitting it out in front of him gives his swing maximum power and enables his eyes to judge the ball better. The front hip must be open and turned quickly to enable the hitter to get around (Figs. 1–11 and 1–12).

Strong wrists, a quick eye and fast hip rotation are all needed to pull the inside pitch. Although some hitters find the closed stance natural for pulling, it sometimes leads to hip locking.

Many hitters experience pulling trouble by committing themselves too quickly and pulling away with the body. They find they can handle only one pitch, the inside fast ball.

There are a number of coaches, including Bobby Winkles, head coach at Arizona State University, who take a cautious view on pull hitting. "I have never been one to advocate pulling the ball if the player cannot do it consistently," explained Bobby. "In fact, I like to see my players hitting the ball all over the park—to all fields. I think a number of hitters have been ruined because they were told they must pull. It is either natural to pull, or it is not natural to pull. Some players can get in front and others cannot."

Just trying to meet the ball

Another common fault of hitters is to try to hit the ball too hard. Young hitters in particular have a tendency to jerk their heads and not watch the ball as they are swinging. If they would cut down on their swing and just try to meet the ball, they would be well on their way to becoming consistent hitters.

The hitter who swings too hard would be a much better hitter if he tried to make better contact. I always try to tell my hitters: "Try and see how good you can hit it, not how hard!" Going back to golf, if a player overdrives the ball or swings too hard, something usually happens. He either slashes the ball or hooks it. With baseball, it is the same way.

"The head is the big key," said Gilliam. "When you turn your head, you don't see the ball as well. So, keep your head on the ball all the time and try to hit the ball where it is pitched."

Too many young players today want to hit home runs, but not everybody is a home run hitter. Instead of trying to pull everything, they should try to hit the ball where it is pitched and just go for a base hit.

Hitting to the opposite field

Major league batting coaches are unanimous in declaring that the pitch on the outside corner can be handled best by hitting it to the opposite field. If the pitch is on the outside corner, the hitter should step toward the plate, pointing his toe toward right field (Fig. 1–17).

To me, the best way to hit the inside pitch to the opposite field is to bring the hands in across the front of the body a little sooner, so that the big end of the bat will get on the ball.

"It is kind of a downward, inside-out swing," said Gilliam. "You try to get the ball down. You don't want to get the ball in the air."

Right-handed hitters find it effective to move the right foot back with the pitch and stride toward right field. "I kept both my feet planted," said Gilliam. "I don't think you should take any foot off the ground."

The main thing is to hit the ball squarely. If necessary, the hitter should push or punch the ball. Stepping in the direction of right field, he should keep his hands ahead of the bat and not roll his wrists. He is just slower with the bat and does not break his wrist. Contact with the ball should be made directly over the plate, not out in front. Although the batter completes a good follow-through, the weight of his body should lean toward the opposite field.

If the ball is on the outside corner, the hitter should go into the pitch. If it is on the inside part of the plate, he should rotate his hip out of the way and bring in his hands and meet the ball in front of the plate.

During batting practice, I like to see a player practice hitting to the opposite field, so that he acquires the knack of moving toward the ball.

Adjusting to game situations

Some hitters find it difficult to adjust to game situations. Many times during a game, the manager wants a hitter just to meet the ball. For some strange reason, it is tough for some hitters to do this.

On the hit and run, the hitter need not necessarily have to hit behind the runner. The ideal thing is for him to hit the ball in the opening made by the second baseman or shortstop moving to cover the bag. The ground ball hit in this spot will put runners on first and third. However, few hitters have the necessary bat control, and instead should just swing and merely try to make contact. By doing so, they will advance the man into scoring position and eliminate the double play.

D

C

Fig. 1–11. LEFT–HANDED POWER HITTER. Being a strong pull hitter, Willie McCovey likes to hit the ball well out in front of the plate, giving his swing maximum power. Notice that McCovey's front hip is turned quickly, enabling him to get around on the ball. Possessing strong wrists, a quick eye and fast

D

C

Fig. 1–12. LEFT–HANDED POWER HITTER. Fundamentally perfect, Boog Powell's batting swing is a picture of great power as he gets around on an inside pitch. Everything—shoulders and arms, hips, wrists and hands—are

Switch-Hitting Since the early 1960s, when Maury Wills popularized the practice of swinging from both sides of the plate, switch-hitting has been play-ing an increasingly greater role in baseball. Certainly his ability to switch-hit changed Maury from a mediocre hitter to a good one. "I had my troubles with the curve ball," related Maury, "and I was often

B   A

hip rotation, Willie has the bat speed needed to pull the ball consistently. His smooth swing finishes with a good follow-through in the direction of right field.

B   A

put together in perfect unison to send the ball soaring for the fences. Popping his wrists with explosive quickness, Boog whips the big end of the bat with maximum drive.

stepping into the bucket rather than into the ball. I was not getting enough leverage in my swing.''

The Dodgers have had more switch-hitters than any team in baseball. In fact, the 1965 club had four infielders who swung from both sides of the plate: Wes Parker, Jim LeFebvre, Gilliam and Wills.

Fig. 1–13. A STRONG FRONT ARM. Many hitters, unfortunately, fail to use the front arm correctly and quite often are weak with the triceps muscle, which is responsible for "whipping the front arm out" (Wally Moses).

Mickey Mantle and Pete Rose have been perhaps baseball's foremost exponents and have done much to promote interest in switch-hitting (Figs. 1–19 and 1–20).

Switch-hitting is more suited to certain players. Coaches surveyed in a 1965 study indicated that it requires a great amount of coordination, timing and ambidexterity not found in the majority of people. A lot depends on just how quickly the individual can adapt to switch-hitting. Some athletes can do such things a little more quickly than others.

The player ideally suited to switch-hitting is one with speed who is having definite trouble hitting one way, often a right-handed hitter with good speed. Players who have good running speed and are not blessed with great power make good prospects for switch-hitting, particularly if they are able to make good contact with the ball consistently.

The chief advantage is that the switch-hitter can hit breaking stuff better. He will not be fooled by the curve ball so much. Secondly, as a left-hander, the player is one-and-one-half steps closer to first base.

The controlled level swing is best for the switch-hitter. He should use a short stroke to start, with a choke grip, and should try to punch

A   B

C   D

Fig. 1–14. BATTING POWER is the result of a smoothly coordinated, well-timed hitting swing. These pictures of Harmon Killebrew prove quite conclusively that the wrists do not break until after contact.

the ball. It should be a short, quick flat swing, even a slightly downward stroke.

Ideally, switch-hitting should begin early in the player's career. Rose was a 10-year-old Little Leaguer when his father taught him to swing from both sides of the plate. Parker and LeFebvre also switched at an early age, but Wills is the real exception, inasmuch as he was 27 years old when Bobby Bragan suggested the change to him in Spokane, Washington. "I think the younger a player can start the better he will be," said Bragan.

Fig. 1–15. A HOME RUN is the result of a smooth, well-coordinated hitting swing such as the style demonstrated here by Billy Williams of the Chicago Cubs. In perfect balance, Billy's body is facing in the direction of the ball he has just hit high over the right field fence at Candlestick Park.

Tips on switch-hitting

When Wills was having considerable trouble at the plate early in the 1960 campaign, Pete Reiser, one of our coaches, took Maury under his wing and started him from scratch, almost like a manager would do with a nine-year-old Little Leaguer. "He selected a new bat for me," said Maury, "one I could whip around faster. He opened my batting stance and worked on fundamentals such as meeting the ball out in front of the plate, taking an even swing and not overstriding. Pete kept driving and encouraging me. Try to hit on top of the ball, just meet it, swing smoothly, choke the bat more and swing level. You have the ability, you can hit to the opposite field, keep swinging!

"Then, it happened as if it were magic. My average started to climb. My entire attitude had changed from that of despair to one of eager anticipation."

"It boils down to practice, practice, and practice," said Bragan, "come out and stand on that side of the plate, and just bunt the ball. Swing easy, and see that ball coming to the plate from the other side. Hit the ball through the middle and to the opposite side of the infield. Just try to make contact and get a piece of the ball."

"Working off a batting tee and the pitching machine will help him get a comfortable stride and feel," continued Bragan. "Have him learn to bunt, then a great deal of straight half-speed batting practice, working later into fast stuff, swinging the bat in pepper games is excellent."

Fig. 1–16. ON–DECK BATTER. As he waits in the on-deck circle, this veteran hitter studies the pitcher intensely and is constantly alert for a possible pre-hitting signal from his coach. Notice the weighted bat which he swings before stepping into the batter's box.

Breaking a Hitting Slump

A hitting slump is one of the toughest things of all to shake. The player has to be encouraged. His manager or coach has to talk to him. If he has a fault, such as uppercutting, the coach should take him out and start him hitting with soft stuff. Just have him meet the ball and more or less start him over from scratch again. Try to get him into stride.

When a hitter gets in a slump, the usual mistake he makes is to become overly anxious to do right. He cannot wait to get up to the plate and get himself a base hit. More than likely, he will stride too quickly. Instead, he should say: "I want to wait until I see where the ball is pitched before I commit myself."

Dixie Walker

"When a hitter is in a slump, the coach should first determine what type of a hitter he is. As a rule, he will be able to get a good idea what this fellow needs. It is very difficult to teach hitting the same way to an entire group because he has to treat them as individuals. In short, each individual has his own style of hitting.

"Some hitters quite often jam themselves simply by reaching, rather than bringing the arms in, in order to bring the fat part of the bat where the ball is traveling. We try to get them to be able to bring their arms in, so that the bat is brought in closer.

"If a hitter has a tendency to pull away from the plate, it will be easier for him to handle the outside pitch if he is leaning in and going

A

B

C

D

Fig. 1–17. HITTING TO THE OPPOSITE FIELD. The hands are brought across the front of the body so the big end of the bat can make good contact (Manny Mota).

toward the pitch, rather than going away.

"Another possible trouble spot is the front shoulder. Some hitters let their front shoulders pull out just a fraction too early. They pull

Fig. 1–18. BATTING TEE. In addition to being raised or lowered, the "T" can be placed anywhere in relationship to the plate so the hitter can practice his weakness or strength from there.

their body away just enough to get the ball on the end of the bat, rather than on the good part of it. If the front shoulder moves just a fraction too early, the batter will likely draw his bat away from the ball.

"Then, there is the problem of not making contact consistently. In this situation, the coach should watch the hitter's eyes to see if he is following the ball. He must watch the flight of his bat and his body movements. He has to determine if his body is getting ahead of his swing or if he is pulling away too much."

Dick Sisler "Most young hitters who come up to the big leagues are so over-anxious to hit. They go out too quickly. They commit themselves too quickly, thereby going after the pitcher's pitch, instead of waiting on a good ball that they can hit. We try to teach these young hitters to stay back, to hold their weight back on their rear leg.

"Most home run hitters usually have a slight uppercut which is a natural uppercut. This is all right for a batter with a lot of power, but for the majority of hitters, I would stress the level swing and have them put more weight forward to prevent uppercutting.

"For some hitters, particularly spray hitters, I suggest that they take a heavier bat, choke up on it some and just try to make contact. The ball will come off the bat sharper than with the light bat.

"My suggestion to most hitters who fall into a slump is to take some extra hitting and hit the ball to the opposite field. This will keep their head in there and it will hold them back a little longer, and they will be able to see the pitch a lot better than if they are overanxious and they go out too quickly."

Harry Walker "Most hitting slumps come from overstriding, trying to pull the ball too much and trying to hit the ball too hard. When this happens, they develop bad habits, and they fail to watch the ball, and the basic fundamentals begin to get away from them. Then they begin to lose confidence.

"First of all, the individual has to get in the right frame of mind to accept what the coach has to talk to him about. The coach should try to pick a time when he can talk to him and get him where he is willing to listen. He can work with him in batting practice with nobody around and try to pick out the things that he feels are causing the trouble, usually overstriding, trying to hit the ball too hard, pulling away from the ball.

"A hitter should be encouraged to forget about swinging hard and just try to make contact. He should consider going through the middle and waiting a little longer. The secret of hitting is being able to wait and still get the bat on the ball. A coach should try to get his hitters to wait on the ball, hit the ball through the middle, and even to the opposite field.

"Encourage him to get a more level swing. Start high and come down and level off just before he gets to the ball and more or less go into the ball. He must keep his weight on the balls of the feet, and keep his eye on the ball and his head and shoulders in so that he will not open up too quickly.

"By doing so, he will let the ball get a little farther up, in the middle of the plate, instead of well out in front. This way he has more room to work on it, and if he is not quite as sharp, he still can get good wood on the ball.

"When a fellow tries to pull too much, he will open up too quickly and hit the ball on the end of the bat or miss the ball completely, and when the ball moves that last ten feet or so, if he has already committed himself, he simply cannot adjust to the ball.

"So, the coach has to get this fellow in the groove, where he can wait and not try to overpower the ball. Keep the ball low, preferably a line drive or ground ball as much as he can. This will get him back in his groove. As soon as he gets a few base hits and gets a little confidence, he will come around and start hitting the ball solidly again."

Drills for Hitters

Batting practice

The most important point to keep in mind is *try not to hit the home run ball.* Hitting sessions should be purposeful and meaningful. The prime concern is making good contact with a level, well-timed swing. Getting the hitters' timing sharp should be the basic purpose of any batting practice. This is also the time to work on any flaws in the hitting swing. In addition, it provides a good opportunity to hit the ball to the opposite field.

Batting practice pitchers should throw at a fairly good speed, perhaps 75 percent of their natural speed. Easy lobs are almost worthless. While a pitching machine can be a good substitute, live pitching, of course, is best.

During batting practice, the hitter should:

1. Try to hit the ball where it is pitched
2. Learn to watch the ball hit the bat
3. Try to hit the ball hard squarely
4. Hit the ball in the direction it comes over the plate
5. Learn the strike zone.

Pepper

This is a game that can help a player educate himself to do certain things. It can be helpful to the hitter who is having trouble holding his body back, if he will take a short stride and go at it just like he does in batting practice. He can learn to guide the ball, hit the ball where he wants to, and even practice swinging slightly down on the high pitches.

Playing pepper can help a player become a better hitter. In addition to developing eye and hand coordination, pepper games can develop much needed bat control, which can help a hitter become a better hit-and-run man.

Pepper can have good carry-over to batting, provided the batter will:

1. Keep the bat back in a ready position
2. Adhere to a short stride
3. Watch the ball hit the bat.

Using the batting tee   The batting tee can be a valuable training aid in developing the swing and snap at the ball. Success with the "T" will not come in five minutes. Rather, it will take hours of practice and effort. The "T" can be placed anywhere in relationship to the plate so he can practice his weakness or strength from there (Fig. 1–18).

The batting tee can be effective in pointing out to the player that he has to hit the inside pitch out in front of the plate more. Conversely, when the ball is on the outside part of the plate, it can prove to him that he can wait a little longer and hit the ball straightaway or to the opposite field.

When the tee is placed inside, it is hard for him to do anything but pull it. Have the player hit from the tee without taking a stride. Then he can progress from the non-stride to a short stride of six to eight inches. Mark a line in front of his stride foot and be sure he does not stride beyond that line.

Dialogue on Batting

Pete Rose

interviewed by Don Weiskopf

DON: Since your arrival on the big league scene, Pete, you have been known for your aggressiveness, perhaps more than any other present-day player. As a hitter, do you try to be aggressive?

PETE: Yes, I do. I definitely feel a ballplayer should be aggressive when he is up at the plate, until he has two strikes on him. Then, he has to shorten up on his swing but still be aggressive. For a hitter, aggressiveness is going after and getting the ball—not letting the ball come and get him. It is important for him to get the bat out in front and hit the ball on the fat part of the bat. That is how the good hitters sting the ball hard and hit it a long ways. They get the big barrel out in front of the plate.

DON: Hustle, aggressiveness and spirited play have been synonymous with your style of play and performance on the diamond. Did these qualities come naturally, God-given, or can you attribute their development to your former coaches or your parents?

PETE: I think that my style of play came from growing up with a type of father I had, and it boils down to hustle. When someone enjoys playing baseball like I enjoy playing it that's just the way it comes out of me. I never feel like stopping running, and when a player can make money playing baseball, which is something that comes natural and easy to do, and something he did every day when he was a kid, he just has to try his very best to stay ahead of the game. That's why I hustle and run around. When I am on the ball field, I try to never stop running. It's not a job to me. It's like fun out there. When it becomes a job, I will have to quit.

DON: Do you feel that hustle and aggressive play can be equally as important to the performance of other athletes?

PETE: Very definitely. I think that a player who is aggressive and is a hustler will take a lot of extra bases and will prove to be a heads-up ballplayer. These qualities have proven to be very beneficial to a number of players I can think of in the major leagues, like advancing from second to third on a passed ball. In short, a player has to be heads-up to play this game of baseball.

DON: Isn't it true that aggressive play can place considerable pressure on the defense?

PETE: Anytime a guy can hustle and run fast, more pressure is placed on the defense. The fielders know they must pick the ball up and throw it quickly in order to beat this type of a base runner. When a ball is hit, they know they must go get the ball in a hurry and get it over to first base. On the other hand, if the runner is big and slow, the fielders can take their time and make sure their throws are accurate.

Speed is so important in baseball, because it is a game of inches. There is no substitute for speed in this sport.

DON: Coming to the qualities of a good hitter, what does it take to become a good hitter?

PETE: First of all, a hitter needs good eyes and strong hands, and he has to have a bat that feels comfortable. In the big leagues, nine out of ten of the good hitters know the strike zone. It is always easier to hit strikes than it is to hit balls. The only two bad-ball hitters I can think of, fellows who can hit a bad ball good, are Matty Alou and Roberto Clemente.

Most hitters have to swing at strikes to become good hitters. Practice is so important in hitting success. No one can take four, five or six swings a day and expect to be a good hitter. We are a big league ball club, and we play every day. Yet, I take from 25 to 30 swings every day. A ballplayer never gets enough hitting.

I don't think that kids today practice enough, and I would highly recommend that they practice on their own, in addition to team workouts. To be an effective hitter, they must work out on their own. I am sure they don't get enough hitting during their regular practice sessions.

A hitter must know what the pitcher's hardest pitch is. A lot of guys are guess hitters, but I try to look for a fast ball every

A

B

Fig. 1–19. RIGHT–HANDED SWING. Cocking his bat in preparation for the swing, Pete Rose aggressively goes after the ball. However, as Pete strides toward the ball, observe that he keeps his weight on his back foot. To prevent

D

C

Fig. 1–20. LEFT–HANDED SWING. "All I try to do," says Pete, "is just watch the ball and get the big barrel of the bat out in front of the plate. This takes

pitch, because it is just common sense. A guy like Tom Seaver is 60 feet from me and I am looking for a curve ball. If he throws me a fast ball how can I possibly hit off of Seaver looking for a curve ball, and he throws his fast ball? The human mind simply cannot adjust that fast. Although some players are guess hitters, I look for the pitcher's hardest pitch every

C

D

lunging, he takes a "casual stride" which results in a well-timed, level hitting swing. His front left arm is straight upon contact with the ball out in front of the plate.

B

A

quick hands and arms. I like to hit the ball when the front arm becomes straight."

pitch, and if he throws something off-speed, I can always adjust to it.

DON: As you look back at your brilliant career, what might you at-tribute your success to? Is it possible to single out a few factors or attributes which have helped you the most?

PETE: The fact that I have been a switch-hitter has helped me the most. Today, there are so many platoon ball clubs and ball-players. When a player is hitting both ways and has the curve ball, which is an out-pitch for a lot of pitchers, and a tough pitch, coming in at him, it has to be easier to hit than it is going away from him.

DON: Would you recommend switch-hitting to the average ballplayer?

PETE: Yes, I would recommend it to any young player, particularly if he has good speed. My father started me switch-hitting when I was nine years old. In fact, I cannot remember ever hitting right-handed off a right-handed pitcher, or vice versa.

Right now, I am much stronger right-handed because I'm naturally right-handed (Fig. 1–19). I started when I was very young, so you can see it takes a lot of developing. A switch-hitter is not going to hit a lot of home runs unless he is a Mickey Mantle. When a player is hitting right-handed one day and left-handed the next, he can't develop a home run swing. Since most switch-hitters can run, they often try to hit the ball where it is pitched and hit it hard.

DON: What are the basic points in learning to be a switch-hitter, that is, when a player first goes to the other side of the plate?

PETE: First, he has to take a lot of practice and start switching in the game. When he first begins, he has to expect that he will make a lot of outs. He will have a tendency to drop his dobber because he won't have too much success at the beginning. Everything we talk about in hitting and in baseball we have to get back to the same old thing—hard work and dedication. A player can never work hard enough in baseball. It takes practice, practice and more practice.

DON: What type of a bat do you prefer, Pete?

PETE: Everyone is different and each hitter has to get a bat that feels comfortable to him. Since I stand pretty far away from the plate, I like to use a long bat. I probably use as long a bat as anybody on our ball club. In fact, I know I do, a bat 36 inches long and 33$\frac{1}{2}$ ounces, and I will try to use the same bat all year long. It's sort of a skinny-handle bat. I think it is so important in the Little Leagues and in high school for a player to get a bat that feels good to him.

DON: Lately, more hitters are being encouraged to use heavier bats, thicker-handled bats, rather than use a thin-handled, whip-like bat. What are your thoughts on this trend?

PETE: The fellow who chokes up on the thick-handled bat has a tendency not to strike out as much as the player holding a light, thin bat down at the end. The object of batting is to hit the ball, and the batter always has a chance if he hits the ball. If he strikes out, he doesn't have any chance at all.

For myself, I just can't use a thick-handled bat. I used a thick-handled bat my first two years, and I hit .273 and .269. I went to the skinny-handled bat and I have hit .300 ever since then. So, I am a thin-handled bat hitter with a big barrel.

Players like Matty Alou and Willie Davis, who don't hit many home runs and are not power hitters, prefer the thick-handled bat and have found success. Everybody is different, though. It might feel good to them. However, no one should want a bat that is too heavy because he won't be able to get it around fast enough.

DON: Do you like to put that pine-tar on the handle of your bat, Pete?

PETE: Yes. I can't hit without pine-tar, whether in practice or in a ball game. I have to get a good grip on the bat. I can't have it wet. Whether this is a mental thing or not I don't know, but the bat has to feel comfortable. A hitter has to feel comfortable up there at the plate.

DON: For the average batter, what type of stance do you recommend?

PETE: I never like to tell a young hitter to spread out too much or take a big step or a small one. I tell him to be comfortable. If possible, when they swing and stride toward the ball, they should try to keep their weight on their back foot. This is an important point in hitting. If they do this, they can still adjust to a change-up, which is so effective against hitters nowadays. The change-up is a real good pitch, especially for a guy like Seaver or Bill Singer, who throw awfully hard. So, I like to keep my weight on my back foot. Take Henry Aaron, for example. He goes out a lot of times on his front foot but he keeps his weight back and his hands back, and he still has everything to hit with.

DON: Where should a young hitter hold his hands as he prepares for the swing?

PETE: Again, this is an individual matter. Some guys have them up high, others prefer holding them lower. It is all according to where they are the most comfortable.

The worst thing a young hitter can do in learning how to hit is to try to copy somebody. Everybody stands differently. Yet when the ball is pitched, everybody ends up the same place. Everybody will end up right back here where the hands start coming forward. Some have their bat up, others down.

DON: Do you recommend a short stride for the average hitter?

PETE: Yes, I do. I take a short stride because I spread out pretty well. It helps me keep my weight on my back foot. But then, there are hitters like Johnny Bench and Henry Aaron who take a big stride, and they have had success.

The coach should not want to change anyone. He does want them to feel comfortable, though. Some guys can spread out and others can't. I can't take a real big stride because I have a tendency to start lunging. As for me, I take a four-to-six–inch stride, and I have had success with it. This is why I am a good change-up, curve ball hitter. I am never in a lunging position. If a hitter has his feet close together, and he takes a big 12–14-inch stride, many times a curve ball or change-up will get him out in front. Since I use a short stride, there is no way a pitcher is going to make me look bad. He may strike me out, but he will never make me look bad striking out.

DON: Generally, most coaches emphasize the level swing; however, lately a number of coaches are teaching a slightly downward swing, more of a chop. Others talk about the slightly upward swing. How would you explain the hitting swing to the average young hitter?

PETE: On the big league level, with the increasing number of artificial fields, the guy who hits the ball up the middle and on the ground is going to collect a lot of base hits and make himself a considerable amount of money. With me, if a ball is inside, I will try to pull the ball. If it is right down the middle, generally I will try to hit it up the middle, and if it is outside, I will try to hit the ball to the opposite field.

It is quite difficult to defense the hitter who hits the ball all over the ball park. If a player is strictly a pull hitter, if he is left-handed, he will always hit the ball to right field. For this type of hitter, a manager can stack his whole defense that way.

A batting coach often tells a hitter too much. When I start thinking about hitting, I don't want to go up to the plate and start worrying about whether or not my hands are right or if my feet are positioned properly. Some hitting instructors make the mistake of getting their hitters to think about all of these things.

All I try to do is just see the ball and get my hands and the bat out in front, the fat part of the bat out in front.

A batter will find it difficult to have a picturesque swing by going up to the plate and starting thinking about taking his stride and worrying if his hips are going to go the same time as his hands and whether the feet are right. He simply can't worry about all of this because the pitcher on the mound will be throwing curves and fast balls, and the batter has to worry about seeing the ball.

So I recommend a short, compact swing. But speed is so important. I like to see a hitter go up there and swing hard, and just hit the ball. Rather than overswing, he should snap his bat and get his bat out in front. That is the secret—hitting the ball hard. It is not how far he hits the ball. He has to hit it hard.

DON: Would you describe your swing as a level one?

PETE: I try to swing level because if I uppercut I will hit nothing but fly balls, and I don't want to hit too many ground balls. So I just try to take a hard, level swing.

DON: What is the most important part of the swing?

PETE: Getting the big barrel of the bat out in front of the plate is most important. I like to hit the ball when the front arm becomes straight. Actually, though, I think it is the hands and arms. Quick hands, good arms and good eyes are the basic essentials of a good swing, plus a hitter should know the strike zone.

DON: Wally Moses believes that many hitters do not use their front arm enough. The front muscles are often weak in many hitters. Do you have a problem with your front arm?

PETE: If anybody is going to have that problem I would have it as much as anybody, because I am a switch-hitter and I don't develop the front arm as much as the normal guy. But if a player has hit the same way his entire career, his arm has got to be stronger. I am a right-hander, that is, I throw right-handed, yet I try to get my left arm as strong as my right arm because I switch-hit.

I believe the most important thing in hitting is getting the bat out in front. I feel the back arm is the most important of the two because a hitter doesn't hit the ball until the back arm locks, and nine out of ten times if he does it correctly, he will have the bat out in front.

DON: Have you always been able to hit to all fields?

PETE: I sure have, and the biggest thing that has helped me during my professional career is the fact that when I am hitting left-handed, on a ball inside, I can hit it inside—out to left field. It Is difficult to defense a batter who hits the ball to all fields. Being a lead-off hitter as I am, I can't be concerned about home runs because they will come no more than three or four times a month, so I don't worry about them.

DON: What are the basic points in hitting the ball to the opposite field?

PETE: The important point is to just go with the pitch. If the pitch is thrown outside, the hitter shouldn't break his wrists. His main concern is putting his bat on the ball and snapping it out there. He shouldn't turn his wrists over. His hands have to lead the way and do all the work. The bat and the hands must go get the ball.

DON: Pete, what is the hardest pitch for you to hit?

PETE: I don't like a guy who throws a good screwball or a good knuckleball, because I think they are freak pitches. I can adjust to the curve, fast ball and slider, but it is difficult to see the rotation on a good screwball, perhaps because of the lights. I think the screwball is a tough pitch. Pitchers like Jim Brewer with his screwball and Phil Niekro, a knuckleballer, are real tough pitchers to hit because of their bread-and-butter pitches. Most successful relief pitchers have a secret pitch like a screwball, forkball or a knuckleball.

DON: Tom Seaver has two different types of fast balls: the high rising fast ball and the sinking fast ball. What is the toughest to hit of these two pitches?

PETE: I am a low ball hitter because I try to hit the ball on the turf. When I bat off of Seaver, I have to lay off of the letter-high fast ball. There are two guys in this league who are similar, Seaver and Bill Singer, and they are both tremendous pitchers. And the reason they are tough is because when they throw the ball down, they throw hard, with exceptional velocity. Most pitchers, when they throw hard, throw letter-high fast balls which will take off, but when Seaver and Singer throw down, they really throw hard. That's the secret to their success. Everybody says, "Keep the ball down. Don't get the ball up!" Well, believe me, these guys do just that. They not only throw hard but they keep the ball down, too.

DON: Has the slider given you very much trouble through the years?

PETE: No, I don't think so. Being a switch-batter, I take a lot of sliders during batting practice, and with a slider, a hitter just has to get his bat out in front a little faster, especially against a pitcher who has a quick-breaking slider who will try to get the ball in on him.

DON: Turning to conditioning, Pete, how do you keep yourself in shape during the off-season? I know you play a lot of basketball.

PETE: Yes, that's what I do. I am not a big drinker, and I don't smoke. I do play a lot of basketball, and I watch my weight. A ballplayer cannot afford to let himself get too fat. The hardest thing in conditioning, though, is during spring training when ballplayers have to get their hands ready for hitting.

DON: How do you get your hands in condition?

PETE: There is very little we can do until we get to spring training, where blisters and calluses have to be developed over again. Naturally, they go away during the winter, and players have to toughen up and get their hands hard again. Take a look at my hand here where the bat lays. The skin is really tough.

DON: Besides playing basketball, how about calisthenics or the use of weights?

PETE: I don't do any of that stuff. I don't believe in weight lifting. I am a firm believer in not using weights because baseball is a game for guys who have to be "loose as a goose." This is what we say. For football, weight lifting is tremendous and great. For a center in basketball, it is good because it makes him strong, but in baseball he has to be loose because it is a game for loose people. The arms and everything else has to be real loose.

DON: Since you have a muscular type of body, I would imagine you could tighten up if you did a lot of weight lifting.

PETE: Yes, I sure could and I have seen some guys who are muscle-bound and just don't make it in baseball. Instead, I like to play a lot of basketball, and I have so much fun.

I am a thick-legged guy, and I have to keep my legs in good shape, therefore I do a lot of running. Ballplayers have to watch their legs closely because they are so important.

DON: As a youngster did you ever try to emulate or try to be like a certain big league ballplayer?

PETE: The only guy I ever tried to be like was Enos Slaughter, the way he ran and performed on the ballfield. I can attribute this to my dad, who kept telling me to "Keep hustling! Keep hustling!" This really helped me as far as my career.

I just think that when an athlete enjoys doing something, when he doesn't hustle when he is on the field, he is cheating the people who are paying good money to watch him play. By not hustling, he is cheating himself and his teammates.

DON: In the 1970 All-Star game, Pete, your aggressive base running paid off with a victory for the National League. Yet, there were a few people, your opponents, who felt that the All-Star game, being an exhibition game, did not call for such spirited, aggressive body contact. Would you comment on this type of criticism?

PETE: All I can say about the All-Star game, is that if I had a place to slide, I would have slid. I did the same thing during a spring training game against our AAA team. I knocked the catcher ten feet behind home plate. He was blocking the plate.

Ray Fosse is a tremendous young catcher, but I feel he was in the wrong position. He shouldn't have been where he was, and if I could have slid around him, I would have slid around him. But there was no way I could have touched the plate if I slid around him. Let's face it. He had the plate blocked, and he did not have the ball. I am not saying that he was wrong. I would say, if anything, that he was just like I was. He was gutty and he was trying to win the ball game. He didn't want me to score, but I did what I had to do, and as everyone could see, I was reaching for the plate when I hit him. I had one thing in mind, and that was trying to score the run. I wasn't worrying about getting hurt, which I did. I got bad publicity from some people, but I missed four games. He didn't miss any games.

I have heard some players say that only if it had been during a World Series or the play-offs, they would have done what I did. I think this should have no significance on the matter. Here are 52 million people watching the All-Star game. Now, if I am going to slide around and give myself up, then I am a pretty dumb ballplayer.

DON: And you play to win, no matter what game you are playing in, whether it be an exhibition or a league game.

PETE: That's right. There again, I am playing in front of my hometown people, and I am trying to win for the National League, and I would do it in the play-offs, World Series, a league game or an exhibition game. It leaves me no alternative. That is what I have to do because I couldn't do anything else. I am not a "give up" ballplayer. If I would have slid, I would have been a "give up" ballplayer.

DON: What were your thoughts as you were tearing down that third base line toward the plate?

PETE: I had one thing in mind, and that was trying to score the run. And I ended up doing that. Amos Otis made a good throw on me, and Fosse had the plate blocked, which he was supposed to do, but it just happened that I hit him just before the ball got to him, and he couldn't catch the ball, but I would do it next year if the same situation came up again.

DON: In closing, Pete, do you have any other advice you would like to give young baseball players?

PETE: Many people say, "It's not whether you win or lose but how you play the game." I am a firm believer that it is the wrong thing to say to a young athlete because there is only one thing in sports and that is winning, and being a good loser if you lose. On the other hand, an athlete should play to win. There is only one way to play the game, and that is to play to win!

Little League ballplayers must practice more on their own. Many people cannot understand how much practice it really takes to become a good athlete.

As a professional, the hardest thing is not making the big leagues, rather, it is staying in the big leagues. There have been a lot of ballplayers who have made the big leagues but they don't stay up there. A player has to work hard to get to the big leagues, and after he arrives he must work even harder.

Helpful Hints in Hitting

1. Know the strike zone and swing at strikes.
2. Take a short stride. Don't lunge.
3. Don't stride too soon but be quick with the hands and wrists.
4. Step *to* hit, not step *and* hit.
5. Hit the ball where it is pitched. *Concentrate on this.*
6. Have a positive attitude. (Every pitch is a strike, and I am going to hit it.)
7. Have confidence you can hit any pitch. (The pitcher must come to me, not I have to go to him.)
8. The level swing has a better chance of contact.
9. Don't hitch with the hands.
10. Try to see how well you can hit the ball, not how far.
11. Be aggressive. Start for every pitch.
12. Keep the front shoulder in.
13. Watch the ball all the way. Don't pull the head out.
14. Use the Instant Replay video-machine to study and analyze your swing.

Bunting /2/

The bunting game can play a vital role in any team's offensive strategy. A varied array of bunts, if used skillfully, can exert the type of pressure that can have an unsettling effect on the defense, particularly when they are executed with the element of surprise and deception. When a runner has to be advanced, the batter must be proficient in executing the sacrifice bunt properly (Fig. 2–2).

A successful bunt is often the difference between victory or defeat in a close ball game. Not only is a well-placed bunt tough to field but the technique of faking the bunt and hitting away can be disturbing to those infielders who like to move in dangerously close. However, the bunt has much more to offer than just in sacrifice situations. Used unexpectedly, it can keep the defense constantly guessing and off balance. The threat of a bunt brings each opposing infielder in a step, and every inward step they take will increase the chances of a base hit.

The present shortage of good bunters can be attributed to a number of reasons. Perhaps the biggest one is the great urge on the part of teams to go for the long ball. The more power a team has, the less likely it will bunt.

There are fewer and fewer Maury Willses who use the bunt anymore for base hits. It should be mentioned that ball clubs are bringing their young players up a little sooner than they used to, with less experience. A player today will play one or two years in the minor leagues, then he finds himself in the majors. And he has not had enough experience or coaching to develop the finer skills of his trade.

Fig. 2–2. WILLIE DAVIS'S BUNT ADVANCES RUNNER. Willie bounces a high bunt in front of home plate in the final game of the 1965 World Series in Minneapolis-St. Paul. The sacrifice advanced Jim Gilliam to second base.

Unfortunately, very little time and emphasis are devoted to bunting practice. Not only should every player learn how to bunt, but he should devote part of his daily hitting practice to laying down bunts. Above all, during bunting practice the pitcher should put something on the ball. Most pitchers just lob the ball in when the hitter is bunting, which creates an entirely different situation than prevails in a game. Indeed, the hours and hours of bunting practice during spring training can pay off with victories later on in the season.

While the sacrifice bunt has to cope with superlative defenses at the major league level, the bunt can produce huge dividends at the lower levels of play. Many supposedly poised defenses have been completely demoralized by a variety of safe bunts in a row. One of the best ways for a team to get going is with a good bunt. When one considers how often bunts can get a team started—getting the first man on base—it is quite easy to respect "the little bunt as a major weapon."

Perhaps the major reason for faulty bunting technique is poor position. Many young players are so interested in reaching base safely and getting a base hit that they neglect to bunt properly. In their haste to get a good start to first base, many bunters are usually not squared around in time.

Consequently, the biggest fault among bunters today is that they want to bunt the ball behind the plate instead of out in front of the plate. In addition, they start for first base too quickly, before the bunt is made. If they would square around, get set and make the ball come to the bat, they would be on their way to becoming proficient bunters.

Good bunters hold their bat fairly high, at the height of the strike zone. Most pitchers are instructed to throw the ball high because the high pitch is the toughest ball to bunt. To combat this, the bunter should be taught to hold his bat at the top of the strike zone. This will enable him to go down on any pitch in the strike zone, rather than coming up. It is easier and quicker to bring the bat down than to raise it up.

Improved Defenses

Laying the ball down can be a difficult assignment, particularly if the pitcher keeps the ball high. The bunt defense has improved considerably. With the first and third basemen drawn way in, the sacrifice can be a tough play to perform. The first baseman is charging and running down your throat. On our club, for instance, we have two or three set bunt defenses. Using signs, we go from one to the other, and we will do one thing on one pitch and another thing on another pitch. The bunt defense has improved to such a degree that the offense really has to have their bunting game down.

I am not surprised that some managers and coaches have questioned the advisability of placing too much emphasis on the bunt. Gene Mauch, manager of the Montreal Expos, explains this point of view: "Just because you put a bunt play on does not necessarily mean it is going to work, because opposing teams spend hours and hours of practice trying to defend against bunts. The situation often dictates a bunt without exception, and they align their defenses in such a way that it is sometimes an impossibility to bunt a man over."

The new artificial turf playing fields likely will have an effect on offensive strategy. Since bunted balls have such a good roll, more than a few managers will have their hitters fake a bunt and then hit away.

While the defense can be difficult in situations calling for the sacrifice, I still maintain that the man who can handle the bat skillfully should not be underestimated. Here again, I think it depends on the club. Take a club like the Dodgers, who are known not to get too many home runs: we have to rely on the sacrifice and the single to score the run, or on occasion the squeeze or the bunt for a base hit. With a Maury Wills on the team, the bunt is a very essential thing. It not only keeps the infield in where the batter can hit the ball past them, but he can get some base hits by bunting too.

Bunting a pitch right over the plate is not a tough assignment, but it takes plenty of practice to put the bat in front of a high pitch. Especially in sacrifice bunt situations, the pitcher will keep the ball high or inside, trying to force the batter to pop the ball into the air.

The major reason for faulty bunting technique is poor position.

Fig. 2–3. BUNTING IS AN ART which demands considerable practice. Here, Manny Mota, one of baseball's premier bunters, works on his bunting technique during pregame practice.

Hitting is a tough assignment to master but almost *any* athlete can become a good bunter if he is willing to practice (Fig. 2–3).

Bunting Stances

There are various types of bunting stances employed in baseball today. More and more coaches are teaching their players to pivot in their tracks, rather than square around with their feet as they did formerly. In fact, most major league players merely square their hips and shoulders and keep their feet planted, whether they are sacrificing or going for a base hit.

If a player can bunt well by just pivoting his hips and shoulders, that is fine, and the ideal way. However, to me, the older method of squaring around is a little surer, especially in colleges and on the younger teams. A player is probably better off squaring around.

Whatever stance is used for the sacrifice bunt, it is essential that the bat be well out in front of the plate.

The biggest fault among bunters today is that they want to bunt the ball behind the plate instead of out in front of the plate.

Fig. 2–4. THE BUNTING TECHNIQUE used by many big league players today involves pivoting on the balls of their feet and remaining in their tracks. They merely square their hips without lifting their feet off the ground (Bud Harrelson).

There are bunters who prefer squaring around with the feet, rather than squaring just the hips and shoulders (Fig. 2–8). They feel they can achieve a more comfortable and set stance if they shift their feet around in a squared position. In fact, some baseball coaches prefer to have their bunters square around with the feet.

Square around

When he squares around, the bunter has a little better coverage of the entire plate. I have observed that when bunters use the "Pivot-in-Tracks" method, at times they fail to get their bat out far enough in front, and it is sometimes a little hard to reach the outside of the plate.

Pivot-in-tracks The bunter remains in his tracks and on the balls of his feet. He merely pivots his feet toward the pitcher. He pivots on the heel of the front foot, so that the toe is pointing toward the pitcher, and on the ball of the back foot just enough to turn the foot a little. This turns the shoulders and hips so he is facing the pitcher (Fig. 2–9).

Actually, the bat position for the pivot-in-tracks is the same as for the square-around position. The bunter can swing his hips around and square them to the pitcher without lifting his feet off the ground.

By using the pivot-in-tracks method, the bunter will help keep the infielders from charging too quickly. However, the defense is frequently anticipating a bunt, so this doesn't play too major a role.

Bunting Technique

There are several theories as to the actual technique of laying the ball down properly. Some coaches teach their players to hold the bat in their fingers, so that when the ball meets the bat it just hits the bat back into their hands. This tends to deaden the ball enough. Another theory is that the bunter has to "give" slightly with the bat when the ball makes contact. The idea is to make the ball come to the bat, and "catch the ball" on the bat.

The thing we do not like our players to do is "jab at the ball." By doing that, they pop the ball up. We like them to just come with the ball and lay the bat on it. Of course, just how hard they should bunt the ball depends on whether they are playing on artificial turf or grass.

Another theory in bunting, designed to get the bat out in front of the plate, is to actually point the barrel of the bat right toward the pitcher as he goes into his delivery. The bunter then flattens the bat out and levels off as the pitch comes in. This will ensure the bat being out in front of the plate—one of the basic rules of bunting.

Body position The bunter's body should be in a slight crouch and leaning toward the plate, to make sure the bat has the plate well covered. The trunk and knees are slightly bent and most of the body weight is placed on the front foot. A bunter should realize that being up in the front part of the batter's box gives him a better opportunity to bunt the ball fair. His knees should be slightly bent and flexible. The weight should be on the balls of the feet, slightly forward (Fig. 2–5).

Arms and hands The arms should be relaxed, out in front of the bunter's body. The bat should be held parallel to the ground, chest-high and covering

The bunter should make the ball come to the bat and catch it almost as if the end of the bat were his glove.

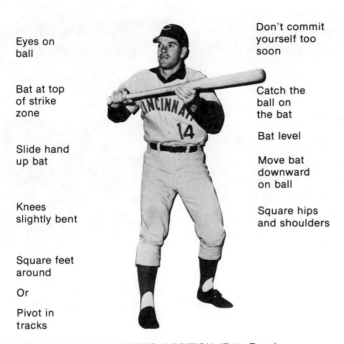

Eyes on
ball

Bat at top
of strike
zone

Slide hand
up bat

Knees
slightly bent

Square feet
around

Or

Pivot in
tracks

Don't commit
yourself too
soon

Catch the
ball on
the bat

Bat level

Move bat
downward
on ball

Square hips
and shoulders

Fig. 2–5. THE CORRECT BUNTING POSITION (Pete Rose).

the plate, with the elbows near the body. The right hand should slide up close to the trademark as the bat is leveled off. The bat should be gripped lightly with the upper hand, keeping the fingers underneath and the thumb on top. The thumb and index finger form a V (Fig. 2–7).

The barrel end of the bat is extended in front of the body and points toward the pitcher. The hands and arms should give as the ball is met, as if the bat were catching the ball. The top hand should cup the bat without curling the fingers around it. The grip on the bat should be mainly with the thumb, index finger and middle finger. The other fingers should be tucked in and under the bat. The more firmly his hands grip the bat, the harder he will bunt the ball.

Eyes

The bunter's eyes should be *on the ball.* From the start of the pitcher's delivery to the actual contact of the ball on the bat, the eyes should be focused on the moving ball. Only good balls should be bunted—those in the strike zone. Successful bunting, like hitting, requires not only good eyesight, but knowledge of the strike zone.

In executing the sacrifice bunt, the hitter should give himself up.

A   B   C

Fig. 2–6. THE SACRIFICE BUNT. The key rule in executing the sacrifice bunt is for the batter to give himself up. Making a good bunt is the main objective. In this excellent demonstration of bunting by Don Money, observe the perfectly level bat which "gives" upon contact with the ball.

Bat position

The bat should be held at the top of the strike zone. It should not be gripped tightly, although it should be held firmly. Let the ball contact the bat, but keep the bat above the ball to prevent pop-ups.

The direction in which the ball is bunted depends on the angle of the bat. In other words, if the surface of the bat faces third base, the ball will be bunted toward third.

The idea is to make the ball come to the bat—to catch the ball on the large end of the bat. The body and arm actions are very similar to those used in catching a ball, so the bunter must concentrate, relax and just "catch the ball" with the bat almost as if the end of the bat were really his glove.

Types of Bunts

There are two kinds of bunts: 1) The sacrifice bunt, and 2) Bunting for a base hit—the drag and the push bunts.

Sacrifice bunt

With runners on first, or first and second, the bunt is still considered good baseball by the great majority of managers and coaches, particularly with no outs. First, the runners can be advanced into scoring

Fig. 2–7. GETTING THE BAT OUT IN FRONT of the plate, Hal Lanier lays down a perfect sacrifice bunt.

position, and second, the double play threat is eliminated.

The sacrifice bunt from first base absolutely can and *should* be made at least 80 percent of the time, if the ball is bunted properly. In this situation, the first baseman should be made to field the ball. Therefore, the ball is bunted toward first. Sometimes, I think, bunters try to make the ball too perfect down the line. They end up having the ball roll foul. If the ball is bunted properly and not too hard, and if it is halfway between the pitcher and catcher, this is a pretty sure bunt.

The key rule in executing the sacrifice bunt is for the hitter to give himself up. The purpose of the sacrifice bunt is to advance the runner at the expense of the bunter. *The bunter is expendable!* Making a good bunt is the main objective (Fig. 2–6).

The placement of sacrifice bunts depends on which bases are occupied, the defensive positions of the opposition and their ability to field bunts. Normally, a sacrifice bunt should not be used unless the runner or runners, when advanced, could tie the score or put the offensive team ahead.

On a straight sacrifice bunt, the batter attempts to bunt the ball *only if the pitch is a strike.* He must realize that he should bunt only good balls that are in the strike zone, unless, of course, the suicide squeeze play is on.

With first base occupied, a bunt down the first base line is considered good baseball. The first baseman, holding the runner on first

A

B

C

Fig. 2–8. SQUARE AROUND. There are still a large number of coaches who prefer to have their bunters square around with the feet, rather than just squaring the hips and shoulders. They feel the bunter then has better coverage of the entire part of the plate (Mark Belanger).

base, will not be in a good position to field the ball, since he does not leave the base until the pitcher delivers. With second base occupied, a hard bunt down the third base line can be a good tactic. When the third baseman comes in to field the ball, he leaves third base uncovered.

While the sacrifice can be a difficult assignment, time and hard work in the cage can provide the skillful execution so necessary for the job. When a runner has to be moved up, the batter must be proficient in executing the sacrifice bunt properly.

Run-and-bunt play

This play is a variation of the sacrifice bunt, in which the base runner attempts a steal of the next base. To protect the runner, the hitter must bunt the ball regardless of where it is pitched. A good time to execute this play is when the pitcher is behind in the count and therefore more likely to make the next pitch a strike. The best game situation is with none out and a runner on first base.

Bunting should not be a lost art in our modern game. It merely takes time and work.

A   B   C

Fig. 2–9. PIVOT IN TRACKS. The large majority of big league players square only their hips and shoulders to bunt and keep their feet planted. This method helps keep the infielders from charging too quickly. The important point is to get the bat out in front of the plate in a position to reach even the outside pitch (Manny Mota).

To surprise the defense and make a safe hit, the batter might attempt to beat out a bunt. The bunt base hit is a beautiful thing to watch because it takes great skill, and plenty of action is involved.

Since sacrifice bunting alerts the infielders, a hitter should not square around toward the pitcher until the very last instant. The drag bunt and push bunt are both attempts at a base hit.

Bunting for a hit is often used when the third baseman, or the other infielders, are playing deep or when the third baseman or pitcher fields bunts poorly. The ball can either be pushed toward first base (right-handed bunter) or dropped down the third base line. The batter conceals his intent until the last split-second and meets the ball on the move (Fig. 2–10).

If the pitcher uses slow pitches and curves, it is easier to bunt the ball on the ground than if he uses fast balls.

There is always danger in base hit bunts, in that once the hitter has decided to use it, he has a tendency to bunt the ball even if it is not

Bunting for a hit

A

B

C

D

Fig. 2–10. BUNTING FOR A BASE HIT (Right-handed hitter) (below). This bunt technique is used when the third baseman is playing deep. The bunter steps one stride backward with his right foot to the left of the plate, as the weight shifts to the left foot. Once the feet are set, the weight should be shifted again to the right foot. The head of the bat points toward first base (Bobby Valentine).

where he wants it. He must learn to snap the bat back out of the way of bad pitches.

The left-handed batter has an advantage over a right-hander in bunting for a base hit, since he is more than a full step nearer first base. The left-handed swinger who is quick on his feet and a skillful bunter can be a real threat to the defense, particularly on a drag toward the second baseman.

Right-Handed Batter *(Push Bunt).* This offensive tactic is used when the first baseman is playing deep. The push bunt is directed toward the pitcher's left, the first base side of the infield (Fig. 2–12). The batter stands at the plate, decoying a possible swing at the ball. As the pitcher cocks his arm in his delivery, the batter rotates his hips to the rear as if he wanted to take a full swing.

Aiming for the hole between first and second base, the batter takes a short lead step with his front foot as the bat is pushed at an outside pitch. He must meet the ball before his right foot hits the ground. The ball is pushed or pulled by manipulating the near hand on the bat handle, sending the ball in the desired direction. This type of bunt must be hard enough to get by the pitcher. It should be used only when the first baseman is playing back.

Left-Handed Batter *(Drag Bunt).* The drag bunt can be a valuable offensive weapon for a left-handed batter, usually when the first baseman plays deep. The objective is to bunt the ball to the left of the pitcher, and hard enough so that the pitcher cannot field the ball, forcing the first baseman or second baseman to do so. Success in the drag bunt comes only when the defense is not expecting it.

The batter stands at the plate, decoying a possible swing. As the pitcher cocks his arm in his delivery motion, he may rotate his hips to the rear as though meaning to take a full swing.

Figure 2–11 shows Maury Wills stepping toward first base with his front right foot, as he levels off the bat. I would say this is a perfect example of how the drag bunt should be executed. He sets the angle of the bat so that the big end points halfway between third base and home plate. The bat is approximately at a right angle with the side of his body. Holding the bat at the end with his right hand, his left hand is on the trademark of the bat. Maury's bat comes in contact with the ball out in front of the plate. Notice the perfectly level bat at contact with the ball. When contact is made, his weight is on his right foot, with his left foot trailing slightly, ready to cross over the right leg.

The biggest fault of many players on the drag bunt is crossing over too quickly with the left foot, since most left-handed bunters run away from the ball. They try to run before they really make contact, because they are more intent on getting a good start than on bunting the ball. It is like catching a ball: the fielder has to catch it before he throws it. Likewise, in bunting, the ball has to be bunted before the play can be made.

In executing a drag bunt correctly, the bunter should step toward the ball with his right foot and meet the ball before his left foot hits the ground. Some bunters prefer to take a short step with the right foot, and then step over with the left.

First Base Area

B   A

D   C

Fig. 2–11. DRAG BUNT (Left-handed hitter). As he levels off the bat, the bunter steps toward first base with his front right foot. The bat is approximately at a right angle with the side of his body. When contact is made, his weight is on his right foot, with his left foot trailing slightly, ready to cross over the right leg (Maury Wills).

Third Base Area   **Right-Handed Batter.** As the pitcher starts his delivery, the hitter should rotate the upper part of his body clockwise and draw his bat back, simulating a swing. When the ball heads for the plate, the hitter should set his feet and bat into position. He should take one stride backward with his right foot, to the left of home plate. As this movement is made, the weight should be shifted to the left foot. However, once the feet are set, the weight should be shifted again to the right foot.

The head of the bat points toward first base, and the handle of the bat is slid between the hitter's right side and his right elbow. It is parallel to the ground and slightly above the right hip.

Left-Handed Batter. A left-handed hitter should follow the same procedure as the right-handed player until the ball is about 30 feet away. He should set his feet in position by crossing the left foot over the right, toward first base, when contacting the ball.

In order to get the bat into position, the left-hander should slide his left hand up the handle of the bat six to twelve inches. The handle

A   B

Fig. 2–12. PUSH BUNT FOR A BASE HIT. This bunt is pushed just hard enough between the pitcher and the first baseman to prevent the pitcher from fielding the ball. The batter takes a short lead step with his front foot as the bat is pushed at an outside pitch (Bert Campaneris).

of the bat should be pointed toward first base when the bunt is being made, and the handle should be held away from the body. The hands can be spread or held together.

Fake Bunt

In a bunt situation, when the infield is in too far for safe bunting, the batter may want to fake a bunt and swing or slap at the ball. This is also effective when a runner is trying to steal a base. This not only bothers the catcher in receiving but in throwing the ball as well.

In still another situation, the hitter may assume a bunting position in the hope that the first and third basemen will charge in toward the plate. If the infielders charge, the batter will move both hands up on the handle of the bat and chop down hard on the pitch. He tries to bounce the ball through or over the charging fielders.

The batter should square around to bunt or pivot in his tracks, and then fake a bunt. His hands should be together but fairly high on the bat. As the pitcher releases the ball, the hitter should rotate his hips slightly toward the catcher and take a short swing, stepping with his front foot toward the ball as he swings.

If the runner on third is stealing home, the hitter may fake a bunt and hold his ground. It will help the runner and make it harder for the catcher to tag him, especially if he is a right-handed hitter.

The batter can also use the fake bunt when taking a pitch or a strike. He should make his move before the pitcher releases the ball because this will upset him and make it harder for him to get the ball over the plate.

Squeeze Play

The purpose of the squeeze play is to bring a man home from third base. The prime objective of the bunter is to meet the ball and to get it on the ground. Usually the squeeze is employed to tie the score, score the winning run or provide an insurance run for the team that is ahead.

Safety and suicide squeeze plays are usually tried in the late innings with a runner on third base, one out and the team at bat ahead, tied or no more than one run behind.

In trying to score from third base, the runner breaks for the plate on the pitch. A quick start is essential. He has to be leaning in the direction of the plate, a walking lead, taking a step or two up the line and having his weight forward. As soon as the pitcher releases the ball, he changes gears and goes into a run.

Safety squeeze

The batter bunts the first good ball he gets—he bunts only strikes. The runner does not run for home until he sees that the ball is bunted.

The runner at third base should make his move only if the ball is bunted on the ground. As soon as the pitcher releases the ball, he is ready to run. If the ball is popped up or missed, the runner does not go.

The batter should try to bunt the ball away from the pitcher. If the first baseman is back, the bunter's objective is merely to tap the ball down the first base line. He does not bunt the ball unless the pitch is a good one. The runner tries to score only if he thinks he can make it.

The bunter must bunt the ball regardless of where it is thrown. He must try just to bunt the ball in fair territory and on the ground. The runner at third base knows the batter will bunt the next pitch, no matter where it is, so he starts for home the moment the ball leaves the pitcher's hand. He must make his move at the right time. The play will be in trouble if the runner is late breaking or is too early. The bunter must protect the runner from suicide by making sure to bunt the ball on the ground in fair territory.

To make sure nobody fouls up on this play, a return sign is given from the hitter to the runner.

The pitching machine is good for teaching bunting fundamentals. There is no fear of the machine and it can be set to throw high strikes.

1. Bunt only *good* balls—those in the strike zone—unless the squeeze is on.
2. Hold the bat at the top of the strike zone.
3. Bend the knees slightly, keeping the weight on the balls of the feet.
4. Keep the bat level on all bunts.
5. Keep the bat in front of the body and in front of the plate.
6. Start high and always come down.
7. Let the hands and arms "give" as the ball is met.
8. Grip the bat lightly, with a "V" between the thumb and index finger.

Suicide squeeze

Drill

Basic Tips on Bunting

Base Running /3/

Although speed is a great asset to a base runner, alertness and sliding ability are equally important. The outstanding base runner is not only quick with his feet but also expert at deciding when to and when not to steal. He is aggressive and full of hustle.

The first half of this chapter will deal with base running fundamentals and instruction, while the second half will consider the various aspects of sliding.

An aggressive offense will make the defense hurry their throws and make mistakes. It is not necessarlly the bases they steal but it is the mistakes they force the fielders to make (Fig. 3–2). I prefer my players to be the aggressive, daring type and occasionally take some chances. I feel that I can always slow them down, but it is tough to take a cautious base runner who runs scared and make him a daring ballplayer.

These fellows do not fit into the Dodger plans. We have had success with good and daring base running. There are times when we have been thrown out, but from the overall picture, speed has played an important part in the Dodgers' success, possibly more than anything else. I have never criticized anybody for being thrown out at third base or trying to steal a base within reason.

Of course, the score is the big factor. When we are three or four runs behind, we do not like to take chances. However, in ordinary circumstances, when we are one run ahead or one behind and the game situation permits, I prefer my base runners to take chances.

Speed and Aggressiveness

Aggressive base running pays off. It is something more or less inborn too. There are some base runners who are just timid and afraid. And there are those who become lazy and then wonder why they are thrown out by one step.

Baseball games can be won or lost through good or poor base running. There is nothing more frustrating for a manager than to see his team rap out a whole flock of hits, but because of poor base running fail to score the runs they should. Then, again, there are few aspects of baseball more exciting than a hustling ball club that knows how to run the bases. The importance of good base running is obvious—more base hits, fewer double plays, more extra base hits and many other advantages.

The Maury Wills era

Base running had been a neglected art until Maury Wills arrived on the major league scene with the Dodgers in 1959. The long ball had dominated the game for years, and because of the lively ball managers were reluctant to place too much emphasis on the running game. Rather than employ such tactics as base stealing, hit and run and bunting, they were more inclined to wait for someone to hit the ball out of the park.

The fleet-footed Maury soon established himself as one of the great base runners in the game's history and, more than any other figure in baseball, helped bring about a return of the exciting running game.

Beginning in 1960, when he stole 35 bases, he went on to win the stolen base crown six consecutive seasons. In 1962, this slightly built, agile infielder electrified the baseball world by breaking the immortal Ty Cobb's record by stealing 104 bases.

Out of 117 attempts, he was caught only 13 times. According to the record, Cobb was thrown out 38 times during his big season in 1915. In 1965, Wills stole 94 bases as he paced the Dodgers to another world championship.

Certainly, the daring, aggressive base running of Wills has given the game much needed color and glamour. He came along at a time when the emphasis in baseball was in power and defied everyone with his speed and skill. To me, this is one of the most remarkable accomplishments of modern baseball.

Although the home run is still baseball's foremost attraction, the daring, aggressive play of Maury Wills has made major league teams more conscious of base stealing. Wills's success on the base paths has brought increased emphasis on base stealing and speed, providing the national pastime with added thrills and excitement.

Speed and quickness

The Dodgers have more or less insisted that the players they sign have speed. We still hold speed as a primary factor, and it always will be in this game. However, in the last few years we have gone more to the power type of hitter.

An aggressive offense will make the defense hurry their throws and make mistakes.

Fig. 3–1. AGGRESSIVE BASE RUNNING such as this demonstrated by Maury Wills gave the Dodgers a big victory over the Atlanta Braves. Braves catcher Joe Torre tried to block him but the fleet-footed Wills slid around the tag.

Basically, this game needs speed. Although I like to have some home runs too, I still think that speed is such a major factor, defensively as well as offensively, that it is pretty hard to overlook.

When we bring up to the Dodgers a young player with exceptional speed, I am not afraid to turn him loose in a steal situation. This is because I know that he has been through our training camp, and we have talked to him about getting leads and stealing bases. We even put some of our real speedsters into a special instruction school to learn how to steal second base.

Instinct and reflexes

Good instincts and reflexes are also characteristics of top base runners—to react without giving it much thought and do the right thing automatically. Junior Gilliam was this type of a player. In deciding to take an extra base on a hit, the coach really cannot tell a player whether or not to go. If a fellow thinks he can make it, he goes ahead and runs. With other players, the manager or coach has to tell them, but there is just so much he can tell a base runner.

A ballplayer can be a good base runner and not necessarily have great speed. Tom Haller is one of the slower ones, yet he knows how to run the bases as well as anybody. Most of all, it takes common sense—taking advantage of any little opportunity he can get.

"Actually, a player does not have to be fast," said Wills, "because, with average speed, he can steal a number of bases. So, the main thing is quickness, speed of foot and quickness in deciding when to and when not to go—and getting a good break."

Fig. 3–2. SPEED ON THE BASE PATHS has played a major role in the Dodgers' success. Above, the hustle and aggressiveness of Maury Wills has forced the catcher to hurry his throw, resulting in another stolen base for Maury. With his eye on the ball, Wills is ready to come up, although an alert infielder backing up the play prevented Maury from advancing. The action occurred in the 1965 World Series against the Minnesota Twins.

Mental approach The proper mental approach is essential in becoming a successful base runner. When stealing a base, the player has to believe that he can make it. He must eliminate the fear of failing.

"In stealing a base, confidence to me is 80 percent of the battle," said Maury, "because I know I can run, have knowledge of the pitcher

A ballplayer can be a good base runner and not necessarily have great speed.

and know how to get a good lead. I feel I am better than the pitcher and the catcher, and I eliminate all fears of failing. I am not afraid to be picked off, and I am not afraid to be thrown out trying to steal a base. But I just feel I am going to make it at all times."

"One of the secrets of my success in stealing bases is positive thinking," continued Wills. "Like batting, stealing bases is a matter of confidence. When I am in this frame of mind, I not only *think,* I *know* I can beat the throws of the pitcher and the catcher."

"A player cannot be a good base runner and practice safety first," advised Wills; "he must take chances. He should not be careless, but he has to be daring. My success in base running can be attributed to the fact that I have eliminated the fear of failure."

Knowledge of the pitcher

The runner must have knowledge of the pitcher, knowing the moves he is going to make. When taking a lead, the runner knows just how far he can go. He wants to keep the pitcher on the defensive at all times.

"I pride myself on knowing every move the pitcher is going to make," asserted Wills. "When I take my lead, I know just how far I can get off, and when I see that he Is going home, I take off for the next base."

As a result, even before they leave the dugout, players should watch the pitcher closely, studying his moves to the plate when he has men on base. As a player moves to the on-deck circle, he should continue to watch the pitcher and study the game situation.

The game situation

The base runner is controlled by the game situation. The number of outs, the score, the ability of the base runner, who is pitching and who the hitter is at the plate, and the arm of the fielders are all factors which determine whether he should attempt to advance or not.

Running to First Base

Base running begins at home plate. Batters should learn to swing so that they can recover their balance quickly in heading for first base; if the ball is hit on the ground, the concern of the batter is to cross the bag as quickly as possible.

The most important thing is to get everybody to run as hard as they can as soon as they hit the ball (Fig. 3–3). Ballplayers have to run only four or five times in a game, and yet when a ballplayer hits a one-hopper to the shortstop or second baseman, and it looks like

The bent leg slide is the safest and most effective slide in baseball.
BERNIE DeVIVEIROS

B   A

Fig. 3–3. BASE RUNNING BEGINS AT HOME PLATE. No matter what side of
the plate he swings from, the batter should try to take his first step with the
rear foot. Observe that Billy Grabarkewitz's body has not pulled away from the
plate following his swing.

an easy out, many players will not give 100 percent going down to
first base.

This is the first mistake the base runner makes because anybody
can kick or drop a ball; even a first baseman can drop one occasionally. If he would run hard from the moment he hits the ball, it
would not be asking too much of him. In fact, that is what the fans
expect, and he should do it. One of my pet peeves comes when runners do not give their very best.

The second fault of a base runner is watching the ball. If there is a
base hit, many batters will keep watching the ball. It is all right to
take a quick glance at the ball to see where it is going, but once he
has decided it is a base hit, the best thing to do is to go to first base
as fast as possible, and make his turn! Pepper Martin was one of the
greatest players I have ever seen rounding first base, and he would
start toward second as though he were going to make it. Then he

would "slide his wheels," so to speak, and go back.

No matter what side of the plate one swings from, he should try to take his first step with the rear foot (Fig. 3–3). As the right-handed hitter starts his swing, his body does not pull away from the plate. His stride is directly toward first base, with his rear foot, as he drops his bat with his left hand. The left-handed hitter takes a full stride with his rear foot, as he drops the bat with his right hand.

The runner should go hard for first, looking only at the bag, unless the first base coach signals and yells that it is "through" and to "take your turn." The runner tries to hit first base without a jump, stepping on the center of the base as he crosses it. This is safer than hitting the front edge of the base with the toe. Even though a continuous run is best, there is no use in running far past first. He should slow down and listen for his base coach.

Rounding First Base

When the batter sees that his hit has gone through or over the infield, he should begin circling toward first base by swerving to his right. He should approach first base at full speed, turning into the bag so that one of his feet hits the inside corner (Fig. 3–5).

We have some fellows on our club who do a pretty good job at rounding first base. Maury Wills is one of them. Ideally, the hitter should take a quick look at the ball, then spend his energy in reaching first base as quickly as he possibly can.

I do not like a player to take the big, wide turn at first base. He should hit the inside part with his inside foot, but if he cannot we do not like him to break his stride. He should hit the base with either foot that comes in stride. As he hits the base from the inside, he should turn as sharply as he can and head for second and keep going until he either sees that he cannot make it or somebody else stops him.

Ideally, it is best for the runner to keep his body leaning toward the infield and to use the inside corner of the base as a push-off point toward second base. It is also easier to hit the base with the inside foot, with the right then crossing over. However, I do not want him to break stride in order to hit it with his inside foot.

The Lead Off

The base runner has to be alert when he is at first base. First, he must look and see whether the coach has a sign for him to take. He should keep one foot on the bag when he gets his signals (Fig. 3–6). He should also check the positions of the outfielders, to see whether they are playing in. He must know the strength and accuracy of the catcher's throwing arm and what kind of a move the pitcher has. This is the type of knowledge that can make him a more effective base runner.

The most important thing is to determine the lead he is capable of taking, and getting back to the base. He must know the pitcher, his

Fig. 3–4. SPEED AND HUSTLE. Batters should learn to swing so that they can recover their balance quickly in heading for first base. In this exciting series of pictures, the speed of Willie Davis is able to turn a slow dribbler into a base hit by beating the pitcher's throw to first base.

habits and manners, and his capabilities of picking him off base. If he studies the pitchers continuously, every day, that is the thing that will help him steal bases.

Stance

The runner at first base should stand facing the pitcher, legs slightly bent, with his feet about a foot and a half apart. He should crouch a bit and let his arms hang loosely in front of him. His weight should be evenly distributed. He should be on the balls of his feet, so that he can go either way. *He must keep his eyes on the pitcher at all times.* He is waiting for the first indication that the pitcher will throw to the plate, and not to first base. He should not jump back and forth. The pitcher may catch him going the wrong way.

Getting the Lead

The factor that determines the length of the lead is: "Can I beat the throw to the bag?" Runners who react quickly can afford to take longer leads.

The length of the lead depends on the game situation. If it is early in the game and our runners have not seen the pitcher's moves, we tell our players: "If you are not going to steal and you want to see what kind of move he has, make him throw over there by more or less getting a good sized lead." This should be a "one-way lead." As he takes a longer lead, he is leaning back a little toward first. Now the pitcher will throw over there a time or two, and the runner will have an opportunity to study his different moves, particularly his shoulders.

In taking his lead, the base runner should always advance his right foot first and then his left foot, keeping both feet close to the ground (Fig. 3–7).

Fig. 3–4. (Continued) The runner should go hard for first base, looking only at the bag. He tries to hit first base without a jump. Rather than curse himself for not hitting the ball solidly, Willie has hustled out a much-needed hit.

There are all types of pitchers who have really good moves to first base. Yet, when they deliver the ball, the delivery is so slow that the good base runner steals on them, in spite of a good move. While a runner cannot take much of a lead, he can still steal the base when the pitcher is delivering the ball because his delivery is so slow.

Then, there is the other kind of pitcher who has a quick delivery but not a good move to first base. With a pitcher like this, the runner has to take a longer lead because he does not have as much time during the delivery.

Basically, the base runner steals on the pitcher, not the catcher. There are a few catchers in the league who are easy to steal on, but Johnny Bench is *not* one of them. Johnny keeps those runners pretty close, and when they do decide to go, he can really gun them down!

Returning to first base

When the pitcher steps on the rubber, the base runner should take a lead just far enough so that he will be able to get back in time to beat any throw. Maury feels that, unless he has to dive back into first base, he has not taken a good enough lead. I think this is all right for Maury, who, of course, has base running down to the fine points. When an experienced base runner like Wills does it, he knows how far he can go and still get back safely. The college or high school boy who tries to do this, however, may get himself picked off.

The runner returns to first base by stepping back on the base with his left foot, and his body leans away from the first baseman. For most base runners, this is the proper way of returning to the bag (Fig. 3–9).

In leading off second base, the runner can take a longer lead. He should always listen for the base coach. In taking a lead, he should

Fig. 3–5. ROUNDING FIRST BASE. On a base hit, the batter begins circling toward first base by swerving to his right. Ideally, he should hit the inside part with his inside foot. He uses the inside corner of the base as a push-off point toward second base (Billy Grabarkewitz).

always advance his right foot first and slide his left foot, keeping both feet close to the ground. He should make sure that a ball hit to the shortstop goes through before going to third base.

The one-way lead The base runner uses this when trying to determine how much of a lead he can take on the pitcher. He tries to make the pitcher throw over there so he can find out a little more about him.

The stance is similar to the normal stance, except that most of the body weight is on the back foot (left). Therefore, he is "leaning" back toward the base.

"I take an exaggerated lead toward second base," stated Maury, "and my weight is shifted to the point where I am ready to go back to first base, regardless of what move the pitcher makes. If he goes home, my first move is still back to first base, and I can still recover in time."

When the runner has determined how much of a lead he can take safely and is flashed the "steal" signal, then he assumes the two-way lead.

The two-way lead The two-way lead means that he can go in either direction, depending on the pitcher's move. He does not take quite as long a lead as in the one-way lead. The runner must keep his weight evenly distributed on

78

Fig. 3–6. GETTING THE SIGNAL, the base runner should keep one foot on the bag. He should also check the fielding positions of the outfielders, to see whether they are playing in (Billy Grabarkewitz).

the balls of the feet and his body in a crouched position, with the knees slightly bent (Fig. 3–8).

"From this position, I take as big a lead as I can," said Wills. "Sometimes I take a big enough lead so that I am forced to dive or slide back to the base when a pick-off is attempted by the pitcher."

In this lead, the runner walks off first base casually as the pitcher is taking his set position. "Just as the pitcher indicates that he is throwing home, I break for second base, without coming to a stop," said Maury.

"This way, I get a good start or jump toward second base," declared Wills, "since my body is moving in that direction. I might add that experienced pitchers will make the runner come to a stop. This spoils the walking lead."

The walking lead

The expert base runner gets the jump on the pitcher by studying his moves and personal mannerisms. Some pitchers have all sorts of telltale things that they do. By watching him closely, the runner can spot his peculiar little habits, which will give the runner the jump he needs. The runner should study how the pitcher lifts his foot and how he comes around with his arm. He should look for a hunch of the shoulders, a move of the elbow. Some pitchers drop

Getting the jump on the pitcher

their shoulder a little. Whatever he looks for, the base runner should remember to be subtle in his looking.

"One of the indications is when a pitcher stands with an open shoulder," claimed Wills. "When he is ready to throw toward home,

Fig. 3–7. GETTING A LEAD. The runner should get his lead by advancing his right foot first, followed by his left foot, keeping both feet close to the ground (Billy Grabarkewitz).

his shoulder is usually on a line to the plate. If he wants to pick me off, he usually turns more toward first."

Sometimes when a pitcher goes to first base with the ball, he will stand with his feet a little closer together, or maybe the other way around. Maury likes to watch the elbow and the head. Willie Mays says he watches the pitcher's head. There have been others who found it effective to study the pitcher's feet, since the feet reveal first where the pitcher will throw.

If the pitcher commits himself with a move toward the batter, he has to throw home or a *balk* is called. As soon as the runner sees the pitcher start his pitch, he can be off and running.

Taking–Off   The base runner should break for the base at the precise second the pitcher begins his move to the plate. Most runners prefer their first move toward second base to be a cross-over step. When they decide to go, they just pivot on the right foot and cross-over with the back

Fig. 3–8. A GOOD READY STANCE. In taking his lead, the runner at first base should be in a slight crouch and let his arms hang loosely in front of him. His weight should be evenly distributed on the balls of his feet so he can go either way (Maury Wills).

foot. They should shove off for second on the left foot while pivoting on the right foot. One's weight should be forward with his legs driving hard (Fig. 3–10).

In shoving-off for second, he should swing his left arm toward the next base in the same way a boxer throws an uppercut. This helps him cross over. The arm action pulls his body around and enables him to take a good first stride with his left foot.

"I always remember to keep my body moving," said Wills. "A runner can get away faster when he is in motion rather than standing still. I shuffle back and forth, bending my knees and trying to keep my weight on the balls of my feet. When the pitcher starts for the plate, I start for second."

Is it easier to steal third base than to steal second base? "It is easier," admitted Maury, "but the only time a player should steal third base is when he is positive he can make it. This is because second base is considered scoring position. To be thrown out trying to steal third base when a player is already in scoring position is a very bad play.

Fig. 3–9. RETURNING TO FIRST BASE. The runner steps back onto the base with his left foot, swinging toward right field with his right foot. This elusive action enables him to lean away from the first baseman (Billy Grabarkewitz).

"Of course, it is much better to be on third base than second base because there are nine more ways a player can score from third than from second."

Touching the bases   The base runner should never have to slow down to make a turn or to change strides in order to touch the bag with a certain foot. The beginning of the turn should be made from 20 to 30 feet in front of the bag.

Tagging up on a fly   The runner should have his left foot on third, with the right foot pointing toward home plate. His body should face the field, with the weight on his front foot.

He goes when the outfielder catches the ball. He should not depend on the third base coach to yell, "Go!" Some players prefer a position similar to a sprinter. When on third base, the runner should tag up on any ball hit in the air, even on all foul balls.

How to Run   Perhaps the fundamental least stressed and one of the most important in baseball is the art of running. While nature has endowed human beings with a basic speed, additional speed can often be obtained simply by executing the basic principles of running (Fig. 3–11).

A runner should keep his head up so he can see the play. Arching his neck, he leans forward without swaying or weaving. All his motion

C   B   A

Fig. 3–10. TAKING OFF FOR SECOND. After getting a good lead, Maury Wills pivots on the ball of his right foot. His first move is a cross-over step with his left foot. Keeping his weight on the balls of his feet, he lifts the heel of his right foot, which enables him to make his pivot smoothly and quickly. Observe how Maury leans toward second base as he generates the necessary momentum for a quick thrust-off with his cross-over leg.

should be straight ahead. His chin should be up and his eyes on the base to which he is running. His arms should be bent at the elbow and relaxed, and the forearm should move directly forward and backward beside the body. The faster the arms are pumped, the faster the legs will move. Taking a good stride, he should run naturally on the balls of his feet.

Most good runners swing the arm forward so that the hand swings almost as high as the shoulder, and then to the rear and to the side of the hip. The right arm should go forward with the left leg, and the left arm with the right leg. In Fig. 3–11, notice the straight line from shoulder to heel as the base runner drives forward with great speed.

A base runner often has the responsibility of breaking up a possible double play. When sliding into second base, the purpose is not to injure the infielder but only to unbalance him and thus prevent an accurate throw to first base. To do this, the runner uses a hard slide with the knees bent at a 45-degree angle. If possible, he should hook the striding foot of the infielder. Some sliders will roll into the defensive player.

In 1959, only by breaking up the double play did we manage to win the World Series. That was one of the key plays in our victory over the Chicago White Sox.

Breaking up the Double Play

Fig. 3–11. PROPER RUNNING FORM. The runner keeps his head up so he can see the play. The arms should be bent at the elbow and relaxed. He should run naturally on the balls of his feet (Bernie Carbo).

The runner on first base, of course, has to run hard to get to second base. Even then, on a fast double play, he does not always get there in time. In certain double play situations where the runner has time to get there, he should slide into the shortstop or second baseman, whoever is fielding the ball. While we do not want to hurt anybody intentionally, we want this runner to slide into the legs of the infielder and try to upset him. He should use a hard slide with the knees bent at a 45-degree angle, and try to hook the striding foot of the infielder.

If the shortstop should move far across the base and toward right field, the base runner should slide after him, rather than the bag. This is an accepted practice in baseball. Of course, the shortstop has the advantage. He knows whether he will cross the bag or stay in the inside, while the runner does not know. The only thing the runner can do is *guess* which side he will go on, and slide into him and try to knock his feet from under him.

The base runner must remember that the slide must be such that some part of the runner is within reaching distance of the bag. Otherwise, he could be charged with interference if he slides more than three feet out of the base line to hit the pivot man or if he deliberately interferes with the throw.

Fig. 3–12. STOLEN BASE NO. 43. Maury Wills, on the way to his base stealing record of 104, steals his 43rd base, shown here against the New York Mets. Fielding the ball is Roy McMillan, Met shortstop.

Use of Base Coaches

Whenever base runners cannot see the ball or a fielder without turning their heads very much, they should use their base coaches. They should use their own judgment as to whether to advance or not whenever they can see the ball or the fielder easily.

Runners use the first base coach for decisions on stopping at first, making the turn at first, going on to second or hurrying back to first. They use the third base coach for stopping at second, rounding it or going on to third, as well as directions at third base.

The third base coach gets blamed for a lot of running situations over which he really does not have control. Actually, the only time he does is when a man is on first and the ball is hit down to first base and on down the right field foul line. This is when the runner has to take a quick look at the third base coach to see whether he should go or not. About 20 to 30 feet from second base, he should cut out and at the same time glance at the third base coach, then go from there. Basically, though, the runner is on his own.

Anytime the play is right in front of the runner, such as in left field, he himself has a better idea then someone else as to whether he can go on to third base. As long as the play is *in front of* him, he should be on his own.

The third base coach might walk up and say: "Now that you are on third, we want you to go in on a ground ball," or, "Make the ball go through the infield," or, "Be sure to take off on a fly ball," and such type of information. Basically, though, the runner plays *himself* and is pretty much on his own.

Base Running Drills

During spring training, we like to work on our base running and hitting together in the same situation. When we take batting practice, we start with a man on first base, and our first pitch is a hit-and-run. The pitcher on the mound is supposed to throw over to first base on occasion, just as in a game situation. As a result, our players get in the habit of executing the cross-over stop and taking-off for second under gamelike type conditions.

Our coaches are right there to make sure the players run the bases correctly. Then, we get the runner to second base on the next pitch and try to advance him to third on a ball hit to the right center part of the field. On the third pitch, we try to squeeze him in. We have a coach at third base telling the runner when to leave.

This goes on all through batting practice. Each hitter takes his turn at bat and then goes to first base and becomes a base runner. This may seem like a silly thing, but it takes a little practice to learn to break just the right way for certain types of balls. And only by *doing* this can we perfect it.

We will put a runner at third base, with one out, and have the batter hit a ground ball. We want our runner at third to force that fielder to throw him out at home. We find that there are certain runners who can do this and others who cannot. A quick thinker and reactor like Maury Wills is the type of runner who will work this play to perfection. Let us say Manny Mota hits a ground ball to the second baseman; even though the infield is pulled in, Wills, with his quickness, alertness and baseball sense, will often score.

Now, if Maury gets caught, the best thing for him to do is hold up until Mota gets to second base, then we still have a man in scoring position. So, it depends a great deal on the game situation and the personnel.

Breaks and leads drill

The Dodgers use this drill to develop base stealing skill. We have a pitcher, catcher and first baseman placed in their respective defensive positions. Then, three players line up one behind the other, with the front player on the base path between first and second.

As the pitcher comes to a set position, the three runners take a two-way lead off the base. Now the pitcher pitches to the plate, or else throws to first base. The runners do not know where the throw is going.

If it goes to the plate, they break for second, using a cross-over step and running hard for about ten yards. If the ball is thrown to first base, they all return to the base or base line. If they break for second, another three players move into the positions.

Drills like these have done much to give the Dodgers their ability to steal bases.

We also have a track where we can work three or four players at a time and teach them the cross-over step. We even have a track coach down at Dodgertown assisting us on speed development.

List of Base Running Drills

1. Running to first base
2. Making the turn at first base
3. One-way lead
4. Two-way lead
5. Straight steal
6. Delayed steal
7. Double steal (when on first and third)
8. Taking the signals (on the base)
9. Squeeze play (running from third)
10. Following coach's directions
11. Tagging up on fly balls
12. Breaking and leading drill
13. Circling the bases (entire squad)
14. Returning to bases on attempted pick-offs.

Practice Tips for the Base Runner

1. Practice getting starts on all hit balls.
2. At every opportunity, practice getting leads and starts off all bases.
3. Practice your jump in leaving first, using the pivot and the cross-over push step.
4. During pregame batting practice, practice this routine after your last swing in the batting cage: run to first, take your turn, hold up, get your lead, and break for second as the pitcher makes his pitch to the next hitter.
5. Practice taking a full swing, then follow-through and try to keep from falling toward third base at the finish.
6. Practice leading off a base. Back off the bag with your rear leg behind your right. Then shuffle off to get the desired length—eight to ten feet.

Base Running Reminders

1. Where is the ball?
2. How many outs are there?
3. Look for a possible sign

4. Do not talk to the opposing infielders
5. Always run with your head up
6. Touch all bases
7. Watch the runner in front of you
8. When in doubt, always slide.

Sliding

A good base runner has to be able to slide, and this comes with practice. Furthermore, he must be able to slide on either his left or right side, as well as go straight in. The sooner young players learn that "it is a slide and not a leap," the sooner they will become proficient base runners (Fig. 3–14).

Sliding is really controlled falling. The runner simply drops to the ground according to the slide desired, and the momentum of his run does the rest.

We stress the bent leg slide because we feel it is the most effective slide in baseball. Besides being the safest slide for a base runner, the top foot is going directly to the bag as quickly as it can. When a runner executes the hook slide and reaches out with his foot and tries to catch the base with his toe, he has to go 93 feet to get to the bag, rather than straight into it.

When one considers that the bent leg also enables the runner to pop-up and run, the value of this slide becomes apparent.

Timing is essential for a good slide. The slide must not start too soon or too late, and the slider should keep relaxed when hitting the ground. As he goes into his slide, he should clench his hands loosely to avoid broken fingers. He must keep his head back, and arms up. Once he decides to slide, he must go through with it. *He should never change his mind!*

John Roseboro always scared me every time he would slide because he waited until he got almost on the bag before he went down. If he did not tear the bag loose, we would wonder why he did not break his leg.

There is a proper way to fall, of course: a controlled fall, rather than a jump, which makes the slider "strawberry" prone and subject to bruises. On the bent leg slide, most players like to take the blow all the way from the calf of their leg up to their thigh so the fall will not be concentrated on one spot.

A player has to have confidence in his ability to slide. To overcome any fear, he should practice in a sliding pit or on soft grass.

Some of the better sliders in the major leagues are capable of watching the fielder to see which side of the base he is going to field the ball on, and they will slide accordingly. During spring training, we work on this point in the sliding pits. Somebody will toss a ball each time a runner comes in, and some of the throws will be on one side of the bag and some on the other. If the slider sees that the ball is on the left side of the bag, he will slide to the right.

Fig. 3–13. BENT LEG SLIDE. In addition to being the safest slide in baseball, the bent leg enables the base runner to spring up quickly, ready to run if the ball goes through (Billy Grabarkewitz).

On several occasions, I can remember losing important runs because a player could not slide on both sides. All he had to do was slide away from the play coming into third base, but he could not, and it cost us. *A player is just as good as the time he devotes to practice.* Only constant practice will make a player perfect in sliding.

The bent leg slide is the safest slide in baseball and the most popular. Young players can become proficient quickly in this method of sliding. Along with the safety factor, it enables the base runner to spring up quickly, ready to run if the ball goes through. Another advantage of the bent leg is the fact that the base runner can get to the bag the quickest possible way (Fig. 3–13).

The bent leg slide is the most practical one because it permits a side approach when the runner must be tagged, and a front approach on force plays. In high school baseball, where erratic throwing is more common than in professional ball, the bent leg slide can be a great asset.

We have an occasional problem when players come down with a stiff arm to lighten their fall; they sometimes get a bruised hand or a stiff elbow. The ideal way to execute the bent leg slide is to come in with both hands in the air. If the player can learn to take the weight

The bent leg slide

Fig. 3–14. BENT LEG POP–UP. As he comes in contact with the base, the bent leg should brace. The runner then rolls inward on his left knee, rising to an upright position. Aided by the speed of his slide, the runner is then ready to continue on to the next base (Danny Cater).

of the fall on the bent leg and all the way up to the thigh, he will not get a "strawberry" or a bruise that he might get through the force of the slide.

Some players like to put dirt in their hands so that, if they slide, they do so with a closed fist. When they put their hands down, they will hit on a closed fist rather than on fingers.

Perhaps the most recognized authority on the bent leg slide is Bernie DeViveiros, former major league infielder and now a scout with the Detroit Tigers. For many years, one of DeViveiros's springtime duties with the Tigers was teaching the rudiments of the bent leg slide to every player in the system.

The base runner should be able to slide on both sides, although it is more natural for 99 out of 100 players to slide on just one leg. With the bent leg, the side he slides on is not as important as it is with the hook slide, where he is fading away from the throw one way or the other.

If the runner is going into second base and the throw is to the short-stop side, he would want to hook slide to the outfield side, whereas if the throw is to the first base side, he may want to slide to the in-field side.

Fig. 3–15. HOOK SLIDE (off the bent leg). The top leg remains straight to the bag until contact is made, and then bends or gives. The catching foot stays on the bag as the body hooks on by. The hooking knee should not be bent any more than is necessary to hook the base (Billy Grabarkewitz).

Therefore, in moving into second base, it becomes more or less necessary for the runner to be able to slide both ways. When using the bent leg slide, in which the runner goes straight into the bag, the chief advantage is the ability to get up and race to the next bag.

The following are coaching points in learning the bent leg slide:

1. Start to slide at least nine to ten feet from the bag. *Do not slide late!*
2. Take-off from either leg (whichever is most natural) and bend it under.
3. Slide only on the calf of the bent leg, which must be the bottom leg.
4. Just sit down, and nature will put the right leg under.
5. Keep low to the ground. Do not leap or jump.
6. Throw the head back as both legs bend, thus preventing the knees from hitting the ground first.
7. Turn the instep of the bottom foot so that it is facing the direction of the slide (preventing the spikes from catching in the ground).

Fig. 3–16. KEY PLAY in the 4–2 Dodger victory over the Houston Astros was Willie Davis's daring attempt to score from first base. Although he was called out by umpire Al Foreman, a clutch hit on the same play drove in runners from third and second base.

8. Always tag with the top leg, which is raised well off the ground and is held loosely and relaxed.
9. Keep the knee slightly bent and the heel off the ground.
10. Just ride the calf of the bottom leg at all times. Use it as a wheel.

Pop-up slide and run
Figure 3–14 shows Danny Cater executing the pop-up slide. Notice that he slides on his left side and braces the bag with his right leg. Fundamentally, this is the correct side for the pop-up slide because it provides greater speed in pushing-off for the next base, particularly at third base. However, in sliding into second base, most base runners wisely prefer to fade away from the throw, which moves them toward the right field side of the bag (Fig. 3–16). Thus, the most effective and natural side is their right one.

As Cater slides along with speed, in Fig. 3–14, he lifts himself up. His left leg remains bent until his right foot contacts the base. As he comes in contact with the base, the bent leg braces. Cater then rolls inward on his left knee. Aided by the speed of his slide, the runner is then ready to continue on to the next base. Some base runners are

Fig. 3–17. THE NINETY–THREE–FOOT SLIDE. The Dodgers discourage the teaching of this slide because of the extra distance the runner has to go. In these pictures of Billy Grabarkewitz, observe that his bottom foot is well past the base but the tagging foot has not even reached the bag.

able to come up to an upright position by pushing off their left hand. Most coaches, however, instruct their players to keep their hands up in the air.

The hook slide is used by a runner primarily to avoid being tagged by a fielder. It can be made to either side of the base. However, we try to stay away from the hook slide, using it only in a special situation in which the runner must evade a tag (Fig. 3–15).

The hook slide

When the base runner hook slides and reaches out with that foot and tries to catch it with his toe, he is going 93 feet to get to the bag, rather than straight into it.

Branch Rickey, whose long career included outstanding work with the St. Louis Cardinals, Brooklyn Dodgers and Pittsburgh Pirates, called the hook slide the "93-feet slide," because the body of the base runner has gone 93 feet and he has not touched the base yet. This is the disadvantage of the hook slide (Fig. 3–15).

The Dodgers discourage the use of the "93-foot slide," by teaching all players to extend both feet when attempting the hook slide.

When hook sliding to the right, the take-off is usually off the left foot. Both legs are extended straight toward the base with the toes pointed, as the body falls to the right side. The right foot is slightly raised and to the right of the base. The body is almost in a flat position as the left foot and left toes touch the right corner of the base. Most of the impact is absorbed on the right hip and the right thigh.

If the runner can keep the touching foot straight as he comes in, and then it hooks, he will be all right. The key to the hook slide is to *keep the touching foot straight until he hits the bag.*

Fig. 3–18. HEADFIRST SLIDE. Sal Bando of the Oakland A's slides safely around the tag of the Minnesota Twins catcher. The runner executes the headfirst slide by lowering the body and then diving toward the plate with his arms outstretched. While considered dangerous, the slide can be effective in certain game situations.

As he starts to hook slide into the bag, he must be sure that his catching foot—that is, the one that will touch the bag—does not bend. He must keep it pretty well straight out until he makes contact with the bag. Then, it stays on the bag as his body hooks on by. From the safety standpoint, he should be sure to get the left foot up so he doesn't jam it into the ground.

In sliding to his left, the runner should take-off on his left foot. Both feet of the runner should be turned sideways to avoid catching the spikes in the ground. Both knees should be bent, with the weight of the upper part of the body thrown left and backward.

As he slides, the left foot should be forward and away from the base, the right leg bent and dragging, and the right foot turned so that the instep faces the base. The toes of the right foot should hook the near side of the base. While sliding, the left hand should be on the ground, palm down, to absorb some of the shock.

"Do not bend the hooking knee any more than is necessary to hook the base," said Wills. "The more the knee is bent, the longer it will take the player to touch the base."

Wills's snake slide

This slide was aptly called the snake slide by Casey Stengel, because it enabled Wills to slip under throws that were only two feet off the ground.

"Unlike many base runners who bend their left leg as they slide," said Wills, "I go in with my legs extended, making a V. If I would bend my leg, I would have to take another three feet, which often makes the difference between being out or safe."

"I move to the right with my right leg and upper body, and hit the outer edge of the bag with my left foot. I twist the balance of my body from my hips, trying to avoid the defensive man. If possible, the only thing I give him to tag is my feet."

Head-first slide

The head-first slide should be used only when the runner is caught off balance and must dive to get back to a base, or if he has an injury to his legs. This slide can be dangerous because of the possibility of injury through body contact (Fig. 3–18).

Tips on sliding practice

A player has to have confidence in his ability to slide. To overcome any fear, he should practice in a sliding pit or on soft grass. When practicing on the grass, he should remove his spiked shoes or use tennis shoes. Sliding pads and practice pants should be used, with long nylon or khaki shorts making good pads. In the early stages, the bases should be loose.

Inexperienced sliders should start sliding at a short distance, to make sure that their legs can be bent. After the technique is mastered, the distance can be lengthened with an increase in speed. *Speed is important* in executing a good slide, but never forget: "You are just as good as the time you devote to practice."

Basic Sliding Rules

1. Once you decide to slide, go through with it. *Never change your mind!*
2. Make your slide with speed.
3. Remember, it is a slide and not a leap.
4. Learn to fall in a relaxed manner.
5. For the straight-in slide, concentrate on watching the base.
6. For hook sliding, concentrate mainly on the hands of the fielder.
7. On all force plays, the runner should employ a bent-leg slide.
8. Clench your hands loosely when sliding, to avoid broken fingers. *Stay relaxed!*
9. Any deliberate attempt on the part of a runner to spike or injure his opponent should *never* be tolerated.

Pitching /4/

In pitching, the name of the game is getting the ball over the plate with good stuff on it. In looking over a young pitching prospect, major league scouts want to see that fast one move a little with good velocity. They want a boy who can throw hard because this is one thing they cannot teach a pitcher to do (Fig. 4–2).

When I think of the pitching game, I think first of proper mechanics and control. Lack of control is generally the result of poor mechanics. Unless his mechanism is good, with everything working together, the pitcher will find it difficult to be ''in a groove.''

How can a young pitcher master control? There is only one solution: practice and more practice. Not just throwing the ball, but throwing the ball *to a target.* Control comes to different people at different times. Sandy Koufax, for example, had to work very hard to get his control, but after years of frustration Sandy finally found the key. He discovered the right method that put rhythm into his delivery, but it came only by working constantly, with Coach Joe Becker at his side (Fig. 4–4).

A pitcher should use a style of his own and throw naturally. The arm angle, particularly, should be one which feels most comfortable and natural. The three-quarter overhand delivery is most used because it is the most natural delivery for the majority of pitchers.

Proper rhythm and timing are the basis of successful pitching. The basic purpose of these elements is to generate speed and momentum in the pitching arm. The pitching greats of baseball, those who have stood up over a long period of time, are prime examples of pitchers

Fig. 4–2. A GOOD FAST BALL comes off the end of a smooth, coordinated delivery, as demonstrated below by Frank Reberger of the San Francisco Giants. The hitter is Pete Rose of the Reds.

who displayed excellent rhythm and timing. Warren Spahn, Robin Roberts, Early Wynn, Sandy Koufax and Whitey Ford are modern-day hurlers who typified well-coordinated pitching deliveries.

Superb rhythm and body coordination enabled Wynn and Spahn to throw hard until they were well past the age of 40. No undue pressure or strain was placed on their throwing arms because they pitched with their entire bodies. As a result, their long and distinguished pitching careers were free of any serious arm trouble.

To have good rhythm and timing, a pitcher's gears have to be meshed. It is a case of meshing the arm and upper body with the striding leg and lower body. The upper and lower halves of the body should come through simultaneously. Like the parts of a machine, when working together, the result will be action with power.

The greatest problem of most pitchers is rushing the delivery. If the body weight moves out in front too soon, a "rushing arm action" will develop, bringing about control problems and inconsistent power. Generally, when the leg stride is too quick, the pitcher has rushed his pitch, or his upper body is too slow. If the striding foot hits the ground and the throwing arm is way back, a pitcher has a pulling motion, instead of action with power. The solution is to maintain good weight retention during the pivot, setting the stage for both the arm and body to come through at the same time. In simple terms, weight retention actually means, "Don't run off and leave your arm." (Fig. 4–3).

Deception is another big factor in the make-up of a successful pitcher. Along with control and a strong, live arm, many authorities believe the key to pitching is deceiving the hitter. Confusing the hitter by throwing the ball at different speeds with the same motion, hiding it until the last possible moment and using good judgment in his selection of pitches are other factors which can increase his effectiveness.

Along with the physical aspects of pitching, mental attitude is most essential to the success of a moundsman. Like the rest of his teammates, he must have confidence in himself, a positive feeling that he can do it. He must have a mental attitude which says, "I know I can do it." He must not let a bad pitch or a lost game discourage him.

Command and poise are qualities possessed by the great pitchers in baseball. A pitcher has to have complete confidence that he will get them out, that he is better than the hitter. He must be in complete control. Koufax was a great competitor. He believed that he could beat anybody who came up to the plate.

I like to see a young pitcher concentrate on what he is trying to do. Whenever he throws the ball, he should have an idea where he wants to throw it. He has to block out everything except the job he is doing —getting the batter out. He must be alert all the time.

A pitcher should not neglect his hitting either. The ability to swing a bat not only can win games for a pitcher, but can keep him on the mound in situations in which he might otherwise be removed for a pinch hitter. If a pitcher can also swing a potent bat, he has just that many more opportunities to win games.

Essentials of Pitching

The three things we look for in young pitchers are ability to throw hard, a good live ball and control. One has to have a good arm. Most big league scouts use a grading system, and they look for the fellow who has an adequate major league fast ball. Throughout most of his career, Sandy Koufax pitched with his powerful fast ball and his excellent curve ball (Fig. 4–4).

Control, the other top requirement, is perhaps the hardest fundamental to teach. Control means more than just throwing the ball into the strike zone. It means moving the ball around, in and out, up and down, keeping the batter constantly off-balance. As a pitcher pro-

The good rising fast ball is the best pitch in baseball.

TOM SEAVER

Fig. 4–3. AN EFFECTIVE PITCHING DELIVERY is one that seems to flow in a smooth, full-arm swing, finishing with a powerful snap of the wrist. In the pictures above, Bill Singer demonstrates good weight retention during the pivot,

gresses in experience and skill, he will learn how to go to work on the hitter, trying to make him hit his best pitch.

Basically, I like my pitchers to keep the ball low. Most hitters like the ball up and out over the plate, which means "belt-high" and on up to the letters. However, if the pitcher can keep the ball down, he is less likely to get hurt.

Another requirement of successful pitching is for the pitcher to have some off-speed pitches and be able to get them over. With hitting being such a time element, off-speed pitches, such as a straight change or taking a little off the curve, can be highly effective. This is especially true today, when so many players are at the end of the bat. The harder they swing, the easier they sometimes are to fool with an off-speed pitch. The off-speed pitch does not strike the man out too often, but it will take some of his power and timing away.

Whitey Ford and Carl Erskine are two former pitchers who were not the overpowering type, but they had great control. In order to make up for the lack of an overpowering fast ball, they had an assortment of pitches thrown at various speeds to get the hitters off balance. Their pitches would break first one way and then the other.

To be a winning pitcher, a player has to have control of the pitches he has.
SANDY KOUFAX

which enables his pitching arm and body to come through at the same time. This helps to prevent a "rushing arm action." Notice that Bill keeps his eye on the catcher's target throughout his delivery.

What type of physical size do Dodger scouts look for in a pitcher? I prefer a well-built boy, with a long arm and supple muscles. Drysdale, perhaps, was the ideal size, although a pitcher does not have to be six feet three inches or six feet four inches. Tom Seaver, at six feet one inch and 205 pounds, has demonstrated not only explosive power but the strength and stamina to go all the way.

Drysdale had long, slender arms, the kind which do not become muscle-bound and provide the real good stuff on the ball. Koufax, on the other hand, was a muscular fellow who had a lot of arm trouble. For Sandy, it took a lot of work between starts.

Koufax had such big hands and powerful strength. In gripping the ball, he could almost reach around it. This is one of the things that gave Sandy his good curve ball. And, too, Koufax had a strong willingness to keep his body in perfect condition. He devoted endless hours toward building and maintaining a healthy body.

Grip

The pitcher should hold the ball so that it feels most comfortable and so that he gets the most life into his pitches. Ideally, the ball

> *Off-speed pitches not only get the hitter off stride but they provide some rest for the pitcher.*
> RED ADAMS

should be grasped in the same manner for each pitch, but this is not always possible.

"Everybody I have talked to who has had pretty good success has held the ball in different ways," said Drysdale. "I have talked with many pitchers since I first came to the Brooklyn ball club, fellows like Erskine, Sal Maglie, Warren Spahn and Robin Roberts, and I have found out that there is really no one way to hold a ball."

We suggest that our pitchers try various grips and let them decide which one feels the best. However, the way the seam is held is not as important as the way the ball is released.

Generally, a pitcher will grip the ball either across the seams or with the seams. If he is *with* the seams, there are two possibilities:

1. His fingers are at the narrow area where they come together.
2. He can slip on around a little further, where he can get the tip of his finger on the seams and still be with the seams.

For the pitcher with the three-quarter delivery, who does not have exceptional power, I would suggest that he grip the ball with the seams to get a little more movement out of the ball. The ball may sink for him when down, or tail in toward the hitter when up.

"When I go down to spring training," stated Drysdale, "I start with the grip and try to move the ball around a little bit. I happen to hold the fast ball across the small seams, primarily because I throw three-quarters and below. Others, like Koufax and Camilo Pascual, who throw over the top, hold the ball over the big seams to get the ball to rise."

Many pitchers grip the ball across the seams at the widest part. The second and third fingertips are placed on the seams, while the thumb is on the seam beneath the ball. Only a slight variation of finger movement is needed to throw the curve or slider.

The thumb plays a very important role in all pitches. It can make the ball go one way or the other.

The young pitcher should watch that he does not choke the ball too much. He should hold the ball as far out on the end of his fingers and thumb as he can, and still have good control and command of it. He should make the end joints work on his fingers, thus getting more leverage and more rotation.

Correct Spin

Successful pitching demands an understanding of correct spin on the ball. "Spin the ball easily and get the ball to spin in the direction

---

A pitcher is only as good as his legs. Therefore, he must do a great deal of running.
EARLY WYNN

---

you want it to spin," explained Johnny Sain, former outstanding pitcher and a highly successful pitching coach. "Then, apply more spin, more spin, more speed, more spin and more speed."

Many pitchers have experienced noticeable improvement by learning how to get better spin on the ball. Additional spin not only can improve breaking pitches but can make the fast ball livelier. "In order to develop more spin on a baseball," said Sain, "a pitcher has to learn the basic idea. And from here, he spins the ball easy, applying more spin and speed until he gets the ball doing what he likes."

In most cases, a pitcher who has trouble applying good spin grips the ball too tightly. When a pitcher grips the ball too tightly with his thumb, it seems to lock his wrist. He does not have that loose, fast wrist and finger action. Actually, it is a combination of wrist and finger action which applies the spin to the ball.

"Every player should practice the correct way of spinning a baseball for all types of pitches," advised Sain. "This practice will give him an understanding of the spin he must apply to make the ball do these things."

The Basic Pitches

Through the years, Dodger pitchers have concentrated pretty much on the basic three pitches. We have had good luck, not having many fellows hurt themselves or develop sore arms.

High school pitchers, particularly, should stay with the fast ball, curve ball and some change-of-pace, whether they take a little bit off the curve ball or throw a straight change. Quite often, a young pitcher thinks he needs another pitch, but actually may not have good command of the pitches he has. He should not consider another pitch until the basic three can be delivered with control, consistency and effectiveness.

After he progresses and can control these pitches, then he might go to a different kind of curve ball or a slider. Lately, more pitchers are turning the ball over with a good sinker—a sinking fast ball, in which the pitcher takes the ball, throws it and, at the last second, turns it over, just slightly, like a screwball, to create a little sinking motion.

If a fellow has a major league fast ball and curve ball, a good change-up, and can control these pitches, getting them over pretty much when and where he wants to, I think he has enough to be a successful pitcher. Coming up with a couple of extra pitches is *not* the answer.

Proper rhythm and timing are the basis of successful pitching.

Seaver, of course, is the *complete* pitcher. He has low fast balls, one that rises, another that sinks. He has the ability to make his fast ball sink, sail or tail, according to the way he holds the ball. Tom also has a good slider, a fine curve, and can change-up on all of his pitches.

The Little League pitcher, particularly, should rely almost completely on the fast ball. It is the only pitch with which he can strengthen his arm with minimum risk of injury.

The slider has attained considerable prominence among present-day major league pitchers. It is a fast ball with a break and is most effective when it breaks outside and hitters go reaching for it, or when it breaks in on a left-handed hitter. However, some coaches do not advise their young pitchers to throw it, claiming it is hard on the arms of some pitchers. Those who come up with sore arms usually throw the slider with a stiff wrist because the rigid wrist transfers strain to the elbow. This is why we advocate a loose wrist for the slider. Unfortunately, some pitchers substitute the slider for their curve ball, and they cease to use the curve and do not develop it.

According to Red Adams, our pitching coach, "There is more contrast in the fast ball and curve ball, in the speeds and breaks, than with the fast ball and the slider. We like our pitchers to change their speeds more. Off-speed pitches not only get the hitter off stride but they provide some rest for the pitcher. They also complement the other stuff. Such pitches as the knuckleball, screwball and forkball should be used only by more experienced pitchers."

Fast ball   There is no substitute for a good fast ball. Indeed, the king of all pitches is still the fast ball. A young pitcher would be wise to rely on his fast ball because of the strengthening effect on the arm. A good fast ball comes off the end of a smooth delivery, a coordinated action of the entire body, in which the strong wrist and forearm play a vital role.

To make the ball hop, a pitcher must provide backspin to the ball. He must exert strong pressure on his fingertips with his wrist, snapping down quickly as the ball leaves his hand. He should never try to throw as hard as he can. The ball will lose its natural break and good snap because the wrist seems to tighten up.

There is no set way to throw the fast ball. The grip that gives the best results, of course, should be the one used. Many big league pitchers throw two types of fast balls:

1. Rising Fast Ball *(across the seams)* (Fig. 4–5).   The forefinger and middle finger grip the ball across one of the wide seams, at a point where the seams of the ball are farthest apart. The thumb is underneath. The ring finger and little finger are bent and curled under the side of the ball. From this grip, the pitcher can get maximum action from the four long seams.

A　　　　　　　　　　　　B　　　　　　　　　　　　C

Fig. 4–4. PITCHING RHYTHM. Working from the set position, Sandy Koufax demonstrates one of the greatest pitching styles in baseball history. After years of hard work, Sandy finally developed the proper rocking and rhythm motion where the body would come through at the right time—the leg lift, stride and arm action, all coordinated.

For a three-quarter overarm delivery, the ball is released out in front with a strong follow-through. When thrown by a right-handed pitcher, this fast ball has a tendency to ride in slightly on a right-handed hitter and away from a left-handed hitter.

When thrown completely overarm by pitchers with good velocity, the fast ball tends to rise, thus earning its title as the "riser."

2. Sinking Fast Ball (with the seams) (Fig. 4–5). The "sinking" fast ball is released with an over-the-top, then outside-in, flip of the wrist. For a right-handed pitcher, this ball drives down and in on a right-handed hitter, and down and away from a left-handed swinger. In releasing the ball, the pitcher has to turn the ball over at the last moment, placing more pressure on the index finger.

This fast ball is gripped with the middle finger and forefinger curled snugly, not tightly, along the two parallel short seams. The thumb underneath pinches across the short seams on the lower half of the baseball.

Known as a sinker, it is a little more difficult to throw than the rising fast ball because of the over-the-top wrist flip. When a ground ball is needed, this pitch can be very effective.

D

The two things big league pitching coaches look for is whether a pitcher's ball has good velocity and whether it moves. Some pitchers have good velocity but their fast ball does not move; it just comes in straight, on a line.

105

Rising fast ball (across seams) Sinking fast ball (with the seams)

Fig. 4–5. THE FAST BALL. Most big league pitchers throw two types of fast balls. The good fast ball must be alive. It must hop, sink, break or sail (Red Adams).

Pitchers of small stature must have more body speed or momentum and extremely good rhythm in order to be fast enough.

Curve ball One of the great curve ball pitchers of all time, Sal Maglie, once stated: "I don't believe there is such a thing as a good curve ball hitter." What "The Barber" actually meant was that no hitter can hit the really good breaking stuff consistently.

The curve ball should be thrown with a little less speed than the fast ball, but with the same motion. When the curve is thrown too hard, the ball will not spin as well. With proper spin, the ball will break correctly. The grip and wrist action should be varied until the most effective break is obtained.

Although there are four or five different ways of holding the curve ball, the majority of pitchers like to hold the ball with the seams, on the narrowest part, where they come together (Fig. 4–6).

The pitcher should wait until his arm is close to the rear of his head before going into his curve ball. The wrist must be cocked back of the head (Fig. 4–6). The elbow starts forward first, and the wrist turns over and snaps downward to put a rapid spin on the ball. "Turn, turn, and PULL DOWN!" describes the wrist and hand action in providing the greatest amount of spin. It is the spin given to the ball that makes it curve.

The wrist should be completely turned over after a very quick reverse snap. The ball is released over the first and second joints of the first finger—like a ball rolling off a table. The first two fingers are close, with the thumb extended and not curled. "Let go of it in front of you," describes the type of release necessary for the curve.

The longer the pitcher can wait, the better curve he will throw. He must stay on top of the ball and put great pressure or pull on his middle finger. The moment he starts coming down is when he must really pull down hard with a sweep of the arm across the body toward the opposite knee. In releasing the ball, he should let it roll over on his index finger. This is how spin is imparted for a good breaking action of the curve ball.

Carl Erskine, a former Dodger who possessed an outstanding curve ball, always thought of tickling his ear when he threw the curve ball. This helped him keep his wrist tucked in and provided good over-the-top spin on the ball. The more the arm is tucked in, the bigger the break. However, the fact that Erskine threw directly overhand should be kept in mind. Each individual should throw the curve ball from the same angle as his fast ball.

The important thing with the curve is that when the pitcher is ready to release it, he must really snap his wrist—as hard as he can, and *make that ball spin!* The stride should be slightly shorter for a curve ball, about six inches, making for a better follow-through and spin.

"The biggest factor with the curve is getting the ball down," says Warren Spahn, the former all-time great southpaw. "The higher you let the ball go, the more chance you have of hanging it."

The curve is a pitch that should be thrown low. A high curve has a tendency to "hang," and a pitcher who keeps his curve high is simply asking for trouble. The stride should be slightly shorter for a curve, making for a better follow-through and spin. An ineffective curve often is caused by not pulling down on the ball enough or letting go of the ball too soon.

Practice

Perfecting the curve ball requires a great amount of practice, learning how to coordinate the speed of spin, the angle of spin and using a natural pitching motion.

Practice to get the correct spin. The pitcher should have a catcher stand 15 to 20 feet away from him and just spin the ball into his glove. He should vary the grip and wrist action and keep turning his wrist over until he obtains the most effective break.

Change-of-pace

A good change-up can be an extremely valuable asset to a pitcher. This is particularly true as he climbs higher in baseball. It takes

Front view

Rear view

Fig. 4–6. THE CURVE BALL. The majority of pitchers like to hold the ball with the seams, on the narrowest part, where they come together. The ball should be held firmly, gripping tightly along a seam with the middle finger. On the left, Coach Red Adams shows how the pitcher should twist his wrist so the palm of the hand and ball will be facing his head. By raising the elbow, he will form an "L" shape with his arm. This is followed by a straight or stiff wrist snap of the ball as his elbow passes the point of his shoulder.

courage to throw a change-up, but it is a pitch that must be learned and controlled by every pitcher. Without a good change-up, a pitcher is definitely limiting his baseball career. By perfecting the technique of his off-speed pitches, he will develop the confidence that he can use them effectively at any time (Fig. 4–7).

The change-up is particularly effective in disrupting the hitter's timing. After all, the essence of pitching is the ability of the pitcher to keep the batter off-stride. Eddie Lopat, the former Yankee pitching great, used a change-of-pace on practically every pitch and threw three or four different speeds.

There are many different ways to throw the change-up, and pitchers on the Dodgers sort of combine three different methods. They use a "dead leg" in back, holding the ball with three fingers across the seams; the wrist comes right down and is stiff. "When I threw my change," explained Drysdale, "I tried to think that my wrist was going to hit the dirt. The reason I used the four-seam rotation is to make the hitter think he was getting the fast ball."

A pitcher should pull down on the ball using a stiff wrist, similar

Front view   Side view

Fig. 4–7. THE CHANGE–UP. Many pitchers like to grip the ball back in the palm of the hand, as shown here by Red Adams. The fingertips are raised slightly as the ball is released. There is greater pressure on the second row of knuckles of the first two fingers. These fingers straighten out.

to pulling down a window shade. The heel of the hand comes down first. The ball must be held slightly looser than on the fast ball, and the wrist is slightly looser on the change from the curve. The fingertips are raised slightly as the ball is released.

Many pitchers prefer the palm ball for their change-of-pace. The ball is stuffed into the palm of the hand (Fig. 4–9).

Again, the motion on a change-up should correspond to that used on the fast ball. If he slows up his motion, the pitcher will tip off his pitch and any illusion he is trying to create will be lost.

One of the easiest ways to teach a change-up is to have the pitcher turn it over a little, like a screwball. The ball is released at the last split-second so it will come off the hand between the second and third fingers, as a screwball, but without too much wrist snap. Even though it will not break as much as the screwball, the change of speed makes this pitch effective.

The slip pitch is taught by some coaches, in which the ball just slips out between the thumb and finger (Fig. 4–11). However, this one takes a long time to master.

Some pitchers find it effective to lengthen the stride on the change-up. Others like to drag the rear foot, using the dead rear leg procedure on a let-up pitch. They hold their foot on the rubber and do not let their weight come through. This reduces the body motion and helps keep the body low. The let-up pitch should be thrown for a strike, in the hope that the hitter will hit the ball on the ground.

The change-up can be a terrific pitch, especially in tough situations. The let-up pitch is often effective on 3–2, 3–1 or 2–0 counts. After two strikes, the batters guard the plate a little more closely.

I try to tell my pitchers, "If you are going to throw an unexpected pitch, on a 2–0 or 3–1 count, it is necessary that you make that pitch a strike. You want the hitter to swing at the unexpected pitch and, therefore, it should be in the strike zone. Otherwise, the hitter will often take the pitch and we will be in worse trouble than before."

For many pitchers, the change-of-pace can be difficult to learn. One reason is that the pitcher tries to develop an entirely new pitching style. Instead, he should stay with the same style he uses for his other pitches. This is why the turn-over change is one of our favorites.

Slider   The slider can be a highly effective pitch and has attained considerable prominence among present-day major league pitchers (Fig. 4–8). Since it is usually accompanied by a hard snap of the arm, the slider must be thrown properly, so as not to hurt the arm.

The slider can be an effective pitch for a pitcher with a good fast ball but poor curve. Unlike the curve, the wrist is stiff. Referred to as a "nickel curve," the slider is a small breaking pitch which breaks (or slides) about six inches. It is held off-center a little, with the middle and index fingers placed to the outside of the ball. The release of the slider can be compared with the passing of a football. The index finger controls the release. Come straight down hard and let the ball come off the second finger. This will cause the ball to spin like a bullet.

The pitcher should use a little inward turn of the wrist as in turning a doorknob, about halfway between a fast ball wrist and a curve wrist. With a fairly stiff wrist, point the index finger at home plate, releasing the ball off the side of the fingertips.

"The slider is a good pitch," says Drysdale, "but it is hard on the arms of some pitchers. I do not believe in throwing a slider until a month after spring training has started. I throw the slider by holding it the same as a fast ball. I cut it right underneath like a nickel curve ball, and it isn't hard on my arm—just natural. It must be thrown hard, though."

To prevent arm trouble, a growing number of coaches are advocating a loose wrist for the slider, rather than rigid wrist, which tends to transfer strain to the elbow. With a limber wrist, the pitcher should cut directly through the ball with his middle and index fingers, ending up with a smooth follow-through.

A slider is good only in certain spots, breaking in and jamming a left-handed hitter or clipping the outside corner. It is also effective

Front view

Rear view

Fig. 4–8. THE SLIDER is held off-center a little, with the middle and index fingers placed to the outside of the ball. The secret of a good slider is to keep the spin as tight as possible. Just before the point of release, the hand should be turned sideways, providing the "football spin." The pitcher should cut across the ball very hard with his big finger, causing the rotation of the ball to swerve laterally.

when thrown so it breaks outside to a right-handed hitter with the hitter reaching for it. But the thing that makes it especially effective is its velocity. It is a fast ball with a break, and should be kept down.

"I do not advise our young pitchers to throw a slider," said Becker. "A number of pitchers will develop a slider if their curve ball is not good enough. Pitchers who have a good slider generally do not have too good a curve."

The general feeling among pitching authorities is that the young pitcher should stay away from the slider until he is physically equipped and has sufficient talent to throw it properly.

Sinker

The sinker is one of the greatest weapons of the relief pitcher, particularly those who throw sidearm. With many of the hitters today swinging for the fences, the sinker pitch has been most effective in making the batter hit the ball in the ground. With the correct motion and sinking rotation, the sinker can be a real "bread-and-butter pitch" (Fig. 4–10).

Many of the game's top relief artists have relied heavily on the sinker pitch, including Ron Perranoski and Elroy Face. Mel Stottlemyre of the Yankees can credit his quick rise to pitching stardom to

Fig. 4–9. PALM BALL. The ball is stuffed into the palm of the hand. The rest of the fingers lie gently and slightly curved around the ball. The pitcher releases the ball with a fast ball motion by letting the ball float out of the hand, controlled by the pressure of the inside joint of the thumb (Dave Guisti).

his natural sinker ball. In throwing this pitch, the pitcher turns the ball over, thus imparting a downward spin. Therefore it should be kept low, otherwise the action of the ball is not as effective. The thumb plays an important roll in the sinker, as it does in all pitches. The ball can be off-centered by moving the thumb up to the side where the little finger is.

There are two types of sinker ball pitchers. First, there is the gifted moundsman, usually with a three-quarter to sidearm delivery, whose delivery makes possible a natural sinker. He is the hard-throwing pitcher who can get on top of the ball to the extent that he does not let it go until it is well out in front of him. He manages to cut the ball just enough in his natural motion so that it will come in and sink.

Then, there is the less gifted pitcher who has to give the ball considerable help when he is releasing it. By bringing his arm clear across the body, he cuts the ball, giving it the necessary reverse corkscrew spin which makes it break downward.

The success of the sinker pitch depends on the following coaching points:

1. Hold the ball slightly off-center
2. Execute the "drop-and-go" body movement
3. Stay on top of the ball
4. Release the ball off the side of the middle finger, well out in front of the body
5. Use a sweeping arm action across the body, which cuts the ball at the last moment.

Fig. 4-10. THE SINKER. The sinker should be gripped within the seams and held slightly off-center, similar to the screwball grip. The middle finger should be resting just inside the right seam. The pitcher flips or turns the ball over, imparting a downward spin (Red Adams).

In throwing a good sinker, the pitcher must utilize a body action which will drive him toward the hitter in a lower position than his fast ball and his other pitches. The "drop-and-go" movement will allow him to stay on top of the ball, cutting and releasing it at the last moment, well out in front of his body.

By bending the right knee, the body drops down and then is pushed forward, a "drop-and-go" movement. The throwing arm is extended across the body, finishing up completely across the body. Most pitchers lengthen their stride as much as six inches more than on the fast ball.

Actually, the turn of the arm is more important than the flip of the wrist, prior to the point of release. The arm movement sweeping across the body gives the sinker a downward rotation. The pitch is released off the right corner tip of the middle finger. The pitcher must stay on top of the ball until the actual point of release.

The sinker pitch is just like a fast ball, except that the pitcher brings his arm on across his body. This gives a reverse corkscrew spin to the ball. Unlike the slider, the wrist is not stiff.

There is a similarity between the sinker and the screwball, although the screwball is much more taxing on the arm. The sinker is thrown harder than the screwball. The screwball is about a half-speed pitch, which is thrown by actually turning the elbow and arm completely over.

Caution should be taken by the young pitcher, in throwing either of these two pitches, in not trying to get too much of an inward arm turn. Too much rotation of the wrist or arm can cause injury to the elbow area.

Fig. 4–11. SLIP PITCH. The key to this pitch is that the heel of the hand comes straight down, like pulling down a window shade. The slip pitch is thrown just like a fast ball, with the same stride, but it does not go very fast (Mickey Lolich).

Screwball   Thrown with an inside-out twist of the hand and wrist, the screwball breaks the opposite way from the curve (Fig. 4–12). Carl Hubbell, a former great southpaw whose success can be attributed to his use of the screwball, had the ability to break his wrist forward more than the average pitcher, thus causing a greater downward break.

The thumb plays a major role in imparting the clockwise rotation to the ball. Screwball pitchers often develop blisters on the top side of their thumbs because of the pressure exerted on the ball.

The screwball is a difficult pitch to master and is considered by many pitching authorities to be hard on a young arm. The clockwise or inward rotation of the arm is unnatural and places undue strain on it. This is the prime reason why coaches and managers do not encourage this difficult pitch by young and inexperienced pitchers.

Jim Brewer, veteran relief pitcher on our club who can attribute much of his success to the screwball, does not share this pessimism. "The screwball has not been hard on my arm because I extend my arm, and I am not using the elbow. From time to time, I have had a problem with my shoulder, but it has not been serious. It is just a tight muscle from throwing the screwball too much." (Fig. 4–13).

"When a young pitcher starts to throw a screwball," continued Brewer, "they must not try to throw it too hard. They should get the feel of it and see that it is rotating properly. As they learn more about the rotation and how to throw it, they can begin to throw it hard. I would not advise them to throw more than one or two screwballs out of six pitches."

Fig. 4–12. SCREWBALL GRIP. This pitch is actually a reverse curve. It is spun out of the hand between the middle and ring fingers and is given its rotation by the reverse quarter-turn of the wrist and the middle finger release. The thumb is used to increase the reverse spin by being given a last-second flip as the ball is released (Jim Brewer).

"Once a young man is out of high school and needs an extra pitch," said Jim, "he might experiment with a screwball. However, I wouldn't recommend it while he is still in high school."

Forkball

The forkball is so named because the index and middle fingers form a fork which encircles the ball. The ball slides from the hand between the spread fingers, with little wrist action. A good forkball comes up to the plate similar in action to the knuckleball. Then, it sinks sharply, as if the bottom dropped out of it.

Like the knuckler, the forkball has little rotation, and because of this, floats toward the plate. Invariably, the break is almost always downward and is more predictable than the knuckleball.

Since the forkball cannot be thrown with great speed, it can be used as a change-of-pace. While several relief specialists have brought recognition to this pitch, the young pitcher should not try to add this pitch to his repertoire.

Knuckleball

The knuckler is the most popular of the unorthodox deliveries and has been used with great success by such modern-day hurlers as Hoyt Wilhelm, Phil Niekro and Eddie Fisher. The name of the pitch, in most cases, is a misnomer because the knuckleball is actually thrown with the fingernails (Fig. 4–14).

The publicity this pitch has received is probably due to the difficulty catchers have in catching it. The knuckler probably takes the

Fig. 4–13. THROWING THE SCREWBALL. This pitch is normally thrown overhand, and breaks down and toward the side from which it is thrown. It has to be snapped just like the curve, but with a reverse spin. The fingers go through first, then the ball, thus creating the effect of a change-up (Jim Brewer).

most erratic course to the plate of any type pitch. Its movement is highly unpredictable, since it may sink, swerve to either side or jump in a crazy manner. It is not only a difficult pitch for the pitcher to control, but is easy to run on. Since this pitch is just about impossible to hide, the success of the knuckleball is due to its action rather than to the surprise element.

There are several methods used in throwing the knuckleball. The method favored by most pitchers is to dig the fingernails into the seams. On release, the fingers are extended vigorously and push the ball toward the plate. While the fingernail pitch can be thrown with one, two or three fingers, most pitchers use the two-finger method. In this technique, the fingers and wrist remain stiff. The ball rarely revolves when thrown in this manner.

The other method is holding the ball cradled against the first joints of the fingers. The first joints of the index and middle fingers rest against the ball between the seams where they are narrowest. The thumb and fourth and fifth fingers encircle the ball and hold it tightly. As the ball leaves the throwing hand, the bent fingers are extended, giving the pitch additional speed. This method requires a good amount of wrist snap as the ball leaves the hand, plus the extension of the index and middle fingers. The result is that the ball revolves only slightly.

The floater or butterfly type of knuckleball is thrown at half-speed,

Fig. 4–14. KNUCKLEBALL. The knuckler is generally thrown by digging the fingernails into the seams of the ball (and not the knuckles). The vigorous extension of the fingers causes the ball to rotate forward and drop when thrown from an overhand delivery (Hoyt Wilhelm).

with a stiff wrist. As it approaches the plate, it seems to dance, reacting to each shift in air currents.

Conversely, the fast knuckler is thrown at full speed. The fingers are extended as the ball is released and the wrist snapped, giving the ball extra velocity and sufficient downspin to make it dip sharply as it approaches the hitter, like "rolling off the table."

Certainly, the knuckleball is not recommended for pitchers in high school or lower age levels. In addition to being difficult to control, development of the pitch usually takes years.

Basic 20 of Pitching

1. Be consistent in your windup
2. Keep the ball hidden throughout the delivery
3. Make a good pivot, keeping the foot parallel to the rubber
4. Retain your weight during the pivot
5. Use your hips properly—activate them!
6. Have a well balanced leg lift—don't start the kick too soon
7. Keep your eyes fixed on the target—*concentrate!*
8. Keep the ball in the glove longer
9. Drive off from the rubber—get a good thrust!
10. Drop and drive right out at the hitter
11. Open up the stride and unlock the hips—don't throw across the body
12. Do not overstride

13. Do not rush the stride
14. Have good rhythm—*put it all together!*
15. Use strong wrist and arm action
16. Throw strikes—stay ahead of the hitter
17. Be quick with the top part of your body—*whip the arm through!*
18. Use a comfortable and natural arm angle
19. Create a consistent point of release
20. Follow-through in a natural manner.

The Delivery

All successful pitchers throw the ball in the way that is easiest and most effective for them. Proper form and delivery are different for each pitcher. Therefore, each pitcher should be able to work out his own natural style. I have never seen a pitcher get to the major leagues by copying somebody else's style.

A good pitching delivery is one that seems to flow in a smooth, full-arm swing, finishing with a powerful snap of the wrist (Fig. 4–19). On the other hand, a half-swing, bent arm, jerky motion will likely place undue stress on the elbow and may ruin the pitching arm permanently.

A well-coordinated and rhythmic delivery will provide extra speed and power, and help him achieve better control. Rather than just the arm, every part of the body will bear the brunt of the effort.

There are four basic types of pitching delivery: overhand, three-quarter, sidearm and underhand. Normally, most pitchers throw overhand or three-quarter style, adding an occasional sidearm pitch. It is the angle of delivery that makes the several styles different.

No matter what style is used, there are certain basic qualities which are absolutely essential. In any type of delivery, the pitcher must have balance, a proper pivot, correct stride and a good follow-through. Practice will give him the coordination and rhythm needed for an effective pitching delivery.

Regardless of which delivery is used, every pitch must be thrown with about the same motion and released from almost the same point. If the pitcher throws his fast ball sidearm and curve ball overhand, the batter obviously will be able to detect what is being thrown.

Getting the Sign

While standing on the mound, the pitcher should keep the ball hidden from the hitter's view. He does this by hiding the pitching hand and the ball behind the thigh of his pivot leg, or by keeping it in the glove. The less the hitter sees of the ball, the better it is for the pitcher.

To take the signal from the catcher, the pitcher must stand on the rubber (Fig. 4–15). In fact, the rules require this. He is also required to deliver the ball to the batter *within twenty seconds* after he receives it.

Fig. 4–15. TAKING THE SIGN FROM A WINDUP POSITION (Dick Bosman).

The majority of pitchers place their pivot foot on the rubber and their other foot a comfortable distance behind it. The spikes of the pivot foot are over the front edge of the rubber, with the striding foot behind and just to the left.

Most of the pitcher's weight is on the back, or striding foot, unless he takes his sign in the crouched position. His shoulders are back or lean slightly forward. Both his pitching arm and glove hand hang loosely to each side. The eyes are fixed on the target.

"When I get the sign," said Don Drysdale, "my weight is on the back foot, because we have pick-off plays where you must have your weight on your back foot to execute properly. I will stand with the weight back, get my sign, and as I go into a rocking motion, I have my grip."

The pitcher then starts his windup, bringing the glove up in front of him to hide the ball from the hitter, the back of his glove facing the hitter.

With a man or men on base, he can stand with his right foot touching the rubber (Fig. 4–16). If he feels he may commit a balk in such a position, he may take his signals while astride the rubber.

Some pitchers take their signals by leaning on the front knee, similar to the style made famous by Bob Lemon and Sandy Koufax. Caution must be taken, however, not to balk, since the weight is leaning in toward the plate. The weight should be kept on the rear foot.

Some pitchers like to angle their feet toward the third base line, which provides for better rotation of the hips and body.

To obtain a better angle in throwing the curve ball, many pitchers find it effective to move to one end of the rubber. The right-hander

Fig. 4–16. GETTING THE SIGN WITH MEN ON BASE (Dick Bosman).

would pitch from the right one-third of the slab, while the left-hander would place his pivot foot on the left one-third of the rubber. However, they would be giving their pitches away if they moved there just for the curve ball.

If the pitcher agrees with the sign, he just gives a short nod of his head. But if he does not like the signal, he can either shake his head "no" or wiggle his glove. Most major league hurlers use the glove.

Occasionally the pitcher might shake off several of the catcher's signals until he comes back a second time to the pitch he really wants to throw. This makes the hitter think and wonder about pitches the pitcher may not even have.

Windup   The primary purpose of the windup is to move the body weight back in order to place power into the pitch. To transfer the body weight effectively to the push-off foot, many pitchers will take an initial step back on the striding foot. In preparing for the start of the windup, the pitcher should "gather his weight" in order to get more power into his delivery.

This pattern of action resembles that of a pendulum. By reaching way back, the pitcher will have the necessary explosive charge to propel the ball toward the plate.

The main thing in starting a windup is to be consistent. As the arms swing forward and upward to a comfortable position above the head, the ball should be hidden in the glove well up into the web, so that

Fig. 4–17. THE PUMP WINDUP. This is the traditional method of winding up. Many pitchers find they can develop better rhythm by using the pumping motion. The pitcher will go into his delivery with a light rocking motion, which first transfers the weight to his right leg as his arms swing in front and then go back (Jack Curtis).

the pitching hand is hidden by the glove. This action conceals the ball so that the batter cannot see the grip and know what is coming. When the pitcher makes his pivot, the ball remains hidden behind the glove and then his body. As a result, the batter does not see the ball until it is coming toward him.

To go into his motion more effectively, the pitcher should place the front spike of his pivot foot over the edge of the rubber. By angling his foot slightly toward the side he will throw from, he will facilitate the pivot and help get his body weight behind the throw. In fact, the pitcher will be more effective by keeping his foot in front of the rubber, rather than on top of it.

The pump

Although some major league pitchers have eliminated the backward swing and pumping action, young pitchers usually find they can develop better rhythm by using the pumping motion (Fig. 4–17). The purpose of the pump is to loosen and relax the arm and shoulder muscles by bending forward and letting the arms swing backward, with the wrists flexing.

As the pitcher makes his pump, his weight should shift to the front foot. It is up to the individual how much he bends over. Some bend way over, while others very little.

A pitcher can upset the hitter's rhythm by varying his pumps, pumping once, twice and sometimes three times. He can also vary the speed of his pump, and the time intervals between pitches.

Fig. 4–18. NO–PUMP WINDUP. An increasing number of pitchers do not utilize a pumping action. The chief advantage is that it takes unnecessary movement out of the early stages of the delivery and allows for greater control (Claude Osteen).

No-pump windup

A growing number of major league pitchers do not utilize a pumping action, or they will limit the action to a small pump. Tom Seaver and Ken Holtzman are two examples of moundsmen using this technique (Fig. 4–18).

This is particularly true of the pitcher who does not get over the top and out in front to release the ball at the right moment. By simplifying his motion, he will very likely get more power behind the pitch. Pitchers who have difficulty hiding the ball in their regular windup should consider the no-pump windup.

The question of using the no-pump method should be an individual matter. For some pitchers, lack of a good pumping motion could destroy their coordination, while for others, it could help them get the most out of their delivery.

The Pivot

A good pivot is essential to an effective pitching delivery (Fig. 4–19). If he fails to pivot correctly, very likely the pitcher will be throwing with just his arm, and he will lack the necessary balance.

As the pitcher's arms come up over his head during the windup, his weight should shift back on his rear foot. For proper balance, his pivot foot must be placed comfortably in contact with the rubber as it is turned.

The actual pivoting is executed without lifting the foot from the rubber. It is performed on the ball of the foot, and when completed, the toe points in the direction of third. This maneuver is very important, in that it makes possible the extreme body pivot to the right and back.

At the start of the pivot, the pitcher's stance should be slightly open, with the toe of his pivot foot pointed out slightly toward third base (for a right-hander).

Pivoting on the ball of his right foot, he turns his pivot foot parallel to the rubber. Keeping the ball hidden from the hitter's view, he pivots his body around and exposes his rear to the hitter. His eyes remain focused on the target.

As the pivot takes place, the pitcher brings the knee of his free foot up high across the body as the arms swing down and back. This leg action bends and pivots the body backward.

The important thing on the pivot is *proper balance*—with the weight of the body over the pivot leg, which is slightly bent at the knee. The body should *not* be leaning forward. Some pitchers have their bodies moving forward during their pivot, and actually start their kick while their pitching arm is still going down and back. The result will be the arm working all alone in the pitch.

Many young pitchers get very little kick in their delivery, because they start their body moving forward before the pivot is completed. Instead, they might take a slight pause, like Seaver, to make sure they have everything together, before they proceed. This will slow them down enough to get their balance and timing together before they throw to the plate.

Weight Retention

A pitcher has to retain his weight during the pivot and wait for his arm to come through (Fig. 4–3). Weight retention, on which Red places so much stress with his pitchers, means, "Don't run off and leave the arm."

If he runs off and leaves his arm, of course, the pitcher will not have time to get his arm up on top, and he will have to shorten up somehow. This could cause him to "shortarm the ball" or throw side-arm. By waiting until the hands get completely to the top, the chance of rushing is lessened.

Another problem is taking too long a stride behind the rubber, in the initial approach to the rubber. This results in a "running start" effect, making it difficult for the pitcher to retain his weight during the pivot.

The coach should be on the lookout for problems of this type. The cause may differ with the individual, but the effect is usually the same: "rushing."

Leg Kick

To obtain good forward drive, the overhand pitcher should bring the knee of his free foot up high across the body as the arms swing down and back. This leg action bends and pivots the body backward, and as the pitcher strides forward with the striding foot, the entire body goes into the pitch like an uncoiling spring, providing maximum power (Fig. 4–4).

There are many different types of leg lifts used by pitchers, depending on their style of delivery. The pitcher with an overhand, erect type of delivery cannot effectively turn his back to the hitter during the pivot, as it creates a horizontal type body action. However, the turning of the back and rear end to the hitter is very effective for the coiling three-quarter or sidearm type pitcher.

The sidearm pitcher will not lift the free knee as high as will the overhand pitcher. Normally, he will use a more horizontal type pivot. With a runner on first base, a left-handed pitcher can raise his leg higher because the start of his leg action is the same for pitching as for throwing over to first base.

A pitcher must execute a well-balanced leg kick with good body control. His weight is more on the ball of his right foot as he pivots into the backswing. He now has the balance necessary for a good thrust forward from the rubber.

As the leg lift takes place, three key points should be kept in mind:

1. The pitcher's body should be twisted back as far as possible without ruining balance.
2. His eyes should remain fixed on home plate or the target. A pitcher should look over his left shoulder as he swings back.
3. The pitching arm should drop well down behind his body and be straightened out.

At this point, the right leg should be similar to a coiled spring. Uncoiling is the movement that pushes the pitcher into the actual pitch, generating drive into the motion.

The size of the leg kick should vary with each individual pitcher. However, he should not kick so high that it ruins his balance, overall coordination and control. For some pitchers, a high leg kick is a big asset because it gives them a deceptive motion and a high angle of delivery. The leg kick gives the hitter more motion at which to look and tends to bother his timing. Unquestionably, Juan Marichal's famous high kick has been a prime factor in his outstanding success.

Not every pitcher, though, feels he is properly balanced with the extra high leg kick. Therefore, each pitcher must experiment until he feels his delivery is smooth and coordinated and has the balance necessary for the push-off forward.

While the deceptiveness of a high kick helps hide the ball longer from the batter, the pitcher should never sacrifice balance for deception.

Hip Rotation

Proper hip action is probably the greatest single factor involved in a powerful delivery. As in batting, this is the part of the body where a great amount of power is generated. While a good push-off from the rubber is essential, correct use of the hips is perhaps the prerequisite of a powerful thrust from the slab.

With the weight on the pivot foot, the hips are rotated to the right. The knee of the free foot is brought up high across the body as the arms swing down and back. The pitcher's eyes are kept on the target throughout the delivery.

The action of the hips is bolstered by driving the rear knee down as the hips are opened and the stride is completed.

"I like to see a pitcher use his hips as much as he can in lifting his leg," said Adams, our pitching coach. "If a fellow will lift his leg and bring his knee back a little toward second base, this will throw the bottom of his foot a little bit out toward home plate. This will activate his hips, and put his hips on a slight tilt. Of course, when he comes on through, it gives him some good leg action and momentum."

"Conversely, if he lifts his knee up and tilts his foot back the other way, back toward second," continued Red, "this will bring his knee out a little away from his body. You can see by looking in the mirror that he will get very little hip action. It doesn't do much to activate the lower part of his body.

"Good hip action comes from the way a pitcher raises his knee. The belt line is the key to watch for. If the belt is on a level plane during his pivot, generally his legs and hips are not activated like they could be. If they are tilted a little, the chances are he has the desired hip action."

Thrust

By bending the knee of his pivot leg, the pitcher lowers his body, thus getting a better position to drive off—*to thrust out!* This forces the pitcher to put extra effort into his pitch. When he drops and bends his knee in order to get the necessary momentum, he has to drive off the rubber (Fig. 4–33)!

A pitcher must not pitch from a lazy pivot let. This leg should be bent in order to get balance and a good thrust forward. Pitchers who are in poor condition or just plain lazy are more apt to pitch from a stiff or dead pivot leg.

Seaver is a good example of a pitcher who uses the "drop-and-drive" technique. He pitches between his hips, keeping his body weight as close under the hips as possible. He drives low and right out at the hitter. When Tom drops and drives, his right knee is dirty from hitting the ground.

As the pitcher pushes forward with the striding foot, the entire body goes into the pitch like an uncoiling spring, providing maximum power and drive.

The pitcher who thrusts out too quickly with the lower part of his body can hold up the thrust by keeping the ball in his glove longer. He might exaggerate keeping the ball in the glove until the upper half of his body is ready for the thrust. Otherwise, the lower part starts too soon—it gets a head start.

Fig. 4–19. THE LEFT–HANDED DELIVERY. A good pivot is the beginning of the coiling action. This is the point in the delivery at which the pitcher gets ready for an explosive thrust off the rubber. He must bend his back knee and bring the pitching arm down to get the body ready for the powerful uncoiling action. He must be careful not to tilt his body too far backward and drop his rear shoulder (Sam McDowell).

Young pitchers often hurry their deliveries by taking the ball out of the glove too soon. When the glove goes, the foot goes. Therefore, he should delay the stride by keeping the ball in the glove a little longer.

While dropping low has been used effectively by many pitchers through the years, it should be remembered that there is a certain advantage in throwing from a more upright position. The flight of the ball, or trajectory, is at a greater angle.

Stride

As the pitcher steps to throw, it is important for him to step almost straight forward with his striding foot. This step will eliminate any possibility of throwing across the body. The stride should be comfortable and natural (Fig. 4–20).

The length of the stride will depend on a pitcher's height and how it suits his size and comfort. Most important, he should guard against overstriding, one of the chief faults in pitching technique. Generally, if the stride is too straight, too long or too far crossed-over, the pitcher will have a tendency to pitch high as well as outside.

Above all, a pitcher should not "lock himself out," thereby throwing against his front leg. He must open up and unlock his hips. By open-

Fig. 4–19. (Continued) The pivot leg should be bent in order to get balance and a strong thrust forward. The stride should be comfortable and natural. He should step almost straight forward with his striding foot. His arm should be loose and relaxed as it swings backward in the windup. The pitcher should snap it forward similar to a whip as he makes his throw. A smooth follow-through should complete his delivery.

ing up more, he gives his throwing arm and the upper part of his body the opportunity to shoot through—to whip the ball!

A pitcher can open up the stride and get his arm on top by moving his lead foot over. A straight overarm pitcher has to open up his stride more. To make sure that he does not throw against his body and that his hips are opened fully, the pitcher's stride foot should land on, or to the first base side of, an imaginary line drawn toward the plate from between the pitcher's feet. Many coaches will draw this line in the dirt with a bat.

The stride should be completed before the pitcher has reached the top point of his delivery. His left foot and leg should be planted firmly in the dirt before he starts to apply the genuine power of the pitch. In other words, he is pitching against the anchor of his left leg which braces his body.

One of the key points in the stride and follow-through is that the knee of the pitcher's striding leg should remain bent to avoid jarring. This bent knee should be flexible so that it will give with the pitch and enable him to obtain the type of follow-through necessary for speed and control.

The toe and heel should strike the ground almost simultaneously, although the ball of the foot should take most of the shock. The

Fig. 4–20. THE STRIDE. The length of the stride should suit the pitcher's size and comfort. Above all, he must guard against overstriding. The left knee of the striding leg should remain bent to avoid jarring. The knee should be flexible so that it will give with the pitch (Mickey Lolich).

pitcher's toe should be pointed toward the plate. It is important that he step in the same spot for each pitch.

Drysdale had a tendency to stride against himself, but he was loose enough in the hips, plus the fact that he threw sidearm. To be effective, Don had to keep the ball low and sinking.

Whenever pitchers stride too far, they might consider raising their front leg a little higher. This should help them come down on the ball of the striding foot a little more.

A pitcher must not rush the stride. He should not rush out with the bottom half of his body. The average pitcher has a tendency to move the lower part of his body ahead too quickly. He wants to start kicking too soon. His leg stride is too quick.

To counteract a tendency to thrust out too quickly, pitchers such as Sandy Koufax, Warren Spahn and Juan Marichal used a higher leg kick. The leg lift not only gets drive into the motion, but gives the arm movement more time to get on top of the pitch.

Arm Angle

Every pitcher has an angle of delivery from which his fast ball is most effective. A change in speed and velocity can be detected by lowering or raising the arm angle even a few inches.

A considerable amount of spin and action on the fast ball can be lost to a pitcher because of a poor angle and impairment of natural coordination. Therefore, it is important for the coach to find the best angle of delivery for each of his pitchers. Normally, the three-quarter overhand delivery is the most natural one for the majority of pitchers.

Essentially, every pitch should be thrown from the same angle, so that the pitcher will not tip his pitches. If he throws his fast ball sidearm and his curve overhand, the hitter will soon know what is coming. Occasionally, however, a pitcher might want to lower the angle of his delivery, even coming around from Port Arthur, i.e., stepping toward the third base line and cross-firing past a right-handed hitter.

"I like to have my pitchers use a natural arm action," stated Sain. "Whenever I want to see what their natural arm action is, I suggest that they catch a fly ball and then run and throw the ball. Wherever they throw from, *right there,* I would say that would be the most natural position of their arm."

Arm and Wrist Action

The arm action of a pitcher should be a smooth, free movement with little muscular tension. His arm should be loose and relaxed as it swings backward in the windup. He should start to cock his arm as soon as his body begins to move forward again.

A pitcher's throwing arm should be away from his body, so he can bring the ball back and throw it in one continuous motion. The arm works as a unit with the back and shoulder. When the arm starts forward, the wrist should bend back. Then the elbow comes through, followed by the forward action of the arm and wrist. He must be sure his elbow is not below his shoulder and that it precedes his wrist as it comes past his shoulder point.

The muscles of the pitcher's hand and wrist must be relaxed prior to the release, so that a maximum wrist snap will take place. Keeping his arm loose, the pitcher should snap it forward similar to a whip as he makes his throw (Fig. 4–19). The release of the ball should be off the first two fingers, with a downward snap of the wrist. A strong wrist action will impart a spin to the ball, which, accompanied by speed, causes it to hop as it is affected by air currents.

A pitcher has to be real quick with the top part of his body. In particular, he cannot be lazy with his arm. He must snap the arm through quickly.

Release

The most effort employed in the pitching delivery comes when he is actually releasing and unloading the ball. Everything before is preparation. Proper release is essential for good control, maximum spin and smooth follow-through. It is wrist action and the release of the ball which is most responsible for imparting good stuff on the pitch (Fig. 4–23).

The arm and wrist are loose and relaxed as the ball is released with good wrist snap. The index and middle fingers pull downward on the ball to make sure that the ball will have plenty of spin.

Although the actual release point is above and somewhere in front of the head, the pitcher must think about releasing the ball well out in front of him to achieve maximum effectiveness. In other words, he must think low when releasing the ball. After coming over the top, he must release the ball with his fingers on top of the ball, imparting strong wrist action.

The pitcher tries to create a consistent point of release, just as

Fig. 4–21. FOLLOW–
THROUGH. A full sweep of the
arm and shoulder and a
complete follow-through will
prove highly beneficial to the
pitching delivery. The pitching
arm should snap straight
across his chest to the knee of
his striding leg
(Claude Osteen).

the golfer tries to create a consistent point of contact. By throwing
the ball over and over, the pitcher will be able to find the correct release point. He can tell *by feel* that he is releasing the ball correctly.

By opening up too soon, the point of release will come too quickly.
The front arm and shoulder will be too far forward, and the throwing
arm will be too far in back of the body. This type of action will result
in poor control and wear and tear on the body.

In short, if the release timing is not perfect, it will be difficult for
the pitcher to be on top of the ball in his pitching.

Follow-Through

A good follow-through is most important for speed, control and a
proper fielding position. A pitching motion which stops abruptly
upon release of the ball will definitely hinder the speed and control
of the pitch. The pitcher's arm should snap straight across his chest
to his left knee, with the pivot foot swinging around to a position

almost parallel to his striding foot (Fig. 4–21). His left leg and foot must remain firmly planted, because pitching against the resistance of the right leg gives·the pitch its final snap.

The pitcher's eyes should be on the target, his back bent and his weight evenly distributed, with the knees slightly bent. His glove should be brought up in front of his body so that he is in good fielding position.

However, there are those pitchers like right-handers Jim Bunning and Juan Marichal, and southpaw Sam McDowell, who really whip the pitch. Consequently, they often end up in poor fielding positions.

Rather than change their natural delivery, it is often best to teach them to make adjustments after completing the pitch, such as getting the feet parallel and ready to move in either direction. Any move which might curtail their motion and deception should be carefully considered.

Control

Control is the prime factor in successful pitching. Whenever I discuss the essentials of pitching success with other major league managers and coaches, we always bring up the tremendous importance of control. To be a winning pitcher, a boy has to have control of his pitches.

The main thing in pitching is to get the ball over the plate with good stuff on it, and be able to get the breaking pitches over. Control is the big difference between a *thrower* and a *pitcher.* The pitcher rarely walks anybody and hits those corners much of the time. When he wants to keep the ball down, he can keep it down.

For good control, a pitcher must be in a groove. He must be mechanically the same. Every pitch must mean something, whether he is throwing in the bullpen, throwing batting practice or in a game itself. He must concentrate and keep his eyes continually on a target (Fig. 4–21).

The mental factor is often the chief reason for poor control. Many pitchers do not concentrate enough on what they are trying to do. Mentally, they have to feel they can get the ball into the strike zone. So, they must "think the ball over the plate."

According to many pitching authorities, low pitching is the secret of successful pitching, because if a ball is down, batters tend to hit the ball into the ground more than they will up in the air. When it is on the ground, some fielder has a chance to catch it.

If a pitcher lacks the necessary control, he should not consider pitching in and out, high and low, or everything low. Instead of throwing to spots, he should aim for the middle of the plate and hope his natural stuff takes care of the corners.

Although good control involves the ability to throw strikes, there are times when the pitcher should throw a ball, either to set up the next pitch or to keep the batter from hitting the ground.

Most pitchers prefer throwing to the glove in the middle of the body. This is the target that enables the pitcher to split the catcher. After giving the signal, therefore, the catcher should move slightly into that area, slightly inside or slightly outside and give his target. It is not advisable for the pitcher to pick spots on the catcher. Instead, he should divide the strike zone into possibly six areas and go for an area, rather than smaller, more difficult to hit spots.

Wildness often comes from a poor stride, either over or under-striding. Landing on the heel, aiming the ball and taking the eyes off the target are all causes of poor control.

Good control takes practice—considerable practice. The pitcher must be sure his grip is correct, that his delivery is the same each time. He must not pitch across his body. "Most important, the release point should be the same," said Adams. "He shouldn't release it here one time and down there another time."

Pitchers should throw from a mound at all times. Throwing or warming-up from flat ground is one way of throwing the pitcher out of his groove or pattern. Getting in the groove is not always easy to do, particularly with so many kinds of variations in soil texture, mound slope and "pitching holes."

The following points are essential for achieving good control:

1. Do not go into your windup without thinking where you are going to pitch the ball.
2. Keep your eye on the target and concentrate on the spot the catcher is giving you.
3. Make sure your catcher is always in a squatting position, and that will make you pitch low.
4. There are four pitching targets: the catcher's knees and his shoulders. Keep your eye on one of these targets during the entire motion.
5. Watch your front foot—where you place your front foot down, and make sure it always lands on the same spot.
6. Make certain you let the ball go only when your arm is in front of you. If you find that your pitches are too high, chances are you are releasing the ball too soon.
7. Be sure you follow-through across your body.
8. Keep ahead of the hitter. *Make that first pitch be a strike!*

Proper Mental Attitude

A pitcher's frame of mind is of great importance to his overall performance, particularly his control. Confidence and poise, when blended with a strong competitive spirit, can be a huge asset to any pitcher. He has to feel he has everything completely under control. He must feel deep down that he is better than the hitter. He has to think positively that "I am going to do it!" "I never pitch a game that I do not expect to win," said Seaver. "I think positively."

Fig. 4–22. HIDING THE BALL. The pitcher must cover the ball with his glove at all times. Concealing the ball is not enough. He must hide as much of his wrist in the glove as possible. Some pitchers change the position of their hand on the ball, and the wrist gives the pitch away as much as the fingers on the ball. Therefore, like Tom Seaver here, the pitcher should lay his wrist across the heel of his glove.

The pitcher has to have courage not to be afraid to throw the ball into the strike zone and be confident that he has the pitches and control to retire any hitter.

Relaxation is of vital importance in acquiring a good mental attitude. Whenever there is fear in the mind of a pitcher, there is tension, and that means he is not relaxed.

Here is how a pitcher can relax:

1. Concentrate on the exact spot you are going to throw the pitch.
2. Take a deep breath before making your pitch.
3. Do not be afraid you are going to walk the hitter.
4. Do not be afraid the batter will get a hit.

A pitcher has a job to do on the mound, and if he places his complete concentration on what he is doing and how he is going to work on the hitter and get him out, there will be no room for fear in his mind.

Every pitcher must work hard on keeping the ball hidden as long as possible. By hiding the ball until the last instant when it is released, the batter has that much less time to get his eye on it.

Many pitchers throw hard, but somehow their pitches come up to the plate big as a balloon. Very likely, their shortcomings can be attributed to a lack of deception and motion. They fail to hide their pitches effectively. The batter is able to pick up the ball early and can follow it all the way.

Hiding the Ball

Then, there is the successful pitcher whose motion and deceptiveness are so effective the hitter is prevented from seeing the ball until it is right on him. Consequently, the batter cannot get around in time to pull the trigger.

A pitcher's glove makes a perfect cover-up for the ball as he gets ready to make his delivery (Fig. 4–22). As a result, most pitchers use as large a glove as possible. Concealing the ball with the glove, though, is not enough. The pitcher must conceal as much of his wrist in the glove as possible. Many pitchers change the position of their hand on the ball, and the wrist gives the pitch away as much as the fingers on the ball. Consequently, the pitcher should just lay his wrist across the heel of his glove.

How to Cover Up Pitches

1. Wear a large glove that will help cover up the pitches.
2. Hold the ball the same way for all pitches.
3. Start every pitch the same way.
4. Cover the ball with the glove at all times.
5. Keep the ball hidden behind the body during the windup.
6. Throw the knee in front of the body.
7. Keep the ball in the glove longer—until the last moment.
8. Swing the glove hand toward the hitter.

Distracting the batter

There are various ways of distracting the hitter. Many pitchers like to swing their gloved hand in front of the throwing hand as they pitch. Certainly, a flick of the glove in the batter's line of vision can prove somewhat annoying.

Kicking the leg higher in the air can provide more deception in the delivery. However, caution should be taken *not* to employ the unorthodox type used by Marichal. Unfortunately, the great majority of pitchers cannot execute this difficult maneuver properly.

Here are other ways to deceive the hitter:

1. A pause in the delivery
2. The double pump (particularly with two strikes)
3. The no-windup delivery
4. Crossfire pitches.

Tipping pitches

Many young pitchers tip off their pitches. Some type of movement gives their intentions away. Therefore, the coach should study each of his pitchers closely to determine whether or not he is tipping his pitches.

To keep from tipping his pitches, the pitcher should strive to throw every pitch in the same manner. He should hide the ball well up in the web of his glove.

The following is a list of other ways pitchers might be tipping their pitches:

1. Pumping higher on one pitch than on another.
2. Raising the leg higher on one type than on another.
3. Spreading the fingers on certain pitches and not on others.
4. Showing more white on certain pitches.
5. Turning the glove differently when delivering certain pitches.
6. Turning the wrist more on one pitch than another as the pitching hand raises up in the glove.
7. Changing the arm angles on different pitches.

Set Position

When there are runners on base, the pitcher should throw from the set position rather than from a windup position. However, he should use the same pitching procedure from the stretch as he does from a windup (Fig. 4–23). He must not vary his style. Some pitchers are not as effective when working from the set position as they are when using their windup. Quite often this is because they do not spend enough time throwing from the stretch position on the sidelines. In the set position, the pitcher keeps his feet comfortably spread, his body turned sideways to home plate, with the pivot foot resting against the front edge of the rubber.

Stretching his arms overhead, he brings his hands down to a set, looks at the base runner, and either throws to the base, steps off the rubber or pitches to the batter.

Most pitchers hold their hands at their belts, while some hold them with their arms straight. Others hold them up by their chest.

The rear leg should be slightly bent, with most of the weight on it, so that a strong push-off can be made. The right-hander, with a runner on first base, should rotate his shoulders slightly toward first base and turn his head down and toward first so that by moving his eyes he can see both his catcher and the runner on first.

Moving a Hitter Back

The inside-outside style of pitching is a regular practice of major league pitchers, particularly for hitters who crowd the plate. This means that a pitcher should learn to throw his fast ball on the inside in order to keep the hitter from covering up the outside of the plate.

Pitchers who throw too much on the outside, without an occasional inside pitch, will soon have the hitters taking picks on the seemingly "perfect pitches" that hit the low outside corner. By keep-

Fig. 4–23. SET POSITION. Sandy Koufax demonstrates how he uses the same pitching style from the set position as he does from a windup. Stretching both arms overhead, he brings his hands down slowly to the belt. This is the set position he must come to and hold for at least one full second before throwing to the hitter. In this series, Sandy demonstrates the timing and rhythm which comes when the arm and upper body are meshed with the striding leg and lower body.

ing all his pitches out over the plate, a pitcher is simply inviting the hitters to take a toehold and swing from the heels.

Larry Sherry, who was a fine relief pitcher with us early in the '60s, had a theory on handling the batter who constantly crowded the plate. "Anyone who moves into the plate or stands close to the plate," said Larry, "you have to pitch tight. I mean you have to pitch around the neck and head inside, not to hit him, but you have to pitch tight in order to make your outside pitches effective."

Occasionally, a pitcher may come in too tight and knock down a hitter. This gives the impression that he is throwing a duster, but more than likely, his fast ball just took off. Drysdale was blamed for many pitches inside that he did not intentionally throw because his fast ball was a live one that would bear in and down. Koufax, on the other hand, seldom brushed anybody back.

When the batter digs in, it is often a good idea to brush him back. A good time to do this is with two strikes and no balls. However, a

Fig. 4–23. (Continued) Young pitchers often hurry their deliveries by taking the ball out of the glove too soon. When the glove goes, the foot goes. Therefore, he should delay the stride by keeping the ball in the glove a little longer. Notice that when Sandy's striding foot touches the ground, his throwing arm is up on top. He now has the necessary body momentum to drive on through.

pitcher should *never* throw at the hitter with the intention of hitting him.

Holding Runners On

Since most stolen bases result from the base runner stealing on the pitcher, it is extremely important for all pitchers to develop a good move to first base. As a rule, the more dangerous the base runner, the more often the pitcher must throw over to keep him close to the base.

"Keep the runner honest," said Spahn. "Let him know you have a deceptive move. His respect for you will keep him closer to the bag."

Before pitching to the batter, many right-handed pitchers make an initial move with their shoulders, arms, body, legs or feet, but when throwing to first base, will always lift the right heel as the starting move. As a result, the base runner will watch the right heel. He will know the pitch is going to the plate if the heel does not lift, thereby getting a good start toward second. The pitcher can remedy the situa-

Fig. 4–24. PICK–OFF MOVE TO FIRST BASE. The right-handed pitcher makes his throw to first by pivoting quickly to the left on his right foot and stepping toward the base with his left foot. His initial move should be the lifting of the rear heel, followed by a quick pivot on the ball of this foot. Here, Bill Singer uses a snap overhand throw. He should never try to just lob the ball.

tion by developing the same initial move for the throw to the batter as the one to first base.

With a runner on first base, the right-handed pitcher should use peripheral vision. He should watch the runner out of the corner of his eye. He makes his throw to first by pivoting quickly to the left on his right foot and stepping toward the base with his left foot. The throw to first should be low and to the inside of the base. Quickness is more important than the speed of the throw (Fig. 4–24).

Aggressiveness is essential in any pick-off move. The pitcher can speed up his action by hopping on his pivot foot as it is turned toward the base. A jump shift, coming down on the pivot foot first and then on the other foot, is quicker than a pivot.

The best time to throw to first is when the pitcher comes down to a set position and just as the runner starts to take his lead. This is particularly true if his first step is a cross-over, which places him in a position from which it is difficult to get back to first base quickly. Sometimes, the pitcher likes to pivot and throw when he is at the height of his upswing on the stretch. Or, he might throw when coming down or after coming to a full stop.

A pitcher must not fall into a pattern. For example, he should not look at the runner the same number of times or take the same amount of time during and after every stretch. A good base runner like Maury

Fig. 4–25. THROWING TO SECOND BASE. When holding a runner on second base, the pitcher should take a normal stance, feet parallel, with the toes pointing straight ahead. In making the throw, he uses a jump shift toward the gloved hand side. Whirling around on his left pivot foot, he makes a snap overhand throw as he steps directly toward the base (Bob Bolin).

Wills or Lou Brock will spot it and will be able to get a good jump on him.

A high leg kick with runners on base can also be dangerous. Instead, it should be a quick kick, or merely a flat, quick stride. Most pitchers like to employ some type of kick, since it allows them to get more hip action into their delivery. Since he is facing first base, a southpaw pitcher is obviously in a better position to hold the runner on.

Many pitchers do not throw to first base often enough, nor do they vary their timing in throwing to the plate or to first. An effective procedure is to throw to first with medium speed to keep the runner close, and with good speed when trying to pick him off.

When holding a runner on second base, the pitcher should take a normal stance, feet parallel, with the toes pointing straight ahead. In making the throw, he uses a jump shift toward the gloved hand side, which is quicker and smoother than turning toward the throwing hand side (Fig. 4–25).

With a runner at second, the pitcher might look back toward second base, look toward the plate, look back toward second again out of the corner of his eye to keep the runner honest, then focus on the target and pitch.

All pitchers should be aware of the fact that they do not have to complete their throws to either second or third, but that they *must* in throwing to first. The rules state that, in throwing to first base, the pitcher *must* step toward the base. Once he moves any part of his body, other than his head, toward first base, the ball must be thrown to first, and he must step toward the bag along with the throw.

If the runner on first breaks before the pitch, the pitcher should back off the rubber by lifting his pivot foot and placing it behind the rubber. He is now out of the box, and cannot commit a balk. He should turn to his left and start toward the runner.

If the runner keeps on going, the throw should be made to second base. If the runner stops halfway, the pitcher should run at him and make him commit himself.

Pick-Off Play A successful pick-off play requires perfect timing, since the throw is usually made before the shortstop actually gets to the bag. The shortstop generally teams with the pitcher because he plays behind the runner. The play is usually attempted when the run, if scored, might have a final bearing on the game. A good time to work the pick-off play is when the count is three balls and one strike, or three balls and two strikes, because the runner is frequently given the "go" sign in these situations.

Unquestionably, the pick-off play must be practiced over and over again until the timing between the pitcher and infielder is synchronized perfectly, so that the throw can be made quickly and accurately.

There are several basic methods of working the pick-off play at second base:

Method 1
The pitcher gives a signal to the shortstop, such as rubbing his shirt with his pitching hand. The shortstop answers with a similar signal. The pitcher takes his pitching position, while looking toward the runner. When the pitcher turns his head toward the plate, the shortstop immediately breaks for the bag. The pitcher looks momentarily toward the batter, then turns and makes his throw.

Method 2
When the shortstop thinks the runner is off guard, he breaks for the bag. The shortstop may break for second base after retreating toward the runner's left. This retreat, in which he backs up slowly, serves as a signal to the pitcher. The runner feels the shortstop has retreated back to his original position, but actually, it keeps him about the same distance from the bag. In either case, the pitcher should watch the shortstop so that he can turn and throw as soon as the break is made for the bag.

Method 3
(The Daylight Play)
The shortstop initiates this play by placing daylight between himself and the runner. The pitcher uses his own judgment. The time to throw is when the pitcher sees daylight between the shortstop and the runner—with the shortstop closer to the bag.

Method 4
(Count Play)
A signal from the shortstop starts this play. When the runner at second takes an extra long lead, he becomes "fair game" for a pick-off play. While the pitcher is looking at the runner, the shortstop flashes the signal. He breaks for the bag as the pitcher turns back to face the batter. As the pitcher turns toward the plate, he counts "ONE–TWO"—and turns and throws on "THREE." The shortstop starts on the count of "TWO."

The throw should be knee-high and directly over the bag, in order for the shortstop to make a sure catch and a quick tag.

Fielding His Position

The pitcher has the important responsibility of being the "fifth infielder." Many times, the difference between winning and losing rests on the fielding skill of the pitcher. Handling batted balls hit up the middle, throwing accurately to the right base, covering and backing up bases are just some of the key responsibilities of the pitcher. The moment the ball leaves his fingertips, the pitcher becomes the "fifth infielder."

The pitcher should follow-through and be ready for the ball to be hit back at him at all times, and be well balanced, with his feet spread, ready to go either way. Balance is the key to a good fielding position.

Indeed, a pitcher can help himself by fielding his position efficiently. His ability to handle batted balls and diagnose play situations can be as important to his success on the mound as the manner in which he delivers the baseball to the plate.

In a single play, he could be called on not only to pitch to the hitter, but handle a batted ball, throw to the appropriate base, cover another base and then back up the play. Failure to perform any of these duties might prove damaging to his cause.

Fielding a Bunt

On bunt plays, the pitcher must break for the ball as fast as he can. As he nears the ball, he should slow down a little, keeping his eyes on the ball all the time.

A right-handed pitcher should try to get in front of the ball. He should jam his right foot hard into the ground, with his body bending at the waist. Using two hands, his eyes follow the ball into his glove. Raising up to a throwing position, he turns to his left and throws.

The left-handed pitcher should face the third base line, with his right foot closer to the line than the left, and turn to his right to make the throw.

On a bunt down the first base line, he should try to get in front of the ball. If it is close to the line, he should make the throw to the inside of first base.

Good judgment by the pitcher is essential in bunts and slow rollers down the foul lines. He must decide whether to field the ball or let it roll, in the hope it will roll foul. As soon as it moves into foul territory, he slaps it with his bare or gloved hand.

If the pitcher feels the bunt is on, he should make his first pitch a fast ball just above the strike zone, hoping that it will be popped up. He should wait until the ball is bunted, and then break.

Throwing to first

When fielding a bunt, the pitcher should use two hands whenever possible. His glove acts as the shovel, with his bare hand scooping the ball into it. Both hands should come up together toward his shoulder, as the pitcher plants his right foot firmly in the ground. He should pivot, look to first, take a little step and throw to the first baseman. He should have his eyes on the first baseman's chest while making an overhand throw. He should never lob the ball, and always put something on the throw.

In fielding the bunt, the pitcher should spin toward his glove hand in throwing to first, second or third. He should make the safe play early in the game, or when in doubt where to throw.

Throwing to second

On a ball hit back to him, or when fielding a bunt, the pitcher must know who is going to cover second. With a runner on first, he should always ask the second baseman and shortstop who will cover.

The catcher directs the action on these fielding plays, and the pitcher must listen to him yell "second" or "first."

On double play balls, the ball should be thrown to the infielder covering the bag, chest-high, leading the shortstop slightly, or to the second baseman, who then makes his pivot.

The pitcher must concentrate on making his throw accurately. Therefore, he must not hurry his throw or make it while off balance.

Throwing to third

One of the toughest plays for the defense to handle is the bunt or slow hit ball down the third base line. On this big play, the defense should strive to get the lead runner going into third. However, if this is impossible, they must go for the out at first or second base.

The pitcher has the responsibility for fielding the ball hit to his third base side, with the third baseman moving back toward the base and receiving the throw.

The key to the play is the third baseman. He must make the decision the moment the ball is hit, as to whether the pitcher can field the ball. If so, he immediately yells, "I got it!" and makes the throw to first or second base.

To get the important force play at third base, the pitcher must practice moving off the mound quickly and making an accurate throw to the third baseman.

Fig. 4–26. COVERING FIRST BASE. Circling into the bag, the pitcher runs to a spot about 12 to 15 feet in front of the base and approaches the base running parallel to the line. On the play below, Skip Pitlock ran a bit too close to the line and suffered a bad spike wound from the runner. On this play, the first baseman has given Skip a good throw, about a stride or two from the bag. He should have had the opportunity to locate the base and tag it.

Covering First Base

On any ball hit to his left, the pitcher should automatically break toward first base. Many games have been lost because the pitcher failed to get off the mound in time.

There are two methods of performing this play:

1. On a ball hit to the first baseman's left, or straight to him, the pitcher should circle into the bag. He runs to a spot about 12 to 15 feet in front of the base and approaches the base running parallel to the line. As he gets near the base, he should slow down slightly and bring his speed under control (Fig. 4–27).

Fig. 4–27. COVERING FIRST BASE. On any ball hit to his left, the pitcher should automatically break toward first base. As he gets near the base, he should slow down slightly and bring his speed under control. In this series, the pitcher has to wait momentarily. Then, he takes a step forward with his left foot and braces with his right foot (Ron Herbel).

The ball should get to the pitcher at a good stride from first base. Catching the ball chest-high, the pitcher now has the opportunity to locate the bag and tag it (Fig. 4–26). He should whirl around over his left shoulder, ready to make a play on any other runner.

2. On a ball hit to the right of the first baseman, or on a slow roller, the pitcher should go directly to the bag and anchor there. This also applies to the first-second-first double play with the shortstop.

On a fumble, the pitcher should stop, place one foot on the second base side of the bag and be ready to stretch or shift to either side for the throw.

On slow hit balls to his first base side, if the pitcher can field the ball himself, he should yell out: "I've got it." Then, the first baseman should answer: "Take it." The first baseman will then cover the base. While this seems quite simple, it is very important.

Covering Home When there is a man on third base and a passed ball or wild pitch occurs, the pitcher must be alert to cover the plate. In fact, anytime the catcher is drawn away from the home plate area, the pitcher must be ready to cover.

Coming in as fast as he can, the pitcher should drop down on his knee, facing the intended throw. He should give the runner the out-

144

side half of the plate. Straddling the inside half of the plate, he gives the runner the outside or foul line territory. He does not want to block the plate, because of the possibility of getting cut up. He tags the runner with the back of his glove facing him.

Backing Up Bases

Every ball that goes to the outfield is a potential backup play for the pitcher, regardless of the number of runners on base. Once he has decided to which base the throw is likely to be made, the pitcher runs to a point 40 to 50 feet behind that base, and in line with the player who is making the throw.

From this position on the diamond, he can easily retrieve all balls which may rebound past the intended receiver. If he is in doubt which base to back up, the pitcher should take a position between the bases until the outfielder makes his throw. He should always be one base ahead of the lead runner.

Pitchout

A pitchout is a deliberate waste ball that the batter cannot possibly reach. The purpose of this pitch is to permit the catcher to throw to one of the bases, for runners who take long leads. Or, it might be used when an attempted steal, hit and run or squeeze play is anticipated.

The pitcher usually throws a shoulder-high fast ball on a pitchout sign. He tries to keep the ball high and far outside the plate. A pitchout is released more quickly, using a snap overhand throw.

One of the cardinal rules of baseball is, "Never walk the tying or winning run intentionally." While there are situations when walking a hitter intentionally can be justified, the percentages are heavily in favor of the defense.

Intentional Pass

In giving an intentional pass, the pitcher should not lob the ball to the plate, but throw medium-speed fast balls about three feet outside and shoulder-high.

Since he cannot leave the catcher's area until the pitcher releases the ball, the catcher makes his target by holding the glove far out to the side and then takes a lateral step to receive the ball.

The primary objective of the intentional pass is to pitch to a more logical opponent, while setting up a force or possible double play. It is used *only with first base open.*

Another time when the intentional pass is considered good baseball is with the winning run on third, and either none or only one of the other bases occupied.

Warming-Up

A pitcher should always warm-up, get good and loose and break a little sweat before he starts to throw hard or run hard, in order not to strain or pull any muscles.

Working on the Hitter

KEY

○ *Fast Ball*

△ *Curve Ball*

⬠ *Slider*

☐ *Sinker*

Fig. 4–28. Tom Seaver (Mets), a right-hander, pitching to Rico Carty (Braves).

Fifteen minutes of warm-up should be enough for any starting pitcher. The opening minutes should be devoted to loosening up from both the windup and stretch positions. The last seven minutes should get the pitcher good and loose, ready to face the first hitter.

Relief pitchers sometimes have to enter a ball game with only a few minutes of warm-up.

The following are tips on warming-up:

1. Always throw at a target.
2. Throw easy at first, but with your whole delivery.
3. Use straight stuff at first.
4. Start throwing breaking pitches by just twisting or spinning the ball.
5. Practice working from the set position.
6. Move the ball around—up and down, in and out.
7. Spend more time on the pitch that is not working right.
8. Make sure you are good and loose before you start throwing hard.

Preventing the Balk

When the pitcher commits a balk, a base runner is allowed to advance to the next base. The following are ways in which the balk can be prevented:

1. The pitcher must have his foot in contact with the rubber when pitching.
2. Once the pitcher has started his motion to the plate, or to first base, he must complete the throw.
3. When throwing to first base, the pitcher must step directly toward the base.

Fig. 4–29. Mel Stottlemyre (Yankees), a right-hander, pitching to Frank Howard (Senators).

4. The pitcher must not drop the ball in the middle of his delivery.

5. When he wants to chase down a base runner, the pitcher must step back off the rubber.

6. The pitcher must pause for one second in the stretch position before pitching the ball to the plate.

7. When he does not have the ball, the pitcher must make no false appearance to pitch.

Working on the Hitter

The ability to work on the hitter plays an increasingly vital role as the pitcher advances upward in baseball. A pitcher can have all the stuff in the world, but without control, a variety of pitches and the ability to set up the hitter, his live fast ball and sharp curve can be greatly reduced in effectiveness. As he progresses in baseball, a pitcher should learn how to go to work on the hitter, trying to make him hit his best pitch (Figs. 4–28, 4–29 and 4–30).

The secret of good hitting is *timing,* so he must be kept off balance. A pitcher can disrupt the hitter's timing by throwing the ball at different speeds with the same motion. The hitter who is kept off balance never seems to get his pitch. When he is set for a fast ball, a change-up will likely cause him to place his weight on his front foot too soon.

A number of factors affect a pitching pattern, including the score, inning, outs, runners on base, type of hitter and the pitcher himself. As a result, the pattern and sequence of pitches should vary from pitch to pitch.

An experienced pitcher will take advantage of the weaknesses of the hitters, and his pitching pattern will be arranged accordingly. It is important that every pitch have an element of surprise.

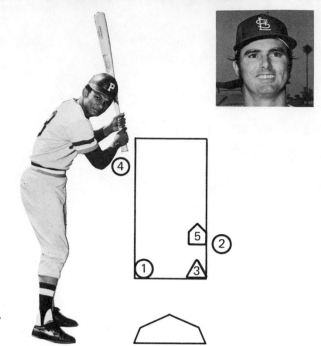

Fig. 4–30. Steve Carlton (Cardinals), a left-hander, pitching to Matty Alou (Pirates).

By establishing a pattern, the pitcher can set up the hitter for his "out pitch," one which the batter is weakest at hitting. By setting him up, the hitter is made more vulnerable.

Pitchers like Jim Brewer and Ron Perranoski, who have a specialty, work in this fashion. To be effective, they rely on their "off-pitches," such as screwballs and sinker pitches. By setting him up, they make the hitter hit their best pitch. Figure 4–29 illustrates how Mel Stottlemyre tries to set up Frank Howard for his favorite sinker pitch.

Even the top pitcher does not always have the good fast ball every time he pitches. This is when he has to be a *pitcher,* and not a thrower. The thrower tries to force his fast ball, even when he does not have it. Instead, he should go to his breaking stuff and begin changing speeds and hitting the corners.

A pitcher should not try to strike everyone out. He will just tire himself out, and will press and often force his pitching. He should use his players. They will know he can get the ball over the plate, and in turn, they will come up with better plays. By conserving his energy and the number of pitches, he can call for a little more reserve energy when he gets into tough situations in the later innings.

Get ahead of the hitter The pitcher should get his first pitch over the plate with something on it. If he can stay ahead of the hitter, a pitcher's troubles will be greatly reduced. He should try to get ahead of the batter and force him to hit his pitch. With two strikes on the hitter, a pitcher should want the hitter to go for his best pitch.

If he is ahead of the hitter, he might push him back once or twice before going for the decisive pitch. In Figure 4–30, on a one-ball-and-two-strike count, Steve Carlton's fourth pitch is high and tight, which moves the hitter back from the plate. He follows with a hard slider to the outside corner. In a crucial situation, the pitcher will either go to the hitter's weakness for a double play, or he may go to his own strength and strike him out.

The following principles should be observed when working on the hitter:

1. Get the ball over the plate with good stuff on it.
2. With men on base, keep your pitches down.
3. Try to get ahead of the hitter. Then, *go to work!*
4. Move the ball around, in and out, up and down, keeping the batter off balance.
5. Change the speeds of the pitches.
6. Learn the batter's strengths and weaknesses.
7. Observe the hitter's position, stance and stride.
8. Work on the corners when ahead of the hitter.
9. A waste pitch should be off the plate but close enough to tempt the hitter.
10. Do not throw the same pitch in the same area too often.
11. Do not show everything. Save your strength pitches for key situations.
12. Do not be reluctant to pit your strength against the batter's strength.
13. Have a reason for throwing each pitch. "Why am I throwing this pitch?"
14. Brush back the hitter who crowds the plate.
15. Do not work too slowly or too fast.
16. After two strikes, make the batter hit your pitch.
17. Use your best control pitch to get ahead.
18. As the old adage goes, "When in doubt—curve him." This is because most ballplayers are fast ball hitters.

Types of Hitters

Type	Suggestion
1. Open stance hitter	Since he likes inside pitches, keep them away from him
2. A long stride hitter	Usually a low ball hitter—pitch him high
3. Uppercut hitter	Pitch him high and tight
4. Crouch hitter	Since he likes low pitching, pitch him high

Fig. 4–31. THE RELIEF PITCHER. Temperament is a key factor in the success of a relief pitcher. He must be in complete control, poised and confident (Ron Perranoski).

5. Lunge hitter	Use a change-up or a high, tight fast ball
6. Hitch hitter	Pitch him fast and tight, although changing-up is often effective
7. Nervous, over-anxious hitter	Take your time and make him wait
8. The bucket hitter	Give him outside pitches, particularly curves
9. Hitter who turns his head	Give him some curves, particularly on the outside pitch
10. The "guess" hitter	Mix up your pitches

Relief Pitching
A good relief pitcher is one who can come in out of the bullpen, without taking too much time to get ready, and be able to throw strikes. He cannot afford to get behind the hitter. He must get ahead of him quickly.

"Temperament is a key factor in the success of a relief pitcher," stated Ron Perranoski, one of baseball's top left-handed relief artists (Fig. 4–31). "You just cannot get excited out there. Even though one mistake can cost your team the ball game, you cannot let this bother you. You just have to feel that there will be another game tomorrow. Actually, though, when I come into a ball game, the percentage is in my favor if I can throw the ball where I want to."

Baseball's most effective relievers have the ability to make the ball sink or keep it down for a possible double play. Ideally, a good relief man should have at least two pitches that he can throw for a strike anytime he wants to. If he can control his third pitch, he will make a good stopper in anybody's league.

"The only way to learn the art of relief pitching is by actually doing it game after game," explained Eddie Watt, Baltimore's dependable reliever. "The more often you are out there, the more relaxed you will be."

Before a ball game

Big league relief pitchers do their conditioning during pregame practice. They arrive on the field early and shag for the hitters, in addition to taking some cuts themselves. Generally, relief men do about eight wind sprints daily, compared to about 12 to 15 for starting pitchers.

"I do an extensive amount of running during spring training and get my legs in shape real good," said Perranoski. "Then, after the season begins, my main concern is to loosen up my leg muscles each day so I do not pull any muscles."

Getting ready

Relief pitching has become such a specialized phase of the game that each major league team has a short man, as well as middle and long relievers. "I know my position is going to be as the short man," said Perranoski, "from the seventh inning on. Therefore, from about the fourth inning, I prepare myself mentally, sitting in the bullpen and watching the ball game. I have to know what pitcher is on the mound and how long my manager will go with him. I must know who the hitter is, and who the next two hitters will be. I have to know how many runs we are ahead or behind."

As far as preparing himself physically to get loosened up, with Perranoski, it varies from day to day. "If I have pitched on four or five straight days," said Ron, "it may take me a little longer to get loose because of stiffness. But if I have had two or three days of rest, I can get ready sometimes after 10 to 12 pitches, plus the eight on the mound. There are, of course, so many variables, such as the weather condition. If it is cold, naturally, it will take longer."

Coming in from the bullpen

The relief pitcher has to know the situation: how many men are on, the score and who are the hitters. "Usually, if a left-handed hitter is coming up to the plate," asserted Perranoski, "I can expect they will switch to a right-handed pinch hitter.

"The first pitch is the most important pitch in a tough situation. It is not a matter of just throwing the ball over for a strike. Rather, it is a matter of hitting a particular spot."

"There are some days you know exactly what you want to do," said Ron, "and you can get the ball right to the spot. Then, again, if you

Fig. 4–32. WIND SPRINTS. Pitchers should run 20 to 25 minutes daily when they are not scheduled to work. Major league pitchers, like these on the Mets' staff above, use the wind sprint method, running hard for 60 or 70 yards and walking back fairly briskly as they get their wind back.

haven't pitched for awhile, like four or five days, you do get a little excited about certain things. It's like human nature. If you have not been out there for a week, you wonder if you can still do the job.''

Getting the job done

''I try to concentrate on throwing a sinking fast ball,'' explained Perranoski. ''I have to keep the ball down because I am not an overpowering pitcher. I will throw an occasional curve, even taking some speed off of it, which makes my fast ball look a little faster.

''My greatest asset is the fact that I have commanding control of my fast ball, slider and curve, which I feel I am able to throw in any situation. Many times, I have had to throw strikes with the winning run on third base, a 3–2 count and the bases loaded. All in all, I think the key to relief pitching is the manner of mixing up the pitches and getting them over when you have to.''

Conditioning of the Pitcher

Some pitchers have the mistaken idea that in order to get into condition, all they have to do is throw, and throw, and get their arms in shape. As a result, after five or six innings, when their legs give out, they rest under a warm shower.

Pitchers should always keep in mind the following phrase: *''A pitcher's legs are just as important as his arm.''* The entire body must be in good physical condition in order to prevent sore arms. Whenever a pitcher does not bend the knee of his pivot foot, he is either a lazy pitcher or a poorly conditioned one. He must have spring in his legs. During the season, pitchers must follow a regular schedule in order to get the necessary throwing and running between starts.

Therefore, we want our pitchers to run a lot. Running is the most important way to exercise (Fig. 4–32). Even after the season begins, we want our pitchers to run 20 to 25 minutes daily when they are not scheduled to work.

Besides their daily running, most pitchers keep in condition through pepper practice, pick-ups and shagging balls. Football pass drills, fungo drills and fielding drills will provide needed variety.

Getting pitchers in shape for the coming season is certainly more simple when they have had a good winter program. Then, some coaches feel the best way to be a pitcher is to throw the ball properly and often.

Many pitchers are now using a weighted ball in strengthening their wrists and fingers. This lead baseball, sometimes called a Medi-ball, is the same size as a baseball, but it weighs about two pounds. Generally, the pitcher does not throw this ball but merely flips it around from ten to fifteen feet. Others prefer moving a five-pound ball around from hand to hand.

Strength development

Many pitchers can attribute their success in part to well planned weight-resistance programs during the off-season. These programs of strength development involve use of weights, apparatus, calisthenics or isometric training. All of these items could be included in a sound program, which must be closely supervised by coaches. These programs are presented in detail in Chapter 14, on "Conditioning."

Stretching is the key to the entire weight training program for pitchers. Without stretching, the program could prove damaging. The pitcher must stretch after each exercise period to maintain flexibility. *Never* allow a pitcher to lift weights without stretching afterward.

In any strength building program, it is important to continually increase the amount of resistance. The part being developed has to be overloaded, starting first with few repetitions, and bringing more muscle fibers into play to overcome the resistance. The result is growth in strength. However, caution should be taken to limit the weight lifted.

Calisthenics alone lack the efficiency of weights and apparatus as a strength developer. It just takes too long to overload a muscle group through calisthenics. However, they do have considerable value in maintaining body flexibility and as a warm-up activity.

Care of the arm

If he is scheduled to pitch the next day, a big league pitcher generally comes in before the previous day's game and gets a massage and stretching, which lasts about 20 minutes.

On the day of a game, a half hour before starting his warm-up, he comes in for a massage and a light stretch. Most big league trainers use Capsolin for this purpose because, when the body perspires, the perspiration comes through the Capsolin. Analgesic, atomic bomb and Logangesic seem to hold the perspiration to the body. Sometimes trainers mix the Capsolin with baby oil.

On the day after a game, a pitcher will likely jog around, throw and play a little pepper. The next day, two days before his pitching turn, he will go out and play "long toss" in the outfield. He will throw 120 or 150 feet, just to stretch out his arm, not worrying about velocity.

Ice bag technique

After the game is over, all of our pitchers use the ice bag technique made famous by Sandy Koufax and Drysdale. Other pitchers, like Bill Singer, use immersion, soaking the arm in ice for about a half hour (Fig. 14–12).

In the case of Drysdale, his arm was elevated and ice bags were used all the way from his wrist to his mid-back for about 25 minutes. Then he was given a very light stretch, which helped him with his elbow problem and got him ready about one day sooner.

A spring training running plan

We start out very gradually. Since we have plenty of time to get in shape, I do not want Red to "kill" the guys the first few days. "The first day we might have them do ten sprints, at least 100 yards or longer," explained Adams, "and we run ten or twelve for two or three days. Generally, after the first four or five days, they start getting the stiffness out a little bit. That second or third day, when they are sore, is really tough.

"After the boys get over their stiffness, we will increase it a couple to 14 or so, and within ten days after training began, we will be running 20 sprints. We will run 20 every day from then on—20 good hard ones.

"When the season begins, the relievers drop back to 10 or 12," continued Red. "The starting pitchers run these with us, then after the relievers finish, they will run maybe 8 or 10 more on their own. Some of the fellows are doing some jogging."

Jogging, though, is better for the off-season. An athlete has to jog so much farther and longer to do the same thing he can do with his sprints.

To avoid arm trouble, my advice to the young pitcher is:

1. Build up a strong arm and body through regular throwing, running and exercise.
2. Concentrate on the fast ball until you have built up a strong, flexible arm.
3. Forget about the breaking pitches, especially the slider, until you have matured physically.
4. Never throw hard until you are completely warmed-up.

5. Do not pitch too often in competition. Make sure you have the proper amount of rest between starts.

6. Regular throwing is not only the greatest deterrent to a sore arm but often the best remedy for it.

Pitching in a Rotation System

Major league starting pitchers follow either a four-day or five-day pitching plan. The pitcher's arm, the schedule and the strength of the staff are the determining factors in the rotation plan.

During the last half of the season, I think the five-day rotation is better, but early in the season, with more rain outs and more days off, a team can get by with a three- or four-man pitching rotation. As the season progresses, with more doubleheaders and fewer off days, it is better to go with a pitching staff of five.

To a large extent, all this depends on the individuals who make up the staff. Some pitchers work better with four days' rest. The size of the staff is a factor too. A team may have only two or three effective starting pitchers. In winning the pennant in 1966, our "Big Four" of Koufax, Drysdale, Osteen and Sutton started all but eight Dodger games. Behind them were two ace relievers, Phil Regan and lefty Ron Perranoski.

"Seaver pitches every fifth day," according to Rube Walker, the Mets' pitching coach. "If he starts on Sunday, he rests on Monday. Then he throws for about 15 or 20 minutes on Tuesday, and rests again on Wednesday and Thursday before he pitches on Friday. There is no throwing in the bullpen or in the outfield on days when we tell pitchers not to throw."

During the regular season, a starting pitcher should work on his weaknesses on the day he does his throwing before the next start. Generally, this is limited to 15 to 20 minutes, and he does not throw at full speed. The coach must insist that the pitcher go at about three-quarter speed, which will allow him to work longer and not tax his arm too much.

Typical pitching schedule

A typical major league pitching schedule is as follows (five-day plan):

Sunday: Pitch a nine-inning game

Monday: Rest (do not touch a ball, but run in the outfield)

Tuesday: Loosen up (15 minutes of light throwing to the catcher)

Wednesday: A good workout (after loosening up, pitch batting practice)

Thursday: No throwing, but good leg work

Friday: Game

Clothing and Equipment

The shirt should be loose, not binding. Pitchers like the arm sleeves to be cut just below the elbow. They should be 50/50 cotton and wool or 100 percent wool in the arms. Professional pitchers have four or five of each. Most pitchers like their toe plate built into their shoe.

Like the majority of players, they like a protective plastic cup inside their supporter.

Drills

Drills must be engaged in vigorously, whether they involve covering first base, fielding bunts, throwing to the bases, throwing for the double play or backing up throws. A pitcher must adapt himself mentally in these drills. The biggest mistake he can make is to just go through the motions. If he performs these skills correctly in practice, very likely they will carry over and become automatic in the game. This is why he must bounce off the mound and hustle after the ball and make this play correctly in practice.

Pitchers who appear bored and handle their assignments sloppily during practice invariably are the ones who foul up in game situations—and one miscue can lose the ball game for him and his team.

Covering first base

The pitchers should line up near the mound, one behind the other, each with a ball. The coach is at home plate with a ball and fungo bat, and the catcher positions himself behind the plate.

The pitcher throws to the catcher, and the coach hits the ball toward first base. The pitcher should then run to cover first, taking the throw from the first baseman. Then the pitcher goes to the end of the line, and the process continues as the catcher gives the coach the ball he caught from the previous pitcher.

The coach can keep the pitcher from cheating by hitting an occasional grounder through the box.

Throwing to first base

This drill not only provides the pitcher valuable lessons in keeping the runner close to first base, but it serves other purposes as well. The base runner gets experience in taking a good lead, and the defense can work on their responsibilities.

The pitchers form a line behind the mound, while the base runners form a line at the first base coaching box. The pitcher tries to prevent the runner from taking too big a lead, and he may throw over to the first baseman, attempting to pick off the runner.

This drill gives the pitcher practice in making the delivery to home plate from his set position. The coach watches the pitcher closely to detect any balk motion.

Backing up bases

A good drill for backing up bases is to put the pitcher on the mound and have him go through various game conditions with runners on base. This is the same procedure used in cutoff play practice. The pitcher also covers a base that is unguarded because the catcher or an infielder has left his position.

The pick-off play

This drill gives the pitcher practice in pivoting and picking runners off second base. The pitchers form a line off to the first base side of the mound, while one of them takes his set position on the rubber. The runner assumes his lead off second base.

The second baseman and shortstop get in their playing positions and work a pick-off play with the pitcher, as described on pages 140–141.

The base runner can allow the pick-off to succeed at first, since the defensive players need practice in executing this play.

Fungo drill

This drill requires a skilled fungo hitter. The pitchers form a line out in right field, and the first one runs toward left field; after he has run a good distance, the fungo hitter hits a fly ball to him. The ball should be such as to make the pitcher keep running to reach it.

The hitter should have several balls available, and after the last pitcher has taken his turn, the line is formed again in left field.

Throw-catch

The pitchers line up at the foul line in right field, facing center field. Each pitcher has his glove and a ball. A coach or reserve player stands halfway to center field.

The first pitcher runs toward the coach. When he is 10 or 15 yards away, he throws him the ball. After catching it, the coach permits the pitcher to run past and then returns the ball to the pitcher by giving him a lead throw.

Pepper

One or more players throws the ball to a hitter, who hits grounders and liners to the fielders, who are about 15 feet away. This drill has more value when the fielders are limited to just two or three individuals.

A game can be made of this fine drill, with the fielders counting how many consecutive times they can catch a ball without error.

Pick-ups

The purpose of this drill is to get the pitcher to move quickly from side to side and to pick up slow rolling balls.

The pitchers pair off about 12 feet apart, one acting as the tosser and the other as the fielder. The tosser rolls the ball first to one side and then to the other side of the pitcher.

Upon fielding the ball, it is returned to the tosser and the fielder keeps fielding the ball until he has fielded 50 of them. Then, they change places.

Fig. 4–33. THE PITCHING ARTISTRY OF TOM SEAVER. The "Drop and Drive" is the biggest power element that a pitcher has. By bending the knee of his pivot leg, Seaver lowers his body and is in a position to really thrust out. Observe the manner in which Tom turns his hips, showing the hitter nothing but his number and rear end. At the top of his motion, he takes a little pause to slow himself down enough to get everything together at the top before throwing to the plate.

Dialogue on Pitching

Tom Seaver

with Don Weiskopf

DON: Tom, what are the key essentials in successful pitching? What do scouts look for in determining whether a youngster is a big league pitching prospect?

TOM: The main thing scouts look for is a good lively arm, a fellow with good size. Since the baseball season is long, a pitcher has to be big enough, strong and durable enough to last the whole season.

    Scouts prefer young kids who can throw hard. While it is difficult to teach a youngster how to throw a good fast ball, he can be taught to throw the breaking ball.

DON: What would you recommend for the young pitcher with a fair fast ball who would like to improve it?

TOM: The best thing he can do is to work on his running and build his legs up. If he lacks body strength, a lightweight program with weights could prove helpful. I did that when I was in college. I used 12-pound weights, and I worked on my shoulders, the triceps muscles as well as the latissimus muscles in the back. I made every effort to develop those muscles in order

Fig. 4–33. (Continued) Pushing hard off the rubber, Seaver tries to drive low and right out at the hitter. One of the key points in the stride and follow-through, according to Tom, is that the left knee of the striding leg should remain bent, thus providing the flexibility so necessary for a smooth, powerful release and follow-through.

to be a little stronger. I think a modified weight program during the off-season could be good for a pitcher.

DON: Do you still use the weights during the off-season?

TOM: No, I don't use them anymore. I used them the one winter while I was attending USC, strictly to help keep me from getting a sore arm. I thought if I got stronger I wouldn't be as likely to get a sore arm or sore shoulder.

    I studied my own anatomy and saw that I was heavy in the thighs and hips. Therefore, I put myself on a weight lifting program designed to build up the bigger muscles along the thighs, back and shoulders, and take the strain of pitching off the smaller muscles in the arm.

DON: What does it take to have a major league fast ball?

TOM: A big league fast ball is a pitch that moves, either up or down, a sinker or a good rising fast ball, one of the two. There are those who do throw straight fast balls but mainly the idea is that the pitcher should have a ball that will move in one direction or another.

DON: What can a young pitcher do in his delivery to make the ball move a little better?

TOM: A young pitcher has to experiment with himself. He should experiment with grips on the ball—holding it with the seams, across the seams, possibly delivering the ball from an overhand or three-quarter position to find out which delivery is best suited for his physical make-up.

DON: Your pitching delivery can be described as a compact type of delivery. In pitching from this style or delivery, what do you try to concentrate on most?

TOM: When pitching, I try to keep in mind using as much of my body as I possibly can, to take the strain off the shoulder or off the elbow. The muscles are bigger in the back and the legs, and these are the muscles that are most important.

DON: Tom, could you describe your pitching delivery (Fig. 4–33), starting with the pictures on the right and going to the left?

TOM: I try to take as much of the excess motion as possible out of the delivery. The old school of thought was that the pitcher with a lot of waving arms would distract the hitter. I think that is a little passé now. I try to be compact and try to keep my balance forward, not getting back too far on my back leg when I go back, and there is a pivot on the right foot. As soon as I come forward, then the right foot and right leg are the power elements in pitching. I try to keep my right knee bent, and I try and pitch on the bent left knee as well. It helps me keep the ball down, and it helps me get my back and shoulder into my pitches.

As we analyze Fig. 4–33, you can see that my legs are bending. When I get out in front and just about release the ball, the left leg is bent almost at a 90-degree angle. I think it is very important to get down low and utilize the legs as much as possible.

DON: You place considerable emphasis on a strong push-off from the rubber, a powerful thrust. Do you call that a "drop and drive"?

TOM: That would be an excellent way to describe it. A pitcher should not pitch off a stiff leg. He simply cannot get a good drive off a stiff leg. The best way to do it is to bend down on that leg a little bit, just as if you were jumping out, and really explode off that rubber. The "drop and drive" is the biggest power element that a pitcher has, and he should try and utilize it to the fullest extent.

DON: Do you agree that overstriding is a prime fault of many pitchers?

TOM: Certainly, that is a big fault of pitching. By overstriding, the pitcher will pitch against a stiff leg, which will make it much more difficult to get the ball down in the low strike zone. If he has that leg bent up front, like in pictures E and F of Fig. 4–33, he will have an easier time to get the ball down in the strike zone. To be an effective pitcher, the pitcher must be able to throw low strikes.

DON: A common difficulty among some pitchers is understriding and throwing more across the front leg. Have you observed this among major league pitchers?

TOM: Very definitely. Quite a few pitchers have a tendency to throw against their body. There is the magic middle ground that a pitcher has to meet. He must find out for himself exactly how far he has to stride. He cannot really put it out in 3'2", or whatever it is. It depends on the individual and the physical make-up, how big his legs are, the length of his arms, his timing, etc. These many elements have to be discovered by the individual.

DON: During the past few years, we have been seeing more pitchers not utilizing a pumping action. With both hands, they move directly from a position out in front of the waist to above their head. What advantages are there in the "no-pump" windup?

TOM: The reason I use the "no-pump" windup is because it takes unnecessary movement out of my pitching, and it provides me with greater control. I have less worry about being on balance when I come through. The key point here in getting through is the turning of the hips and resting on that right leg. That is the most important thing. A big pump might throw a pitcher off balance, going backward or forward or to the side. Actually, I think a big pump is passé.

DON: As for the hip rotation, how much do you rotate your hips?

TOM: I don't know how far I turn my hips but the hitter can almost see my number coming at him and my rear end coming, and I look back over my left shoulder, keeping my eye on my target at all times. I have big legs and a big waist, and I try to utilize these as much as possible. I think it is important that if a pitcher is going to pitch a lot of innings, he is able to make use of all the body parts he has, including his legs and his hips.

DON: In pitching between your hips, you keep your body weight as close under your hips as possible. You drive low and right out at the hitter. After the game I notice that your right knee is dirty, from hitting the ground. Is this a result of the "drop and drive"?

TOM: Yes, that is the "drop and drive." That is getting down on that right leg and really pushing off. I am not only pushing out but pushing down, and I try to go right at the hitter's knees. This is actually where I am trying to drive. As a result, I get down and get that right leg dirty. Jerry Koosman does that very well. He gets down and drives on that back leg of his. Being left-handed, it is his left leg. It is a good sign to see a young pitcher get down and get that knee dirty. Then, he knows he is really getting down and getting his leg into the pitch.

DON: Have you always had that bent left leg, the 90-degree angle?

TOM: Where I got it, I don't know. I just seemed to fall into it. I didn't have anybody teach me, but for me, it seemed to be the most natural way for me to throw. And I have always used it.

DON: Pitching rhythm is so vital to pitching success. How can a pitcher get good rhythm?

TOM: There are several elements. One is not to hurry himself. A pitcher should not rush or get his leg and hips out in front. Another element is getting the pitching hand out of the glove and back up.

I have a slight pause after I come forward and rotate my hips and bring my leg up. The reason for the pause is to make sure that everything is together. Then I will go from there. I hit upon this little pause at the top of my motion to slow myself down enough to get my balance and timing together before throwing to the plate. Rube Walker, our pitching coach, looks for this because he knows that if I miss that pause it will likely throw my timing and control off. It is like a golf swing. The golfer gets everything together at the top and then he goes. Well, a pitcher does much the same thing. He gets everything together, and then he goes for the plate.

DON: Many pitchers rush out too much with the lower half of their body, and they begin their stride too quickly. As a consequence, they rush the stride. This can be bad, can it not?

TOM: That can be very bad. It is a good way for them to hurt their arms too. By getting his arm behind, he is placing a lot of strain on his shoulder—the front of the shoulder in pulling through. That is why it is important to take a small pause at the top of the motion which enables everything to get together and have the hips and legs all in the right position.

DON: To get the necessary momentum, isn't it true that the pitcher has to be quick with the top part of the body?

TOM: Yes, it is a sudden movement, really, at the end. He must move quickly at the end, after his pause, and then it is almost like an explosion going to home plate.

DON: Coming to your pitching repertoire, what pitches do you like to use?

TOM: First, I place considerable emphasis on my sinking fast ball and the rising fast ball. Along with a change-up, I have my hard curve, and the slow curve. In addition, I throw a slider. Actually, it involves about six or seven different pitches when you consider all the changes of speed. But the four basic pitches which I have are the fast ball, curve, slider and change-up.

DON: Some coaches feel the number one pitch in baseball is the sinking fast ball. Do you agree?

TOM: No, I don't. In my judgment, the good rising fast ball is the best pitch in baseball. A pitcher has to be strong and be able to get that rotation—get that ball going up. I certainly don't have it every time I go to the mound, but I look for it, and if I don't have it, then I would say that the sinking fast ball is the next best pitch. A good fast ball will keep the hitters honest. It really makes your curve and slider. If the pitcher has a good fast ball, it will make his other pitches that much more effective.

DON: Would you describe the rising and the sinking pitches? What is the grip and technique for each?

TOM: The rising fast ball is held across the seams. I try to get a backward rotation and get four seams going for me and get the ball to rise as it gets to home plate.

The sinking fast ball is held with the seams, with the two small seams, and thrown off of the middle finger. I try to get that ball to run down and in to the right-handed hitter. Of course, the pitcher doesn't want to snap the wrist or snap his elbow to get that ball to run down and in, but he should get the rotation coming right off his hand so the ball will go down in a natural manner.

DON: Do you try to turn that ball over?

TOM: No, you don't want to turn the ball over. A pitcher doesn't want to put that pressure on that elbow. That is an easy way to get a bad elbow. But if he can get the rotation off that finger in a correct manner, the ball is going to sink.

DON: As for control, how do you account for your excellent control?

TOM: It just takes a lot of hard work and a lot of running. Control comes in the legs and from the deep concentration when you are on the mound. It comes in confidence. The pitcher has to think that he can throw a pitch to a particular spot. He has to think a spot. He cannot aim the ball. He just has to say, "I am going to throw this ball up and into this right-handed hitter." Then he must go through his motion and concentrate on that spot and throw the ball. It takes a lot of work. It comes easier for some people than it does for others, though. It is a combination of hard work, confidence and just believing that you can do it yourself.

When I was only twelve years old, I learned that the difference between good pitchers and bad pitchers was that the good ones got the ball over the plate—they threw strikes. Later, in my teens, I figured out that the really good pitchers not only threw strikes but threw strikes low. Then I started aiming at corners, and finally I began hitting spots.

From Little League to college and professional competition, control has always remained at the heart of my approach to pitching.

DON: Do you agree with the pitching premise—low pitching is the secret of successful pitching?

TOM: I think that is one of the big secrets of pitching. The ball is much easier to see when the ball is up, therefore, pitching down is going to be most helpful to a pitcher. He will get more ground balls, and fewer home runs.

DON: Do you move the ball all over, that is, in and out, up and down, moving the ball all around?

TOM: On the big league level, pitchers have to move the ball around. We cannot pitch one way. We cannot pitch strictly in or strictly out. We have to move the ball around, up and down, and have to continually appraise the situation on what we think the hitter is going to be thinking.

DON: Tom, you certainly employ strong arm and wrist action. Could you explain how you get that arm up on top and whip it through?

TOM: It is a combination of making sure that I get the arm up in time to come around just a fraction behind the rotation of the hips. Quickness in getting the hand out of the glove and getting it back on top is most essential. I try to get the hand back up where I am able to throw and keep my arm above my shoulder, being an overhand or three-quarter delivery pitcher.

DON: You have mastered not only the fast ball but your breaking pitches as well. When did you actually begin throwing curves and breaking pitches?

TOM: I started throwing the breaking pitch when I was about 13 or 14, and it has taken considerable work. I am not a natural breaking-ball pitcher, and it just takes time and hard work, and continuation of doing the same things over and over. A pitcher has to refine his muscles to get them so he can throw the breaking ball and keep it down in the strike zone.

DON: When did you begin as a pitcher?

TOM: I started pitching when I was nine years old in Little League, but I threw just fast balls and that's where I first learned control. I started young, and the repetition of learning how to throw the ball over the plate probably is one reason why I have decent control now.

DON: I see quite a few Little League pitchers throwing a lot of breaking pitches. Now, when should a young boy start throwing curves and breaking pitches?

TOM: It depends upon the individual. I would say as soon as his muscles develop and are big and strong enough. The muscles can take up the strain so that he doesn't put the strain on the elbow and the shoulder joints. For some kids, it might be 14 years old. Other kids might have to wait until they are 16. I think somewhere in that age category. They should not start too young. When the bones are still growing, it is too early and they can place too much strain on the very delicate joints, especially the elbow.

DON: How do you work on a hitter? Let us say, for instance, you have a typical right-handed hitter up at the plate. What is a good way to get him out, to have him hit your pitch?

TOM: It would depend, of course, on the individual and what type of hitter he is. For a normal right-handed hitter, we may start with the good rising fast ball up under the letters, up in the right corner of the strike zone. Then, we may throw a slider on the outside corner, and we may come back with another fast ball up and in, and a sinker down and in. Then, we might come back with a curve ball to the outside corner (Fig. 4–28).

The slider would be outside, breaking the slider away from the hitter on the outside part of the plate. The sinker would be on the inside part of the plate, and the fast ball on the inside, and the breaking ball could be away.

To be effective, pitchers should use different combinations. They should mix in a change-up. The pitches will continually change, depending on the type of hitter.

DON: Is there anything else you would like to tell young pitchers?

TOM: Most important, if they really enjoy pitching and want to pitch and be in the big leagues, they will have to devote a lot of time and hard work. Nothing comes easy in this game. There is no secret to quick success. It takes hard work, continually concentrating and trying to make the best of your abilities.

The only thing an individual owes the world, and himself, is his best effort—to take what talents he has and make the most of them.

Quite often, the dividing factor between the one who wins and the one who loses is mental attitude, the effort they give, the mental alertness that keeps them from making the mental mistakes. Concentration and dedication are the deciding factors between who wins and who loses. I firmly believe that.

I love to pitch. It is a personal challenge to me. Every time I go out to the mound, I have to prove to myself that I am better. I never pitch a game that I do not expect to win. I think positively. A pitcher cannot win them all but he can't play this game unless he expects to win them all. When I lose, I write down the mistakes and try not to make them again. The big thing is not to let a bad pitch or a lost game discourage you.

A good set of training rules is all a part of hard work. I don't think a pitcher can go out in the field and work, and get all his running, exercises and stretching, and then go off somewhere and not get his rest and not eat the right food and expect that his good work on the field will pay off.

It is a combination of on and off the field. An athlete has to combine his good eating habits and his good sleeping habits, along with the hard and diligent work that he puts in on the playing field.

DON: In closing, what has been your biggest thrill in sports?

TOM: It is an accumulated effort. The biggest moment in my life undoubtedly was the winning of the World Series. The biggest single thrill might be between two things: pitching in my first All-Star game and pitching and winning my first World Series game, the fourth game of the 1969 World Series against the Orioles in New York.

DON: How about the 19 strikeouts in one game?

TOM: That is a big one, but I think the more you play this game the more you find that the thrills come in the team efforts.

Catching /5/

The catcher has to be the leader, a take-charge sort of person who can direct the play of his team. His performance behind the plate in handling his pitchers, keeping the runners honest with a strong and accurate arm, setting up the hitters and keeping the whole team inspired and alert by being aggressive and full of drive, contributes to the effectiveness of the pitcher out on the mound. The catcher, perhaps, is the key to a strong defense, a bulwark of strength through the middle.

Indeed, a team's greatest need is a skilled, clever and spirited catcher. I do not think a team can rise to championship heights without an able and durable receiver. The confidence of not only the pitcher, but the entire defense, rests on the catcher. He must know the weakness of opposing hitters, be able to handle all types of pitchers and fielding plays, and be able to throw with strength and accuracy.

The Essentials

A strong arm can be a great asset to the catcher and his team. This has been true of Johnny Bench and the Cincinnati Reds, as well as other ball clubs who have been fortunate enough to have receivers with powerful throwing arms. In fact, a player cannot hope to be a successful catcher if he does not have a strong throwing arm. He must be able to throw base runners out with consistency and keep opponents from stealing and taking extra bases.

On some occasions, the catcher may have to go out to the mound and give his pitcher some encouragement and suggestions. "Don't

---

A good catcher is the quarterback, the carburetor, the lead dog, the pulse-taker, the traffic cop and sometimes a lot of unprintable things, but no team gets very far without one.

MILLER HUGGINS

---

try to throw too hard,'' or, ''Don't rush your motion'' are typical of the little reminders the catcher can give the pitcher.

A receiver often has to remind his pitcher to throw to first base and be alert for a bunt play. If the ball is hit back to him, where will he throw the ball? How many outs, and what is the score? This is why the catcher has to be a good leader and a quarterback on the ball field.

Catching the low ball and throwing to the bases are two of the most important skills of a good catcher. Therefore, the receiver should practice catching the low ball as much as he can, and work diligently on his throwing. Correct footwork in shifting for the throw is essential.

Catching is a vigorous activity and demands considerable endurance. Stopping a low pitch with the body and getting a foul tip on the ''meat hand'' goes with the job. Perhaps this is why the catching job calls for more dedication than any other position in the game. Former big league receiver Bob Scheffing once remarked, ''He has to *want* to catch!''

While catching is probably the toughest job in baseball, it offers the best chance for advancement, simply because good catchers are usually in short supply. I suppose this is because of the physical abuse they take. Although they have protective equipment on, there are still a lot of bare arms, shoulders and legs left unprotected. Unquestionably, a foul ball off a receiver has got to hurt. I have seen catchers like John Roseboro, Roy Campanella and many other fine receivers get hit right on the fat part of the arm. They merely shake it a little bit, and go right on as if nothing had happened.

Great Dodger catchers

Down through the years, the Dodgers have been blessed with some outstanding catchers. Campanella not only had a strong arm but he had the knack of catching the ball and throwing it quickly. He had the great ability of blocking the low pitch and keeping it out in front of him. ''Campy'' was one of the best at catching the pop fly. Many times, he would run a long way, reach over the railing and catch the ball with one hand. Of course, in addition to his fielding capabilities, he had the bat to go along with it. Campy's combination—bat, throwing arm and catching ability—was the thing that made him a great catcher.

Roseboro was another of the great Dodger receivers. He had a bit more mobility than Campanella. When he first came up, John had difficulty with the low pitch. He even had trouble with Koufax's high hard one. Roseboro broke in with a pitching staff that was a little hard to catch. Maybe this was good for him, because he became a fine receiver and learned to catch the low ball with the best of them. His arm was great too.

I think Roseboro was the best I have seen at blocking the plate on a thrown ball from the outfield. He thrived on body contact. The slider coming in did not bother him at all.

Both Campy and Roseboro were cagey fellows back there, in regard to what pitch to call for and how to set up a hitter. Campy had more or less a veteran pitching staff, with Carl Erskine, Don Newcombe and fellows of that kind. We did not have to worry about the sequence of pitching with Erskine on the hill and Campy back of the plate.

Qualifications

A catcher has to be able to catch the ball. While this basic skill sounds elementary, the ability of the receiver to handle all types of pitched and thrown balls, bunts and pop fouls can be a major factor in a "sound defense."

Being able to catch low throws, particularly, is of great importance in instilling the confidence of the pitcher in keeping his pitches down. Quite often, a pitcher is reluctant to throw a low curve ball with a man on third base, fearful that it might bounce in the dirt and get past the catcher. With a good receiver behind the plate, the pitcher will feel, "If I throw the breaking pitch in the dirt, I know my catcher will handle it."

Talking to and encouraging the pitcher can help make the pitcher think he can get the hitter out. Jeff Torborg has that encouragement quality. He will go out to the mound and say, "Come on, Bill, let's get this guy!" When he makes a good pitch, Jeff will say, "That was a great pitch!" Or, when coming in to the bench, I have heard him say, "You made a hell of a pitch! Keep it up!"

A catcher has to be kind of a cheerleader. His confidence actually will reflect on the pitcher. To me, this is one of the most important attributes of an outstanding receiver.

In a tight situation, I like to see my catcher go out to the pitcher and talk over the game situation. Tom Haller is good in this respect.

A strong, accurate throwing arm is a quality possessed by all the great catchers. The catcher who does not have a powerful arm, has to make up for it in quickness. I would not trade quickness and accuracy for the fellow who just throws hard.

A catcher must learn to understand each and every pitcher as a different individual. He must converse with his pitchers at all times to develop good rapport, a relationship necessary for a smooth-working battery.

Another requirement is the ability to block the plate—a rugged, rough catcher who is not afraid of a little body contact. Those runners come in there with a full force, and he has to block the plate, catch the ball and tag the runner, all at the same time. Therefore, the catcher has to be a rugged individual, with a lot of courage (Fig. 5–1).

A good receiver has to have fair size in order to take all the abuse that he will have to take. Yet, *mobility,* the ability to bounce around fielding bunts, shifting on bad pitches and getting foul balls, is even more important.

Finally, to be a good catcher, an individual must catch *all he can and whenever he can.* Catching in games, in the bullpen or in batting practice will help keep his reflexes sharp. Above all, he should work on his weak points; the strong ones will take care of themselves.

Type of Glove

Basically, there are two types of gloves worn by catchers today: 1) the nonhinged glove, and 2) the single-break glove. As a result, there are two schools of thought as to the type of glove a catcher should use.

Nonhinged Glove

Many veteran receivers believe a young catcher should use the non-hinged or nonbroken glove (Fig. 5–2). They contend that this type of glove will force him to become a better "two-handed catcher." A nonhinged mitt will force him to catch with two hands and execute proper footwork. This means that he will have to shift to his right and left. Therefore, he will learn the rhythmic footwork and obtain the proper balance necessary for accurate throwing.

"I use a glove that doesn't have a break in it," said Torborg. "There is no mark that makes a glove break like a first baseman's glove. This is basically what they call a two-handed glove."

Single-Break Glove

Big league receivers such as Haller, Bench and Jerry Grote all use a glove with a break in it, one a little more flexible. This is more of a "one-handed glove," like the type used by the first baseman (Fig. 5–2).

"I like the one-hinged glove because of two advantages," asserted Bench, regarded by most diamond observers as the game's top receiver. "With a one-handed glove, I can keep my meat hand away from or behind the glove," said Bench. "In fact, I don't want that hand around my glove. Secondly, I seem to have more maneuverability with a single-break mitt."

The trend

The trend today is toward the single-break glove because it is easier to catch with the more flexible one-handed mitt. However, in catching one-handed, catchers can develop some lazy footwork by failure to shift properly.

For years, the Yankees have used a one-handed glove, and their receivers have been very successful with it. Some people believe it

Nonhinge (Jeff Torborg)   Single-break (Tom Haller)

Fig. 5–2. TYPES OF GLOVES. There are two basic types of gloves worn by catchers today. The single-break mitt is more of a "one-handed glove," while those who use the nonhinge glove generally become better "two-handed receivers."

is more difficult to get the ball out of the glove, but I would say the trend is toward the one-handed glove.

Torborg has found he has had difficulty adjusting to the single-break glove, explaining: "Any ball down, I have a tendency to go for the low ball exactly opposite the way I would with the old firm nonhinge mitt, grabbing and picking at the ball. I sort of pick at the low ball, instead of turning the glove around and bringing it to me. That is why I don't use the one-handed glove. But these other guys like Bench and Haller use it very successfully."

"Catchers have to learn one thing," observed Torborg. "They do not want to start grabbing at the ball, even if they use the one-handed glove. It should be a real relaxed motion as they reach for the ball, and their hands give as they catch the ball. Do not go stabbing at the ball because, the minute you push out, it is one force against the other force, and the ball will bang out of the glove."

Even though catchers use the one-handed glove, they still should use the same two-handed method of shifting and footwork. They must let the ball come to them and catch it with a relaxed hand.

Giving Signals

There are many different methods of giving signs. Generally, our receivers use a combination of signals. They might give the location with the flaps, and then give the pitch with the fingers.

With nobody on base, most catchers use the single series; that is, one finger for the fast ball, two fingers for the curve ball and a wiggling of the fingers for the change-of-pace. For the slow curve, two

171

fingers are slowly flexed and extended. Some teams use a fist for a pitchout.

If there is a runner on second base, the catcher should use a sign series which is more difficult to understand, so that the runner cannot relay the pitches to the hitter. One method is to give a series of three signs, with the first, second or third the actual sign. Another method is to add the first and third signs. If they total two, it is a fast ball; three, a curve; four, a change; five, a pitchout.

Many big league catchers use a hand sign to indicate whether they want the ball to be high, low, inside or outside. These are called *location signs.* If our receivers want the ball high and inside, they give one sign for that location and then the type of pitch it is. However, the catcher should not get his glove up to the desired target too soon, so that everybody in the ball park knows where that pitch is coming.

The catcher should signal first the *type* of pitch, then give the *direction* of the pitch. Sometimes, however, catchers will signal the location first, and then the pitch.

Before the game, as well as between innings, the catcher should go over the hitters with the manager and pitchers.

Hand signals are often used for night ball and whenever the pitcher has trouble seeing them because of shadows. The catcher can "flick" his fingers out a certain number of times for the various pitches. Whatever signs are used, they should be kept relatively simple and yet not easy enough for the opposition to pick up.

Signals can also be given by the catcher when attempting to pick runners off base. Signs that can be used are wiping a hand across the chest protector, grabbing the face mask or throwing dirt off to the side. The infielder should give an answer back that the play is on, so the ball is not thrown away. After the pick-off sign is flashed and answered, the receiver then gives a pitchout sign to the pitcher. Fielders should not leave their position unless the pitchout is given.

Switching signals

To switch a signal, a sign is given that alters the meaning of the signs in the series. This prevents the opposing team from picking up the signal pattern, particularly with a man on second. The catcher may hold the right hand on the knee with the fingers together to shift the sign from the second to the third showing of the fingers.

The pitcher should indicate to the catcher that he has observed the switch by returning a prearranged signal, possibly by touching the peak of his cap. Still further, the battery can use the switch signal to change from a curve to a fast ball.

Stance

Catchers have two sets of stances: a signal-giving stance and a ready stance, the receiving position. Regardless of the type of stance, it must be comfortable, since catching is a very tiring job. The more comfortable the catcher can be, the better off he is. Since every

A. Glove up   B. Glove flat

Fig. 5–3. GIVING SIGNALS. The catcher must assume a stance in which he can hide all his signals. Hanging his glove over his left knee, he gives the signs over his right leg, deep in the crotch. The left forearm rests comfortably on the thigh, with the glove blocking the view of the third base coach (Jeff Torborg).

catcher has a different physical build, what will work for him might not be best for another receiver.

Signal position

In giving signs, the catcher must assume a stance in which he can hide all his signals and prevent his opponents from stealing them (Fig. 5–3). This is *not* the same stance he catches from. He merely gives his signs from this position. Hanging his glove over his left knee, he gives the signs over his right leg, deep in the crotch. The left forearm rests on the thigh, with the mitt hand in front of and next to the left knee, with the force of the glove facing in toward the crotch.

"The right leg must go straight to the pitcher," explained Torborg, "and that blocks out all the signs from the first base coach. To block out signs from the third base coach, the glove hand, the left hand, should be held a little past the knee of the left leg. Some catchers sit a little higher than others, but they should be sitting down easily."

"When you start to give the signs," continued Jeff, "you have to keep your right arm in tight toward your body. You don't want the elbow sticking out away from the body because, if you do, your arm will move and increase the chance of giving away the signal. Therefore, you clamp it down tight."

Receiving position

After he comes out of the sign-giving stance, the catcher gets up into the ready position to receive the ball (Fig. 5–4). To be able to throw or field a bunt, he must have a stance which is not only comfortable but

Fig. 5–4. PROPER RECEIVING STANCE. The catcher must make sure his glove hand is relaxed, and not locked. The wrist can get locked if the face of the glove is held too perpendicular (glove up) to the pitcher. A locked wrist makes it difficult for the receiver to turn the glove when catching a low pitch. Rather than see a full pocket, the pitcher should be shown more or less the top half of the glove (Jeff Torborg).

which he feels he can get out of quickly. Normally, the feet are more than shoulder-width apart. The toe of the right foot is about on a line with the heel of the left foot, and pointing toward first base.

"In this position, your thighs and lower part of the legs form almost a right angle," explained Torborg. "Your weight is slightly forward on the balls of your feet, however, you don't lift the heels. You are up on the toe of the right foot, and the left foot is planted a little more solidly than the right one."

The catcher should move up under the hitter, but not so close that he interferes with his swing. There are a number of advantages in staying as close to the plate as possible. Among them, he will be in a better position to throw on steals, to move out quickly on bunts and to handle low pitches easily.

He must have a feeling of readiness, to be *ready to go.* He has to get his weight planted so that he has pretty good weight on his right foot, with a certain amount on the ball of his left foot. He is balanced, ready to move in any direction.

When he crouches down ready for the pitch, the catcher should strive for the most comfortable position he can obtain. Too low a buttocks will definitely restrict his lateral motions. Conversely, if his tail is too high, he will have difficulty looking up and getting his arms up on high pitches. Consequently, he must find the happy medium, assuming a position about knee-high. This will provide the mobility necessary in moving to his right or to his left.

The hands and arms are relaxed, and the upper arms and forearms form almost right angles. The arms and elbows should be kept outside his knees, never between them. The mitt is held in the lower

Fig. 5–5. A GOOD, LOW TARGET. As he crouches down ready for the pitch, catcher Johnny Bench has a low stance which is not only comfortable but enables him to move out quickly. The toe of the right foot is about on a line with the heel of the left foot and pointing toward first base.

area of the strike zone, moving when necessary to either corner of the plate.

In giving a target and getting ready to receive the pitch, the catcher must make sure that his hand is relaxed and not locked (Fig. 5–5). Torborg explained that, "The wrist can be locked if the face of the glove is held too perpendicular to the pitcher. A locked wrist may cause trouble turning the glove to catch a low pitch."

"If I were facing the pitcher," continued Jeff, "he wouldn't see my full pocket of the glove. He would see more or less the top half of the glove pointed toward the pitcher. From this position, the glove can be moved up or down with the quickest and smoothest results."

While the buttocks should be up, a catcher's rear end should not be too high. According to the old theory, the catcher should keep his tail up so he can move better. The first thing that happens when he puts his tail up high is that his shoulders go forward, and then it becomes a real strain to look up at his pitcher. Furthermore, on any ball that is high over his head, he will have difficulty in getting his arm up to it.

Catching on one knee may cause a catcher to take foul tips on the inside of his leg, which is left unprotected.

Target

The catcher should give the pitcher a good target (Fig. 5–5). Above all, he should give him a *full* target. After giving the signal from his crouch, he moves slowly into his ready stance, with the glove in the middle of his body. He should keep the target arm away from his body, flexed and with encouraging gestures. He also gives his target at the spot where he wants the pitch.

To give an outside target, the catcher merely has to move about six inches farther than the normal target over the middle. When he wants to give a target on the inside, he merely has to move over six inches to his left. Many pitchers prefer this type to that of merely extending the glove into the area desired.

"If I want the ball slightly on the inside corner," said Del Crandall, one of baseball's former great catchers with the Milwaukee Braves, "I will move over prior to giving my signal. If you remain in the middle of the plate to give the signal and then move your body and glove over, you will likely tip off the hitter.

"Furthermore, if the catcher can keep his body in front of the pitch, plus his target, the pitchers seem to have better control."

Holding the Hand

There are several ways that catchers hold their bare hands, depending largely on whether they are using one-handed or two-handed gloves. Some receivers like to "cut their hand," with the fingers bent a little and the thumb touching the index finger. Another method is to close the fingers loosely, with the index finger folded over the thumb. However, the hand should not be clenched tightly.

"Most catchers today like to keep their bare hand pretty close to the glove," said Torborg, "either in back of it or right up along the thumb of the glove. I hold my index finger close to my thumb, holding it lightly on the back of the glove (Fig. 5–6). As the ball hits the pocket, I will automatically move in with my bare hand."

The important point in holding the hand is that the fingers are not pointed toward the pitcher, but are curled. "I try to keep the hand loose," said Bench, "sort of a relaxed fist, like you are holding a piece of cotton, with your thumb inside your fingers to keep them from get-

Fig. 5–6. HOLDING THE HAND. Most catchers like to keep their bare hand pretty close to the glove, either in back of it or right up along the thumb of the glove. The receiver should keep his "meat hand" loose and relaxed, and not clenched tightly (Jeff Torborg).

Fig. 5–7. RECEIVING THE LOW PITCH. The catcher's hands should be held out away from his body in a relaxed manner. He must not be rigid. He handles pitches below the waist with the fingers pointing down. Observe how Jeff Torborg follows the ball all the way into his glove. He never turns his head on a pitch.

ting damaged. Should the ball hit them, you will have some cushion on your fingers so that they will give."

A catcher is asking for trouble when he holds the meat hand up to the side and away from the glove hand. But if both hands are up there close together and relaxed, the ball, as it comes off the bat, has less chance to hit the fingers.

Receiving

The catcher who can come up with all types of pitches, rising fast balls as well as low curves and sinkers in the dirt, will give the pitcher much needed confidence.

The catcher's hands should be held out away from his body in a relaxed manner. He should handle pitches above the waist with the fingers pointing up (Fig. 5–8), and those below the waist with the fingers pointing down (Fig. 5–7). The belt-high pitch can be handled from either above or below. However, he has to be *relaxed with the hands!* If he keeps rigid, he will go down with the heel of his glove on low pitches.

In receiving the pitch, the catcher should give slightly with his mitt as the ball hits it, at the same time drawing the ball toward his belt buckle. If done smoothly, this will prevent borderline pitches from being moved out of the strike zone. Sloppy catching of pitches may lose a pitcher the strike he deserves.

Catching pitches with two hands will give the receiver a chance to adjust the ball in his throwing hand while he is drawing the arm and mitt back into throwing position. This will enable him to get the throw away more quickly.

The one-handed catcher has less time to get his throwing hand on the ball. Therefore, he must develop an effective method of picking the ball out of his mitt as he moves the glove and the ball back into throwing position.

Fig. 5–8. RECEIVING THE HIGH PITCH. The fingers point up in handling pitches above the waist. The belt-high pitch can be handled from either above or below the waist. The receiver can raise or lower his body by straightening or bending his knees and hips (Jeff Torborg).

"The mental aspect of getting ready to receive the ball is very important," said Torborg. "If you are calling a curve ball, you hardly are thinking about the ball being high. You are thinking of it being low. Therefore, you must prepare yourself to catch the ball down and be ready to stop the ball if it is in the dirt."

"The same is true of a fast ball. Some pitchers have a real hard fast ball," explained Jeff, "and because of this, you must be conscious of the fact that the ball may be up. So, keep your head up and your hands relaxed."

Caution should be taken by the receiver not to block the umpire's view of the ball by excessive jumping movements or body-raising. Too much movement laterally, or up and down, will often take strikes away from the pitcher. A good receiver is smooth and fluid, making as few motions as possible.

On the high pitch, the receiver must remember to get his body in position so that he can field the high ball where he is not cramped. He must get his head and shoulders up, and his tail down. Otherwise, the ball is a pretty easy pitch to miss.

"The problem is the low curve ball," stated Torborg. "First of all, it has a difficult spin on it and does not act normally. It does not bounce directly at you. It usually bounces off to the right or to the left, depending on the spin when it hits the ground."

Catching the low ball and throwing to the bases are two of the most important skills in becoming a good catcher.

A big shortcoming of the average receiver is not being alert on every pitch so that, when the runner goes, he is ready to throw. On too many occasions, when the base runner attempts a steal unexpectedly, the catcher is not alert and ready. *The catcher has to get into the habit of being ready to throw on every pitch.*

Even with no one on base, the good catcher will automatically catch the ball and get in position ready to throw. This becomes a good habit.

Catching more foul tips

Some catchers catch more foul tips than others mainly because they catch up close behind the hitter. In fact, the really good catchers catch as close as possible right behind the hitter. This way, foul tips do not have a chance to veer off that bat as quickly as they would if he were further back.

Many young catchers catch too far back, and that is the ball that always gets away from them. Of course, there is a danger zone too. A catcher can be too close. However, if he can be up there where his arms are outstretched, where he can keep them from getting in the way of the bat, he will be a good catcher.

On third strike situations, when there are foul tips off the bat, the ball that is tipped downward has a good chance of being caught. Therefore, a foul-tipped ball is more easily retained when caught with the back of the glove facing the ground.

Handling the Low Pitch

One of the most crucial plays a catcher has to perform is handling the low pitch. Many a ball game has been decided by a receiver's ability, or lack of it, in stopping the low one in the dirt. The receiver who can handle the low pitches will win the confidence of his pitchers.

For years, baseball coaches have been telling their catchers to "block anything in the dirt." As a result, the accepted practice among most catchers today on the ball in the dirt is to automatically drop their knees first (Fig. 5–10). This is particularly true in some crucial situations. With a man on third base, naturally, the defense does not want to score, so the catcher is instructed to try to block the pitch any way he can. The chief concern is to block the ball and keep it in front of him.

Therefore, the catcher is taught to fall to the ground on both knees, with the glove in the middle. By getting the shin guards out of the way, he leaves the soft part of his body for the ball to hit. He keeps his body facing the ball.

Lately, there has been a trend among major league catchers to try to catch the ball first, and then follow it up with a block. After he

Fig. 5–9. DROP ONE KNEE to ground and catch ball (Tom Haller).

moves his hand for the ball, his body comes in with a blocking motion (Fig. 5–9).

This new approach in handling the low pitch can perhaps be attributed to the number of speed merchants on the base paths of big league diamonds. In the past, when catchers tended to block the ball, a fast runner on first would take a base, whether the ball was blocked or not.

Now, many receivers, rather than automatically dropping to their knees, will try to catch the ball cleanly, but their body will still be in a blocking position if they should miss.

"In my case, if the ball is slightly to my right in the dirt, I will go down on my right leg first," explained Torborg, "and try to block it. I will try to twist my body so that both of my shoulders are even and facing the ball. If I have to, I will bring down the other leg to cut off all holes."

The catcher must keep his body square to the pitcher. If the body is on an angle—say, to the right—and the ball hits him, it will still go toward the right.

"The important thing here is to keep your mask and chin right in tight to the body," said Torborg, "and looking at the ball all the way. The shoulders and body are square so that if it does hit you, generally, it will bounce out in front of you."

Throwing

For most throws, good body balance is essential for accuracy. Accuracy and quickness of the throw depends largely on how quickly the catcher can achieve proper balance of his body, along with speed at releasing the ball. The catcher should use the overhand delivery. The only exception is when he fields a bunt or a slow roller while off balance, and must throw sidearm to first or third base. He always uses the overhand throw to second base.

Fig. 5–10. DROP TO BOTH KNEES and block ball with body (Bob Barton).

In throwing from the catching position, two important points should always be kept in mind:

1. Try to get the ball off the best way you can
2. Have a good grip on the ball.

A receiver cannot rush either of these points. Although he would like to make the throw as quickly as he can, he should not rush it to the point where he does not have a good grip on the ball.

"I just make sure I get the ball out of the glove properly," said Torborg, "and just try to throw it all in one easy, fluid motion. The catcher who does not have the great arm has to make up for it with quickness."

Correct Grip

Gripping the ball across the seams has proven most effective for the majority of catchers. The two fingers are right on top of the ball. While it is not always possible to do this, by working at it, the catcher will be able to grip the ball across the seams most of the time (Fig. 5–11). Otherwise, he may throw sinkers or sliders, which are difficult to handle by his teammates.

A receiver should always be concerned with getting the ball out of his glove as quickly as possible. By catching with both hands and bringing the throwing hand and glove back into the throwing position, he will be able to grip the ball across the seams and get rid of it more quickly.

Throwing Technique

The overhand throw is not only the most accurate way to throw but is more easily handled by the receiver (Fig. 5–11). The catcher's throw is made from the shoulder, and is not a complete sweep of the arm.

Fig. 5–11. CORRECT THROWING TECHNIQUE. Keeping his eyes constantly on his target, the catcher cocks his arm just back of the ear and completes an overhand throw as quickly as he can. The step with the left foot is made in the direction of the throw, and not across the body (Bob Barton).

A receiver cannot afford to wind up. His delivery must be short and quick. A catcher who gets rid of the ball quickly and accurately generally is more effective than one who throws hard but takes too long to throw.

A catcher should perfect three types of throws:

1. The full overhand throw
2. The snap throw
3. The sidearm flip.

To make the overhand throw, the catcher should shift his weight to his right foot and rotate his shoulders to the right while the ball is brought back over the right shoulder with both hands. He brings his throwing hand and mitt back together, giving him a better chance to adjust the ball in his hand. He tries to get a grip across the seams in order to give the ball the necessary backspin.

Keeping his eyes constantly on his target, the catcher cocks his arm just back of the ear and completes his throw as quickly as he can. The ball is released with a vigorous wrist and arm snap while pushing off his right foot onto his left (front) foot (Fig. 5–12).

The snap throw is like the full overhand throw, except that the arm is not taken back as far. This is the short and quick type of delivery. The sidearm flip is used when balls are bunted or tapped out in front of the plate, and the catcher does not have time to straighten up for the overhand throw.

Shifting and Throwing

The footwork of the catcher, the manner in which he shifts his body into the throw, will determine his effectiveness to a great extent. By shifting his body correctly, he will have the rhythm, power and quick-

Fig. 5–12. REAR VIEW OF JOHNNY BENCH'S THROWING DELIVERY (above). Bringing his throwing arm straight back to a position behind the ear, Bench releases the ball with a vigorous wrist and arm snap. To gain needed momentum, he pushes off his right pivot foot as his weight moves forward onto his front foot.

ness to get rid of the ball in a hurry. It is essential for the catcher to get as squarely in front of the pitch as possible in catching the ball. Knowing the steal situation, he must get as close to the batter as possible and come out into his throwing position every time.

The one-handed glove has probably spoiled catchers to the point that they do not shift their feet as much as they used to. The old-time catchers did a better job of staying in front of the ball and shifting their feet. As a result, they were in better position to throw on every pitch.

Catchers are becoming reluctant to shift simply because they can reach out and backhand that ball with the one-handed glove. If they can do it, that is fine, but sometimes they get too relaxed by not shifting and some of the balls get through them. I still prefer my catchers to shift, even though they catch the ball with one hand.

On an outside pitch, by shifting and catching the ball with two hands, the catcher is in a much better position to throw the man out (Fig. 5–15). By backhanding it, he has to switch the ball from there to his throwing arm and take turns getting his body into throwing position.

Some veteran catchers maintain that, with the one-handed glove, it is not necessary to get in front of all the pitches. They feel that a natural stance will easily protect the 17-inch–wide home plate, even an additional six inches on each side of the plate. The catcher just has to reach for the ball.

Crandall, who managed one of our top farm clubs, has an excellent theory on getting the ball away quickly. "When receiving the ball," said Del, "you do not catch the ball and then get your body in motion. If you do wait until you actually catch the ball, you are going to waste a lot of time. So, the thing to do, when you know where the ball is going and you know what you called for, get your body into motion and be ready when the ball hits the glove. Then, get it up there beside your head and throw it."

A catcher should learn to carry the ball and glove to his right ear all in one motion, adjusting the hand for the throw as it is brought up. Crandall believes, "This gets your left side in motion, and when you do turn to throw, your left side is in position; and it will bring your right side around, getting more on your throw."

"Practice going into the ball," continued Del. "It is very important not to catch the ball flat-footed. You want to be on your toes and leaning a little bit toward second base."

Types of Receiving and Throwing

When throwing to second base on an inside pitch, many catchers take a lead step left and slightly forward with their left foot to receive

Fig. 5–13. RECEIVING INSIDE PITCH (below). The catcher takes a lead step left and slightly forward with his left foot to receive the pitch. After placing his right foot behind his left, he steps straight forward toward second base (Jeff Torborg).

A

B

C

the pitch. After getting their right foot behind their left, they step forward toward second base (Fig. 5–13).

Other receivers prefer to step to the left with their left foot, catch the ball, then step forward with their right foot, shifting their weight to the right foot. Then they step forward with the left foot for the throw.

If a left-handed hitter is at bat, and the pitch is to the left of the catcher, the catcher steps to the left and, if possible, slightly forward with the left foot. The right foot is then swung behind the left or a step is taken in front of the left foot, the weight shifting to the right, and the left foot strides out for the throw. This type of shift clears the batter. The shift becomes a jump shift as it increases in speed.

"Catching the ball inside to a right-handed hitter can be a difficult pitch to catch," says Torborg, "unless you reach out for the ball and cup it into you.

"Catchers who use the old way, step over with their left foot, step behind with the right and then move forward on the throw. Basically, that is what you still do, but you do not have time to step behind because your momentum laterally will carry you off, and you will throw with a wide open body.

Fig. 5–14. RECEIVING OUTSIDE PITCH (below). The catcher will step right and slightly forward with his right foot, catching the ball and then stepping forward with his left foot for the throw to second base (Jeff Torborg).

A

B

C

"Johnny Roseboro gave me this advice on the pitch inside to a right-handed hitter: 'Catch the ball and flip your body around so that your weight is more or less on your back (right) foot, the one you push off of. You have caught the ball and you have executed the same "step-behind" footwork. However, you have kept your body down, and your shifting is similar to a crow hop. You move both your feet around, but actually, it is not a step behind because that pulls you back away from the throw to second base.'"

"While it involves the theory of stepping behind," said Jeff, "actually, it is a shuffle behind. You receive the ball and get your body into a throwing position by shifting, yet you keep your weight over your legs."

Receiving pitch down the middle

On a pitch over the middle of the plate, the receiver will catch the ball and then step forward with his left foot and throw. He should not move forward to catch the ball and then throw.

Receiving inside pitch (inside alley)

"We do one of two things," said Torborg. "First, he can receive the ball and not take any steps at all, just turn and throw it. Or, he can do the same type of shuffle where he turns and throws to second base, just by having his body moving slowly through this little shuffle."

Fig. 5–15. THROWING TO FIRST BASE. On a pitch over the plate, the receiver catches the ball and executes a little jump shift to his right. He places his right foot behind his left foot, at the same time shifting his left foot in the direction of first base (Jeff Torborg).

C

B

A

In throwing to the bases, the catcher must get his body into motion and be ready when the ball hits the glove.

On an outside pitch, with a right-handed hitter at the plate, the receiver will step right and slightly forward with his right foot, catch the ball, then step forward with his left foot for the throw to second base (Fig. 5–14).

If a left-handed swinger is at the plate, and the pitch is also to the catcher's right, he again steps to the right with his right foot, catches the ball, then shifts all his weight back to his left foot. He then steps diagonally forward and toward home plate with his right foot, then forward with his left as he makes the throw. This shift will clear the batter.

"On the ball away to a right-handed hitter," said Torborg, "I just step over with the right foot, catching the ball at the same time, then stepping forward with my left foot for the throw."

Receiving outside pitch (outside alley)

Fig. 5–16. THROWING TO THIRD BASE. The catcher takes his first step to the left, and then swings his right foot behind his left foot. He then steps toward third base with his left foot for the throw, thus clearing the batter and moving behind him (Tom Haller).

A

B

C

Fig. 5–17. TAGGING THE RUNNER. In this exciting action, catcher Jeff Torborg has blocked off the plate a few feet from home plate and places the tag on the Pirates' Roberto Clemente as he hooks for the plate. It is to the advantage of the catcher to make the runner hook to reach the plate. He doesn't want to get injured blocking the plate.

Throwing to second base

In throwing to second, the catcher should try to throw above the bag, right to the shortstop or second baseman, knee-high, instead of trying to throw exactly to the bag. By throwing above the bag, he has a leeway. The infielder might be on the bag, and then again, if the ball is a little high, he will still be able to handle it.

Throwing to first base

If the pitch is away from a left-handed hitter, the catcher steps to the left with his left foot to take the pitch. His next step is forward with his right foot. Then he steps toward first base with his left foot. This action puts him in front of the hitter as he makes the throw (Fig. 5–15).

With a right-handed hitter at bat, the catcher should step to his left if the pitch is to his left. After the catch, he shifts his weight to the right foot, then steps out with his left foot toward first base.

On a pitch over the plate, he catches the ball and merely steps forward with the left foot for the throw to first base. If the pitch is inside to a left-handed batter, the catcher may step behind the batter for his throw. If he finds this difficult, he should step right with his right foot, make the catch, then shift his weight to his left foot, step forward with his right, then forward with his left toward first for the throw.

The important thing is for the catcher to keep his balance and keep his weight over his leg so he can push from his right leg to his left leg.

"If you want to throw down low," said Jeff, "you have to stay down. A catcher cannot stand up and throw to a base without the ball going up. He has to keep his body and shoulders down."

Throwing to third base

With a right-handed hitter, on a pitch to his left, the catcher takes his initial step to the left and then swings his right foot diagonally backward behind his left foot. He then steps toward third base with his left foot for the throw, thus clearing the batter and going behind him (Fig. 5–16).

If the pitch is away but not too wide, with the right-handed hitter still at the plate, the receiver steps to the right for the catch, then shifts his weight back to the left foot. He then steps diagonally in back of the left foot, shifting his weight to the right foot, and stepping out with his left foot for the throw.

He can make this throw in front of the hitter by stepping diagonally forward with the right foot as he makes the catch. The hitter's position in the box, of course, will determine the exact footwork the receiver will employ. As he catches the ball, he will step either in front of or in back of the batter.

Some receivers who have the necessary height do not use any footwork for clearance. Wherever the ball is pitched, they throw from there, if necessary over the batter's head. At times, though, they have to extend their arm a little higher as they throw over the batter.

Everything has to be automatic. The important point is for the catcher to learn to throw under all circumstances, because he never knows what the hitter will do.

First and third steal situation

This play is used more often at the high school and college levels. A catcher should look for this play when the opponents need a run and, generally, when a weak hitter is at the plate.

The catcher has three alternatives: he can throw to second base, throw high to the pitcher or throw to third base. "If I see the runner moving forward or toward me as I am getting ready to throw," said Torborg, "I will immediately adjust and throw to third base."

Some catchers like to make an arm fake to second, retaining the ball, and then throw quickly to third base. However, in executing this play, they take the risk of throwing the ball into left field.

The simplest of signals should be used in the first and third situation. Most teams use word-of-mouth signals. If the catcher wants the pitcher to cut it off, he will tell him so as he goes halfway to the mound. Or, he may tell the pitcher to "let it go."

The throw to second base has the same trajectory whether or not the pitcher cuts it off, the second baseman handles it in front of the

Fig. 5–18. OUT AT THE PLATE! OR WAS HE? Catcher Dick Dietz goes quickly to his knees in an effort to make the tag as the base runner hook slides across the plate. Although the umpire ruled that the runner was out, the Cubs thought otherwise.

bag or the ball goes all the way down to the base. *Every player must be ready to adjust to any throwing situation.*

Tagging the Runner

A catcher must be aggressive when tagging a runner at the plate. If he has the ball, he must hang tough, especially if it is an important run or a "boom-boom" play (Fig. 5–17). After judging the flight of the ball, the catcher should move out and place his left foot in front of home plate on the third base line. His right foot is the moving one. His heels are on the plate, and his shin guards are facing the runner.

"Basically, I will use two or three ways to tag the runner," said Tom Haller, "depending, of course, on how the runner approaches the plate. Generally, he will use a hook slide, a straight-in slide, or he will try to bowl you over."

"Let the runner see part of the plate," said Haller, "preferably the outside. This way, he has more of a tendency to use his hook slide, which is to the catcher's advantage. You might come up on the line a foot or two to receive the ball and make contact there, where he has less of a chance to get to the bag. So, let him slide in and then tag him."

"Wait for the ball to come to you," advised Tom. "Do not go out after the ball and then come back. Be on balance and mobile until you get the ball, then go into action."

As he catches the ball, the catcher turns to his left and brings his left knee down to the ground. "You do not have to reach out," said Tom, "all you have to do is make contact with the runner. Make sure

Fig. 5–19. DISCARDING THE MASK ON A POP–UP. The catcher holds on to his mask until he has located the ball. Then he tosses it off to the side and moves under the ball. He must keep his eyes on the ball at all times (Bob Barton).

that the ball is in your glove, with your bare hand holding the ball snugly. When you make contact, just make sure that you hold on to that ball and tag him with the back into his stomach. Do not tag the runner just with the ball. Use the glove and the ball!

"The easiest kind of runner to tag out is the one who goes into a hook slide. When he starts sliding, you do not have to worry about much of an impact because most of his weight is going away from you. All you have to do is go down on one knee and tag him, similar to the tag used by infielders at second or third base (Fig. 5–18)."

The most important thing is for the catcher to make sure he has the ball first, and he must hold it tight, particularly on the "bang-bang" play. When he does make contact, nine times out of ten, the umpire will call the runner out because the catcher has made the contact with the runner.

"The throw from right field to home can be a little more difficult," said Haller, "as well as dangerous for the catcher. Try not to get hit from the blind side. Give the runner the inside of the plate and make sure the shin guards face the runner."

The catcher should know the speed of the runner coming home, the arm of his outfielder and the approximate distance to home plate. Normally, the catcher must have possession of the ball, or he will be called for blocking home plate. Under the heat of action, however, this is often overlooked. Very seldom is obstruction called at home plate, in which the catcher blocks the plate before he has the ball. Most catchers like to block the runner by forcing him to make an outside hook slide. They often block him a few feet from home and put the tag on him as he scrambles for the plate.

"The catcher should make the runner commit himself first, and then he counters," said Haller, "Remember, the runner has his momentum

Fig. 5–20. CATCHING THE POP FLY (glove flat). Although most catchers have their gloves pointing upward when catching the pop-up, receivers like Tom Haller, above, prefer keeping their hands close to their belt and opened up. The face of the glove is up and the hands are flat.

built up. Therefore, the catcher should put his left foot right on the base line, and if he hooks, he will hook right into that shin guard."

Forcing the Runner

With the bases loaded and the throw coming into the plate from an infielder, the catcher has the assignment of forcing the runner and trying for the double play at first base.

On a good throw, the catcher will place his right foot on the plate. As he catches the ball, he will step forward with his left foot, and throw. Throws that are received wide of the plate are caught by stepping to the side on which the ball is thrown.

"If I touch the plate with my left foot," said Haller, "then I have got to take two steps and throw. You do not have that long if you want to double that man up at first base."

"Make sure the throw is to you," advised Tom, "that your foot is on the plate. I try to extend myself a little bit like a first baseman, not too far out, though, because you need good balance to make your pivot and throw. Sometimes, you do not know how much time you have, but make sure you get the first out. Then, as you step toward first base, try to keep the ball inside of the runner so the first baseman can handle the ball easily."

In throwing to the first baseman on a possible double play, the receiver must be sure to get clearance from home plate. If not, he could

Fig. 5-21. CATCHING POP-UP (glove up). This is the technique used by most big league catchers. The glove of the receiver is pointed upward, similar to the technique used by outfielders. The hands are positioned about eye-level.

get racked up by the runner, and his throw might end up down the right field corner.

Catching the Pop Fly

Most big league catchers like to catch pop flies with their back to the infield; because of the rotation of the baseball, the ball usually comes back toward the infield. This is known as the *infield drift,* and the catcher must allow for it. The higher the foul ball, the more drift it will take, which can be as much as three to five feet. This is what makes pop foul balls hard to catch.

Experience is most important in catching high pop-ups, and it comes only after handling many pop flies during practice and games. In doing so, the catcher can build up the necessary confidence. Catching pop-ups is a matter of practice and allowing for the rotation of the ball.

"The more you catch, the more you know when the foul pop-up is in play," said Haller, "just by the sound of the ball. If a ball goes over your right shoulder, you should then turn to your right, and vice versa if the ball goes over your left shoulder."

The high pop-up hit directly over home plate is particularly difficult to catch. After judging the ball, the catcher throws his mask away and moves into the ball. His back is toward the infield (Fig. 5-19).

"Many catchers will go out and have the ball come back into them," said Haller. "Then, there are those who will stay there, and move out facing the infield. They know the ball will move out, and then they will overplay it somewhat, and the ball will come out in front of them."

If the pop-up is moving into the infield away from the plate, one of the infielders should handle the catch. The catcher should go after

Fig. 5–22. FIELDING A BUNT. The catcher must move out quickly on bunts. He should always be ready to pounce on the ball in front of the plate. He should try to field all rolling bunts with two hands. Placing his glove out in front of the ball, he scoops the ball into his glove with the throwing hand. Although catcher Bob Barton is shown circling the ball in this series, many receivers prefer turning their back toward first base and approaching the ball directly.

every pop-up until he is called off by either the third baseman or the first baseman, who might have a better angle and a better shot at it.

The pitcher can play an important role in these situations. As soon as he realizes who should catch the ball, he will yell the last name of the player, and his teammates will react accordingly.

After getting a good sight on the ball and judging its return, the catcher should be sure to throw his mask in an opposite direction (Fig. 5–19). He should avoid turning around too much.

"Most of the balls are usually away from the plate," explained Tom. "So, you do not have to worry about stepping on your mask. On those balls hit directly overhead, you should hold on to your mask for a moment and discard it to either side, depending on which way you have to move."

Catching the ball
Most catchers point their gloves upward when catching the pop-up. This technique is similar to that used by outfielders, with the hand and glove up at about eye-level, with the fingers of the glove pointed up (Fig. 5–21).

"I prefer the other method," stated Haller, "with the hands close to my belt and opened up. The face of the glove is up and my hands are flat (Fig. 5–20). I just feel that if a ball hits the edge of my glove in that manner, I will have another shot at it before it hits the ground. I like to catch the ball this way. For me, it has been much easier, and I have had good success with it."

Fielding Bunts
In fielding bunts, the catcher must move out after the ball as quickly as possible. He has to get a good jump on the ball (Fig. 5–22).

The speed of his moves will depend, of course, on how fast the batter is running down to first base. If he is a real fast runner, it could be a desperation play. If he is only an average runner, he will have more time to get set and throw him out.

"Try to field all rolling bunts with two hands," advised Haller. "Placing your glove out in front of the ball, you want to scoop the ball into your glove with the throwing hand. Do it all in one motion and make sure you have good control of the ball. Never take your eyes off the ball!"

In throwing, some catchers like to come back over the top, while some prefer to throw sidearm. If it is a hurry situation, they have to throw from their fielding position and make a quick, sidearm throw.

The bare hand should be used only if the ball has stopped rolling and it is a "do-or-die" play.

Down the third base line

There are two different theories on fielding the bunt down the third base line. Most catchers prefer to turn their back to first base and approach the ball as quickly as possible, rather than take the time to circle the ball. It is generally believed to be faster for the receiver to turn his back on the play. Others like to circle the ball, since this method helps keep the play in front of them at all times.

The pivot-and-whirl method

On a rolling ball, the catcher places his left foot as close to the ball as possible, allowing him plenty of room to field it as it rolls to his right. If the ball stops rolling, he places his right foot close to the ball and makes a turn to his left on his right foot, then steps out with his left foot as he throws to first base.

The primary task is to place the glove in front of the ball to stop it. As he pivots on his right foot, he uses his glove to flip the ball into his throwing hand. As he fields the ball, his right foot is placed ahead of his left foot, thus cutting down his angle in turning around for the throw.

Circling the ball

Some catchers like to have the play in front of them at all times, circling to the left of the ball, if possible. "I prefer circling the ball because I can snap the ball to first base as fast and hard as I can in turning and pivoting around," said Haller. "While it takes another step as far as the runner is concerned, I think it is the surest way. You always have everything in front of you. If the throw is to go to second base, he does not circle as much." (Fig. 5–22)

Down the first base line

The catcher should move out as quickly as possible, buff the ball with his glove, take one step with his right foot, step with his left foot and throw sidearm to the first baseman. He remains low to the ground when fielding and throwing, and by keeping the play in front of him, he should be able to make an accurate throw to the first baseman.

Run-Down Play

On a run-down situation occurring between home and third, if he has the ball, the catcher should run the base runner as hard as he can toward third base. When the runner is about halfway down the line, he should bring his throwing arm to the area of the shoulder. As soon as the third baseman moves into the play, he should toss him the ball about chest-high, with the receiver placing the tag on the runner. One throw should be all that is necessary.

After the toss, the catcher should get out of the way to his outside and go back. The catcher and third baseman must be on the inside of the base runner, keeping the runner on one side. They should never let him bisect their view or throwing procedure. Catchers, like infielders, are advised not to make more than one fake throw.

Covering and Backing Up

Whenever a ground ball is hit to the infielders with no runners on base, the catcher should move quickly down the first base line in foul territory, and back up the first baseman. Generally, he runs parallel and about 35 to 40 feet from the line as fast as he can.

When the first baseman goes after a short fly ball, the catcher often covers first base. He also covers third base when a bunt or slowly hit ball is fielded by the third baseman with only first base occupied.

Cutoffs

If the throw from the outfield is accurate and if the catcher does not want the infielder to cut the ball off, he should remain silent. However, in an exciting game with plenty of noise, he will often yell, "Leave it alone," or "Let it go!" If he wants the infielder to cut the ball and make a play, he will yell, "Cut." The catcher will yell, "Relay" if the throw coming into home is to be cut off and thrown home.

Working with the Pitcher

The catcher must call the game according to the type of pitcher with whom he is working. In sizing up a hitter, a catcher, above all, must remember his pitcher's ability, even more so than the hitter's weakness. It is particularly important to work more around the pitcher's strength if the catcher does not have a "book" on the hitter.

The type of control his pitcher has will be a big factor in what pitches the catcher will call. He does not want to get his pitcher in a hole. He should want the pitcher to work in front as much as possible. Therefore, he should try to go with pitches of which he knows the pitcher has good control.

If his fast ball is good on a particular day, he might start out with a fast ball. But he must mix up the balls, especially with some off-speed pitches. Otherwise, the hitter will learn just what to expect.

Fig. 5-23. BEFORE A GAME, the catcher should get together with the starting pitcher and the manager to determine how he will pitch to opposing hitters. Here, Thurman Munson of the New York Yankees talks things over with veteran righthander Mel Stottlemyre.

The big thing is to *get ahead of the hitter,* and work from that point. In a tough situation, the catcher should call for the strongest pitch that his pitcher has on that particular day.

Just because the hitter is weak on a curve does not necessarily mean to throw him curves, UNLESS the pitcher can throw a good curve ball. If he has a poor curve, perhaps it would be best to waste that pitch, or merely "show" the curve.

Quite often, what is effective for one pitcher may not be effective for another. A letup pitch on a 3-1 count can be a good call for some pitchers and will often force the hitter to hit the ball with his timing slightly off.

On 3-1, as well as 2-0 situations, many catchers will call for an "off" pitch. This pitch, though, must be a strike, preferably low and away. The pitcher wants the hitter to hit this ball, not miss it, hoping, of course, that the batter's timing will be off.

Should the pitcher shake the catcher off now and then? If he is a young pitcher, I would prefer that he pitch basically what the catcher calls for. If he is a veteran—a Claude Osteen, for instance—who has been around a long time, I want my pitcher to have the right to throw the pitch that he wants to. He will do a better job of throwing the pitch he wants in this situation.

Both the pitcher and catcher must make a thorough study of the opposing hitters and discuss them freely (Fig. 5-23). They should study the hitter's stance and remember what pitch he went for and where he hit the ball in previous appearances. Batting practice is a good time to watch the opposing hitters. It does not take long to find out who the pull hitters are, those who hit straightaway, and the opposite field swingers.

However, young battery combinations are advised not to worry too much about stances and batting positions. After they get ahead of the

Studying the hitters

A. The target

B. The pitch

Fig. 5–24. THE INTENTIONAL PASS. Since the catcher must keep one foot in the catcher's box until the pitcher releases the ball, he has to hold his glove straight out to his left and then move out quickly to receive the pitch (Dick Dietz).

hitter, though, they could consider his stance and his relationship to the plate.

If the batter crouches over the plate, the catcher should advise his pitcher to keep the ball high and inside. The batter who steps away from the plate should be pitched outside, while the hitter who stands up straight should be given pitches down low.

Some hitters will crowd the plate, because they want the tight pitch. Those who stand far from the plate invite the outside pitch.

Setting up a hitter

Setting up a hitter to make him hit the pitcher's best pitch is very important (see "Working on the Hitter," in Chapter 4). However, to a large extent, this depends on the control of the pitcher. Personally, I do not like to be beyond a 2–2 count on a hitter.

In the National League, we try to teach our pitchers to get the low strikes, and work from there. We encourage them to move the ball around and get the breaking ball over, if possible. If they can, they will likely be consistent moundsmen.

Should the catcher talk with the hitter? I think there is nothing wrong with that. It might have an effect on some hitters. The only thing you are doing is taking the hitter's attention, keeping him from concentrating on the pitch. This is one of the tricky ways to try to get a hitter out.

Going out to the mound

When going out to the mound, the catcher should have something definite to say to the pitcher. Some pitchers need a few harsh words, for them to get going. The catcher might have to make them a little angry at times. Other pitchers may need a pat on the back and a few words of encouragement.

More than likely, if a pitcher runs into control trouble, he is basically high and usually is doing one of two things wrong. First, he could be rushing, which would cause him to be high with his pitches.

"We usually look for this, and if we see it," said Haller, "we will go out and talk to him and say, 'You are rushing. Stay back and don't rush the delivery.'

"If you pinpoint one or two things wrong, very likely it will settle him down. Pitchers have a tough job. The biggest job is to concentrate for nine innings. Quite often, when a pitcher gets in trouble, he is not concentrating enough on what he wants to do."

Sometimes it is effective for the catcher to go out and talk to his pitcher just to slow him down a little. A little humor or a joke might be good at this time to help him relax.

In their relationship with umpires, catchers generally fall into three groups:

Relationship with the Umpires

1. The catcher who lets the umpire know that he has missed a pitch
2. The receiver who argues on every close pitch called against his pitcher
3. The one who does not say a word, and gives the impression that he is not in the ball game.

We like our catchers to practice more the first point listed. When a catcher is sure the umpire missed the call, without turning around, he should let him know that he has missed this pitch. In our league, a catcher is not allowed to turn around and argue with him. If he misses another one, he has to raise hell again, but within reason, of course. The catcher has to be *sure* that he is right, though, before he makes too big an argument about it.

Crandall had this to say about his relationship with umpires: "I did not particularly like to argue with umpires, but when I thought I was right, I had my words. If a catcher feels that he is right, he has to say something because, if he does not, the umpires will feel they are not in the ball game. Then they might get a little careless. I am not saying they do not bear down all the time—they *do,* but I know as a player, if the manager did not get on me once in a while, I would get a little careless, and I think the same thing goes for umpires."

"I believe you should have a cordial relationship with umpires," said Haller. "To have their respect, you must respect them. As long as I know that he is consistent, that he is that way all the time, I do not often get disturbed. But I do not like to see a fellow changing his mind all the time. For one hitter, he will call a particular pitch a ball, and then for the next hitter, he might call the same pitch a strike. This can be very disturbing to me. Generally, though, in our league our umpires are very consistent.

"Being a habitual griper can hurt you more than it can help you," Haller believes. "You do not get many birds with salt. You get a lot more out there if you try to butter them up. If you want the respect of umpires, do not try to show them up. Then they will have a little more respect for you."

Practice Tips for Catchers

Young catchers should work on the basic fundamentals of catching, practicing the correct techniques of the position over and over, and always striving for perfection. The more a young receiver can catch, the better off he is going to be.

No one has ever learned how to catch overnight—it takes *years*. Experience is often the best teacher. During batting practice, he should try to imagine situations and react accordingly. By being lazy in the bullpen and during batting practice, a catcher can very easily develop bad habits.

In particular, a young receiver should learn how to catch low pitches. When catching batting practice or warming-up a pitcher, he should always remember to execute the correct fundamentals in catching the low ball in the dirt. Likewise, he must work on his throwing, using correct footwork in shifting for the throw.

Many catchers experience difficulty handling pop-ups. Quite often, their troubles stem from a lack of practice in catching pop flies. Therefore, if they would have a coach regularly hit them foul pop-ups from all angles, there would be a noticeable improvement in their execution.

Drills for Catchers

One-step drill

This is an excellent drill for catchers who take too many steps and overdo their footwork. In this drill, the catcher receives the ball with his weight already on his right foot, steps with his left and throws.

Footwork warm-up drill

This is a drill to be used just prior to infield practice, in which the catcher uses correct footwork in shifting for the throw. He and another catcher play "hard" catch from a distance of 65 to 75 feet away, in which they execute the same shifting footwork they will use during the game.

Throwing drill

Practice catching low throws with full equipment on.

Rules in Working on the Hitter

1. Find out as soon as possible which pitch is working best.
2. Always try to get *ahead* of the batter. Get that first ball over for a strike.
3. Watch the hitter's position in the box, and call your pitches accordingly.

4. Make a thorough study of opposing hitters, and discuss them freely with the pitcher.
5. If the pitcher is wild, slow him down occasionally.
6. Call for pitches that will throw a batter off his timing or fool him.

Basic Catching Rules

1. Be the field general, and direct the play on all batted balls.
2. Keep check on the defensive positions of the infielders and outfielders.
3. Give the pitcher a good target at all times, crouching low.
4. On the intentional pass, keep one foot in the catcher's box until the pitcher releases the ball.
5. Learn the most effective pitch for all the hurlers you will handle.
6. *Talk to your pitcher!* (He may be lonesome.)
7. Be alert for any possible steal or hit-and-run play. A pitch-out may be called.
8. Back up first base with the bases unoccupied on all batted balls that might result in overthrows.
9. On throws from the outfield, call "CUT" to the cutoff man if a throw to the plate is wide or if the runner cannot be retired.
10. If the bunt is in order, have your pitcher pitch high.
11. Study the hitter's stance, and remember what he went after and where he hit the ball in previous appearances.
12. Make your signs simple and understandable, especially to your pitcher.

The First Baseman /6/

Some people exclaim, "Anybody can play first base." Well, that is not really true; there is a lot more to first base than most people think. In fact, I believe a good fielding first baseman can *save* as many runs as the big, powerful hitter, who cannot field, will drive in. As a fielder, the good glove man can prove just as valuable to his team as the slugger whose fielding woes often lead to defeat.

Actually, the first baseman has *many* duties to perform. This is why he should possess, in addition to impressive physical attributes such as good hands, agility and quickness afoot, the mental capability to make quick decisions. There are numerous plays at first base, such as in bunt and cutoff situations, in which he has to make split-second judgments. Playing first base may call for more varieties of talent than some of the other positions. Therefore, the first sacker should be a player who can hustle, one who wants to play and likes to play first base (Fig. 6–2).

Nothing can instill greater confidence in an infielder than a first baseman who is capable of leaping high to grab the high ones and scooping low ones out of the dirt. Indeed, one of the most artistic sights in this great game is watching an agile, coordinated athlete stylishly performing his duties at first base.

The big glove used by modern first basemen has tended to change somewhat the style of play at the initial sack. First baseman gloves today are much bigger than those used by such old-time greats as George Sisler, Charley Grimm and Bill Terry. Using the long glove

A good fielding first baseman can save as many runs as the big, powerful hitter, who cannot field, will drive in.

Fig. 6–2. A GREAT SAVE. This fielding gem by Wes Parker is typical of the plays this outstanding first baseman has executed for the Los Angeles Dodgers. In this World Series action in 1965, Parker stopped the ball with a backhand stab, skidded on his belly, got to his knees and threw to the pitcher covering first for the out.

with big webbing, first basemen now catch the ball in the web, rather than in the palm of their hand as they used to. This has led to more one-handed catches. Frankly, with the present style glove, there is nothing wrong with a one-handed catch at first base, particularly if the player keeps his other hand close by, ready for a possible throw.

The young player who aspires to become a topnotch first baseman must spend more practice time with the glove. Skill will not come any other way. A good example of what I mean is our own Wes Parker, who has won the "Golden Glove Award" often for his fielding excellence.

"From the time I was about eight years old," recalled Wes, "I was fortunate; I grew up with a home with a big yard. So, my Dad and brother would get out with me and hit me ground balls all day long. I spent on the average from two to three hours every day just standing at the end of our lawn and having my brother and my Dad just smash the ball at me! And I honestly feel that is how I developed the fielding skill I now have. There is no question the work I did in the backyard of our home is what helped me become a 'Golden Glove' winner."

Wes still takes 20 to 25 ground balls every day before a game. With the artistry of a musician, he still devotes hours of practice working on the basic techniques of his position. Wes performs his position so easily and naturally that we sometimes take it for granted and do not really appreciate the greatness of his glove. Having strong pride in his glovework and fielding skills, Parker does not want to lose his sharpness and rhythm. Significantly enough, Wes does not use a particularly large glove, simply more of an average-sized first baseman's mitt.

A ballplayer can improve *only by practice.* Sometimes it is difficult to get ballplayers to do this. They want to do things they do best. If they are good hitters, they want to hit all the time, thereby neglecting their fielding responsibilities.

Picking up ground balls, receiving all types of thrown balls and catching pop-ups should be a part of every first baseman's daily chores. These are the fundamental skills which need to be developed and continually worked on to keep players sharp and effective.

Having a Wes Parker play first base will help the other infielders, too. They know that if they get the ball over there within reach, this guy is going to catch it. Then, they can go ahead and hurry their throws and put something on the ball and not have to worry.

The Dodgers have been fortunate to have a long string of outstanding fielding first basemen. Prior to Parker taking the job in 1965, such greats as Dolph Camilli in the 1940s and Gil Hodges in the 1950s performed brilliantly at this position. Hodges, for a big man, had pretty good agility and great hands. Anything he would get his hands on, he would hold. He could make the pivot and throw to second very well for a big man of 200 pounds. Of course, Hodges' bat was one of the things that made him a great star.

Qualifications

Size is a definite asset for a first baseman, because a taller boy makes a better target and has greater reach. Preferably, he should be at least six feet tall, in order to stretch and get the high throws. However, a smaller player who is quick and agile can often make up for his height disadvantage.

The first instinct of the first baseman is to get to the bag as quickly as he possibly can.

The ideal man for this position is tall and rangy—the Willie McCovey type, who can reach sky-high and take any throw. In addition, he has to be agile, quick and alert, and have a strong arm, which is why I like the Wes Parker type at this position. The big, powerful slugger who is in the lineup because of his bat will not cover the ground that Parker covers, nor will he be able to handle the bunted ball play that Wes makes. The first baseman must have a good pair of hands. He has to be able to catch the ball with sureness and dependability. This is where strong hands play a key role. He must be coordinated and agile enough to maneuver quickly and nimbly while performing his fielding responsibilities.

His legs have to be in excellent shape. Getting in position on the ball plays a vital role in fielding the ball, and the first baseman needs his legs to do this.

The ability to make quick decisions is another important quality of a good first baseman. A good example of this is when charging a bunted ball. Should he throw the ball to second base, or go to first base and play it safe? He does not have much time to make up his mind.

"Besides taking hours and hours of practice," said Parker, "it takes a lot of thinking and planning ahead when you are in the field during a game. You have to be ready to do the unusual because there is always some time during the season when a play will come up which is different from any you have seen before. So, you have to be ready to adjust."

Defensively, the left-handed first baseman has a fielding edge over the right-handed player because he has more natural advantages, especially on the double play, when he can catch the ball and throw naturally to second base. Also, on the bunt play down the first base line, the left-hander is in a natural position to throw the ball to second base.

Getting to the Bag

When the ball is hit on the ground to other infielders, the first instinct of the first baseman is to get to the bag as quickly as he possibly can. Ideally, he should play as deep as he can, which makes it necessary for him to run as quickly as he can to first base.

"Getting to the bag quickly is the whole secret," said Parker (Fig. 6–3). "That is why speed is so important in playing first base. The faster you can go from where you are playing to the bag to receive the throw, the farther you can play away from the bag initially."

Arriving at the bag, he must find the base, get his feet in position and then turn and look for the throw.

Fig. 6–3. HEELS TO BAG WHILE WAITING. Most first basemen like to straddle the bag and place both heels in contact with the bag, at the front part of the base. By keeping both heels on the base, they know exactly where the bag is (Rich Reese).

Fig. 6–4. AWAITING THE THROW WITH LEFT FOOT IN CONTACT. Wes Parker is among those first basemen who prefer to always place their left foot on the front edge of the bag in the middle. Parker places his left foot on the bag at all times. He is in a position to shift for all types of throws from his infielders.

A   B

Fig. 6–5. SHIFTING TO THE RIGHT. On balls thrown to his right, the first baseman shifts to his right and touches the base with his left foot.

Awaiting the throw   Standing directly in front of the bag, the first baseman is in a position
to shift for all types of throws from his infielders.

Most first basemen like to straddle the bag and place both heels
in contact with the bag, at the front part of the base (Fig. 6–3). This
position enables them to have a feel of the bag.

However, some of our greatest fielding first basemen, including
Parker and Hodges, employ a different position when waiting for the
throw. "I always put my left foot on the bag," stated Wes. "I put my
toe right at the middle of the bag, not on top, but on the front edge
in the middle. (Fig. 6–4)

"I am standing almost in a straight-up position, with a slight bend
of my knees, with my hands up. As I look for the throw, I am always
anticipating a bad throw."

Footwork   The footwork involved in taking thrown balls is probably the most
important phase of first base play. By shifting his feet correctly, the
first baseman will be able to handle the ball more smoothly and
quickly, with a greater natural motion.

The shifting of the first baseman is often called a "waltz-step." If
the ball is to his left, he shifts to his left and touches the bag with his
right foot. If to the right he shifts to his right and touches the base
with his left foot (Fig. 6–5).

First basemen like Parker and Hodges, instead, prefer coming into
the bag and placing the same foot on the bag at all times. They know
exactly where the bag is (Fig. 6–6).

On a ball hit directly at the second baseman, the first baseman has
to come in, turn around and put his right foot on the bag. Then, he is
facing him and can see where the throw is coming from.

A   B

Fig. 6–6. SHIFTING TO THE LEFT. If the ball is thrown to his left, he shifts to his left and touches the base with his right foot (Wes Parker).

"The only time I might not use my left foot is when I cross over the bag and move into foul territory. I might use my right foot because it does not matter too much here.

"Gil Hodges proved to me," recalls Wes, "that a left-hander can stretch further by putting his left foot on the bag and stretching out with his right foot. He can stretch a foot farther than doing it the other way.

Fig. 6–7. STRETCHING FOR THE THROW. On the ball thrown directly to him, the first baseman places his toe against the side of the base and steps well out into the diamond with the other foot and reaches for the ball (Wes Parker).

A   B

The majority of big league first basemen try to use two hands whenever they can.

"If the throw is toward the home plate side, and I am stretching out," explained Parker, "I will slide my foot right to the corner closest to home plate. If it is to the other side, then I will slide my foot to the corner closest to right field and, in this way, I can get a longer stretch."

If the ball is thrown directly to him, the first baseman places his toe against the side of the base, steps well out into the diamond with the other foot and reaches for the ball (Fig. 6–7). Occasionally, he may have to leave the base to catch the ball and make a tag play on the runner coming to first. This is done with a sweeping motion.

On close plays, he has to stretch out as far as he can, so that he can get the ball as quickly as possible.

One of the faults of many young first basemen is committing themselves too soon. On a close play, they stretch out too quickly. If the ball should happen to sail a little bit, he finds that the throw is not exactly where he thought it would be. He is all stretched out, and if the ball is off to the side, he cannot reach it.

So, he must not commit himself too soon. He should wait a moment, so that he can shift and stretch any way that is necessary to catch the ball.

Catching the Ball

Although there is nothing wrong with the one-handed catch at first base, the first baseman generally should use two hands in catching the ball (Fig. 6–8). However, there will be times when he will have to grab the ball with only his glove hand.

While the large glove has led to more one-handed catches, the majority of big league first basemen try to use two hands whenever they can. According to Parker, "Ninety per cent or more of the time, it is better to use two hands. Whenever you have a play where you have to stretch more than normally, where the stretch is important, I would recommend the one-handed catch. The chief reason is that you can stretch farther when you use one hand."

Two hands are surer, too, and also enable the player to move more quickly into throwing position. Even if he does use one hand, though, he should have his other hand close by, so that he can get the ball out of the glove if another throw is necessary.

In receiving the throw, the first baseman should try to follow the flight of the ball right into the mitt. "This is a major weakness of many young first basemen who are starting to learn the position," according to Wes. "On a low throw, for instance, they will stand almost straight up and merely reach down to catch the ball. This is the worst thing they can do because as the ball approaches them, their head

Fig. 6–8. TAKING A THROW FROM AN INFIELDER. Although the big leaguer uses one hand on many plays, the young first baseman should use two hands whenever he can. As Wes Parker demonstrates here, two hands are surer than one hand. Notice that Wes has his head just behind his glove as he looks right over the top of his mitt. He follows the ball right into the glove.

has to move down very quickly to follow the ball right into the glove. Many first basemen are lazy this way, and they will lose sight of the ball and drop it.

"So, what I do," continued Parker, "on a low throw—or any throw, for that matter—I try to get my head just behind my glove so I am looking actually right over the top of my mitt. Naturally, on a throw higher than my eyes, I cannot do this, but on a low throw, I will just get my body right down as low as I possibly can and try to look over the top of my glove at the ball, and I will follow it right into my glove.

"Every infielder throws differently," said Parker, "so before you play a game with a group of infielders, you should know how each one of those guys throw and how his ball is going to move. Maury Wills probably has the most accurate arm in our infield. His ball will go relatively straight. Usually, at the end, it will move in toward the home plate side of the bag, just slightly. Some infielders will throw a ball which will sail sometimes because they do not hold the ball across the seams."

The throw into the runner is possibly the toughest play for the first baseman to catch, especially coming from the third baseman who has come in to field a bunted ball or swinging bunt. There is a tendency for that ball to break in toward the base runner.

This is a tough play because it will be close. The first baseman will either have to tag the runner or keep his foot on the bag. Quite often, the runner and the ball will arrive at the same time. The good first baseman will know whether he has a chance of catching the ball standing on the bag or if he has to tag the runner.

A   B

Fig. 6–9. CATCHING LOW THROW (two hands). The first baseman has to give with the low throw, as he cups the glove under the ball. With the palm of the glove facing up, he draws the glove and hand in toward the area of his belt. In cushioning the ball, he makes the impact softer.

Or, he might cross over in front of the runner and tag the bag with his other foot. Parker does this very well. He makes it look so easy; he has the knack of knowing what he should do with the ball.

In going after wild throws, the first baseman often has to make a quick decision as to whether or not he can stay on the bag and still

Fig. 6–10. CATCHING LOW THROW (one hand). Although the first baseman should use two hands whenever he can, on less accurate throws he may have to use just one hand, particularly when greater reach is needed. He should pull his hand back into his body the moment the ball enters the glove (Wes Parker).

A   B

catch the ball. If he cannot, he should move off the bag and catch it, then tag the runner.

The fielder has to "give" with a low throw. Rather than let his hands and glove go out toward the ball, he has to pull his hands back into his body the moment the ball enters the glove (Figs. 6–9 and 6–10).

Low throws

"The reason for this is that you are 'cushioning' the ball," explained Parker. "You are making the impact softer. So, the ball is more likely to stay in the glove when it hits it. If you are moving out toward the ball the same time it is moving toward you, then the impact is going to be greater, and the chances of that ball bouncing out again will be greater."

Fig. 6–11. LEAPING FOR THE HIGH THROW. A first baseman like Wes Parker can time his leap to catch the ball and come down on the base. When reaching for a high throw, the first baseman should use the bag to get the greatest possible height. If he doesn't have to jump, he merely rises up on his toes to make the catch.

A   B   C

The good fielding first baseman has a nice, easy "give" motion to the scooping action, a soft touch to the catch. His head is down, and his eyes follow the ball right into the glove. While beginners have a tendency to lift their head up, they must learn to keep it down.

The in-between hop can be a difficult play for the first baseman. A ball within two feet of him is not considered too tough because the ball does not have enough room to take a bad hop.

The tough play is out in front of him, anywhere from five to ten feet, because the ball has to take almost a perfect hop for him to be able to catch it.

There are some situations when the first baseman might not take a chance on the ball taking a good hop. With the tying run rounding third base, he should flop down in front of the ball and just block it altogether, or else he has to rush out and catch it without even being on the bag.

High throws

In catching a high throw, the first baseman must decide whether he has to jump and come back down on the bag, or stay on the bag and try to reach it (Fig. 6–11).

Before he does anything, he has to know *where the bag is*. If the throw is fairly straight and high over the bag, there are two ways he can go after the ball:

1. If he has to jump for it, he can jump straight up in front of the bag and come down with his foot on the bag.
2. He can shift behind the bag into foul territory and take the throw without jumping. This is because the majority of the throws he will get are the type which will be coming down. Therefore, on low throws the ball will be lower behind the bag than it will be in front of it. This is why the first baseman can stretch behind the bag and not even have to jump for it. However, to do that, the throw has to arrive in plenty of time. Otherwise, he will either collide with the runner or the throw will be too late by the time he catches it behind the bag.

Fielding Position

The fielding position of the first baseman depends on a number of factors, such as the game situation, the score, the base runners, the pitcher, the hitter at the plate and—*very important*—the speed of the first baseman himself (Fig. 6–12).

The depth will depend on the hitter and the speed of the first baseman. With nobody on base, the normal fielding position for major league first basemen is approximately 15 to 20 feet in back of the bag and about the same distance from the base line. This is the deep fielding position. However, the depth is not so great in the lower leagues. The important thing is for the fielder to get to first base in plenty of time to take the throw.

Fig. 6–12. PROPER FIELDING POSITION. Knowing the hitters and where to play them is a major fielding responsibility of the first baseman. As the pitch is being made, he drops his glove down close to the ground. He must be alert and ready on every pitch (Wes Parker).

"I will change my position according to the score," says Parker. "If we are way ahead and a runner is on first, Walt will have me play behind the runner. In this case, I would play three to four feet behind him and two to three feet off the line. If the game is tight and this guy is likely to steal, I have to hold him just as close as possible."

With men on first and second, and only one out, the fielder should assume a double play type of situation. In this case, he still would be 10 to 15 feet off the first base line but only about five to eight feet behind the runner. In other words, he has to move up closer to the hitter in order to increase the speed of the double play.

With a left-handed hitter at the plate, he plays as deep as he can, but still so as to be able to get to the bag. With a man on, he either holds him on or plays close behind him. If men are on first and second, he does not have to hold him on, so he moves back halfway or to the deep position.

The first baseman can play deep on hitters who are not fast runners, but with the speed merchants, he has to be ready for a possible drag bunt.

Knowing his second baseman is of particular importance to the first baseman. If the second baseman does not have good range, for example, he will have to go out and get a few more balls in the hole. With a left-handed pull hitter at the plate, he has to play close to the foul line.

If he has speed, he can play a wide or deep first base. He can play further away from the bag before the ball is hit and still get there in time to make a put-out. Being able to play far off the base gives his infield better defense.

Fielding Ground Balls

The first baseman should think of himself as an all-round fielder, and not just as a fellow who guards first base. He should not be afraid to get away from the bag and make an attempt to field all ground balls hit into his territory, except those hit to his right which the second baseman can play. He should try to get in front of the ball and then keep the glove low to the ground.

"I try to keep my glove low," said Parker. "When I assume my position as the pitch is being made, I actually drop my glove right down on to the ground so that it is practically on the dirt. This has become a good habit for me because it helps me stay low when the ball is being hit hard at me. (Fig. 6–12)

"I always work to get a big hop," said Parker, "and not the in-between hop. A first baseman can do this more than any other infielder because he has more time to make the play. He can always throw the ball to the pitcher who covers first if he cannot get there in time. But he should go to the base himself whenever possible."

When the first baseman cannot make the put-out himself after fielding a ground ball, he throws to the pitcher covering first base. On a ball hit to his right, the first baseman will often field the ball and have to make a quick throw from his fielding position.

Fig. 6–13. FIELDING A SACRIFICE BUNT. The first baseman must move quickly the first few steps, then as he approaches the ball, he should start slowing down to get his balance. Hard bunted balls are often played to second base, whereas slow bunted balls are thrown to first base, with the second baseman covering (Wes Parker).

A

B

C

Possibly the toughest play for the first baseman to make is the ground ball to his right. This is definitely a judgment play. Let us assume he is playing a normal position and a ball is hit hard between him and the second baseman. Now, should he go after the ball or go to first base? Many times he feels foolish if he goes to first base and the second baseman cannot get there. He will ask, "I wonder if I ran away from that ball?" This is the worse of the two evils.

It is better to go after a questionable ball between first and second than let it go through for a clean base hit. If he goes after it and cannot get to it, the pitcher is still responsible in getting over there. Also, the second baseman has a chance to make the play.

Once he commits himself, he will not have time to get back to first base; therefore, it becomes a judgment play.

In fielding a bunt, the first baseman should always assume that he will make the play at second base. Otherwise, it will be too late. If a bunt is likely, he should move in quickly toward the batter as the ball is pitched (Fig. 6–13). When charging the bunt, he should be saying to himself: "Second base, get him at second base!"

When charging in on a bunted ball, the first baseman must be able to make quick decisions. Should he throw the ball to second base,

Handling Bunts

Fig. 6–14. RIGHT–HANDER'S THROW TO SECOND (pivot to outfield). On the ball hit to his left, the first baseman pivots with his back to second all the way around to his left and steps out toward second base to make the throw. He makes one continuous motion as he whirls around (Don Mincher).

A B C

A   B   C

Fig. 6–15. RIGHT–HANDER'S THROW TO SECOND (jump shift to right). Anytime the first baseman can get in front of the ball, he should field it off his right knee. In this series, he makes a jump shift to the right and uses a snap overhand throw (Don Mincher).

or go to first base and play it safe? He does not have much time to make up his mind.

Although some people say the catcher should call this play, basically, I think the first baseman must make up his mind whether he can get the man at second or not. He knows whether a slow runner or a Lou Brock is running. He knows how hard the ball was bunted, how smoothly he fielded it and whether he still has time to throw it to second.

"When I field the ball and intend to go to second," said Parker, "I will lead with my left foot so that my hips are open and I am not closed. This is particularly important. The first baseman must know where second base is, and then make a strong throw.

"You have to move quickly the first two or three steps, then, as you get about halfway, you start slowing down to get your balance. This will help you keep your body weight under control and be able to make a good throw to second base."

With runners on first and second and a bunt expected, the first baseman plays on the grass in front of the runner on first. The force play at third base is the prime objective.

The Unassisted Put-Out

Since the pitcher runs to cover first base on all balls hit to the left of the mound, the first baseman, after fielding the ball, must decide immediately if an unassisted put-out is possible. If so, he should call to the pitcher or wave him away at once, saying: "I have it," or, "I'll take it."

"When you wave the pitcher off," said Parker, "do not wave him off with the glove of the hand that the ball is in. I have seen it happen, when a guy will wave and drop the ball accidentally."

A   B

Fig. 6–16. TEAMING WITH THE PITCHER. The first baseman should move toward the pitcher and lead him with a smooth underhand toss. The fingers of the hand are stretched out, and the hand movement stops about chest-high. Show the pitcher the ball! (Wes Parker).

If he fields the ball away from the line, he should tag the second base edge and either cross the base ahead of the runner or back away a step. If the play is close, he may use a straight-in slide.

Throwing to Second

All throws by the first baseman to second base should be made quickly. It is quickness and accuracy that count. The throw should be made overhand, if possible, and high to the shortstop's face, right over the bag or to the third base side of the bag. In making this throw, good timing is essential. The play should be timed so that the ball reaches the shortstop about one-half step before he steps on the base.

A right-handed first baseman can make this throw two different ways, depending on how far from second base he fields the ball and how much time he has. Generally, a right-hander will pivot to his right side a quarter-turn of the body. If the ball is hit to his right, he has to backhand it and, at the same time, make a jump shift to the right. He uses a snap overhand throw (Figs. 6–14 and 6–15).

In executing the 3–6–3 double play, the left-handed first baseman has a definite advantage over a right-hander, since he can throw to second without pivoting and can do so by taking a normal step toward the base. As he picks up the ground ball, he is already in good position to make a quick sidearm throw.

"In making this throw, the left-hander should try to keep his hips open," advised Parker. "He cannot lock his hips. Ideally, he should field the ball with his left foot slightly ahead of his right foot. Keeping his hips open will accelerate the throw to second base."

After making his throw, the first baseman should always hustle back to the base to take the return throw. On a ball hit to his right, he

219

might have difficulty getting back in time for the return throw. In this case, the pitcher should be at the bag to take the throw from the shortstop.

Teaming with the Pitcher

After picking up the ground ball, the first baseman should move toward the pitcher and lead him with a smooth underhand toss, about chest-high, and at least two steps from the bag. The fingers of the hand are stretched out, and the hand movement stops about chest-high (Fig. 6–16).

"Get the ball to the pitcher as soon as you can," advised Parker, "usually 10 feet before the bag. This way, the pitcher does not have to worry about catching the ball and stepping on the bag, both at the same time.

"When you underhand him the ball," advised Wes, "do not hide the ball from the pitcher. Hold it out in front so that he can see the ball, and do not throw it too hard or too soft."

As he releases the ball, the first baseman does not stop running. He continues running toward him, which adds a little momentum to the throw itself, and also helps him make a straighter throw.

Cutoffs and Relays

The first baseman generally takes all the cutoffs from right and center field, even left center when he has time to get there. The only one he does not take is the base hit directly to left field. In this case, we like our third baseman to take the cutoff. He should dash in and take up a position between home plate and the mound so the throw can be cut off if necessary. He should be in a position to catch the ball and throw it to second base.

"On throws from center field," said Parker, "I prefer a position about where the pitcher's foot lands after he makes his pitch. Go to a spot right in front of the mound, about four to five feet down from the rubber.

"When a throw comes in from right field, I like to be about halfway between home and first base, a little toward home. A straight-up stance is best in this fielding situation. He might hold up his glove in the air to serve as a target for the outfielder."

Watching the base runners closely is most important on these plays, so that he can anticipate making a play either at the plate or cutting the ball off and throwing to second or third base. In other words, the first baseman should try not to rely on the catcher or someone else telling him what to do. Usually, the crowds are screaming pretty loudly in these situations, and he will not be able to hear instructions anyway. So, he has to use his own visual information in order to make the play. Some coaches, however, prefer having him listen to the catcher's instructions as to letting the ball go through or cutting it off.

A   B

Fig. 6–17. TAGGING THE RUNNER. Facing the pitcher with his body slightly crouched, the first baseman extends his glove hand as a target about waist-high. In tagging the runner, he places his glove down by the bag and forces the runner to slide into the ball (Wes Parker).

When he lets the ball go through, the first baseman should fake catching it in order to confuse the base runners, at least momentarily.

Many first basemen make the mistake of just standing there and letting the ball come all the way from the outfield and having to catch it on the short hop. I prefer my cutoff men to be a bit closer to home plate than necessary and move into the ball. Then, they are in a position to throw to second base or wherever the play might be.

When the ball comes that far, there is no reason for him to catch the ball on the short hop. He should have time to either maneuver in or back and catch it on a big hop or on a fly—and the ball is much easier to handle.

Pop Flies

The first baseman should call for and take any pop fly to the right side, where he will move in on the ball and make the catch. He should take all the fly balls that he can possibly reach, within reason.

Pop flies midway between first base and home plate are plays that are easier for the first baseman because the spin of the ball is bringing the ball toward him but away from the catcher. It is easier for him to catch the ball coming into it, than for the catcher to attempt it when the ball is breaking away. Besides, the first baseman's glove is better than the catcher's glove for catching pop flies.

"If the ball is anywhere near the stands," said Parker, "you should always run first of all to the retaining wall. If there is any doubt in your mind as to whether that ball will drop into the stands or into foul territory, get over to that wall! And once you get there, you can either move away from it to catch the foul ball, or stand there and make a play into the stand. This is much better than going over there and

Fig. 6–18. TAKING THROW FROM PITCHER. The first baseman gives a clear inside target for the pitcher or catcher fielding the ball in front of home plate (Tom McCraw).

looking up at the ball all the way and feeling your way to the stands. You think you are at the stands, but you are not quite there and you are reaching.''

By using this procedure, the player will avoid dropping the ball, which often happens when a fielder bumps into a fence as he attempts to field the ball. So, we try to get everyone to go as quickly as he can to the fence. It is like an outfielder going back up against the fence. Go to the fence and take a look at the ball. Then, if necessary, come in a step or two.

''If the ball is popped up behind you or down the first base line,'' said Wes, ''it is also a better idea to run past the ball. Run beyond it and then come back into it. If it is a pop-up behind you, down the line that is closer to the stands, I would run behind it and then over to the stands so that I am always moving into my catch.''

We want our pitchers to be over there, directing traffic, rather than having someone yell from the dugout. He should yell: ''Wes!'' or, ''Haller!'' Everyone should be quiet except the pitcher and the two players involved: the first baseman and the catcher.

Holding the Runner On

Assuming a position next to the bag enables the first baseman to catch throws from the pitcher just in front of the bag, and requires only dropping the glove to the ground to complete the tag.

Most players like to have their right foot to the right side of the bag, with their left foot about on the foul line. Facing the pitcher, with his body slightly crouched, he extends his glove hand as a target about waist-high. He is now in a comfortable position, ready to handle throws to either side and tag the runner's foot in the same motion. By turning to his right, he sweeps his glove down and into the runner.

"In tagging the runner, he should just get his glove down by the bag," said Parker, "and not sweep it down and then through again (Fig. 6–17). Some runners can be pretty tricky when they return to the base."

Parker will have his foot almost six inches from the bag. By doing it this way, it is a little easier for him to turn and tag the runner, even though his foot is six inches away, rather than go right down to his foot.

"I will tell you why I put my foot toward the home plate side of the bag instead of on the side of the bag that faces directly toward second base," stated Wes. "A runner returning to the bag can spike you. That is why I have my foot where I do. It also makes it easier to make the tag from that position."

Occasionally, the first baseman will play two or three steps behind the runner but close enough to hold him near the base.

If he feels a bunt is likely, he will not even stand close to the bag, but about four or five feet toward home plate. He might even take as big a lead as the runner does, and he will stand almost in a sprinter's position. This facilitates his running to home plate.

In moving off the base, the first baseman may take a cross-over step with the left foot, a step with the right foot and a shuffle step into fielding position.

Fig. 6–19. PICK–OFF PLAY. Playing behind the runner, the first baseman gives the pitcher a sign for a throw, such as rubbing the numerals. After confirming the signal, the pitcher goes into the stretch, and when he looks back to second, the first baseman breaks for the bag. The pitcher tries to throw him the ball directly over the bag (Wes Parker).

A

B

C

When a runner starts for second, he should alert the catcher by calling, "There he goes!" Parker will call the catcher's name. If it is Tom Haller, he just yells, "Tom!"

In receiving a throw from the catcher, the first baseman should put his left foot on the base and his right foot out toward second base. His glove is held slightly to the outside of his right shoulder as a target (Fig. 6–18).

Driving the runner back

When the pitcher is in the hole on a right-handed pull hitter, the first baseman might break in from his deep position to drive the runner back, with first and second bases occupied. This increases the chances of making a force play at second base on a routine grounder.

Pick-Off Play

While holding the runner on base, the first baseman must be ready for a pick-off throw from the pitcher at all times. When he is playing behind the runner, he gives the pitcher a sign for a throw, such as hitching his pants or adjusting his cap (Fig. 6–19).

"I will give a sign," said Wes, "and he will give an answering sign. Either one of us can initiate the sign, and the other one has to confirm it. Otherwise, the sign is not on."

We work it like this: The pitcher will go into the stretch, look back to second and see Wes break out of the corner of his eye. He then turns and tries to throw him the ball directly over the bag.

Cooperation between the pitcher and first baseman is essential on any pick-off play. When the play is on, the first baseman must feel free to break for the bag. We do not like to see him break toward the bag and then have the pitcher make a pitch to the plate. By having signs between the pitcher and first baseman, there is no reason this play should get messed up. We do not like them to be obvious, yet the signs have to be simple enough so that both players are able to pick them up.

The Dodgers also employ a pick-off play with the catcher. It could be with a man on first, first and second, or with the bases loaded. In this type of play, the first baseman might rub his leg and the catcher might go to his shin guards.

Setting up the run-down play

If a runner is caught off first base and breaks for second, the first baseman should throw the ball to the second baseman as soon as possible, unless there is a runner on third. This will set up the defensive players for the fastest and most effective way of handling the run-down. The key to this play is to get the runner moving back to the base from which he came.

Backing Up and Covering

When the bases are unoccupied, the first baseman backs up second base on all throws from the left field side or the second base side.

After a single to left field, for instance, he should be ready to retrieve overthrows to second base. He also covers second base and the plate when these bases are left uncovered.

Breaking in the Glove

Big league first basemen break their gloves in fairly well before they use them in a game. Otherwise, the ball will have a tendency to hit and bounce out. "I always have a minimum of two mitts with me," explained Parker. "One is my game glove, which I never use except in games. The other is my practice glove, which will become a game glove later."

To break in a brand new mitt, many players use this routine: Put a ball in the glove and either tie it or put a heavy rubber band around it. This helps to form a good pocket.

Neets foot oil will tend to soften it but many first basemen prefer a firm glove.

As for Parker, he does not put anything on his glove. "The only thing that I might do," said Wes, "when it gets dirty, I will take a damp towel and wipe the dirt out."

First Baseman Drills

1. Footwork drill—shifting to the left, right, and stretching forward; using the cross-over step while touching the base.
2. Tagging the runner returning to the bag (throws from the pitcher and catcher), and other pick-off plays.
3. Feeding the pitcher when covering first.
4. Catching pop fly balls.
5. Fielding bunts down the first base line and in front of the plate; working with the pitcher in fielding drag bunts and hits.
6. Practicing the 3–6–3 double play.
7. Handling cutoff and relay plays (working on use of the voice for the direction of the throw).
8. Mastering the run-down play (with the second baseman and shortstop).
9. Fielding ground balls (to the left and right).
10. Throwing to second base, to the plate, and making long throws to third base.
11. Receiving all types of throws (low, high, wide, straight-in and in the dirt).
12. Leaving the bag to catch wild throws and making the tag.
13. Infield practice.

The Second Baseman /7/

When I realize that one of the keys to championship baseball is the double play, and that the second baseman is in more double plays than anybody else, I have to believe that this is a very important man.

The keystone combination must be able to make the double play *consistently* if a team is to play championship baseball. This is why the shortstop and second sacker must practice making this play over and over, until they know all the moves each one makes at his position. The longer they work together, the better they will be.

The Essentials

Quickness is most essential! The second base position demands quick hands, a quick throwing arm and quick foot action. The day is coming when speed and quickness will be at more of a premium than it is right now. This is particularly true when playing on fields with synthetic turf, where the ball comes through with surprising quickness. The player who can start in a hurry, take a quick cross-over step and reach his full motion on his second or third step is the type of player I want at second base.

The individual who performs at second base should practice throwing the ball from every position. He must even practice throwing with a man sliding into him. While a strong arm is vital to his success at making the double play, a quick snap throw is also important. He handles a variety of slow bouncing balls, which require quick snap throws to first.

Like all players in the field, the second baseman must learn to play the hitters properly. This can be a major asset to him. The more

The second base position demands quick hands, a quick throwing arm and quick foot action.

knowledge he has of a particular hitter and the pitcher on the mound, the better he will react. He must know where the batter will likely hit the ball. Experienced infielders get a good start on a ground ball because they know what pitch is being thrown and the type of hitter at the plate—a pull, opposite field or straightaway type.

In addition to covering second base on steals, he serves as a relay or cutoff man on throws to various bases.

During batting practice, when our coaches hit ground balls in the infield, I like to see my second baseman and shortstop work on the double play. In spring training, they go through drills almost by the hour. These drills not only provide good footwork practice but they also serve as ball handling practice.

The footwork involved in the double play pivot has to be done automatically; the infielder has to hustle into the bag and then be ready to go either way, depending on where the ball is. The key to a second baseman's footwork is not to commit himself too quickly. He has as many as four or five ways of making the pivot, but he should not commit himself until he sees where the ball will be thrown to him.

Star pivot men The Dodgers have had many exciting second basemen who have given baseball fans numerous thrills with their glovework and speed afoot. Junior Gilliam was one of the most knowledgeable ballplayers in the game. Game strategy—what to do, and when—Junior had all this, plus quickness, agility and speed. The only thing that Gilliam lacked was a really strong throwing arm—but he more than made up for it with his agility and knowledge of how to get rid of the ball.

A second baseman who has the entire quota of important qualities is Bill Mazeroski of the Pittsburgh Pirates. Along with agility and a great throwing arm, he is the greatest I have ever seen at catching the ball and getting rid of it quickly. He has the uncanny ability to get into position to throw as the ball is approaching. As he sees the ball, he has his body turned so that he gets into position to throw the ball as soon as he catches it. This has been one of the major reasons for his outstanding success: getting his body into position to throw as soon as he catches the ball.

Bobby Richardson, who played on several championship teams with the New York Yankees, was one of the cleverest performers ever to play second base. His ability to range far to his right led Casey Stengel to exclaim: "Bobby does that better than anyone I have ever seen, plus the fact that he makes the double play better than any player in baseball."

Carry your glove low. It is easier to come up on the ball than it is to go down.

In teaming with shortstop Don Kessinger, Glenn Beckert gives the Chicago Cubs the down-the-middle strength so necessary for pennant contention. Beckert has the ideal size for a pivot man, at six feet, one inch and 190 pounds. He not only possesses a powerful throwing arm but has the agility to make all the moves expected of a topnotch pivot man.

Qualifications

Quickness is the second baseman's greatest asset. He must have speed and agility to cover the bag on double plays and be able to throw from any position. He has to be able to move to his right or left for hard hit balls. He must be a good judge of fly balls, and of pop-ups behind the second and first base areas.

Along with speed, agility and aggressiveness, he should be the type of athlete who does not get upset too easily by the runner who slides into him. The timid infielder sometimes becomes spike-shy and has a tendency to watch the runner instead of the ball.

Since he often fulfills the role of team leader, the second baseman should be an intelligent, alert individual who can anticipate every type of play. He has to have a sound knowledge of the game in order to make the many types of decisions that have to be made during the game.

Stance

The second baseman should assume a stance which is comfortable to him, one in which he can maintain good control of his body. He keeps his body low and more or less relaxed. Most infielders keep their feet approximately shoulder-width apart and pointing slightly outward, not straight ahead. This will make it easier for them to turn or jab-step as they start to move to their right or left. The hands are on their knees until just before the pitch, at which time they hang down loosely at the side.

As the ball is being pitched, most infielders like to move forward a step or two. They do this so they will not be caught flat-footed or on their heels in the event the ball is hit their way. The hands which were on the knees now hang loosely as they shift forward.

"I like to have my feet under me," said Mazeroski, "so I can move quickly in any direction (Fig. 7–2). First, I will go into a preliminary stance, with the heel of my hands above my knees. Then, as the pitcher goes into his pitch, I drop down low so my glove hand is almost on the ground.

"On every pitch, I move or step forward," said Bill; "I will always step forward with the left foot about a foot, followed by a slight shuffle

A   B

Fig. 7–2. INFIELDER'S STANCE. The weight of the second baseman is distributed evenly and comfortably on both feet, which are approximately shoulder-width apart. By having his feet under him, he can move quickly in any direction. On every pitch, he steps forward with the left foot about a foot, followed by a slight shuffle with his right (Bill Mazeroski).

with my right. I time this movement with the anticipation of the batter hitting the pitched ball."

The glove and bare hand should hang relaxed, close to the ground (Fig. 7–3). Both knees are bent, and the fielder is on the balls of his feet, *not on his toes.* He keeps his arms close to his body in the event he has to move laterally. He will be able to move faster because his arms are close to the body.

By being comfortable and staying low to the ground, he can get a quicker start in any direction. As he goes for the ball, he gradually rises up into a running position.

Basic Fielding Positions

With no one on base, the second baseman should pay as deep as he can, his position being determined by such factors as his arm and the speed of the hitter. The condition of the playing field should also be a factor. Other points to consider are where the batter usually hits the ball and how his pitcher is working on the hitter. Normally, he plays approximately 30 feet from second base and 25 feet behind the line.

With a runner on first base and less than two outs, he will move to his double play depth. This will bring him in four or five steps toward home and move him toward second base by one or two steps. This fielding position should put him about 20 or 25 feet from the base and approximately 20 feet behind the line. Of course, these figures will vary according to his speed and quickness and the hitter at the plate. It will be to his advantage to play as far from the base as he can and still be able to get there in time to make a play.

Fig. 7–3. KEEP THE GLOVE LOW. The hands are relaxed and kept close to the ground. It is easier to come up on the ball than to go down (Billy Grabarkewitz).

The left-handed pull hitter should be played three or more feet back and a few steps closer to first. With a right-handed pull hitter at the plate, he will likely move in and position himself as much as 15 feet closer to second.

Fig. 7–4. FIELDING GROUND BALL. The infielder should field the ball with two hands out in front of him, and with a continuous motion, he "gives" with the ball and brings both hands back into a throwing position. He has his legs apart, his knees are bent and he steps toward the base (Glenn Beckert).

A   B   C

More often, it is better for the second baseman to charge the ball than to lay back or back up.

With a runner on second or runners on first and second, he is responsible for keeping the runner close to second. Generally, he will be at double play depth, particularly if the bunt is not expected. By breaking for the base occasionally or making fakes toward the base, he can help keep the runner close to the bag.

Percentagewise, the second baseman generally will find it to his advantage to play closer to the base. First, he can go to his left more easily than to his right, and more base hits go up the middle than through the hole.

The experienced infielder wants to know every sign that his catcher gives, and he will shift with the pitch. However, he must not shift too soon because he could thereby tip off the pitch.

Fielding a Ground Ball

Perhaps the key points in fielding a ground ball are to watch the ball, keep more or less relaxed and stay low on the ball. The ball is fielded with the hands out in front, loose and relaxed. Most infielders like their hands to "give with the ball." They have to use soft hands to catch the ball properly (Fig. 7–4).

As the player fields the ball, his tail is down and his knees bent. He is in front of the ball. *His head must stay on the ball.* He must not lift his head. Recall that, in hitting the ball, if the batter pulls his head away from the plate, he will not hit the ball with consistency. The

Fig. 7–5. A LITTLE BIT OF ROBBERY. Second baseman Dick Green makes a diving grab of a hard hit ball. He came up with the ball and threw the batter out at first base. A fielder should never give up on a ground ball.

same rule applies to fielding. If he takes his head off the ball, he will have less chance of catching it (Fig. 7–5).

Generally, an infielder should move in on all ground balls except the hard shots that do not require coming in. The reason a good infielder rarely gets a bad hop is that he makes every hop a good one by the way he plays it.

An infielder must remember to play the ball, and *not* have it play him (Fig. 7–6). "Naturally, it is easier to catch a big hop than it is for a short hop," said Richardson. "So, as soon as the ball is hit off the bat, if you can kind of take a couple steps in and play the ball where you will get a big hop, it is easier. Now, a short hop is also easy to catch. The one bad ball that seems hard to catch is the in-between hop that you sometimes cannot avoid."

Richardson, who is now head baseball coach at the University of South Carolina, then went into the "secret" of getting rid of the ball quickly. Bobby said: "First, it should be said that an infielder should make sure he has the ball before he tries to throw it. You cannot throw the ball if you do not catch it! Now, in getting rid of the ball quickly, you catch the ground ball with two hands out in front of you, and with a continuous fluidlike motion, you 'give' with the ball, bringing both hands back into a throwing position. As your hands go back, your right hand has a chance to grab on to the ball securely and you find yourself ready to throw. You save time by having the catching maneuver continue right into your throw, but again, *make sure you catch the ball first!*"

Fig. 7–6. PLAYING THE BIG HOP. The infielder should play the ball, and not let it play him. He can usually get the big hop by taking a couple of steps in (Hal Lanier).

A   B

One of the hardest plays for a second baseman to make is the ball hit hard directly at him.

"The main thing in fielding a ground ball," according to Pee Wee Reese, for many years a great shortstop with the Dodgers, "is to watch the ball and stay low on the ball, because it is much easier to bring your hands up than it is to take your whole body down."

Pee Wee also suggests this: "Charge the ball—always keep coming in on the ball. If you are weak on going to your right or on balls being hit directly at you, practice at it. Practice the things you do not do well!" As one of his managers, I know Pee Wee practiced what he preaches.

More often, it is better to charge a ball than to lay back or back up. If an infielder backs up, he will likely field the ball between hops. This often lets the ball play him.

One of the worst habits that infielders develop is trying to be too sure. They will wait for the ball to come to them, wanting to be really sure, and they find themselves letting the ball play them. For the great majority of ground balls, they should charge the ball, unless it is a real "hot shot" which doesn't give them time to do anything.

By charging the ball, they will have more time to recover a fumbled ground ball. They will have time to pick it up and still throw the man out at first.

"Watch the hops and try to get it on the big hop," advised Beckert. "If the ball is not too hard, I like to round off slightly so I can field, step and throw to first base.

"Never give up on a ground ball. If you fumble a ground ball, go after it as quickly as you can. There may still be a chance to make the play. However, do not make a useless throw."

Basically, we keep yelling at our men to "Stay in front of the ball," "Stay low," "Charge the ball," "Go toward the ball," "Go after it" and "Be aggressive."

Hard Hit Ground Balls

Strange as it may seem, one of the hardest plays for a second baseman to make is the ball hit hard directly at him. This play can be difficult because he does not have a chance to gauge the hop of the ball. He cannot see the hops as well as he can on balls hit to his side. He just has to try to get in front of it, knock it down and throw the man out. Actually, it is often hard for an infielder not to charge the ball coming directly at him. The main thing is to try not to let the ball play him.

On hard smashes, the infielder may drop to one knee or go into a squatting position with his heels together. He might even have to use his body to help block the ball. Usually, he will have time to pick it up and beat the runner with his throw.

A   B   C   D

Fig. 7–7. FIELDING THE SLOW ROLLER. The second baseman must field the slow grounder on the run. The throw is started from where the ball is fielded. Coming in fast, he scoops the ball up and makes a sidearm throw across his body while straightening up on his right foot. Fielding the ball with two hands, he takes a step with the right foot to make the throw (Glenn Beckert).

Fielding Slow Rollers

A slow roller can be most difficult, since the ball must be fielded on the run and thrown while the second baseman is off balance. For many youngsters, this is one of the most difficult of all infield plays to execute. The throw must be started from where the ball is fielded. Coming in fast, the fielder scoops the ball (Fig. 7–7) and makes a sidearm throw across his body while straightening up on his right foot. He keeps his eyes on the ball until it is safely in his glove. This fielding play will occur on drag or push bunts, or with slow hit grounders.

In making this play, it is best to field the ball with the left foot forward. Field it with two hands, then take a step with the right foot to make the throw.

The infielder races in with his body bent at the waist. He moves with his feet apart so that he has good balance. After picking up the ball, he has to throw it sidearm, across the body. He cannot waste time straightening up, because that split-second might cause his throw to be late.

"Getting the jump" on the ball is essential. He must charge in and go right after the ball.

For the most part, I do not advocate picking up a ground ball barehanded. Naturally, in a "do-or-die" situation, an infielder has time only to come in and grab the ball with one hand and throw it across his body. If at all possible, he should go down with both hands to make the play. To make plays barehanded, he will need good, relaxed hands as well as excellent playing facilities. The barehanded play has its place in professional ball, but even there, it can be overdone.

If the ball should stop or almost stop rolling, however, the bare-handed pickup can be effective. With a scooping motion of his hand, the player fields the ball about even with the toe of the left foot and in line with the right foot.

Going Far to the Right

The most difficult play for most second basemen to make is the ground ball hit to their right side, behind second. In fielding the ball, the player has to move away from first base. There is no question but that this play takes a great deal of practice and ability.

In making this play, he should turn on his right foot and take a cross-over step with the left foot. He pushes off with the left foot and takes a step with his right foot. Then, he crosses over and digs after the ball. If he can, he should try to get in front of the ball. However, if he cannot, he has to make a gloved, backhand stab of the ball and come to a full stop. His weight is braced on his right foot as he turns and makes his throw. The body should follow-through in the direction of first base as he completes his overhand throw.

It is important to keep the glove face "square" with the ball. Failure to do this will result in balls hitting the face of the glove and bouncing off to the side. Bringing the left elbow in close to the body will help correct this situation.

If he has to backhand the ball, he should try to keep his right foot forward as he fields it so he can move quickly into throwing position.

Some second basemen try to round the bag and go deep behind the base, where they cannot make the play anyway. They get to the ball, but they cannot make the play. Consequently, we encourage our fielders to go straight across and take the short route. Then, if they get to the ball, they still have a chance to throw the man out.

Fig. 7–8. GOING TO THE LEFT. Moving quickly to his left, the second baseman follows the path of the ball right into his glove. By bending his knees and waist, he is able to stay low on the ball and field it with his left foot forward. Turning his body to the right, he brings the ball and his glove up into throwing position (Glenn Beckert).

Like all fielders, the second baseman should catch the ball with both hands whenever possible.

Going to the Left

On a ball hit into the hole, the second baseman must move quickly to his left. Since he is driving quickly toward the first base line, his throwing motion can be difficult. In fielding the ball on his left side, he has to pivot his body around so that he can make the throw to the first baseman (Fig. 7–8). This is similar to a right-handed first baseman throwing to second. If he is able to handle it, he should be sure to call for it so the first baseman does not have to make an unnecessary attempt and can go immediately to the bag for the throw.

"If the ball is to my left," said Beckert, "I like to stay as low as possible and dig with my arms as I cross-step my right leg over the left. Actually, I do not lift my foot. I merely turn the left foot, just so the spikes barely clear the ground. Then, I take a cross-over step with my right foot as I break to my left for the ball, making sure to stay low."

In approaching the ball, the second baseman makes a quick one-two step directly behind the ball. He takes a step with his right foot, and then brings his left foot down. This places the heel of his left foot in line with the right toe.

He takes a short, quick step with his right foot while turning his body to the right as he brings the ball and his glove up into throwing position. Since he does not always have time to get set in front of the ball, he should try to field it with his left foot forward.

Catching the Ball

"Watch the ball into your glove" is a phrase worth repeating over and over when catching the ball. A fielder should always keep his eyes on the ball.

The ball should be caught with both hands whenever possible. This places the throwing hand on the ball as it hits into the glove. Too many young players make the mistake of catching the ball with one hand and then having to reach into the glove with their bare hand to make the throw. Catching the ball with two hands is not only surer but the fielder can move more quickly into throwing position.

In addition, they should be in the correct position to throw the ball as soon as possible. This can be done by moving as the ball approaches. In this way, they catch it on the throwing arm side of the body.

The fielder who reaches out or across his body and catches one-handed wastes valuable time, which may cost his team the ball game.

Keeping the hands relaxed is most important in handling a ball. Do not jab at the ball. The fielder should "give" with the catch, and as he catches the ball, he goes into his throwing motion.

"Quickness of the hands can be improved with practice," said Mazeroski. "By practicing constantly, an infielder will soon be able

Fig. 7–9. A STRONG THROWING ARM. Most infielders who throw well have a good forearm and wrist snap, which gives the ball good carry. Keep the arm loose and snap it forward like a whip as you make the throw. Always throw at a target (Jim Lefebvre).

to get the ball out of his glove quickly and smoothly. As the ball is caught, the hands should give a little, and as he gives with the catch, he takes the ball from the glove.''

Throwing

The second baseman's throw is more of a snap throw than the throws of other infielders and outfielders (Fig. 7–9). This is because he almost always has to get rid of the ball from the position in which he fields the ball. Quite often, he will not have time to straighten up.

Although he may use several methods of throwing, the overhand throw has more carry and is more accurate. However, if he has to hurry, he should come up only part way and throw with more of a sidearm motion. On a long throw, he will plant the right foot so that he can get a full throwing motion and greater force.

Above all, the fielder must not hurry the throw. After straightening up for the throw, he steps toward the base with the left foot and completes his throw.

Grip

An infielder holds the ball with his fingers well spread across the seams where they are widest, and his thumb underneath. This will help prevent the ball from sailing or sliding and it will generally go in a straight line. The pressure is on the tips of the fingers.

As the ball is being taken out of the glove, the player can quickly twist it around to the proper grip. Sometimes, though, he has to grab and throw the ball regardless of how the ball is gripped.

Throwing technique

Most infielders who throw well have a good forearm and wrist snap which gives the ball good carry (Fig. 7–9). They keep their throwing arm away from the body and throw the ball in one continuous motion. The elbow not only comes back first, but it leads the forward drive as well.

Keeping the arm loose, the fielder snaps it forward like a whip as he makes the throw. He uses a powerful wrist action with the wrist rolling over just as the ball is released off the ends of the first two fingers. He should follow through with his body to get the proper power behind the throw.

To obtain a good push-off, the fielder must turn his body to the right. He does this by turning his pivot foot to the right so he can push off the entire inside edge of the foot. Many players fail to turn their pivot foot properly. As a result, they find themselves throwing off the toes or balls of the foot. They lack the strong push-off necessary to make a strong throw.

A fielder should not ease up on his throwing. This usually happens when he has excessive time. He must keep everything in rhythm. When he fields the ball, he should execute his footwork, grip the ball across the seams and throw it in a fluid motion.

When warming-up, infielders should throw at each other's face or chest. Remember to *always throw at a target.*

Taking too many steps before throwing the ball can be a dangerous habit for all fielders. Too many steps are unnecessary, and should be discouraged by the coach. As he throws the ball, an infielder need take only one step in transferring his weight from the rear foot to the front foot. Those who have a tendency to take too many steps should practice the "one-step-and-throw" drill while warming-up.

Making the Double Play

The good infielder is always looking for the double play. In fact, he wants to make it. In a tight situation, a good double play combination actually wants the ball to be hit to them, rather than to someone else.

The secret of a successful double play is getting to the bag early, so that the pivot man is waiting, rather than running across the base. Most young infielders are usually too far from the base when trying to make the double play. Invariably, they end up sprinting for the base, providing a difficult, moving target. Then they try to catch and throw the ball off-balance.

A veteran infielder gets to the bag as early as possible. He must strive for perfect control of his weight so he can step inside or outside the base line. He should be able to execute either of these options because he knows the runner will attempt to slide into him to prevent a double play. With his weight balanced evenly on both feet, he makes the necessary adjustments and completes his pivot and throw to first base.

Fig. 7–10. GET TO THE BAG QUICKLY. The pivot man should move to the base as soon as the ball is hit. He receives the ball chest-high (Bobby Knoop).

We want the second baseman to get there as fast as he can. His footwork will be governed by the throw and by the way the runner comes into the base.

Proper Position In covering for the double play, it is important that the shortstop and second baseman move a few steps in and over closer to second base. To execute a good pivot, the infielder must reach the bag and be on balance before the ball arrives. Since this is difficult to do from a regular fielding depth, the second baseman must shorten up or cheat toward the bag in a double play situation.

Some teams, however, have their keystone combination cheat by shortening up on the play, rather than moving close to the bag. In double play situations or steals, they will cheat toward home plate. This will bring them closer to the bag.

First, it must be decided who will cover second base. Use the voice to let each other know who is going to cover. The closed mouth says, "Me," which means, "I will take the bag." The open mouth, "You," is the signal for the other infielder to cover.

On a normal double play, the man who is not fielding the ball covers the bag. However, when the first or third baseman fields the ball, then the man who is playing nearest the bag covers.

The manager or coach has to analyze the batter, score, pitcher, runner and the count on the hitter, plus the number of outs. Then he must set up his defensive pattern.

In making a double play, the first thing a second baseman should think about is getting to the bag as quickly as possible (Fig. 7–10). Then, as he approaches the base, he should shorten up his stride a little so that he is capable of adjusting himself to the particular situation. He will go either to the left or the right side of the bag, across the bag or possibly touch the bag and back up.

Actually, he has as many as four or five ways to maneuver at second base, but he must not commit himself too quickly—not until he sees where the ball is going to be thrown. If he comes in and decides the ball is going to be on the inside, he commits himself to touching the bag with his right foot. Now, if the ball happens to end up somewhere else, he will find himself in a difficult position. Therefore, as he nears the bag, he should slow down by means of short, choppy steps, to get on balance and be ready to shift in either direction for the throw.

The second baseman should try to round off a little as he approaches the bag. When he gets within three or four steps of the bag, he should round off. This will make it easier for the third baseman and the shortstop in the hole to throw to him. By rounding off slightly, he can get more momentum on the throw, providing, of course, he receives the ball over the bag or slightly in front.

A difficult double play situation is when the runner gets to the bag at the same time the ball does, such as on the hit and run. The pivot man has to use some really quick footwork on this play.

Getting to the Bag

There are at least five ways in which the second baseman can make the pivot. As in the case of the shortstop, one way of pivoting is not sufficient. The footwork he uses depends on where the throw is caught and how much time he has.

Once the pivot man sees where the ball is, he should not find it too hard to use the proper pivot. The pivot man may hit the bag with his left foot, drive back off it and throw to first. Or, he can go on across the bag, drag his foot across the bag and make his pivot on the other side of the bag.

Any number of ways can be used but many players will find that one method is easier than the others. The young infielder should learn several methods, so he will know eventually which one is his best. However, if he always goes the same way each time, the base runner will know which way to come into the base.

There are no set rules in making the pivot. Each fielder should make the pivot the best way suited to his physical ability. While Bill Mazeroski can back off and make his throw from behind the bag, other pivot men whose throwing arms are not as strong as Bill's, should consider other pivots.

The pivot man should strive for perfect control of his weight so he can step inside or outside the baseline. He wants to be in position

Second Baseman's Pivots

to use all of his options because he knows the runner will attempt to slide into him to prevent a double play.

"Always anticipate a bad throw," said Bobby Knoop. "I always expect a bad throw, not a good one. This way you are on guard, ready to move quickly for the errant throw."

Taking out the pivot man in a double play is not only a legitimate play in baseball, as long as the runner does not go outside the base path to accomplish it, but it is something every smart base runner tries to do.

In the big leagues, teams play each other numerous times during the season and if an infielder can make the double play in only one position, the base runners will soon realize this and will start after him. Therefore, the pivot man must know how to pivot several different ways, and must be able to pivot on either foot.

While most second basemen will touch the bag with either foot, Mazeroski prefers to use only his left foot. "On all pivots, I always touch the bag with my left foot," said Bill. "Generally, I will use the push-back pivot, since I have found this to be the best method of keeping away from the runner. After hitting the outside of the base with my left foot, I will push back on the right, and step toward first base on the left foot for the throw."

Fig. 7–11. STRADDLE AND DRAG. The second baseman must get to the bag quickly and straddle it. If the throw is accurate, he steps out toward first base with his left foot and drags his right toe over the bag (Bobby Knoop).

A

B

The footwork used in executing the mound side and backing-off pivots carries the second baseman away from the path of the slider. A prime objective of the pivot is to *move away from the path of the slider.* Unless he avoids contact with the slider, the double play throw is less likely to be successful.

Again, the key to the whole thing is where the ball is thrown. This will determine what type of pivot to use. Therefore, he should know two or three types.

One of the easiest and surest ways to make the pivot is to ease into and straddle the bag, then drag the foot over the bag (Fig. 7–11). The second baseman takes the throw and makes a fast flip to first. Pivot men of the New York Yankees, from Richardson back to the days of Tony Lazzeri and Joe Gordon, have been executing the straddling technique.

The straddle and drag with the right toe

"On the straddle and drag," said Richardson, "it is particularly important for the pivot man getting to the bag quickly. If the throw is accurate, he steps out toward first base with his left foot and drags his right toe against the left field side of second base as he makes the throw to first."

Fig. 7–12. MOUND SIDE OF SECOND BASE. The second baseman steps on the base with his left foot and into the infield with his right to throw. He pushes off his right foot and steps toward first base, making an overhand throw (Bobby Knoop).

A

B

"If the shortstop's throw is to the pitcher's side of the bag," said Bobby, "he hops to the left toward the mound. If the throw is to the left field side of the bag, he should drag his foot over the bag and throw from behind it."

As soon as a ground ball is hit to the third baseman or the shortstop, the idea is to get to the bag quickly, straddle it and then be in a position to go either to his left or right. If the throw is to his left, he takes one step with his right foot, placing his right foot on top of the bag, turns and throws all with the same motion. Naturally, he jumps from his left foot as he avoids the runner.

However, if the throw is to his right, he can hook onto the bag with his left foot to provide a little more momentum to bring him back, and get a little something extra on his throw to first.

Is it difficult to get to the bag in time to straddle it properly? In answering this question, Richardson said: "The only time you would have trouble getting to the bag is on a ball that is hit sharply at either the shortstop or the third baseman. On this play, though, you would not have to get to the bag quickly because it would possibly be an easy one."

"I try to get to the bag a fraction of a second before the ball," stated Mazeroski, "so that I can use the bag for leverage and push off it to

Fig. 7–13. BACKING OFF. The second baseman steps on the base with his left foot, then pushes back toward right field as he throws. He steps toward first base with his left foot to complete the throw. This pivot is effective when the runner is close (Bobby Knoop).

A   B

get more zip and accuracy on my throw to first base. The throw must be quick, with the body moving toward first base for speed and accuracy.

"When you arrive too late," explained Bill, "you give the thrower a moving target at which to shoot. You will either miss the ball, be undressed by the runner or make a poor throw yourself."

Although the straddle technique is the surest way, the chief drawbacks are the vulnerability of the second baseman to being jarred by the runner and the lack of force on the throw to first.

"As soon as you release the ball," suggested Roy Hartsfield of our coaching staff, "you should jump in the air and relax because the runner coming into you could collide with you. If you can clear your spikes from the turf and relax, you will have less chance to get hurt than you would if you had your feet firmly planted and some big 210-pounder comes barreling into you."

The second baseman steps on the base with his left foot and into the infield with his right to throw. A favorite of many infielders, this pivot is used when the runner is close to the base and on the outfield side of the base line.

As shown in Figure 7–12, Knoop receives the throw chest-high as he steps on the base with his left foot. After catching the ball, his right

Mound side of second

Fig. 7–14. STEPPING WITH RIGHT AND THROWING. A simple pivot, the second baseman merely steps on the base with the right foot. He then steps toward first with the left foot for the throw (Glenn Beckert).

A  B

Fig. 7–15. HOW FAR CAN A RUNNER GO? While the runner is allowed to try to break up the double play, according to the rules, he is permitted to slide as far out of the base line as he can while still able to touch the bag with some part of his body. Obviously, this runner should be guilty of interference but it is rarely called. Shortstop Hal Lanier still got his throw away, although nearly in right field.

foot comes down two feet past the bag in on the infield. He braces on his right foot and steps toward first base, making an overhand throw to first.

"The throw will determine where he will go," said Knoop. "Usually, the shortstop feeds the ball to the second baseman only on the inside part of the bag so that his momentum coming across will enable him to complete the play. However, if the throw is to the outfield side of second base, he cannot come on across because he will be fielding the ball across his body and off-balance."

Backing off This pivot is effective when the runner is close and on the infield side of the base line. During his career, Mazeroski has used this pivot almost exclusively in making the double play. This is his favorite pivot. "By throwing from behind the base, I am able to keep away from the sliding runner," asserted Mazeroski. "I might add that my arm is strong enough to do it this way. Someone else, though, might not have a strong enough arm to throw from behind the base."

The second baseman steps on the base with his left foot, and as he is catching the ball, he pushes back off the base, landing on his right foot. He steps toward first base with his left foot to complete the throw (Fig. 7–13). By pushing his weight back onto his right foot, he can get rid of the ball more quickly and get something on it. He should bring the left side of his body back vigorously toward right field.

"If the throw is to the left field side of the bag," said Mazeroski, "I will hop to my right, dragging my left foot over the bag, and then I will make my throw from behind the base."

Fig. 7–16. UNDERHAND TOSS. If the second baseman is close to the bag, he will use a simple underhand lay-up. He immediately pulls his glove hand away from the ball so that the shortstop can see the ball. He uses only his wrist and forearm (Glenn Beckert).

A simple pivot to make is to step on the base with the right foot. The fielder plants his foot right on the bag and accepts the throw at the same time. He then steps toward first with the left foot for the throw (Fig. 7–14).

Stepping with right foot and throwing

This seems to be one of the quickest and most popular pivots used by the second baseman. He can get rid of the ball immediately after catching it chest-high.

Fig. 7–17. SIDEARM THROW. Beyond twelve feet or so, the second baseman has to turn and throw, a quick sidearm throw across his body. He pivots to the right on his right foot and steps toward the bag with his left foot. It is a snap throw with the wrist and the forearm (Glenn Beckert).

247

"Once again, on this pivot," said Hartsfield, "he should jump in the air and relax a little and get his spikes loose because he never knows exactly where that runner is going to be."

The straddle and kick with the left foot

If the throw is to the left field side of the base, the second baseman hops to his right, dragging his left foot over the bag, and throws to first from behind the base. After stepping away from the base runner, he braces on his right foot and steps out with his left foot for the throw.

Right foot, leap and flip

This is one of the fastest ways to make the double play but difficult to perfect. The second baseman jockeys into second base and straddles the bag with his right foot, just touching it. Upon taking the throw, he makes a fast fliplike relay to first. As he throws, he lifts his left foot or leaps into the air off his right foot to avoid the sliding base runner.

The left foot, leap and throw is another way to make the double play pivot. When he has to take the throw a few steps before arriving at the bag, he will hit the bag with his left foot and throw as he comes across the bag, leaping and throwing at the same time to get accuracy and power on the ball.

Fig. 7–18. BACKHAND FLIP. Similar to a basketball type pass, the second baseman can backhand the ball accurately from twelve feet away. The fielder is more accurate when executing the flip with a stiff wrist. Let the shortstop see the ball all the way (Bobby Knoop).

A

B

The success of a double play usually depends on the manner in which the ball is fed to the pivot man. Therefore, the throw must be executed accurately and as quickly as the situation calls for. Speed and control is, of course, vital in handling the ball.

The second baseman uses as many as three types of throws to the shortstop: the underhand toss, the sidearm throw and the backhand flip. Whatever the type, all his tosses should be made letter-high for easy handling. He should throw in front of the shortstop so that, if possible, the shortstop receives the ball one step away from the bag. We call this "leading" the shortstop with the ball. Generally, the second baseman will throw to the outside corner of the bag.

Sidearm throws are used by the second baseman more than by any other player on the field. This is because the sidearm delivery enables him to get rid of the ball more quickly. Very few second basemen throw really overhand because they cannot always position their body to get something on it that way. Quite often, they have to move quickly to the side, reach down low for the ball and, without straightening up, make an accurate throw to the shortstop. A little snap with the wrist and forearm helps to get something on the ball and get rid of it quickly.

The farther he is away from the bag, the more speed he can put on the ball. The closer he is to the shortstop, the softer the toss.

If the runner stops to delay the tag, the second baseman should not chase him. Instead, the throw to first should be made to retire

Second Baseman's Throws

Fig. 7–19. TAKING THE RELAY THROW. To save valuable time, the second baseman should catch the ball on his throwing side. Taking the throw with his body turned toward the infield, he steps forward with his right side in the direction of the throw (Joe Morgan).

the batter, then the play is made on the runner. If the latter runs out of the base line to avoid the tag, he should not be chased—*he is automatically out.*

Why has Mazeroski been so successful in making the double play at second base? "Well, I make it the way other second basemen do," said Bill, "but I believe my arm has proven to be a little stronger on the sidearm throw, which is so important at second base."

Does Mazeroski find it difficult to get out of the way of those fellows who try to break up the double play? Bill remarked: "It is at times, but you are not usually taken out before you get rid of the ball."

Underhand toss   If he is close to the bag, the second baseman should field the ball with both hands and use a simple underhand lay-up, similar to a bowler's throw (Fig. 7–16). We want our pivot men to keep the ball chest-high and to throw it firmly, not just a "lollipop" toss.

"As soon as I start my throw," explained Beckert, "I pull my glove hand away from the ball so that the shortstop can see it. Then, using only my forearm and wrist, I toss the ball underhand to him. I flip my wrist in an upward motion, the palm of my hand facing the shortstop upon release of the ball. A little farther out, I use a long lay-up, or else half-turn and throw sidearm."

Sidearm throw   Beyond twelve feet or so, the second baseman has to turn and throw, a quick sidearm throw across his body. It is a short arm throw and requires a great deal of wrist action to get speed behind it (Fig. 7–17).

"Whenever possible, be in a position to throw when you field the ball," suggested Beckert. "Practice picking up fast grounders and getting rid of them in a hurry, yet accurately, from any position. Farther from second, you will turn the same way, but you will cock your arm and put more shoulder into it."

From a medium distance, the second baseman pivots to his right on the balls of both feet, so that his toes are pointing toward the base. Then, he makes a short sidearm snap from a squat position.

On a ball hit slightly to his left where he still can get in front of the ball, he should field the ball with his left foot ahead. This makes a pivot to the right easier. He will pivot to the right on his right foot and step toward the bag with his left foot to make the throw. It is just a twist of the body and a snap throw with the wrist and forearm. This has proven to be quicker. As this play is speeded up, it will become a jump-shift. The right foot should come down first, as the left foot steps out in the direction of the throw.

Some infielders like to make a jump pivot or a little hop in the air. They turn their body around so that they are in a position to throw and be able to put something on the ball. Generally, they will release the ball from a low body position with a forearm snap.

Or, the player will pivot to his right on his left foot and bring the right foot in back of the left. Then he steps out with his left foot to complete the throw.

If he moves far to his left and back and is unable to get in front of the ball, he pivots to the left, and turning his back to second base, makes a half-turn of the body to throw. He usually catches the ball with the weight on his left foot and makes a little hop in the air to turn his body. When he comes down, he is in a position to throw.

Backhand flip

This type of throw is executed similarly to the way a basketball player passes to a teammate on his right. Big league infielders like Knoop and Beckert can backhand the ball accurately from twelve feet away (Fig. 7–18). They find they can get rid of the ball more quickly and throw it faster than they can by laying it up.

The backhand flip, however, requires a good amount of skill. By executing it with a stiff wrist, the fielder can be more accurate. In addition, it is essential that the shortstop see the ball and be able to follow it.

In the Dodger organization, we never shovel with the glove because it is very difficult to control the ball this way. The ball will roll off the glove at different angles.

On a ball fielded directly behind second base, some big league second basemen will occasionally backhand it from the gloved hand to the shortstop. "Do not make a practice of doing this unless you absolutely have to," advised Knoop. "Throwing from the glove can never be as accurate as when you throw with your free hand."

While an infielder must be constantly reminded to get rid of the ball, he must know when hurrying the play will result in more damage than good.

Relays and Cutoffs

Relays and cutoffs are team plays which require a great deal of practice to be executed properly. Failure of the second baseman to carry out his part of these plays will result in a serious breakdown of team defense which could mean the ball game.

The most important thing to remember, in taking a relay, is to be sure that he catches the ball on the glove side, the side on which he is going to pivot (Fig. 7–19).

On a base hit to right center field, for example, the second baseman will go out to take the relay throw. Raising his hands in the air, he should yell, "Here!" In order to catch the ball on his throwing side, he should take the throw with his body turned toward the left. He steps forward with his right side in the direction of the throw. This maneuver turns his body slightly toward the infield, to his left, enabling him to make his throws more quickly. Failure to turn his body more into throwing position will merely use up valuable time.

Most teams use a double cutoff. They will send out the shortstop or the second baseman. They will put either one behind the other players, in case there is a bad throw. The outfielder has to hit the first man who comes out for the throw. It must be a good throw, quick and on a line.

Use of the voice is important in this defensive situation. The shortstop is the backup man, about thirty feet or so behind. He should tell the relay man where the ball should be thrown. He should call out: "Home!" Second base!" or "No play!" depending on where the play should be made.

On routine ground balls to right field, we instruct our second basemen to go directly to the bag, and the shortstop to back him up. We feel this is better than going out for just a short relay. The proper maneuver depends entirely on where the ball is hit, though.

We have been making throws directly to second base or real short relay plays especially when speedsters like Lou Brock or Pete Rose get a base hit and make their turn at first base. Figuring that we will hit that relay man, they often keep on running. Thinking this is a sure single, the outfielder will nonchalantly pick up the ball and throw it to the cutoff man. With the runner speeding into second base, the poor second baseman frantically hollers, "Give me the ball!" Then, it is too late to get the runner.

Tagging the Runner

All infielders must remember that the runner actually *tags himself out.* After breaking for the bag, the fielder should straddle it with both feet. He catches the throw from the catcher with two hands whenever possible, but the tag is made with the gloved hand only. He tags the runner by sweeping the ball across the line of his slide, snapping the ball down and in front of the base. By keeping the ball between the runner and the base, the runner will tag himself.

If he has to wait, an infielder should not plant his glove because the runner has a better chance of kicking the ball from the glove. He holds the glove cocked to one side and times his sweep. When the base runner slides, he snaps it down and across his foot.

Fielding Fly Balls

Besides handling fly balls hit in his general direction, the second baseman must have the range to move behind second base and into the outfield, and even behind first base in foul territory. These fielding responsibilities call for speed and quickness, in addition to the ability to judge high, twisting pop flies which can be difficult to handle. This is particularly true when he has to cope with a glaring, bright sun or adverse wind conditions.

The second baseman and the shortstop are the logical fielders of most short fly balls in the outfield territory. If the fly should move out near enough for an outfielder to grab, they should back off, since the outfielder coming in has the better play on the ball. But they should keep going until the outfielder calls for the ball. Furthermore, the outfielder is in a better position to throw. On pop flies behind first base, the second baseman has a better angle than the first baseman be-

Fig. 7–20. A SPECTACULAR OVER–THE–SHOULDER CATCH. Jim Lefebvre makes a brilliant catch in the top of the tenth inning to prevent a go-ahead run by the Braves. As far as an infielder is concerned, every pop fly in the outfield is his play, and he should move out after it unless called off by the outfielder.

cause he is often coming in on the ball. If the sun tends to bother him, he should use his gloved hand to shade his eyes. On sunny days, an infielder should consider painting black charcoal on the skin below his eyes to lessen sun glare.

If a pop fly is hit over his head to his left, his first step is backward with his left foot. On a pop-up to his right, he steps back first with his right foot. It is important to keep after the ball unless another player calls for it or the catch cannot be made (Fig. 7–20).

In chasing fly balls, the fielder should run on the balls of his feet. Running on the heels tends to make the ball appear to jump with every step. Therefore, he will see the ball more clearly and follow it better by not running on his heels. He makes the catch with his hands just below eye-level and in front of his right shoulder. The fingers of his glove point upward.

Outfield flies can be difficult to handle unless the infielders and outfielders work together and communicate with each other. It is essential that the fielder who has the best play on the ball call for it. If he can catch the ball, he should simply wave his arms, while yelling, "I have it!" If the outfielder calls for the ball, the infielder will step out of the way and yell, "Take it!" An infielder should always be listening for the outfielder calling, "I have it!", or "Take it!"

Good communication

The second baseman should cover second base on all ground balls and most fly balls that are hit to the left field side of second base. He

Covering and Backing Up

also covers the bag on attempted steals with a right-handed hitter at the plate. With a right-hander at the plate, he should be prepared to drive a runner on second base back to the bag.

On a single to right field with no one on, he should move quickly to the base, face the right fielder and take the throw-in. The shortstop will back him up.

On a single to left field in which the shortstop will go to the bag, the second baseman must back him up on the play. On a base hit to center field, generally, the player closest to second base will handle the throw-in.

On a bunt situation, he should move closer to first base and be ready to cover first and make the put-out. He should run straight to the bag as quickly as he can and place his left foot on the bag to receive the throw.

The second baseman should be alert to back up throws to first and second bases unless he is handling some other duty on defense. On throws from the catcher and pitcher with a man on third, he should be in the proper backup position.

The Infielder's Mental Attitude

When he is on the playing field, the infielder has to concentrate on his fielding. *He cannot let his mind wander.* He must be alert and thinking all the time he is on the field.

"You have to watch the hitter," added Mazeroski, "and see where the pitch is—whether he is going to pull it or not. We have to see how he swings."

The good infielder is one who is hoping that, when his team needs one or two more outs in a tough situation, the ball will be hit to him.

A ballplayer must have confidence in himself, a positive feeling that he can do it! He has to have a mental attitude which says, "I know I can do it."

The positive approach to the job was recommended by Red Schoendienst, manager of the St. Louis Cardinals. Said Red: "If a youngster goes out and fields the ball with the wholehearted intention that he is going to make the catch—if he goes at it in a positive way—he will surprise himself that, nine times out of ten, he will do it!"

The young player so badly wants to be sure not to make a mistake. As a result, he is a little too cautious. Being cautious, he is reluctant to charge the ball.

With more experience and practice, he will become more positive and aggressive. The moment he sees the ball hit, he will know what he has to do. If he must charge the ball, his instinctive reflexes, developed by habit, will direct him to move in for it.

When an infielder makes an error, he should not let it get him down. *It is just one of those things.* Even the greatest players in the game will make an occasional error. Nobody is expected to catch them all—so a ballplayer who commits an error has to forget it. He must make sure he grabs the next one.

Pepper practice is considered an excellent drill for infielders, the same as it is for players in every other position. In playing this popular game, they have many opportunities to field all kinds of hops, plus going to their left or right.

Infielders should field ground balls by the hour, with someone to fungo balls hit to their right, left or directly at them. The infielder involved in the drill should not know where the ball is being fungoed.

The second basemen and shortstops practice the various pivots every day. The shortstop will field the ground ball and feed it to the second baseman. He then moves to the second base position and takes his turn at second base.

Runners should be placed on first base, or on first and third. This drill can be started by putting a ball at first base near the runner. Or, the coach can fungo balls to the second baseman with the runner going so that a run-down situation is created. Another play can be created by having the runner at first break while the pitcher is taking his stretch. This gives the pitcher practice in backing off the rubber and making the correct play.

Drills

Pepper

Fielding grounders

Double play drill

Run-down drill

Practice Tips for the Second Baseman

1. Practice constantly with the shortstop, playing catch, throwing to each other and working together on double play drills.
2. Spend 15 minutes a day picking up ground balls.
3. Get daily practice on pop flies hit in all directions.
4. Practice going to your left, pivoting around and throwing to first base.
5. Practice the slow roller, coming in, picking a ball up and throwing, while still bent down.
6. Practice going far to your right behind second and making the long throw to first.
7. In warming your arm up, keep moving back until you are throwing from the same distance as that from your deepest area behind second base.
8. Every day when your legs are loose, work at stopping and starting quickly.
9. Squeeze a hard rubber ball several minutes each day to develop your throwing arm and wrist.
10. Do a lot of running to strengthen your legs.

The Shortstop /8/

The shortstop, even more than the second baseman, is the key man in the infield. Actually, it takes a more specialized ballplayer to play short, for the simple reason that he must have a great arm. The real test of a shortstop comes when he has to go into the hole toward third base and backhand the ball. Then, we can see how good an arm he has.

Indeed, the shortstop must have a strong throwing arm and be quick on his feet in plays of all kinds. He must be able to make the double play consistently. In addition to going deep into the hole, he must possess the ability to charge slowly hit balls, and also to go far to his left behind the bag to get the runner going to first base.

The throwing arms of the little wiry guys have always been one of the surprising aspects of this game. I am speaking of the Maury Wills and Bud Harrelson type, who have amazing throwing arms for their small size. Freddy Patek is another infielder who surprises everyone with his arm. Even though he is the smallest player in the league, he throws the ball as hard as any shortstop. In fact, I have never seen too many heavy-muscled shortstops with good arms.

The Essentials

Quickness, plus speed and a strong, accurate arm, are the prime requisites of a good shortstop. *He has to cover a lot of ground.* The Maury Wills type, at 5 feet 10 inches and 168 pounds, is the ideal type for covering ground. True, there are shortstops who may have stronger arms than Maury—and *his* arm is pretty good—but his speed afoot is such a tremendous asset.

Quickness, plus speed and a strong, accurate arm, are the prime requisites of a good shortstop.

A good example of his importance to our ball club was the final play of the 1963 World Series, when we beat the Yankees four straight. There was a high bounding ball over the pitcher's head, and I was so thankful that Maury had the speed to get in there and make the play.

In the beginning of his big league career, Wills had a little trouble with his hands because they are not too big. He had a habit of catching a lot of balls between hops, but through practice and hard work, Maury has corrected this fault.

A leader on and off the field, Maury has gained a vast knowledge of the game. Certainly, he has been the captain of our infield.

Playing the hitters is essential to the play of a good shortstop. All major league shortstops keep a mental "book" on every hitter in the league.

"I have spent a lifetime learning the hitters in the American League," said Luis Aparicio of the Boston Red Sox. "If they traded me to the other league, I would quit because I couldn't be one-half the shortstop that I am now."

Great double play combinations

Down through the years, major league baseball has been blessed with some brilliant double play combinations. I know that old-time followers of the Dodgers, when we were in Brooklyn, will always remember Pee Wee Reese and Jackie Robinson. The Yankee teams, during the time of Joe DiMaggio and Bill Dickey, had Frankie Crosetti and Joe Gordon roving around the pivot positions, followed by Phil Rizzuto and Gil McDougald, and then Tony Kubek and Bobby Richardson. The great St. Louis Cardinal teams of the early 1940s had Marty Marion and Red Schoendienst.

The present era, likewise, has produced keystone combinations equally as great as their predecessors. When shortstop Jim Fregosi teamed with Bobby Knoop, the California Angels fielded one of the top double play combinations in the American League. Spectators in Chicago have marveled at the youthful double play duo of Don Kessinger at shortstop (Fig. 8–2), and Glenn Beckert at second base. In Pittsburgh, Pirate fans felt that Gene Alley and Bill Mazeroski in their prime worked together like the parts of a clock.

Glove

Most major league infielders like a "flat glove," one with minimum padding. A deep glove only gives the ball a chance to get buried. When the fielder takes the ball deep in the pocket, it seems to get lost in there.

Fig. 8–2. GET TWO! The shortstop must always think of the double play. Whenever there is a man on base, it should be the first thing on his mind. This is the play that has to be made consistently if a team is to play championship baseball. Above, the Cubs' Don Kessinger executes a fast twin-killing which stops an opposing rally.

Qualifications

A shortstop, as mentioned, should have a strong throwing arm and be quick on his feet. He must have exceptional speed in covering and fielding ground balls to either side of him. From a variety of positions and areas in the infield, he must be able to throw accurately with either a sidearm or an overhand movement.

The athlete who plays shortstop is often the team leader, the "take charge" type of player, and the one to keep his teammates on their toes. Therefore, he must be a resourceful player with sound baseball sense and a talent for anticipating plays—something which Pee Wee Reese excelled in for many years.

The history of baseball shows that few teams have risen to championship heights without a smooth-working, dependable double play combination. Certainly, the success of any baseball team lies in its strength down the middle.

A shortstop not only has considerable ground to cover, but because of the long throws he has to make, it is essential that he field the ball cleanly. Contrary to the shorter throws of the second baseman, the shortstop cannot afford to fumble. He must often throw without straightening up, although when time permits, he should raise up and get his normal movement into the throw.

Stance

As he takes his position before the pitch, the shortstop should stand with his feet comfortably spread shoulder-width apart. His eyes are on the pitcher. Both feet should face out just a little, not straight ahead. This will make it easier to turn or jab as he starts to go right or left. The knees and hips are bent slightly, and his back is straight. His hands are placed on the knees, with the upper part of his body resting comfortably on them.

As the pitcher goes into his delivery, the shortstop takes his hands off his knees and lets them hang loosely between his legs. He shifts his weight a little forward to the balls of the feet, while still keeping his heels on the ground. He moves his eyes from the pitcher to the hitter at the plate.

As the pitcher throws to the plate, the infielder will step or hop forward with the left foot, about a foot, and a slight shuffle with his right. This process is timed with the anticipation of the batter hitting the pitched ball.

In moving laterally to his left or right, I recommend that a player use a cross-step. Many players have a habit of lifting their right foot high in the air and stepping with it before crossing over with their left foot. Instead, they should keep everything low.

The important thing is to take *short, quick steps* when starting for the ball. The shortstop may jab to the right and then cross with the left.

"If the ball is hit to my left," said Kessinger, "I will keep as low as possible, dig with my arms as I cross-step my right leg over the left. If the ball is to my right, I will push off my left foot, jab-step with my right foot, cross-step and dig after the ball."

Playing the Hitters

The basic fielding positions of the shortstop depend largely on his own strengths and weaknesses and the type of batter at the plate. Generally, he will play about 30 feet from second and about 20 to 25 feet behind the line. He can play deeper for slow runners.

With a right-handed pull hitter, he should play more toward third base. Likewise, with a left-handed swinger, he should move over toward second four or five steps. He should move in a couple of steps for the fast runners.

With a runner on first base, the shortstop moves into his double play depth, perhaps three to five steps toward the plate. Although he should play as far away from the bag as he can, he must get to the base in time to complete the play.

When runners are on first and second bases with no one out, and the bunt situation is in order, he should move in directly in back of the base runners but should not leave his fielding position too vulnerable. His big responsibility is to keep the runner close to second base, to prevent him from getting too long a lead.

Playing the ball in the hole is probably the most difficult play for the shortstop. This is why a strong arm is such a great asset at this position. If he lacks the outstanding arm, then he must play in closer to compensate for it. With a man on first and third and a double steal is attempted, he must move quickly from his normal position after the ball has passed the plate, and go to a spot approximately one step in front of second base. There, he must watch for an attempt by the runner on third base to score. If the runner breaks for the plate, the shortstop should charge in fast to cut off the catcher's throw and return the ball to him.

Fig. 8–3. BASIC FIELDING POSITION. As the ball approaches, the infielder has his glove close to the ground and his bare hand next to the glove. He keeps his elbows and hands away from his body when fielding ground balls (Don Kessinger).

If the runner on third decides not to go, the shortstop, in his position one step in front of the base, should wait for the catcher's throw and pivot around to make the tag at second base.

Using another method to defense the double steal, the shortstop runs quickly to a spot about halfway between the pitcher's mound and second base. There, he watches for an attempt by the runner on third base to score. If the runner decides to go, the shortstop will catch the ball thrown by the catcher and return it to the plate.

If the runner does not make a break, he will be in position to let the throw from the catcher go through to the second baseman, who is covering the base.

The score and the inning of the game will determine if the shortstop should try to cut the runner off at the plate or try to get the runner attempting to steal second base. If the run is the winning or tying run, the play should be made to the *plate,* by all means.

Fielding Ground Balls

The main thing in fielding a ground ball is to watch the ball and stay low on it. The infielder's glove should be close to the ground. It is much easier for him to bring his hands up than it is to take his whole body down. He must get in front of the ball quickly, plant his right foot and make the throw. His eyes follow the ball into his glove (Fig. 8–3).

Ground balls, like fly balls, should be fielded with both hands if at all possible. Using the glove hand and throwing hand together is not only surer but it enables the fielder to move into his throwing motion more quickly. He will have much better control of the ball and will make fewer errors.

As the ball approaches, he has his glove close to the ground and his bare hand next to the glove. He keeps the glove facing the ball.

"Charge the ball," advised Pee Wee Reese. "Always keep coming in on the ball. Most often, it is better to charge a ball than to lay back or back up. If an infielder backs up, he will likely field the ball in between hops. This often lets the ball play him."

However, on hard hit balls directly at him, the infielder has to be less aggressive. He cannot see the hops as well as he can those from an angle. Consequently, his judgment and timing may be off.

The real test of a shortstop comes when he has to go into the hole toward third base and backhand the ball.

"You have to watch the ball go right into the pocket of your glove," said Maury Wills. "Keep your eyes on the ball until you see it in your glove. Above all, do not try to throw the ball before you get it."

Since the shortstop seldom has time to straighten up to throw, he must make throws from the position in which he fields the ball. Often he must charge balls hit directly at him and play them as quickly as possible. He has to throw across his body in order to get rid of it quickly enough. By fielding the ball quickly, he will have more time to throw the ball.

A slow-bounding ball hit just past the pitcher calls for a quick off-balance underhand flip throw. A play deep in the hole near third base requires a long, more powerful throw. By moving in or charging the ball, the infielder will get the hop that he needs by either speeding up his forward motion or by slowing it down.

If the ball is not hit hard, some infielders like to round off slightly so they can field, step and throw to first base.

To cover the most ground quickly, the infielder's first step should be a cross-over step. Keeping his body low, he gets to the line of the ball quickly. After fielding the ball, he plants his right foot and makes the throw.

Coming in for a Slow Roller

A slow roller is always tougher to field than a hard hit grounder because the fielder must run in faster and throw it to a base while on the move. If he waits for a slow grounder to reach him, a fast runner will take advantage of the time loss and reach base safely. The fielder must charge the ball at full speed, catching and throwing it without straightening up (Fig. 8–4).

On this play, the underhand throw has to be strong and accurate, and the fielder has to get rid of the ball as quickly as possible. He must make this play with two hands if he possibly can.

If he has to approach the ball from the side, the shortstop should field it with the gloved hand only and in front of the left foot. The glove should be used as a scoop, with the ball rolling into it.

The barehanded grab and running throw should be used only as a last resort, in a "do-or-die" situation. The difficulty of the barehanded pickup is increased greatly on a poorly maintained field filled with rough spots. Even on big league diamonds, the barehanded grab requires considerable skill and finesse.

If the ball has stopped rolling, the infielder should charge it from the left side and field it with the bare hand only, and about even with the toe of the left foot. With a scooping motion of the bare hand, he picks the ball up and makes the throw.

Fig. 8–4. COMING IN FOR SLOW ROLLER. The slow roller must be fielded on the run. The fielder must charge the ball at full speed, catching and throwing the ball without straightening up. Fielding the ball with his left foot forward, he then takes a step with the right foot to make the throw (Jim Fregosi).

Going to His Right

The toughest play for the shortstop is going to his right (Fig. 8–5). Since he has to move far to his right, he has to go for the ball very quickly. Then, he has to plant his right foot, sliding in the dirt and fielding the ball at the same time. Since he is a great distance from first base, he has to get control of his body very quickly and really get something on the ball. The braced leg gives a firm support as the fielder steps out with his left foot in the direction of the throw. This is a very tough play.

In the Dodger organization, we teach our shortstops to get in front of the ball whenever possible. We want them to backhand it only when necessary. We want them to get in front of the ball and handle it with two hands. Just as he gloves the ball, the shortstop has to put on the brakes, placing his weight on his right foot. He then pushes off his right foot and makes the long overhand throw. With the right foot sliding the last few inches as he gets the ball, he has to grip it and get the necessary body control to deliver the ball to first base.

However, on the ball that he cannot quite get to with both hands, the shortstop has to backhand it with his glove hand. For most infielders, this is more difficult than getting in front of the ball and fielding it with two hands (Fig. 8–6). First, he backhands the ball and then plunges his right foot into the dirt to make the play.

Maury has become very proficient in using the backhand technique. He believes he can field the ball more easily this way, without the sometimes sluggish slide in the dirt characteristic of the accepted method.

Of course, Maury has played shortstop a long time, and although this may be easier for him, young infielders do not possess the skill and finesse to use this technique regularly in going far to their right.

A   B   C

Fig. 8–5. GOING FAR TO THE RIGHT. On the ball that he cannot get to with both hands, the shortstop has to backhand it with his glove hand. After fielding the ball, he stops his momentum by bracing on his right foot. The braced leg provides a firm support as he steps out with his left foot in the direction of the throw. This play is perhaps the shortstop's toughest play (Chris Speier).

If a shortstop can get in front of the ball, this is what we want him to do.

Going to His Left

This is the play toward or behind second base in which the shortstop does not always have time to get in front of the ball. If not, he should try to field the ball with his left foot forward. Then, he takes a short, quick step with his right foot while turning his body to the right. At the same time, he brings the ball and the glove up toward the throwing position.

On a hard hit ground ball, the big league shortstop will start by turning, rather than pivoting, on his left foot. The foot is not lifted, merely turned so that the spikes barely clear the ground. Then, he takes a cross-over step with his right foot as he breaks to his left for the ball. He wants to stay low to the ground as he makes his move for the ball.

As he catches the ball, he should step forward and in front of the left foot with his right foot to check his momentum. He then steps forward with his left foot in the direction of the throw.

Making the Double Play

The success of any keystone combination rests upon a vital question: Can they make the double play? This is the question asked of every shortstop and second baseman because the double play is believed to be the key to championship baseball. Therefore, these two infielders must be able to make the double play consistently.

Fundamentally, the double play pivot is not a difficult maneuver to learn. Although some infielders have trouble executing it properly,

A   B

Fig. 8–6. GOING TO HIS RIGHT. The shortstop should get in front of the ball whenever possible and handle it with two hands. He slides his right foot in the dirt and fields the ball at the same time. Putting on the brakes, he places his weight on his right foot. He then pushes off his right foot and makes the long overhand throw (Jim Fregosi).

their difficulty usually results from poor execution before the pivot, not the fundamentals of the pivot itself. Actually, the pivot is easier for the shortstop because he comes into the bag moving toward first base, while the second baseman is almost always moving away from first.

For maximum efficiency, the shortstop and second baseman should know all the moves each one makes at his position. This is true in the Kessinger-Beckert and Alley-Mazeroski combinations, and likewise with the Kubek-Richardson combination of a few years back. These players have spent all their major league careers together. They know each other like a book, i.e., their running speed, the type of ball each one throws, their mannerisms and their mutual reactions to various situations.

"As far as cooperating," explained Mazeroski, "we have signs back and forth which signify who is covering with a man on first base. As a general rule, the shortstop covers on left-handed hitters and the second baseman on right-handed hitters. There are exceptions, of course, like for the hitter who goes a lot to the opposite field. On a steal, we try to watch the signs from the catcher if it is a curve ball or fast ball. On a ball hit back to the pitcher, we want to know who will receive it from the pitcher."

The double play is the most intricate and difficult maneuver in the infield, but surely the most rewarding. Like any other play, young infielders should learn to make the double play in a fundamental manner. Before they try to be fancy, they should master the basic maneuvers. *There is no substitute for executing baseball skills in the fundamental way.*

Getting to the Base

In order to execute a good pivot, the infielder must be able to get to the bag and be on balance before the ball arrives (Fig. 8–7). However, for most infielders, this is difficult to do from a regular fielding depth. Consequently, in double play situations, the shortstop and second baseman must shorten up, or "cheat," toward the bag.

"Of course, your speed will determine how much you can shorten up," said Fregosi, "but I find I can reach the base in plenty of time by moving three or four steps closer to it."

As soon as the ball is hit, the infielder who is responsible for covering the bag should break for second base at full speed and try to get there as quickly as possible. The shortstop will often sprint toward the bag and slow up as he nears it. When he sees the throw coming, he will increase his speed again and hit the bag at a fairly good speed.

Generally, the big league shortstop likes to run hard until he is four or five feet from the bag, then jockeys in, bouncing from one foot to the other like a boxer. His knees are bent so he can move to either side for the throw.

"As I get near the bag, I like to slow down by using short, choppy steps to get on balance," explained Fregosi. "I want to bring my body under control. I want to see where the throw is. Then, I am ready to shift in either direction for the throw.

"I like to have the ball over the base and about chest-high," said Fregosi. "I want the ball thrown pretty hard, firm and accurate. I do not like to see any mushroom throws."

Shortstop's Pivots

The shortstop has no standard pivot because a good double play man will pivot a number of different ways. Otherwise, the base runner will know where to slide to upset the shortstop's throw and break up the double play.

Much of the time, on perhaps 98 per cent of the plays, the shortstop will use two basic ways of making the double play pivot: 1) to the right field side, dragging with the right foot as he glides across the base; and 2) to the infield side, touching with his left, stepping with the right and throwing.

On the other plays, his footwork is the result of his reactions to the various situations, i.e., the type of throw, the speed of the base runners, and his position when the ball is released to him.

The majority of the time, the shortstop is going into the play and his momentum is carrying him toward first base. Generally, he will drag his right foot across the back corner of the bag and get into position to make his throw. Actually, instead of moving directly toward the base, he angles off between first base and the outfield, thus keeping him away from the runner.

For the shortstop to come across the bag in this manner, the throw must be just right. If the throw is to the pitcher's side of second base, he will go to the "infield side," touching the base with the left foot and stepping with the right and throwing to first base. Or, he can hop to his right, brush the bag with his left foot, and throw to first from inside the base line.

A simple but effective pivot is for the shortstop to step on the base with his left foot and throw. He receives the throw in front of the bag. One of the fastest ways is to straddle the bag, take the throw and make a fast fliplike relay to first base. Another way is for the shortstop to come in, hit the bag with the left foot and then back off toward left field as he throws to first base.

Occasionally, when he is close enough to the bag, the shortstop will handle the force play himself, rather than risk the possibility of the second baseman dropping his short toss. One step from the bag, he will take a stride with his left foot and make his throw as his foot makes contact with the base.

When throwing to first base, most shortstops use a three-quarter natural throwing procedure. *Under no circumstances should they throw around the runner.* It is the job of the base runner to get out of the way or hit the dirt early.

Across base to the right side, dragging with the right foot

Considered the most popular pivot among major league shortstops, this maneuver is most effective when the shortstop has very little time, and quick action is needed to get away from the approaching slider.

"I like to receive the throw from the second baseman a step in front of the bag," explained Fregosi. As shown in Figure 8–7, the ball arrives as Fregosi straddles the base. "As I catch the ball, I place my left foot down a foot past and to the right field side of the bag. Dragging my right foot through, I kick the corner of the bag. As I drag the right foot over the base, I place it behind my left foot and I hop in the air, placing my weight on the right foot.

"Meanwhile, I am moving the ball into throwing position," continued Jim, "and I step toward first base with my left foot and make a three-quarter delivery throw to first base." Fregosi finds himself past second by several feet, making his throw outside the base line.

If the runner is too close for the shortstop to make the throw on this step, a short hop or shuffle-step is made to the left (Fig. 8–9). This footwork carries the shortstop farther out of the runner's path. He makes his throw to first as his right foot lands, thus stepping toward first base on his left.

Touch with left foot, step into infield with right

If the runner is outside the line, the shortstop should make the double play by going to the inside of the base. He can touch the bag with his left foot, then step into the infield with his right and make his throw to first base. The left foot is the one which makes contact with the base, either with a drag or a step (Fig. 8–10).

Fig. 8-7. ACROSS BASE TO RIGHT FIELD SIDE. This pivot is effective when the shortstop has very little time and quick action is needed to get away from the oncoming slider. He drags the corner of the base with his right foot as he glides across the bag (Jim Fregosi).

"Catch the ball one step in front of the bag," said Kessinger. "Then step forward with your left foot, placing it immediately in front of the base. As you hop into the infield on your right foot, you drag the left foot over the bag."

By making his hop toward first base, the shortstop will transfer his weight to the right foot. Then, pushing off on the right foot, he steps toward first base with his left foot.

Fig. 8-8. PROTECTING HIMSELF FROM THE BASE RUNNER. Rather than be a stationary target, some shortstops, after completing their throws, will jump in the air to avoid the runner. Others will sidestep to the left or right, depending on the path of the base runner (Eddie Leon).

Fig. 8–9. EVADING THE HARD SLIDER. A short hop or shuffle step can be made to the left if the runner is too close for the shortstop to make the throw. Below, the footwork of Bert Campaneris carries him out of the path of hard sliding Cesar Tovar.

Actually, the shortstop is in a better position to make a good three-quarter delivery throw when he goes to the right. By dragging with his left foot, he can be more sure of the force play, while the step method can carry him farther away from the bag and out of the path of the runner.

Touch with left foot and throw

This pivot is used when the shortstop has more time. He can straddle the base and make his throw in front of the slider. He receives the ball chest-high, one step in front of the base, with his weight on his right foot. As he brings the ball into throwing position, he lifts his left foot and places it on the right field side of the base. Pushing off the right foot, which is behind the base, the weight of his body moves up onto his front foot, which remains rested on the bag.

"If the runner is close to you," said Kessinger, "make your step with the left foot away from him."

A similar maneuver is to step on the middle of the base with the right foot; then, as he takes a normal stride with the left foot, he completes his throw to first base.

The drag method can also be used with this type of pivot, and is one of the surest ways to make the double play. The shortstop takes the throw while straddling the base, and with his right foot forward, he drags his left foot across the top of the base as he throws to first base.

Right foot, leap and flip

Although this is a quick maneuver in making the double play, it is one of the most difficult to learn. The shortstop hits the base with his right foot and makes a flat, flip throw to first. He then jumps in the air to avoid the runner.

Young infielders might find it difficult getting much power behind the flip throw, and until skill is achieved, they might toss a few in the first base dugout.

269

Fig. 8–10. INSIDE PIVOT: LEFT FOOT AND THROW. When the throw is on the inside of second base, the shortstop touches the bag with his left foot, steps into the infield with his right and makes his throw to first base (Don Kessinger).

Backing off   On a close play, the shortstop comes in and hits the base with his left foot. Then, he steps back with his right foot and braces it for the pivot and throw to first. The step toward first base should be away from the runner.

One disadvantage to this pivot is that it places the shortstop farther away from his target at first base, and unless he has a strong arm, he might lack the carry to throw out some of the fast runners.

Using a variation of this maneuver, the shortstop will hit the bag with his left foot and back off toward left field before stepping toward first for the throw.

Shortstop's Throws   The shortstop actually has four types of throws he can make when feeding the ball to the pivot man. A successful double play depends as much on the accuracy of his throw as on the pivot man's throw to first.

A young shortstop should learn how to throw overhand, sidearm and underhand. However, in throwing to the second baseman, I recommend just the sidearm and underhand throws. Then, as he gains more experience, he might find the backhand toss or flip quite effective in getting the ball to the pivot man.

Because of the nature of the second baseman's pivots, the throw by the shortstop is difficult to execute. It has to be just right, approximately chest-high, directly at the bag.

If a second baseman is close to the base, he will use a simple underhand lay-up. A little farther away, he has to use a long underhand toss, or a half-turn and sidearm throw. Many big league infielders like to use a backhand flip from twelve feet away, because they can get rid of it more quickly and throw it faster than by laying it up. Beyond twelve feet or so, they usually turn and throw, with a quick arm flip across their body. Far from second, they will turn the same way, but in cocking their arm, they will put more shoulder into it.

The shortstop should train himself to field a ball and throw it to second base with the same motion. The play should be made without straightening up, and the glove should be pulled away from the ball in order for the second baseman to get a good view. Practice will develop the timing and teamwork so necessary for perfection.

"I always throw at the bag," said Fregosi, "because a moving target will be at different spots on different plays. I expect the second baseman to be at the bag when the ball arrives. I figure, the better throw I make to him, the better throw he will make to first."

A fielder should never ease up on his throwing. He must keep everything in rhythm and make his delivery as smooth as possible, finishing with a good snap of the wrist.

If he can remember to execute his footwork correctly, grip the ball across the seams and throw the ball in a fluid motion, he will seldom make throwing errors.

The grip

The infielder should hold the ball with his fingers well-spaced to avoid throwing sliders. When the ball is grabbed with the fingers too close together, it has a tendency to slide off to one side or the other and curve a little.

The ball should be held the same way for every throw. It is gripped with the index and middle fingers on top, the fingers spread about one-half to three-quarters of an inch. The thumb is directly under the index finger. The infielder should make sure there is a space between the ball and the "V" formed by the thumb and index finger, to get good wrist snap as the ball is released. *He does not grip the ball too tightly.* A tight grip will often prevent good wrist snap.

Sidearm throw

On a ground ball hit to his right, the shortstop should stop squarely in front of the ball by bracing his right leg and sliding the inside of his right foot in the dirt.

"Begin the sidearm throw immediately after you field the ball," explained Fregosi. "Then, step with the left foot in the direction of the throw. Do not be deceptive. Show him the ball all the way."

As shown in Figure 8–11, Fregosi brings his glove and the ball up into a throwing position. He grips the ball as he brings the glove up. When he uses only arm action, sometimes he has to throw from a squat position.

Many times the sidearm throw is made without the shortstop taking a step with his left foot, but merely throwing from the position in which he received the ball. This enables him to get the ball away quickly.

If the ball is hit sharply, the shortstop may have time to straighten up a little and take a step with his left foot.

Underhand toss

When close to the pivot, the shortstop should lay the ball up clean and simple. It is a simple, stiff-wristed, underhand toss. This throw has

Fig. 8–11. SIDEARM THROW. The shortstop begins his throw from a fielding position. He brings the glove and ball up together into a throwing position. He takes the ball out of his glove and throws sidearm across his body. Keeping the arm loose, he snaps the ball forward like a whip, stepping with his left foot in the direction of the throw (Jim Fregosi).

little arch, because it goes in a straight line to the second baseman's chest. Staying low to the ground, his legs bent sharply, he comes up with the ball from a fielding position (Fig. 8–12).

"Give him the hand," said Fregosi, "and then let it follow-through after the ball. It is a simple, stiff-wrist, underhand toss chest-high. Do not let the arm follow-through any higher than waist-high."

Backhand flip When fielding the ball far to the left and behind second base, many big league shortstops such as Luis Aparicio use a backhand flip (Fig. 8–13). The throw should be aimed toward the third base side of the base. It is made either on the run or from a non-moving position, in which the shortstop flips the ball with his wrist to the second baseman covering.

Giving Signs The shortstop usually gives the sign to the second baseman as to who will cover second on a possible steal. This is done by hiding his face from the opponents with the glove, and giving the "open" and "closed" mouth signs.

The open mouth means the second baseman will cover, while a closed mouth indicates that the shortstop will cover. These two infielders must get in the habit of glancing at each other after every sign given by the catcher. Generally, the shortstop covers the bag on left-handed hitters and the second baseman on right-handed swingers.

They can also cross their letters or their belts, which will indicate, "You take it," or, "I take it."

272

Fig. 8–12. UNDERHAND TOSS. The lay-up is used when the shortstop is close to the pivot man. He makes the throw clean and simple, a stiff-wristed, under-hand toss. He does not let his arm follow through any higher than waist-high (Jim Fregosi).

There are two basic ways in which an infielder can tag a sliding runner:

This is perhaps the safest way to tag the runner. Straddling the base, the infielder places his glove on the ground in front of the bag and lets the runner slide into it. Closing the thumb over the glove, he lets the runner slide into the back of the glove. As a result, there is less chance of the ball being kicked out.

Tagging the Runner

1) The stationary tag

Fig. 8–13. BACKHAND FLIP. This throw is made either on the run or from a nonmoving position, in which the shortstop flips the ball with his wrist to the second baseman covering (Luis Aparicio).

Fig. 8–14. THROWING ON THE RUN. On high bounding balls over the pitcher's head, the shortstop has to move in quickly and throw on the run. Here, Larry Bowa of the Philadelphia Phillies, after grabbing the ball, straightens up and throws off his right leg. With a good snap of the wrist, he employs a quick arm flip across his body.

2) The sweep tag

Standing with his feet on both sides of the base, the infielder sweeps the ball across the line of his slide. In receiving the throw, he sweeps the ball in an arc, down across the foot and up again. If he has to wait, he should not place his glove in the runner's path with the ball exposed; this is a good way to have it kicked out. Instead, he should hold it cocked to one side and time his sweep. When the base runner slides, he snaps the glove down and across his foot.

Catching Pop Flies

The shortstop, like the second baseman, must work hard on fly balls hit back of the infield. He must learn to keep going back without calling for the ball until the outfielder calls him off the play. The outfielder should take every ball that he can take because it is much easier for him to catch it than for the shortstop going back. If a throw has to be made following the catch, the outfielders moving in will have the better play. All pop flies hit directly behind the first and third baseman are the responsibilities of the second baseman and the shortstop.

Whenever possible, fly balls should be caught with both hands, thumbs together and fingers pointing up (Fig. 8–15). The infielder uses his glove to shade the sun on pop flies. In calling for the ball, he yells, "I have it!" and uses one hand to wave his teammate away.

If the ball is hit over his head, the shortstop should turn his head and run as hard as he can back after it. This procedure will enable him to position himself under the ball, rather than timing the ball.

Fig. 8–15. CATCHING A POP FLY. Whenever possible, pop flies should be caught with both hands, thumbs together and fingers pointing up. They should be caught approximately eye-level on the throwing arm side (Ed Brinkman).

On extra-base hits to left and center fields, the shortstop serves as the relay man. He moves quickly out to a position where he will be in line with the throw from the outfielder and the base to which the throw is to go. He should be close enough to the outfielder so that the relay can be caught on the fly.

When he takes a relay from the outfield, he should listen for instructions from the second baseman or third baseman on where to make the throw.

Cutoffs and Relays

Covering and Backing Up

The shortstop covers second base on all bunt plays and all ground balls, and on most fly balls hit to the right field side of second base. He is partly responsible for keeping the runner on second close to the base. In addition, there are some situations when the shortstop should cover third base. With a runner on second and a base hit to left, the third baseman is usually the cutoff man to the plate and the shortstop covers third.

The shortstop should back up second base when the second baseman covers the base on throws from the catcher or pitcher, and on throws made by outfielders. He also backs up third base on throws from the catcher.

Pick-Off Plays

We have found pick-off plays to be very helpful. The number of runners picked off is not the prime objective of this play. Rather, it is trying to keep runners close, so if there is a base hit, we have enough time to throw them out. The fact that the Dodgers have a reputation for good pick-off plays is often enough to keep the runner close to his base.

The shortstop and second baseman play a very important role in setting up the pick-off play and giving signs to the pitcher. After all, the pitcher can be concentrating so much on the hitter that he sometimes forgets there is a possible pick-off play which can get him out of a tough jam.

The pick-off with the pitcher is usually a signal play, worked in either of two ways: on a "count," or by the "daylight" method. Maury uses the "daylight" play on occasion, plus the "count" or flash systems. Four methods of the pick-off play are presented in detail in Chapter 4, on "Pitching."

Practice Tips for Shortstops

1. Practice constantly with the second baseman, playing catch, throwing to each other from all angles and executing double play drills.
2. Spend 15 to 20 minutes daily on picking up grounders.
3. Practice fielding the slow roller. Over and over, come in and charge the ball.
4. Concentrate particularly on coming in, picking the ball up and throwing while still bent down.
5. Get plenty of practice going to your right, using both techniques, i.e., getting in front of the ball and using two hands, and employing the one-handed backhand method.
6. Get plenty of practice on pop flies hit in all directions.
7. Practice the play behind second base, moving quickly to your left and throwing to first base.
8. Do a lot of running to strengthen your legs.

Drills

1. *Double play drill*   The shortstop and the second baseman should practice the various pivots four or more times each, then changing to different ones.

2. *Fielding grounders*   The fungo hitter should hit ground balls in all directions, i.e., to the right, to the left, the slow roller and the hard hit grounder.

3. *Run-down drill*   (*see* DRILLS for the second baseman).

4. *Pepper*   (*see* DRILLS for the second baseman).

5. *Pick-off play at second*   The second baseman and shortstop get into playing position and work the pick-off play with the pitcher. The runner assumes his lead off second base. The pitchers form a line to the first base side of the mound, while the runners form a line in shallow right center field.

6. *Double steal defense*   The infielders, pitcher and catcher should assume their regular positions. One group of runners goes to first base, another to third. After the ball is thrown to the catcher, the runner on first tries to steal second. The catcher has three choices: throw to second, throw to the pitcher, or fake a throw to second and throw to third. The runner on third makes his move, depending on what the defense does. The runners should be told not to slide in this drill.

7. *Bunt defense*   The defense practices against all possible bunt situations. A runner is placed on first base, and the first baseman must play on the bag. The pitcher takes his set position and then throws the ball to the plate. The defense, with the catcher, pitcher, third or first baseman fielding the ball, makes a play at first or second base. The second baseman must cover first base, and the shortstop moves to second base. The defense tries to make the play at second base, if possible, then to first.

8. *Relays and cutoff drills*   These team drills give the defense important practice in handling relay, cutoff and backup assignments in all game situations. The coach will hit the ball between the outfielders. The runner will attempt to score, and the batter will try to reach second or third. The infielders and pitcher will take their proper relay, cutoff and backup positions.

The Third Baseman /9/

Third base is called the "hot corner" because there is never a dull moment around the bag. The third baseman often has to react automatically, both mentally and physically. He has to be able to field slow rolling bunts, block hard hit balls and make long, accurate throws.

A third baseman must have a strong, accurate arm, sure hands and quick reactions. Of course, the ideal man at third is the fellow who has the agility *plus* speed—the fellow who can come in on bunted balls and make the one-handed throw, like Brooks Robinson and Clete Boyer.

I am sure that, with more fields using artificial turf, those balls will be coming faster and faster. It will take quickness and courage on the part of all third basemen to defend against those hard hitters.

More and more hitters in baseball today are using their speed and agility to get on base by using drag or push bunts. Therefore, a third baseman has to be alert at all times. He has to move around and vary his position, anticipating every possible play. Brooks and Clete certainly know how to play the hitters, too. They know the fellows who might bunt on them and who cannot, the hitters who will pull the ball, go up the middle or to the opposite field. These two great glovemen know when to guard the line and when not to.

With a runner on third, the third baseman must stay alert to receive pick-off throws from the catcher. Occasionally, he will have to run out to catch high pop flies that sail into short left field, or he may have to move into foul territory to grab pop fouls.

The third baseman has been described as a steel trap, always poised, waiting to spring in any of several directions.

During the past two decades, the Dodgers have had some truly fine glovemen at third base, such as Billy Cox, Don Hoak, Jackie Robinson and Junior Gilliam. Cox was one of the very best, having a good glove and a strong arm. He could catch bad hops, good hops and everything else. Billy was blessed with exceptional body control and quickness of hands.

Perhaps the most memorable play I have ever witnessed took place in the 1965 World Series against the Minnesota Twins. This was the great play in which Gilliam backhanded the ball and made a highly crucial put-out at third base (Fig. 9–7). With runners on first and second, a base hit would have tied the ball game, or put the Twins ahead. The ball was hit sharply down over the bag—but, fortunately for the Dodgers, Gilliam went over, backhanded the ball, spun around and tagged third base. It was a great play and was a key factor in our winning the World Championship.

Qualifications In playing third base, quickness is more essential than great speed afoot. Since balls are hit so sharply at third, the first two steps of the third baseman have to be quick. They either "do or they don't" down

Fig. 9–2. QUICK REACTIONS AND SURE HANDS are perhaps the greatest attributes of an outstanding third baseman like Brooks Robinson. Since the balls are hit so sharply at third, his first two steps have to be quick. Here, Robinson moves quickly to his right, backhands the ball in time to throw out the hitter at first base.

An aggressive athlete is needed at third base who is willing to dive after balls and stay in front of hard hit balls.

there. Quick hands is another great asset, and can make up for mediocre running speed (Fig. 9–2).

The third baseman must have a good arm to make the long throw to first with plenty of speed and carry on the ball. This is why, in addition to the bunt threat, he must play in closer than other infielders in order to field the ball as soon as possible and get it across the diamond ahead of the runner. Playing that close when a powerful pull hitter smashes a drive his way certainly can make things hot for him.

A sure pair of hands and the ability to handle the ball with speed are valuable assets of the third sacker. Since his fielding position often brings him close to the hitter, hard hit ground balls cannot always be fielded cleanly.

Consequently, an aggressive athlete is needed at third base who is willing to dive after balls and stay in front of hard hit balls. He should have the agility to retrieve them in time to throw out the hitter. Every manager likes a fielder who will knock a hard hit ball down with his chest like Pepper Martin used to do, then pick it up and throw the runner out. Pepper could dive sideways and knock a ball down and then get up quickly and throw the man out.

One of the mistakes made most often by third basemen is the assumption that a hard ground ball between third and shortstop is not their ball. Everything they can reach cleanly on either side is their ball.

It takes a tough competitor to play third base in the manner it should be played. Hard work and considerable practice will improve every player's game. He must have someone hit him ground balls of all types, directly at him, to his left and right, hard shots, along with medium and slow rollers.

The Glove

A player's glove can be his best friend. A good glove, well taken care of and broken in, can improve his fielding a great deal. Most big league third basemen prefer a long one, an outfielder's glove.

Generally, infielders take most of the padding out of their gloves. They feel they can grab the ball more securely this way and have more feel and touch when catching it.

Most infielders use two gloves each year. They break in a new glove during spring training, and then put it away when the season starts. From the opening game until July, they use their glove from the previous year. Then, early in July, they discard this glove for the one they broke in during spring training.

A. Preliminary stance   B. Set position

Fig. 9–3. STANCE. After taking the preliminary position, the third baseman moves a half step forward as the pitcher releases the ball. He lowers his hands and gets into a set position. This places his body in motion so he can jump in any direction the moment the bat meets the ball (Brooks Robinson).

Stance   A third baseman should use a semi-crouch stance, with his legs spread shoulder-width apart. He keeps his knees bent slightly because sudden adjustments, forward or backward, left or right, can best be made from this crouch.

An infielder should be a little bit on the move when the ball approaches the plate. It is a lot easier to control the body from a moving position than it is from a dead, standstill position. Just a little movement in toward the hitter is always good. He must not be caught flat-footed or on his heels if the ball is hit his way.

All good fielders say that the glove should be low because it is easier to come up with the glove than it is to go down. By starting low with the glove, they can keep their tail a little low, which is good. The weight is evenly distributed. The legs are spread in a comfortable position so that they are ready to go in any direction.

"I like a stance that feels comfortable to me," explained Brooks Robinson, regarded by many as the greatest fielding third baseman in baseball history (Fig. 9–3). "After taking my preliminary or ready position, I will move a half step forward as the pitcher releases the ball. On every pitch, I move that half step forward when the ball is sent to the plate. I will take my hands off my legs and get into a set position. My arms are loose, and I am low and ready on every pitch."

I want our infielders to get down low enough so their back is straight or parallel to the ground. The left foot is slightly ahead of the right foot. As demonstrated by Robinson in Fig. 9–3, both feet should face out just a little, *not* straight ahead. This will make it easier to turn or jab as he starts to go right or left.

The third baseman must be ready at all times, and have his mind made up as to what he is going to do with the ball before it gets to him. He must expect every ball to be hit to him. If he does, he will be ready.

The fielding position of the third baseman depends on a number of factors. Of course, he must consider the type of hitter at the plate, whether he is a pull hitter or a late swinger. Does he often bunt for a base hit? What kind of running speed does he have? These are the questions he must ask himself throughout the game.

There are three basic positions, or depths, which the third baseman assumes:

Playing the Hitters

1) Normal to Deep Position

This position is approximately four or five steps from the line. The depth is anywhere from a spot even with the bag to about two or three yards beyond the base. With a pull hitter at the plate, he plays closer to the line. If he hits straightaway, he can play further over from the foul line. His position, however, will depend on the ball-and-strike count on the hitter, as well as the score and inning of the game.

2) Halfway (Double Play Depth) Position

The fielders play squarely on the base line, and not behind the bases. A batted ball will take less time to reach them. Thus, the execution of the double play can be made more quickly.

3) In Position

The third baseman moves in close to the front edge of the grass, with the idea of trying to stop a runner from scoring from third on a grounder. In a sacrifice situation, the third baseman will want to be positioned in on the grass.

"I have to know the hitters," said Brooks, "and that actually governs my position. However, it should be kept in mind that more balls go by a third baseman on his left than on his right."

This is why a third baseman has to think ahead on every play. What will he do with the ball when he gets it? Hesitating for even a split-second can make the runner safe at a base or allow him to score a run. So, he must think over each play before it happens.

"Although some second basemen and shortstops shift positions as much as 20 or 30 feet for certain batters," explained Robinson, "I rarely shift more than a yard to either side of my normal position. I move back on pull hitters and forward when I expect a bunt. Of course, when my shortstop plays close to second base for a left-handed pull hitter, I will move over toward the hole."

With a bunt in order and a runner on first base, the third baseman will move in on the grass a step or two as the pitcher delivers the ball.

With men on first and second, the third baseman has a real judgment play on a bunt, considered by many to be the toughest play at his position. He has to decide whether to charge the ball or go back to the bag. I like the third baseman to be three or four feet in front of the bag, but he should not commit himself until the ball is actually

Fig. 9–4. FIELDING THE LOW GROUND BALL. By staying low, the third base-man will be able to maintain good body balance and will stay with the hops and bounces much better. By using both hands in bringing the ball into throw-ing position, he can get the proper grip on the ball (Sal Bando).

bunted. We will discuss how he should handle this bunt situation later in the chapter.

Fielding a Ground Ball

An infielder must get as low as he can when fielding ground balls. Certainly, it is easier to go up for a high hop than to go down for a grass cutter. Therefore, he must keep his glove low (Fig. 9–4).

When fielding, the third baseman must keep his eyes on the ball, not the runner. He should follow the ball right into the glove. "Have the glove open as soon as possible, facing the oncoming ball," asserted Robinson. "Do not wait until the last second."

The ball should always be fielded with both hands. By using both hands in bringing the ball into throwing position, the fielder can get the proper grip on the ball. The weight should come back on the right leg, which braces and pushes the body forward in a position to make a hard, accurate throw. Some fielders often take a hop step while throwing.

In going after a ground ball, most infielders jab step and then cross step. They try to stay as low as possible in going short distances after ground balls. By staying low, they can judge the hops or bounce of the ball better.

Generally, the fielder will have more success if he moves in toward the ball rather than lay back or back up. If he backs up, he will likely have to field the ball between hops and the ball will often play him.

On balls hit to his left, the third baseman often finds it necessary to cut in front of the shortstop and field the ball with his glove hand.

Fig. 9–5. FIELDING THE HIGH BOUNCE. The third baseman moves in and fields the high hopper with two hands. In fielding the ball above his waist, the fingers of his glove are pointing up (Don Money).

This is particularly true of slow hit balls which the shortstop finds difficult to field and throw out the runner at first.

Since he has many opportunities to start a double play, the third baseman must always be thinking in terms of "two" with runners on base and less than two outs.

The ball hit directly at the third baseman is one of his toughest plays. "I try to stay as low to the ground as possible," said Robinson. "I feel I can judge the hops or bounce of the ball better."

Hard hit ball directly at fielder

If the ball is hit right at him, he has to keep his body right in front of it so that if the ball hits his glove or any part of his body, it will drop down in front of him. Then, he has a chance to pick it up and throw the batter out. Quite often, the ball is hit so hard the third baseman does not have a chance to field it cleanly.

"If it must hit you," explained Brooks, "let it hit you, but do *not* let it get by you! Knock it down and go after it quickly. Then pick it up and throw the man out."

On hard hit balls to his right along the foul line, he has to pivot on his right foot before grabbing the ball. On hard hit balls to his left, he pivots on his left foot and crosses over to the spot where he can field the ball.

On the play to his right, the third baseman handles it pretty much like the shortstop's play to his right. He usually has a little more time, though, than the fielder has at short. This is a play that requires good

Going to the right

The third baseman should take any ball to his left which he can reach.

---

reflexes and the infielder's ability to keep his eyes on the ball. He steps to his right, reaches out and backhands the ball. He then braces on his right leg and makes the throw across the diamond (Fig. 9–6).

Using the cross-over step with his left foot, he moves quickly to his right. On this type of play, most third basemen will veer back at a 45-degree angle when they pivot, in order to be in a better position for the throw. When he gets in front of the ball, he braces with his right leg and gets low to the ground. If he does not have to reach out and backhand the ball, he should pick it up with two hands, in front of the right leg. He throws off his planted rear foot with an overhand motion for the long throw.

Going to the left We tell our third basemen to take any ball to their left they can reach because this usually is an easier play for them than for the shortstop. A third baseman has a shorter throw to first base and is going with the throw. However, if the grounder is hit fairly hard and cannot be reached in a balanced position, the third baseman should let it go through to the shortstop.

The fielder starts his move to the left by using the cross-over step. He must not raise his pivot foot too high. As he moves over and in

Fig. 9–6. GOING TO THE RIGHT. Using the cross-over step with his left foot, he moves quickly to his right. If he can get in front of the ball, he picks it up with two hands, in front of the right leg. He throws off his planted right foot with an overhand motion for the long throw (Brooks Robinson).

Fig. 9–7. GAME–SAVING PLAY. With runners on first and second, Junior Gilliam performed the fielding gem of the 1965 World Series. On a ball hit sharply down the line, Gilliam made a sensational backhand stab, spun around and tagged third base.

front of the ball, he should be low to the ground, grabbing the ball with both hands if he can. He must be sure to keep the open face of the glove toward the ball. Since his momentum is still going to the left, he places his right foot behind the left and steps off the right foot in the direction of first base. He makes a sidearm to three-quarter delivery to first base (Fig. 9–8).

Once in a while there will be a play in which the third baseman will attempt to field the ball and just get the top of his glove in it and not come up with it. However, I still feel a coach has to tell his third baseman to go ahead and get everything he can. If he does boot one or two of these plays a year, it is still better than staying back on balls which the shortstop will not have adequate time to field.

To be aggressive, a third baseman must try to get everything to his left. However, the shortstop might yell the third baseman off if he feels he is in better position to field and throw the ball. This does not happen very often, though, because a third baseman will usually be in a better throwing position than the shortstop. He has a shorter

Fig. 9–8. GOING TO THE LEFT. The third baseman should take any ball to his left he can reach. He starts his move by using the cross-over step. After fielding the ball, he places his right foot behind the left and steps off the right foot in the direction of first base (Sal Bando).

throw to first base and is going with the throw. Therefore, he should get everything he can reach.

The slow roller   Most big league third basemen rate the slow roller down the line as the toughest play at their position. This is the unexpected slow hit ball which comes as a result of a bunt or a topped ball. Hours of practice must be spent in order to learn the play properly. Those who cannot make this play will be in for a lot of bunting.

Fig. 9–9. SLOW ROLLER: TWO–HAND PICKUP. Coming in quickly, the third baseman fields the ball with both hands. In this series, Brooks Robinson is shown fielding the ball with his right foot forward. As he comes down with his left, he moves the ball up into throwing position.

The speed of the ball and the closeness of the play determine whether the third baseman uses his glove or his bare hand to scoop up the ball. Although the one-hand technique is an exciting and picturesque play to watch, most bunts and slow hit balls should be fielded with two hands because there is less likelihood that the ball will be fumbled.

Young third basemen should employ the two-hand technique whenever possible, and resort to the one-hander only in "do-or-die" situations when the split-second speed of the one-hand pickup is demanded.

To make plays barehanded, an infielder will need good, relaxed hands as well as excellent fielding facilities. The barehanded play has its place but it can be overdone.

Coming in quickly, the third baseman fields the slow roller with both hands. In Figure 9–9, Robinson is shown fielding the ball with his right foot forward. As he comes down with his left, he moves the ball up into throwing position and makes the throw while straightening up on his right foot. The arm swings up and across his chest for a sidearm throw to first base.

When he is able to field the ball with his left foot forward, he merely takes one step onto his right foot and makes his throw off

Two-hand pickup

Fig. 9–9. (Continued) Robinson maintains a fairly wide stance as he fields the ball. This gives him the necessary balance in throwing off his right foot and making a hard, accurate throw. The arm swings up and across his chest for a sidearm-to-overhand flip to first base.

the right foot. This footwork is particularly effective when he has to hurry his throw.

If he wants to field the ball with just his gloved hand, he should pick up the ball off his left foot. Then he makes the throw while straightening up on his right foot. A good follow-through is essential.

One-hand pick-up The third baseman races in as quickly as possible. His eyes are squarely on the ball. He places his left or right foot down close to the ball (whichever comes natural). In Figure 9–10, this happens to be his left foot. As this foot comes down, Robinson's bare hand comes in contact with the ball. His leg bends in order to get his body low to the ground. Notice that Brooks's hand is open and acts like a cup, letting the ball roll into it. Moving his right foot forward, he goes into throwing position by pushing off his right leg to make the throw to first.

"The slow hit ball should be fielded on the run," says Robinson, "and in front of or just outside the right foot. I like to have the ball roll into the palm of my bare hand while I have my left foot forward. I will then make the throw as I step onto my right foot.

"Always field a bunt with your glove," said Robinson, "unless it is coming to a stop or has stopped. That is the only time you should use your bare hand."

Fig. 9–10. SLOW ROLLER: ONE–HAND PICKUP. Third baseman Brooks Robinson races in with his eyes on the ball. As his left foot comes down, his bare hand comes in contact with the ball. His left leg bends in order to get his body low to the ground.

The third baseman should throw overhand to first base whenever possible. An overhand throw is generally faster and more accurate than other types of throws. It carries better and is also easier to handle. Sidearm throws have a tendency to sail away and down. However, the sidearm and snap underhand throws are used in making the double play at second base and when moving in quickly to field a slow roller. When the fielder has to go into the hole toward second base to field the ball, sometimes he has to throw across his body to make the play. When he has plenty of time, though, the third baseman should throw from a three-quarter to directly overhand delivery.

One of the biggest mistakes of young players is to just "lollipop" the ball over to first base. Thinking they have a lot of time, they want to be so careful with the ball, so they let go with a mediocre half throw, instead of turning the ball loose. This is the ball they are more likely to throw away than the one with something on it.

"When fielding a grounder, practice bringing yourself into position immediately to throw overhand," asserted Robinson. "When you can do this without wasting any time, you will be a better third baseman."

The third baseman has five different ways of throwing:

1. Overhand (on balls hit directly to him, to the right or to deep third)
2. Sidearm (in making the double play and when fielding bunts)

Throwing

Fig. 9–10. (Continued) Moving his right foot forward, Robinson goes into throwing position by pushing off his right leg. Although he comes over the top with an overhand flip on the run, he often whips the ball sidearm across his body.

Fig. 9–11. CORRECT GRIP. Big league third basemen like Clete Boyer like to grip the ball across the seams for proper rotation, carry and accuracy. The top two fingers are spread, and the pressure is on the tips of the fingers.

3. Underhand (in fielding bunts)
4. Fielding ball with bare hand, jumping and throwing off right foot
5. On the ball hit slowly to his left, he throws either underhand, sidearm or overhand, depending on the position in which the ball is fielded.

Grip (Fig. 9–11)   Most big league third basemen favor gripping the ball across the seams for proper rotation, carry and accuracy. The first two fingers are on top, the thumb underneath, with the third finger along the side of the ball. The first two fingers are slightly spread across the seams, with the pressure on the balls of the fingertips.

Throwing technique   As stated before, I recommend that the third baseman throw overhand to first base whenever he can. It might often be easier to use a sidearm motion, but an overhand throw is generally faster and certainly more accurate.

When throwing to first base, the fielder usually has time to crowhop before making the throw. He will hop forward on his right foot, push off it and step forward on his left as he throws. This maneuver enables him to get more time to grip the ball, and by transferring the weight back to his rear leg, he can push off with greater power.

The following key principles apply to throwing:

1. The throwing arm should be away from the body so that the ball can be brought back and thrown in one continuous motion.

2. The elbow should come back first, while the forearm lays back from the elbow.

3. Bring the arm, wrist and right hand forward, with the elbow leading.

4. Keep your arm loose and snap it forward like a whip as the throw is made.

5. Use powerful wrist action with the wrist rolling over just as the ball is released off the ends of the first two fingers.

6. Execute a good follow-through with the body to get the proper power behind the throw.

In making the double play, the third baseman must give the pivot man the ball quickly, about letter-high over the base. If possible, he should lead the second baseman to the bag by throwing a step in front of him on the first base side of second base. A young infielder should *not* concentrate on throwing directly to the bag. As he picks up the ground ball, he braces on his right foot and uses a sidearm delivery across the front of the body. His elbow should move back and then quickly forward as the wrist snaps the ball toward the target.

Generally, the third baseman will take a short step toward second base, sometimes just a jab step. If the ball is to his right, he will field the ball, step and throw to second base. If the ball is directly to him

Throwing to second base (Fig. 9–12)

Fig. 9–12. THROWING TO SECOND BASE. In making the double play, the third baseman must give the pivot man the ball quickly, about letter-high over the bag. As he picks up the ground ball, he braces on his right foot and uses a sidearm delivery across the front of the body. Generally, the fielder will take a short jab step toward second base.

or to his left, he will step with his right foot toward second base, either in front of or behind his left foot, depending upon the angle at which he receives the ball. Then, he steps with his left striding foot and completes his throw. This enables him to put something into his throw. Those with strong arms often can throw without stepping, but this is not recommended for the young player or the fielder with an average throwing arm.

Making the double play

With the bases loaded, the third baseman has several ways to make the double play. If he is near enough to his base when he fields the ball, he should step on third, and then relay the ball to second or first. This route is the easiest. But if there are none out, and the situation warrants it, he should try to make the first out at the plate, by throwing to the catcher. With one out, he can forget about the man going home and start the double play by throwing to second, which is the shorter throw.

With a man on first, or men on first and second, he should always go for the double play starting at second base.

The Bunt Situation

With a runner at first and the sacrifice on, the third baseman comes in a couple of steps on the grass; then, as the hitter squares around, he charges in a little more. When the batter drops his bat, he starts toward the plate for a bunt.

Most offensive teams in this situation will make the first baseman field the ball because they know the third baseman is right up there close. If they bunt the ball down to the third baseman, he may force the man out at second base, or even make a double play.

So, most big league managers say, "Make the first baseman field the ball." Therefore, with a man on first, the third baseman does not have as many good chances to field the bunt.

In a bunt situation with men on first and second, it becomes a judgment play for the third baseman. He must decide whether to move in to field the ball or return to the bag and let the pitcher handle it. Ideally, of course, he would like the pitcher to play the ball so that a force play can be made at third base. I like him to be three or four feet in front of the bag. The important point is for him *not to commit himself too soon*. He must stay there until the ball is bunted. He must be ready to come in or go back to the bag.

"The third baseman must know his pitcher," said Brooks, "that is, how much ground he can cover. I like to angle my stance so I can see the runner on second as well as the batter. I will take a step or two in as the ball is bunted and decide who can make the play. If the pitcher can field the ball, I will cover third base by placing my right foot against the base.

"If it is a hard bunt, I will yell the pitcher off and field the ball and make my throw to first base," continued Brooks. "If it is the pitcher's ball, I will keep my mouth shut and cover third base. The catcher will

Fig. 9–13. TAGGING THE RUNNER. Bringing his glove down quickly in front of the base, the third baseman looks for the runner's foot, then tags it with the back of his glove. Never place the glove in the runner's path with the ball exposed in the glove. This is a good way to have it kicked out (Aurelio Rodriguez).

then control the pitcher and yell at him whether to throw to 'third' or 'first.' "

We do about three different things in a bunt situation. The old-fashioned way is for the pitcher to make the pitch and break toward the third base foul line. The third baseman has to stand there and wait and see if the ball is bunted hard enough to get by the pitcher. If the pitcher cannot get it, he must charge the ball and make the play to first base. Of course, this is exactly what the offense *wants* the third baseman to do: field the ball.

However, from the defensive standpoint, the pitcher has to get over there in time to field the ball. Then, the third baseman has to go back to third base and make the force play at third.

In this same bunt situation, we may signal for a different type of execution, for example, if there is a slow runner on first base and the pitcher is at bat. We will have our third baseman ignore the runner and just charge in for the ball. We are gambling that the third baseman will get the ball.

We tell our pitcher to cover the pitching area. The first baseman covers the area in front of him, and the third baseman is going to charge in. Then, if the ball is bunted toward third, the third baseman may have time to go to second for the double play.

The third possibility has the shortstop covering third base. With the third baseman charging in, the shortstop will move over to third for the force play.

This is one reason why the bunt defense is so tough today, why it is more difficult to get a man over than it used to be. Many clubs have the shortstop go to third in a bunt situation, and the baseman goes ahead and charges in.

On throws from the right side of the diamond, most third basemen like to straddle the bag, facing second base, with their feet on either side of the base, an inch or two behind the front edge. Many like to bring the glove down in front of the base and then look for the runner's foot, tagging it with the back of the glove.

Other Plays at Third

Tagging the runner (Fig. 9–13)

In taking throws from the catcher, the fielder should also straddle the bag. His left foot is placed on the left field line but he turns his body a quarter-turn to the right so he can face the catcher's throw. Bringing the glove down quickly in front of the bag, he looks for the runner's foot. Some infielders like to tag the runner with both hands, providing they can catch the ball with both hands.

Cutoffs

On base hits to left field, the third baseman acts as the cutoff man for the throw to the plate. The cutoff position on the play is in direct line from the left fielder to the catcher and between the mound and the third base foul line. It depends, of course, on where the ball is hit. He listens to the catcher for directions whether to cut off the ball and throw to a particular base or home, or let it go.

We prefer the cutoff position to be a little deep, so that the fielder can move toward the ball in order to make any necessary adjustments. The ball definitely should be caught on the fly or on the big hop. There is nothing more disgusting than to see a throw come in all the way from the outfield and have the cutoff man just stand there as the ball travels 200 feet and hits on a short hop. By taking one step forward or backward, he could make an easy catch.

So, we prefer him to start closer to the plate so he can go into the ball. Then, when he cuts the ball off, he is in a better position to throw to second base or elsewhere.

While the third baseman takes the cutoff throw, the shortstop covers third base.

On throws to third from the outfield, the third baseman should assist the cutoff man (shortstop). If the throw is wide, or if there is no play, he calls, "Cut!" If he thinks the runner can be caught, he does not call.

Covering and backing up

The third baseman covers third base in almost all play situations. On a hard hit ball to left field with a runner on second, he will act as the cutoff man for the throw to the plate.

On throws from right field, the third baseman backs up second base unless he has a possible play at third. He also backs up the pitcher on throws from the first baseman.

When both the shortstop and second baseman go for a fly ball with no one on base, it is the third baseman's job to cover second. In this case, the catcher moves down to cover third.

Catching pop flies

I want my third baseman to take any questionable ball between third and home plate. He should call for any ball he can reach. This is because he is coming in and has a better angle than the catcher does in going out. He should "run" the catcher off on any pop fly he can handle. He should always call for the ball in a loud, clear voice.

On fly balls back of the infield, he should keep going back without calling for the ball until the outfielder calls him off the play. All pop flies hit directly behind the first and third basemen should be the responsibility of the second baseman and the shortstop.

On a foul fly close to the grandstand fence, he should follow the same technique as explained for the first baseman. He should move to the fence as quickly as possible. Then, after locating the ball, he can move back to the spot where it will come down.

Run-down plays

On run-down plays between third and home, the third baseman should get the ball to the catcher in plenty of time to keep the man from scoring. Then, it is the catcher's job to drive the runner back toward third base.

The fewer throws made the better, in these run-down situations. The catcher should run the base runner as hard as he can toward third. As soon as the third baseman moves into the play, the catcher tosses him the ball about chest-high, and he places the tag on the runner. Actually, one throw should be all that is necessary.

The catcher and third baseman must be on the *inside* of the base runner, keeping the runner on one side. They should *never* let him bisect their view or throwing procedure.

Pick-off plays at third

With a runner on third, the third baseman and the catcher should have a signal when a pick-off play is in order. There is usually a pitchout on this play. The third baseman must wait until the catcher receives the ball before he breaks for the bag.

Practice Tips

1. Spend 15 minutes daily picking up ground balls.
2. Practice continually at fielding the slow roller properly, and use two hands whenever possible.
3. During your daily ground ball session, field many balls going both to your left and to your right.
4. Do not make any long throws until your arm is completely loose and warmed-up.
5. Devote considerable time to perfecting throws of all kinds. This work will not only strengthen your arm, but give you the necessary accuracy.
6. Have your coach hit plenty of hard ground balls directly at you. *This is one of your toughest plays.*
7. Have your coach hit pop flies regularly to you.

Drill

The Slow Roller (one-hand pick-up) The third baseman should place four or five balls on the ground halfway between the pitcher's box and the foul line and halfway between third and home. He should run in as hard as he can, pick up a ball with his bare hand and underhand it to first. Then, he should go back and repeat the procedure with the second ball, then the third and fourth.

The Outfielder /10/

The outstanding outfielder is a great asset to his team, just like the slugger at the plate and the star pitcher on the mound. The jump he gets on the ball, his speed, the manner in which he plays grounders and the intelligent throws he makes back to the infield prevent the opponents from scoring runs. A bobble, a slow return or an inaccurate throw are all enough to give the hitter an extra base, and the difference between a runner on first and a runner on second can mean the ball game.

No wonder Lefty Gomez, the former pitching great of the New York Yankees, once admitted: "I owe my pitching success to clean living and a fast outfield."

The Essentials

To be a good outfielder, a player should have speed and the ability to get a good jump on the ball. I like a fellow who can judge the ball, an aggressive individual who wants to get to the ball as soon as possible. I do not care for a loafer. Some players have the knack of more or less knowing where the ball is going the instant it leaves the bat. As soon as that ball is hit, they are off and running.

The outfielder with an average arm who can field and throw the ball quickly and accurately will make just as many assists as the fellow who has a great arm but has to take a couple more steps to get rid of the ball. This latter individual always catches the ball on the wrong side and, consequently, takes longer to throw it. Actually, it is a simple thing to catch the ball on one's throwing side and having his body in position to throw.

I just get the biggest thrill when I see a guy warming-up in the bull-pen and a pitcher in a jam, and I make a catch to keep him in the ball game, and he goes on to win.

JIMMY PIERSALL

An outfielder has to have a little bit of "infield" in him. There are times when the winning run is on second base in the late innings and a ground ball goes through the middle. He must come in and charge that ball, pick it up and throw it as an infielder would. He must get rid of it quickly.

Getting the jump on the ball is mostly a matter of habit, and an outfielder will master it only if he practices constantly. The more a player plays the outfield, the better he will be able to judge every fly ball.

A good outfielder must continually be alert and on his toes, especially with men on base. He must always be thinking ahead, and should know what he will do if the ball is hit to him. Indeed, ball games are often won or lost on the judgment of the outfielder on a throw to the right base, or to the wrong base.

An outfielder should be a good hitter with adequate power, plus throwing and fielding ability. If he can swing the bat and has a strong enough arm, constant practice on fly balls and grounders should make him a respectable fielder.

Fig. 10–2. WILLIE THE ROBBER. Center fielder Willie Davis of the Los Angeles Dodgers makes a one-handed leaping catch of Boog Powell's long drive in a 1965 World Series game at Baltimore. Exceptional running speed is the key to greatness in the center fielder. He must be a quick starter in any direction.

Check every pennant-winning team, and you will find a deer-footed "fly-chaser" in center field.

BOBBY BRAGAN

Great fly chasers

Down through the years, major league baseball has seen many truly outstanding fielders, but the matchless Joe DiMaggio was perhaps the finest of all. His speed and grace in fading back at the crack of the bat for a long drive enabled him to make outfielding look simple. He was a model of grace and skill as he roamed center field. He had everything—anticipation, speed, great hands, throwing power and accuracy.

There have been numerous fielding standouts of the Dodgers who have won the admiration and respect of fans in Los Angeles, and back in Brooklyn. For judging the ball, Ron Fairly would have to be recognized, while for speed, I have to say Willie Davis.

Carl Furillo, unquestionably, had the strongest throwing arm. He not only charged balls well, but he had an excellent throwing arm. Carl played the right field wall as it should be played, and got rid of the ball as quickly as anyone I have seen. Runners were very careful when they made a base hit to right field because Carl often threw back to the first baseman so quickly the runner was caught off base.

What was the greatest fielding play during my managerial career with the Dodgers? Although it is rather difficult to pick out one particular fielding gem, the most famous would have to be Sandy Amoros's great catch in the 1955 World Series against the Yankees. The fact that it came at such an opportune time made it an even greater catch than it actually was. Yogi Berra, the batter, was pretty much a pull hitter. Yet, on this particular pitch, he hit the ball to the opposite field. Amoros, our left fielder, was playing Yogi a little to left center, and he had to run "a country mile" for the ball.

The great part of the catch, to me, was the fact that he was getting so close to the fence. For everyone in the ball park, it was a question whether he was going to bang into the fence or not. Well, Sandy kept on going and that fence did not "back him off" any. He made the catch, stopped quickly, and with amazing agility, turned and threw back toward the infield. Even though Amoros was never known to have a good arm, he got rid of the ball very quickly. He hit Reese, our shortstop, in the cutoff, and Pee Wee made the return throw to first base for the double play. This play got us out of the one serious spot we were in.

Qualifications

The prime requisites for a competent outfielder are good fielding, a strong arm and powerful hitting. From there on, the qualifications of the three positions are judged on the basis of the duties to be performed.

Generally, if he has three outfielders, the coach would put the fielder with the weakest arm in left field. The strongest arm would go to right field because the throw to third base is longer. The center fielder would very likely be the best outfielder of the trio. This is the guy who covers the most ground and is more or less the captain of the outfield. He takes all the fly balls that he can reach. However, I think that center field is possibly the easiest field to play because balls hit to center field do not have the slice or hook on them that they do to left field. Any ball hit by a right-handed batter down the line is likely to have a hook on it, and it will go toward the line. The left-handed hitter who swings late on the ball will also cause the ball to slice toward the left field foul line.

Speed can be the great equalizer. Even if they misjudge the ball slightly, fly chasers like Paul Blair and Reggie Smith can make up for it with their exceptional speed. Speed can overcome some of the mistakes of judgment.

Left field

The left fielder needs reasonable speed and a good arm, and he must have the ability to judge curving line drives. Because the left fielder has the most difficult plays to make on balls hit to his right, the right-handed thrower has the advantage, since he is in a better position to make the throws after fielding the ball.

Center field

The center fielder should be the top outfielder because he has the most territory to cover. Exceptional running speed is the key to greatness in a center fielder. He must cover the maximum ground to his right and left, and in order to do this successfully, he must be a quick starter in any direction.

The center fielder must have a strong throwing arm. He should be a roamer, always alert and ready to race back for the long drives and to dash in for the short ones.

Right field

The player with the best arm should be placed in right field for double protection. He must guard against the scoring play from third to home, and against the all-important man on first going to third on a single.

The art of hitting behind the runner, when successful, enables a runner on first to reach third base on a single. This factor emphasizes the need for the strongest possible arm in right field to protect against this extra base.

Stance

The outfielder should use a comfortable stance, one that enables him to go in either direction with the quickest possible speed (Fig. 10–3). Using a semi-crouch, he positions his right foot slightly back, with his hands on or in front of the knees. His toes are pointed slightly out to move laterally as quickly as possible.

Fig. 10–3. STANCE. The outfielder should use a comfortable stance. He uses a semicrouch, with his hands on or in front of the knees. He is set, but not tense, and always alert. As the pitch is made, the fielder rocks forward on his toes and is ready to cross over in either direction with the quickest possible speed (Paul Blair).

"An outfielder should use a stance that he prefers and which gives him confidence," said Pete Reiser, former great Dodger outfielder and for years a successful coach. "Through confidence, he will relax, which is so necessary in obtaining quick starts. I like a stance which has one shoulder nearer the batter than the other. Generally speaking, a right-handed thrower will have his left shoulder pointing more to the batter, and vice versa with left-handed outfielders."

As the pitch is made, the fielder rocks forward on his toes, ready to move in any direction. It is just a matter of shifting the weight off the heels and relaxing. He is ready to cross over either way.

Glove

The majority of big league outfielders recommend a long-fingered glove with considerable webbing and a deep pocket. While infielders must catch the ball and throw it quickly, outfielders are not required to do this. They prefer a deeper-pocketed glove in order to make any necessary one-handed catches.

"Learn to catch the ball in the webbing," said Reiser, "and it will not jump or slide out. I more or less like to trap a ball like a first baseman would, making the catch in the web, instead of in the pocket."

Hank Aaron, an accomplished glove man as well as a brilliant hitter, also prefers a soft, long-fingered glove, and stated: "It enables me to scoop up ground balls better. I can make the catch in either the pocket or the web."

Playing the Hitters

Every good outfielder I have known was good not only because of his abilities, but because he knew where to play each batter. Three major factors determine how the outfielder will play a hitter:

1. The batter
2. The pitcher
3. The game situation.

Fig. 10–4. CALLING FOR THE BALL. As soon as he is sure he can catch the ball, the outfielder must call for the ball, "I've got it!" "I've got it!" In turn, the other fielder should answer in a loud, clear voice, "Take it!" "Take it!" Below, two outfielders are shown communicating with each other.

The outfielder has to know who is on base at all times, and must try to remember the speed of the base runners.

Usually the outfield shifts as a unit, so there are no gaping holes between them. If there is a right-handed hitter at the plate, the left and center fielders move over toward the left and deeper than their normal straightaway positions. The right fielder moves toward center field and a little closer to the plate.

The outfielder should study every batter to learn his hitting habits. To do so, he watches his opponents in batting practice, analyzing each batter, i.e., long ball hitters, off-speed hitters, pull hitters, late or straightaway hitters. Since his pitcher and catcher also will know the batter's habits, they will throw to him accordingly.

During the game, various factors will determine how the outfielder will shift his position. When the double or triple will hurt his team, he will play deeper. He must gamble at times and play shallow when the winning run is on second base, in order to throw out the base runner at the plate.

The type of hitter is probably the biggest factor in determining the position of the fielders, plus the score of the game.

An outfielder will shift according to the count on the hitter. If it is two and nothing, or three and one, he plays deeper and more around to pull. If there are two strikes on the hitter, he does not play quite so deep.

Some coaches have their outfielders take a sign from the shortstop or second baseman for the coming pitch. For the infielders to relay signs to the outfield is mostly a thing of the past.

Calling for the Ball

Outfielders should help each other by calling in a loud and clear voice for all fly balls (Fig. 10–4). As soon as he is absolutely sure he can catch the ball, the fielder must call for the ball, "I've got it!," "I've got it!" and keep on calling. He should call more than once because the other fielder may be yelling at the same time. He should be answered in a loud clear voice, "Take it!," "Take it!" They must talk back and forth. Whenever I hear two fielders communicating with each other, I know that there is not going to be a collision. So, remember to repeat calls, and to answer them.

Calling for the ball too soon is sometimes dangerous in the outfield. There are so many balls hit between the outfield and the infield, that if a fielder calls for the ball before he is absolutely sure, it can lead to trouble, particularly in windblown Candlestick Park. Quite often, an outfielder will call for the ball and the other fielder will answer, "Take it." Now the responsibility is with the one who made the call, and even if the wind takes hold of the ball, he has to stay with it and make the catch.

On long drives near the fences, the outfielders should tell each other how much room there is near the fences and where to make the throw. One may call out: "Lots of room, you take it," if a ball can still be caught.

In calling for the ball, a center fielder, for example, may use his right hand to motion his left fielder away from the area. The same practice should prevail when an infielder and an outfielder are both involved in a play. In this case, the outfielder runs the infielder off the play whenever he can. It is usually an easier catch for him, since he is coming into the infield and the play is in front of him.

Catching the Ball

An outfielder should catch every fly ball with two hands, unless it becomes necessary to catch it with one hand. Using two hands will enable the outfielder to have his throwing hand on the ball just as soon as he catches it. This is particularly true on ground balls, when he has to charge the ball and make a quick throw.

I have observed that the best place to catch a routine fly ball is above eye-level (Fig. 10–5). If he can, the fielder should catch the ball facing it, in a stride position. The glove should be up in front of his face and on his throwing side. Youngsters should not try to make fancy catches—the simpler, the better.

We often think of the belt, or sometimes the chest, being the dividing line. On any balls above the belt, the fingers are up, while on balls below the belt, the fingers are down. While Willie Mays's basket catch has been effective for him, I would not recommend this technique for the majority of players.

Good outfielders will learn to catch balls both ways. Usually, when a fielder comes in hard for a fly ball or line drive, he will catch the ball with fingers down; when going back or handling a big drive, he will catch the ball with fingers up. Handling balls between these two areas is a matter of preference and confidence.

The outfielder should learn to run immediately to the spot where he thinks the ball will go, and wait for it. Some fielders like to thrill the fans by drifting on the ball, making their catches on the run. Joe DiMaggio had a style that all fielders should try to emulate. He made them all look easy.

The outfielder should run on his toes, since running on the heels makes the ball "dance." By running on his toes, he will make a smooth approach to the ball and eliminate the dancing ball.

An outfielder should catch the ball on his throwing side whenever possible, with the body in position to throw. If he is right-handed, he should keep his left foot forward.

True, the great arm does not always make it possible to throw out the runner. However, the player who fields and throws the ball quickly and accurately will make just as many assists as the fellow who has to take a couple of extra steps in order to get rid of the ball. In the latter case, he is always catching the ball on the wrong side, thus taking longer to throw it. Actually, it is a simple matter for an outfielder to catch the ball on his throwing side and have his body in position to throw.

As the ball starts to settle into the glove, there should be a slight give of the outfielder's hands and wrists. This softens the impact of the ball when it hits the glove.

The fielder should be relaxed when he makes the catch. The arms should be extended, thumbs together, and his hands loose. He should not try to "box" the ball.

Coming in for a low fly ball (Fig. 10–6)

Most major league center fielders rate low line drives the toughest balls to handle. These balls tend to sink rapidly. Some veer away from

Fig. 10–5. CATCHING A HIGH FLY BALL. An outfielder should catch every fly ball with two hands, if at all possible. He should try to be facing the ball, in a stride position, and catch a routine fly ball above eye-level. His fingers are up for any balls above the belt (Jim Northrup).

the fielder. It is not only a difficult play but a dangerous one because if the fielder does not get the ball, it will go through him and allow the hitter to get an extra base or two.

The best way to play the low liner is to wait an instant before moving. Then the fielder will have a better idea whether to go back or forward. If it is a sinking low liner in front of him, he has two alternatives: 1) hold up and catch the ball on a long hop, or 2) continue in for a possible shoestring catch. If he charges and goes for it, he should try to lower his body as he comes in to get his eyes as much in line with the ball as possible. If the fielder decides not to try for it, he should shorten his steps and try to get his feet together and his body under complete control. He gets his glove quickly down in front of the ball, the fingers pointing down. His prime concern is keeping the ball in front of him, and if he has to, he will block the ball with his body.

The low liner which is particularly troublesome is the one on which the fielder has to go to his right and move in to make a low catch, reaching across his body. If the fielder, for instance, is a right-handed thrower, and the glove hand is on his left side, he must go to his right and in, at full speed, and catch the low drive as he reaches across his body. This play often becomes a shoestring catch, which is, indeed, a tough play.

Generally, an outfielder will not attempt a shoestring catch unless the winning run will cross the plate on a base hit in the late innings of a game. He should be very careful in attempting this type of catch. Mickey Stanley, who has made countless game-saving catches

Fig. 10–6. CATCHING A LOW FLY BALL. In catching the ball below the belt, the fingers of the outfielder should be pointed down. The dependable fly-chaser uses two hands whenever he can. As he follows the ball into his glove, there should be a slight "give" of his hands and wrists (Jose Cardenal).

Fig. 10–7. GOING TO THE RIGHT. Whenever an outfielder moves laterally, he should use the cross-over step. He breaks for the ball by pivoting on the foot nearest the ball and crosses over with the other foot. In going to his right, he brings his left leg over his right and shoves off with his right foot (Bill Russell).

Fig. 10–8. GOING TO THE LEFT. A good push-off in the direction he is going is essential in getting the proper jump on the ball. In moving laterally, the outfielder uses his natural running motion (Bill Russell).

during his outstanding career with the Detroit Tigers, said: "To make a diving catch, stay relaxed, double-up and roll as you hit the ground. Tuck your chin and one shoulder in and roll over. By doing this, you can usually come right up on your feet and be in position to make a throw."

The cross-over step is recommended whenever an outfielder has to move laterally. It should be kept in mind that all balls going to left and right field have a tendency to break toward the foul lines. For instance, a right-handed hitter will often get out in front of the ball and give it a counterclockwise spin, and the ball will hook around toward the left field foul line.

If the outfielder has to go to his right, he brings his left leg over his right and shoves off with his right foot. This enables him to cover a much greater distance on his first step than if he were to lift his right foot and push off with his left (Fig. 10–7).

The fielder will get quicker starts to either side by using the cross-over step. A good push-off in the direction in which he is going is most important. He should try to run quickly to the spot where he feels the ball will come down.

By using a little wider stance, an outfielder can get a quicker start sideways. To his right, he merely pivots on his right foot, cross-steps and goes after the ball, and vice versa to his left.

Going to the left or right (Figs. 10–8 and 10–7)

A   B   C

Fig. 10–9. GOING DEEP FOR A FLY BALL. The outfielder pivots on both feet in the direction he is going and takes his first step with the foot nearest the ball (Bill Russell).

D

"Learn to put on the brakes just before you reach the ball," asserted Reiser. "Extend your left foot if you are going to your left, or your right foot if you are going to your right, and slide the last few inches as you reach the ball. By doing this, you will step as you glove the ball and be prepared to throw."

Fig. 10–10. AN OVER–THE–SHOULDER CATCH. This catch is actually not as difficult as it looks to the fan in the stands. It is very much like a football catch, in which the outfielder follows the ball all the way and into his glove (Frank Johnson).

Going back for a fly ball (Fig. 10–9)

To be a good outfielder, a player must be able to go back for a fly ball. Then he can afford to play shallower. In going deep for a fly ball, an outfielder will find his job easier if he runs to the spot where he thinks the ball will come down and wait for it. In moving back, he should make one or two quick glances over his shoulder to check on the ball's flight. By playing it this way, he will be in the proper position for the catch.

Can an outfielder go back as fast as he can forward? I do not think he can, but he certainly can improve his ability to go back through practice. The only way an outfielder can go back as fast as he can forward is when he turns his back on the ball and takes his eye off it.

While the veteran fielder can turn his back on the ball and run to the spot, the younger player should keep his eye on the ball as long as possible. With practice, he will learn to turn his back completely on the ball and run to the spot where he thinks it will fall, making one or two quick glances over his shoulder to check on the ball's flight.

We asked Willie Mays whether his famous over-the-shoulder catch was really a tough one. He answered: "I don't think so. I thought it was when I first started doing it, but I practiced it during spring training and I didn't find it too hard because actually it is just a football catch."

Theory of shallow outfield play

According to this theory, the outfielder should play as close to the infield as his fielding ability will permit. The great outfielder plays closer to the infield than the poor one, because he is able to go back better for a fly ball.

During their brilliant playing careers, Tris Speaker and Terry Moore played the shallowest center field in the game because they were

Fig. 10–11. PLAYING THE BALL NEAR THE FENCE. The outfielder turns and runs as fast as he can to the fence. Then he is ready, even if he has to come back five feet and catch it. When the fielder runs from grass to the cinders of a warning track, he will know he is nearing the fence. Above, Jim Northrup goes directly to the fence and places his hand on it for possible leverage.

masters at racing back. Blair is the best at this among fly chasers today.

Terry Moore, who gave St. Louis fans plenty of thrills when he was with the Cardinals, explained the theory this way: "If you are a center fielder, it is an advantage if you can play close and go back on a ball because the majority of the hits are hit in front of you. You have that short line drive which you can come up with, and you have the ground ball. The man is on first, and he is trying to go to third. You are in close, that ground ball is going through there and you can charge it. You can be closer to the infielder, you can be closer to your target and it is the big advantage of playing shallow. Of course, there is a certain time in the ball game when you have to move back to protect a one- or two-run lead."

While Terry's theory is still a sound one, I do believe outfield play is much deeper now than when he played over 25 years ago. I have to feel the ball is livelier, and with artificial turf, ground balls seem to "shoot through" the infield with greater speed. Therefore, outfielders have to play deeper in order to cut off ground balls up the alleys, plus the long drives off the bats of some of today's hefty sluggers.

As soon as the ball is hit, I like to see an outfielder turn and run as fast as he can to the fence. He should really *hustle* to that fence! Then he is ready, even if he has to come back five feet and catch it. That is so much better than backing up into the fence, when he is backpedaling the last four or five steps and is not sure when he will hit the fence.

Playing the fly near the fence (Fig. 10–11)

Fig. 10–12. SHADING THE SUN WITH THE GLOVE. The fielder sights the ball, either above or below the glove. His flip-down sun glasses are kept in the up-position until he must look into the sun. At this time, he merely taps the peak of his cap, which forces the glasses down (Rick Monday).

What often happens is that the fielder catches the ball one or two feet in front of the fence and then backs into the fence, and the collision knocks the ball out of his hands.

Many parks today have a "warning track" made of cinders or skinned dirt, so that when the outfielder runs from grass to cinders, he will know he is nearing the fence. If the ball is the line drive type, the fielder has to judge the distance by the warning track.

The outfielder should know how the ball will rebound from fences or walls. If a fly ball cannot be caught and hits the wall, he runs three or four steps toward the playing field and then turns around and faces the fence, ready for the rebound.

The fielder should *never* try to rush in and smother a ball that is coming off the wall. Instead, he should play back a few feet and let it show him in which direction it is going before he tries to pick it up. After he scoops up the ball, he whirls in the direction of the glove hand to make the throw.

During the pregame outfield drill, a fungo batter should hit several balls against the wall in order for the fielders to learn how to determine the manner in which they will rebound.

Playing the sun field (Fig. 10–12)

The majority of ball fields are layed out with the sun facing the right and center fielders, but occasionally the left fielder has to cope with the sun.

Catching balls hit into the sun can be very troublesome, especially for the individual who neglects to work on this important phase of outfield play. Flip-down sunglasses which reduce glare from the sun can be very beneficial to an outfielder. However, it takes practice to get used to them.

Whether sunglasses are used or not, the glove should be used to shield the eyes. If the sun is low, the fielder should hold his glove on the sun as the pitch is made. He then sights the ball, either above or below the glove, and makes the catch.

Fig. 10–13. GETTING A GOOD JUMP. Concentration on the hitter is perhaps the key to getting a good jump on the ball. By watching the ball, he sees how it comes off the bat. Paul Blair, the Orioles' fleet-footed outfielder, above, uses a cross-over step to get a quicker start laterally.

The most widely used sunglasses have an adjustable band which fits around the back of the head. The glasses are kept in the "up" position until they are to be used. When the outfielder wants to snap the glasses down to look into the sun, he merely taps the peak of his cap. This action forces the glasses down.

"I play the sun slightly to the side," said Mays. "This may make it a little more difficult because you may be overplaying a certain hitter. Even with sunglasses, I cannot play or field a ball going directly into the sun. If at all possible, I like to play the sun by sighting the ball from an angle, that is, getting a side view of it."

During spring training, we have our outfielders go out in the sun field and practice using their sunglasses and flipping them down. After practicing with them, it becomes a habit; then, when a fly ball comes out to them, they automatically knock their glasses down.

The outfielder who gets the fastest start catches the most balls. In order to do this, he must be alert and ready to move in any direction as the ball leaves the bat. Getting a jump on the ball is mostly a matter of habit, and he will master it only if he practices constantly. The good jump has to come through experience. The great outfielders have that sense of where the ball is going.

Concentration on the hitter is perhaps the key to getting a good jump on the ball (Fig. 10–13). In order to be ready to go, the fielder must get up on his toes so that the instant the ball is hit, he will make his move. Even though he is as far as 350 feet away from the plate, he should be able to tell the type of pitch as it travels toward the plate.

"When the ball is pitched," said Bill Virdon, a former great center fielder and now a coach with the Pittsburgh Pirates, "the outfielder should be in a semi-crouch, with his knees bent and the weight on the balls of his feet. He must be ready on every pitch."

"As soon as the pitcher starts his windup," continued Virdon, "he should take his eyes off him and place it on the hitter. In order to get

Getting the Jump on a Fly Ball

Getting the jump on the ball is mostly a matter of habit, and you will only get it if you practice constantly.

DOM DIMAGGIO

---

the direction the hitter is hitting the ball, he has to watch him all the way to see the general direction in which he is swinging the bat and the direction in which he might hit the ball.''

Dom DiMaggio, a truly great fly chaser when he played for the Boston Red Sox, cites six basic rules in getting a better jump on the ball:

1. Find a comfortable position
2. Be in position on every pitch
3. Know the batters, and play them accordingly
4. Do not listen—look!
5. Follow every pitch to the plate
6. Be able to tell the type of pitch.

One of DiMaggio's rules brings to mind an interesting point. Some outfielders have claimed that they could tell the direction of a ball just hit by the sound it made against the bat. This is sheer nonsense, of course! There never was an outfielder who could tell anything with his eyes shut, unless he had been skulled by a fly ball.

''A player has to be alive and be in the game,'' asserted Mays. ''He must know his pitcher and the hitter at the plate. By watching the ball, he sees how it comes off the bat. During practice and in a game, he cannot stand around in the outfield just daydreaming. He must be ready all the time, physically and mentally, and stay in the game.''

On any ball that is hit—whether it be foul, fair or whatever—if an outfielder has not made a move of any kind, then he is not in the game 100 per cent. If a manager or coach looks out toward the outfield and sees that he has not moved, he had better tell him to start moving and bear down.

One of the toughest balls to get a good jump on is the line drive directly at the outfielder. For awhile, he does not know whether the ball is the sinker type that will drop in front of him or the one that is hit extremely well with a little backspin and that keeps on rising as it goes. The worst thing that can happen is for the fielder to charge the ball and have it go over his head.

The difficult aspect of the ball hit directly at the fielder is that he has no side view of it. It is like an individual watching a train coming at him. He cannot see how fast the train is going if he is standing on the tracks, but if he gets off to the side, he can tell. A fly ball presents practically the same problem. The fielder cannot tell immediately how hard the ball is hit.

Backing up　Outfielders have a key responsibility in backing up thrown balls to the bases and balls hit to the infielders and other outfielders. If possible,

Never lag behind on a ground ball—charge, get set and make the throw.

DOM DIMAGGIO

they run to a point behind and in line with the fielder and the player who is hitting or throwing the ball.

The left fielder backs up second on all plays from the right side. He backs up third on all bunts, pick-offs and run-downs. He should back up third when a bunted ball is played to first base for a possible return throw to third. The center fielder backs up second on all bunts and plays at that bag. The right fielder backs up first on all bunts, pick-off plays and throws made there. He backs up second on all throws from the left side. On run-downs between first and second, he should move in quickly and back up first base.

Fielding Ground Balls

The outfielder fields ground balls in much the same manner as an infielder. Unfortunately, however, very few outfielders spend enough practice time picking up grounders. As a rule, I doubt if they devote enough practice to charging grounders, in which they have to field the ball and throw it quickly and accurately. This is something that has to become a *habit.* There is no question but that the majority of errors by outfielders occur on ground balls.

When no quick throw is necessary, he may field the ball with his heels together, or he may drop to one knee to block the ball (Fig.

Fig. 10–14. BLOCKING A HARD GROUND BALL. The outfielder tries to play all ground balls in front of his body. Here, Jim Northrup drops to one knee to block the ball. Using two hands, his eyes follow the ball into his glove.

Fig. 10–15. FIELDING A GROUND BALL. An outfielder must never lag behind on ground balls. He must charge the ball, pick it up and make an overhand throw. Fielding the ball with two hands enables the fielder to move into throwing position faster than if he went down with just his glove hand (Bill Russell).

10–14). If the fielder is trying to throw out an advancing runner, he has to charge the ball and either play it with both hands (Fig. 10–15) or scoop it up with his glove hand and then throw (Fig. 10–16).

The fielder should approach and field ground balls to his left or right in a semicircle, fielding them in front, at the maximum height of the bounce. By bending his knees, he will be able to stay low and follow the ball all the way into his glove. His weight is transferred to the right foot with a hop. Outfielders, as well as infielders, should remember to *play the ball, and not let the ball play them.*

"Never lag behind on ground balls," advised Stanley. "Even before the play begins, you should know where the throw is to be made. Charge in, then get set and make your throw. When I played sandlot ball, I was an infielder, and I often was puzzled why outfielders would wait for grounders to come to them. I thought if they would charge a ball the way we do in the infield, they would be twice as good."

Stanley's observation about outfielders not charging grounders is a good one. This is why I believe an outfielder has to have a little bit of an "infield instinct" in him. There are times in the late innings when the winning run is on second and a grounder will go through the middle. This is the time when an outfielder must come in and charge that ball, pick it up and throw it as an infielder would. He has to get rid of the ball quickly. Fielding the ball with both hands will enable the fielder to move into throwing position faster than if he went down with his glove hand.

If he fumbles the ball or it gets by him, the outfielder must hustle after it, *keeping in mind that the runner is running.*

Throwing the Ball

One of baseball's most thrilling plays occurs when an outfielder makes a perfect toss into a base or home plate and nips the runner who is sliding in. Base runners soon learn to respect the fielders

Fig. 10–16. FIELDING A GROUNDER WITH ONE HAND. When they have to pick up a grounder quickly in an attempt to throw out a runner, some outfielders, like Ron Fairly of the Montreal Expos, feel they can make the play more quickly by using a glove-hand pickup. Young players, however, will find that fielding the ball with both hands is not only safer but probably just as fast.

who have the real "shotguns" in the outfield—fellows like Roberto Clemente, Reggie Jackson and Al Kaline.

The main factors in throwing from the outfield are accuracy, a strong arm and ability to get rid of the ball as soon as possible. This does not mean, however, that the fielder should rush his delivery and try to get too much on the ball. By hurrying his throw too much, he will very likely miss the cutoff man, which is the worst thing that can happen.

The overhand delivery, in which the ball is held across the seams, is recommended for all outfielders because of the carry and accuracy it provides. In addition to good backspin, the ball does not veer sideways when thrown overhand.

In addition, the low throw has a better chance of being accurate, and will not lose as much momentum as the one with high arc on it. I believe the use of artificial turf will encourage more outfielders to make low throws.

An outfielder should try to get into throwing position while fielding the ball. Just before the ball comes down, he moves into it with his body in proper position to throw. Therefore, the ball should be caught as his left foot comes down on the ground.

Throwing technique (Fig. 10–17)

On a routine fly ball, I like him to stay back of the ball two or three steps, so that he is coming *into* the ball to catch it. As he catches the ball, the weight is shifted to the pivot foot (the right foot, if he is right-handed). The striding foot points in the direction of the throw and the body moves forward against the braced front leg.

The throwing arm is away from the body so that he can bring the ball back and throw it in one continuous motion. The elbow comes back first, and the forearm lays back from the elbow. Then, as the

The main thing in throwing from the outfield is accuracy, a strong arm and getting rid of the ball as soon as possible.

HANK BAUER

elbow leads the way, the arm, wrist and right hand are brought forward. His throwing arm is whipped through in a free and easy follow-through, coming straight forward and then down across his body. In fact, his entire body follows through to get the necessary power behind the throw.

One of the biggest faults among outfielders is that they often over-throw the cutoff man, which eliminates all possible cutoff plays. By throwing the ball over the head of the cutoff man, he will not get the man at home and the offense will have a man in scoring position again. This is a bad situation. When the throw is kept low, the infielder acting as the cutoff man may be able to intercept the ball and keep runners from advancing.

Even if the ball is thrown too low, the defense will not get hurt because the ball can still be cut off. He might not throw the man out at the plate but he can still prevent the hitter from going to second base.

Throwing to the bases Another common error of outfielders is to throw to the wrong base. This will seldom happen if he will keep his mind on the ball game, and know *where* he is going to throw the ball when he gets it. He must

Fig. 10–17. BASIC THROWING TECHNIQUE. After catching the ball, the fielder shifts his weight to the pivot or push-off foot. The throwing arm is away from the body so that he can bring the ball back and through in one continuous overhand motion. Pushing off the back foot, the fielder's entire body follows through to get the necessary power behind the throw. He throws on a line to hit the relay man coming out for the throw (Bill Russell).

make his throws to the base *ahead of the runner,* never behind him.

"Throw overhand and low on the line to the relay or cutoff man, chest-high," asserted Jim Northrup, veteran outfielder of the Detroit Tigers. "Throws to a base that take a hop will usually be low enough for good tagging position."

Training

The outfielder, like any other player, must take good care of his throwing arm. During spring training, his arm should be worked into shape with as much care as that taken by a pitcher.

Then, during the season, his arm must be given enough work to keep it fit. It is a standard practice in major league baseball for the outfielders to throw between innings and during delays in the game.

Virdon gave this advice on keeping the arm sound and healthy:

"Keep your arm warm by throwing before each inning starts. If the dugout is on the first base side, the bullpen catcher throws with the right fielder, and the left and center fielders warm-up together."

Frankly, I do not like my outfielders to throw batting practice. It is too short a throw, and I think it will do your outfield throw-in more harm than good.

Drills for Outfielders

1. *Throwing to the bases* Prior to the infield drill, the outfielders should throw to the bases. The coach should fungo flies from near the pitcher's mound, and each outfielder should make several throws to

second, third and home plate. These throws must be low and hard, and come in on one bounce. Cutoff plays should be practiced on these throws. The coach should make the flies easy to handle because, here, throwing is the main concern. The outfielders should be thoroughly warmed-up before it becomes necessary for them to cut loose.

2. Catching fly balls   While the infielder drill is going on, the coach should have someone hit fungos to the outfielders. On the high school and college levels, the fungos should be hit from foul territory and well beyond first and third bases. If the hitters are good enough to hit balls over the infield, the method practiced by big league teams should be used.

The outfielder should practice catching all types of fly balls, to his right, left and front, as well as longer drives over his head in which he has to back-pedal. Also, fielders should get practice going laterally, moving to their left and right.

Since the hard hit liner is regarded as one of his toughest plays, the outfielder should devote much of his fly-shagging to catching liners.

3. Footwork drill   We use a very simple drill to have the outfielders practice quick starts and move in various directions.

The outfielder stands in his regular stance, approximately 30 feet from the coach, who tosses a ball over his head and shoulder area.

If the ball is hit over his right shoulder, he should turn to his right, and if the ball is hit over his left shoulder, he should turn to his left.

4. Ground ball drill   This drill gives the fielders practice in picking up ground balls. Have them back up and then charge in to field these grounders.

5. Relay and cutoff drill   During the team defensive drills, the outfielders are able to practice their throws to the relay and cutoff men. These throws must be accurate, as well as sharp and crisp.

6. Playing balls against the sun   Outfielders should get regular practice catching fly balls in the sun. This drill should not only include using sunglasses but also shielding the sun with the glove.

7. Playing rebounds   Playing a ball rebounding off the fence is a definite skill which requires ample practice. Since fences vary, an outfielder should handle several balls off the fence before every game on the road.

8. Pepper (see DRILLS in Second Baseman chapter)

Practice Tips

1. Work out in the infield to learn how to handle ground balls.
2. Practice going after fly balls that are hit over your head.
3. Drill continuously in judging fly balls, especially line drives.
4. When engaged in a long fly-shagging drill, have a halfway man handle your throws. Use him as your cutoff target.
5. Practice catching fly balls in the sun. Get used to your glasses.
6. Do not spend all of your time fielding fungos. During batting practice, practice fielding balls hit directly off the bat of the hitter.
7. Do not spend all your time on fly balls. Get plenty of practice at picking up ground balls and hops of all kinds.

Psychology of Coaching /11/

Handling 25 different players on a baseball squad is not a simple matter. Each one has his own personality and character traits which must be handled individually. Keeping in mind the strengths and weaknesses of his players, the coach has to utilize various approaches and techniques to bring out the most effective performance of his team.

Some athletes have to be patted on the back, while others have to be coaxed or even needled. Then, there are the problem athletes with their negative forms of behavior which must be skillfully dealt with if there is to be the team unity so necessary to win.

This is why the coach must be continually alert to notice the personal characteristics that distinguish the problem athlete from the good competitor. In this way, the coach will achieve a better psychological insight into the personality makeup of the player, which can be extremely valuable in motivating the athlete toward maximum effort.

Indeed, the athlete himself is the one who makes or breaks the manager or coach. Generally, the coach fails only when he does not get 100 per cent out of his players.

Role of the Coach

The coach, or manager, has to be able to recognize talent when he sees it on the ball field. He has to be able to find mistakes and "see the faults of a player." The coach must first recognize the fault, and secondly, he must try and correct it in such a way that it is acceptable and will get across to the boys (Figs. 11–2 and 11–3).

Fig. 11–2. ROLE OF THE COACH. Most coaches know how the game should be played, but their chief problem is communication, the ability to relate to the player, to instruct and show him in such a manner that he understands what the coach means. In short, baseball needs more coaches who are good teachers.

The league standing does not necessarily indicate how good or how bad a coach really is. If he has gotten 100 per cent from his men, maneuvering them skillfully, using the proper defenses and changing pitchers when he should, he can feel he has done a most satisfactory job.

First impression
The first impression that a coach makes on his squad is important. *Organization* is the key to the whole thing. When practice is first called, the coach must be ready.

The first meeting with his team should be fairly brief. He should give them a general idea of what he expects them to do, and what they can expect of him. He may talk about some of his theories and ideas of how they can develop a winning ball club.

There is nothing more damaging to a team than for a coach to have his first workout, and not know where to go and what to do.

Generally, the coach or manager should spend more time with his planning for the first three or four practices. The rest will follow as he goes along. He will know what he needs to work on and what requires less work. But the first three or four practices are the important ones.

Ballplayers are a lot like kids in a school class. When a new teacher comes into his class, the first three or four days, they are pretty well-behaved because they do not know what to expect. But after the fourth or fifth day, they start testing him out and try to find out what they can get away with.

If they can get away with something on the fourth day, the students try a little more on the fifth day, and the first thing he knows, they are

Fig. 11–3. ABILITY TO COMMUNICATE. After diagnosing the causes of the player's mistakes, the coach must then give the player instructions in the right kind of way, to get him to correct his faults. (Don Drysdale).

completely out of hand. And if he waits two weeks, the teacher has let it go much too far. Now, he cannot straighten out the situation. If the teacher can jump on somebody about the fourth day severely, very likely he will go through the entire year without much trouble.

I believe ballplayers operate the same way. They want to test the coach to see how far they can go. After all, they are only grown boys, and the sooner the coach can achieve discipline, the better off he is.

Anytime he has his club working out, the coach should be in uniform. Then he is better prepared for work, and will command better respect. Off the field, he should be clean and presentable, not necessarily a fancy dresser. Both on and off the field, the coach should set an example for his squad.

Coaches' dress

Instilling in his players a positive approach to the game is an important responsibility of the coach. This is true more with young players than with the veterans, who know they will have hot streaks and slumps. The young player who is just trying out for the team needs more of this than anyone else.

Instilling confidence

Sometimes it is difficult to encourage a player who is going 0 for 10 or 1 for 19. Here is the problem—the fellow who is in a slump. The coach keeps telling a player that he can *do* it, yet he continues to fail. This is when he is susceptible to a few instructions, such as, "Try this," "Try that" or, "We think that you can do it."

This individual should be brought out to practice a little earlier to hit as many balls as he can. The coach should show interest in him.

While teaching in the Ohio school system, I learned how to make suggestions tactfully enough so that they would be kindly received.

Then the coach must hope and pray that, the next game, he will break loose. The only way to really build confidence is through *practice, practice and more practice.* It does not come any other way.

When Maury Wills first came up, he was having trouble with the bat. He had just started switch-hitting, and it was quite a task for him. Maury is such an emotional fellow, and his pride is so great, that this was continually "eating away at him."

One day, following a game, Maury came up to me in the shower room and said: "Why don't you send me back to Spokane, Skip? I'm not helping the club!" He actually felt that he was not helping the club with his bat.

However, I had seen things in his makeup and in his aggressive spirit and his overwhelming desire that led me to believe that he would eventually be a pretty good ballplayer. The only thing I said to him was: "Maury, if you have as much confidence in yourself as I have in you, everything is going to be all right." That is about all I said to Maury, and I kept him in the lineup.

The confidence I showed in Wills at that time gave him the needed confidence in himself, and he began to pick up. Actually, the only thing we did was to open up his stance slightly. He still could hit the ball to all fields, but he just opened up more or less to get his knee out of the way so that he could get the bat through. I do not know whether it was the confidence that we gave him or the opening up of his stance, but he started to hit and, of course, anyone close to baseball knows the rest of the Maury Wills story.

Patience

Not only should the coach be patient but he should insist that the player also be patient. Quite often, when he tells a player to change his stance or his swing a little bit, it is bound to feel awkward to him in the first few attempts.

"If we have to tell a player fifty times that he should do it a certain way," said Bobby Winkles, head baseball coach at Arizona State University, "then we tell him fifty times. We do not tell him ten times, and then say: 'Well, he cannot get it. Why mess with him?' If a player needs that much, the coach must tell him fifty times. Keep reminding him!"

Encouragement

Words of encouragement can be more helpful to a ballplayer than finding fault with him. I definitely believe a player can be encouraged to greater performance (Fig. 11–4). I am sure that the compliment I gave Willie Crawford one night for his all-out hustle did him more

Fig. 11–4. WORDS OF ENCOURAGEMENT can be more helpful to a ballplayer than finding fault with him. The more his athletes are encouraged, the more a coach will get out of them and the better they will play (Ted Williams).

good than criticizing him for the times he failed to hustle.

When a player makes a great play or executes a particular play correctly, the best tonic is for the coach to let him know that he, as a coach, saw this. If a player gets a man from second to third by sacrificing, or hitting the ball to the opposite field, I think the coach must let this individual know that he appreciates his effort or his sacrifice of his own hitting ability. Maybe he would have gotten a base hit if the coach had let him hit away, but he has done the thing that his coach wanted him to do.

Fig. 11–5. THE POWER OF SUGGESTION. The coach will often find it effective to make suggestions, such as, "Try this and see how it works out." When a player comes to him for help, he should give him some suggestions. Here, pitching coach Red Adams offers a mound tip to Don Sutton, Los Angeles pitcher.

Therefore, the coach must let him know that he saw this, and in anybody's book, it is a big plus. This is not only a coach's way of showing his appreciation but at the same time an encouragement for the ballplayer to do it again.

Suggestive power   The coach will often find it effective to make suggestions, such as, "Try this and see how it works out" (Fig. 11–5). He has to start out with suggestions as to how the player might improve or how the coach thinks he will improve. He must get the idea across that *this is the better way.*

The coach cannot just walk out and say: "Look, you have to do it this way." More or less, he has to sell the player on the idea that this might help him and then work on it. The coach must get him to practice enough so that it becomes natural for him. At first, however, he should not make too many suggestions, certainly not during the game, when the hitter has to concentrate and not have to worry where his little finger or his toe is.

How should the coach handle the player who does not want to take suggestions? First, it depends on what kind of an athlete he is and what his problem is. If he does everything well and hits the ball well, we do not try to change him too much. If he is successful doing something his way, I would be reluctant to try to change him. The best time to try to help him is when he gets in a little slump. This is the time to make suggestions, such as: "Why don't you try it *this* way?"

A coach can go only so far in trying to get the best out of a ballplayer. If he will not take his advice, there is not a lot he can do with the player. He should try and talk to him about it, but if he will not listen, the coach simply has to let him fail or make it on his own. If he fails, more than likely the player will start to listen.

Suggestive power sometimes involves forcing a fellow to do something that he does not really believe in. Possibly, he has tried it twice, and inwardly he feels it does not work. More than likely, he will disregard the coaching point, saying: "This will not help me." However, the coach could suggest that, rather than try it in a game, he might achieve better results if he tried it during practice. "Try it and see how it feels to you," he could say.

When Jimmy LeFebvre first came up, he had a terrible uppercut swing, so we tried to level him off. During a game when he was in a little slump, he walked by me and I said: "Hey, Jim, why don't you just level off and don't swing too hard." Well, he did this and he got a base hit. I am not sure whether or not this tip actually helped his swing, but I do feel it served to help him mentally.

"Maybe the skipper is right," Jim might have thought. "Maybe he saw something that I was doing wrong." A little later, LeFebvre came down to sit beside me before he had to hit and asked if I had anything else to tell him.

Fig. 11–6. INSTILLING CONFIDENCE. An important responsibility of a manager like Sparky Anderson of the Reds is instilling in his players a positive approach to the game. Here, Sparky talks to his great young receiver, Johnny Bench.

Sometimes, a suggestion like the one I gave Jim can get the seed planted pretty well. Then, he will start working on it, and this is even more important.

Too often, we, as coaches and managers, do not realize that once those kids go on the field, we cannot do a thing. We can only sit in the dugout and watch them. If we have not taught them correctly, it is out of our hands once they take the field. So, what we have to do is prepare them to mentally think for themselves in the various situations which may occur during a game.

Some coaches have as many as 40 automatics. Well, I do not think anyone should have more than three or four automatics in coaching baseball. If his coach makes everything automatic for his players, a kid never thinks for himself. If a nonautomatic situation ever comes up, he will not know what he should do. Therefore, the coach or manager should not "over-coach." Instead, he must require his players to think for themselves and concentrate on teaching them the fundamentals of the game.

Teach them to think for themselves

The first thing a coach must do is to demand hustle from his players (Fig. 11–6). Ballplayers are not asked to run too often. Maybe four or five times, they will run from home to first. Therefore, the coach should insist that they always hustle.

Demand hustle

On the other hand, when a player does hustle and gives a little extra effort, the coach should compliment him the same as he would if he rapped out a base hit or a home run.

I remember an evening last season when Willie Crawford hustled as much as he possibly could. He made a great catch in the outfield, when he almost ran into the left field fence. He hustled on the ball

Fig. 11–7. GAME CONCENTRATION. By concentrating and thinking about what he should do, the manager or coach will find that the emotional aspects of the game are more or less secondary. His intense concentration can often override his emotions.

that he hit and dove into second base. He ran hard on every play that he had. He backed up everything. I complimented Willie on it. I did not have too many things to compliment anyone on that night, but I made sure Crawford knew that I saw him hustling.

Now, this does more good than raising hell a time or two in previous games when he did not hustle. Following the game when talking to a writer, who obviously did not have much to write about, I pointed this out by saying: "Here is a guy who sits on the bench for two weeks and does not complain or moan, and when he got into this game, he did not hold any grudge. He went out and hustled his fanny in an effort to stay in the lineup. This is the type of spirit that we need on this club."

If I see a player not hustling, generally I will wait until the following day to talk to him. Quite often, I will pull him aside and talk to him privately. Willie Davis is one player who hustles most of the time, but one day, for some reason or other, he took it easy going down to first base, and it cost us an important run. So, when Willie came back to the dugout, I said to him: "Come here, Three-dog! Willie, you hustle for me 99 times out of 100, but what happened this time?"

The first thing I wanted to tell him was that he had hustled in the past, then to find out what happened this time. This is much better than saying: "What's the matter, Willie? Why didn't you run it out?" In other words, I wanted to pat him on the back for being a hustler and then kick him in the fanny for the time he did not hustle.

This is better psychology than just taking the negative side, which makes him feel that "Every time I do something wrong, you are on me." When a player takes a defensive attitude, you have to tell him: "Look, we are on you, we are finding fault with you, but this is our business, to find fault with you." In fact, I want my coaches to tell him, "You did this wrong." Hartsfield, Ozark and Gilliam will all tell him, and before long he has been told four or five times.

When a coach is always finding fault with a player, he has to tell this fellow: "Don't worry. When we find fault with you, we are interested in you and want you to improve. You should start worrying when we ignore you, when we do not say anything to you. So, don't take it the wrong way."

Let them know who is boss

The players have to know who is boss. In my case, I might be a little more lenient than most managers, and this may be a fault. I am not saying that this is the right way. But when I do have a meeting and I want to raise hell, I want it to *mean* something. I like to think that they all know when I have had enough. They know how far they can go.

As a manager and coach, I do not want too tight a rein, with everybody either afraid to move or afraid of me. This is where respect comes in. They know, too, that I will go just so far, and when that happens, I have had enough.

In severe cases, the coach may take the uniform away and say: "Look, if you do not want to do it this way, then just leave your uniform in the locker." Of course, with professional players, the pocketbook is where it hurts the most, more than anywhere else. However, this should be a last resort.

Early in my big league managing career, Don Newcombe told my pitching coach that he would not pitch batting practice. Of course, Don and I are great friends today and we joke about it every once in a while. He possibly respects me more for treating him as I did, although at the time, he was ready to kill me.

Newcombe had just been discharged from the service, and he was having a little trouble. He was not winning, so I told Coach Becker to have Don throw batting practice. Well, he told Joe he was not a batting practice pitcher, that he would not do it.

So, I called Newcombe in and told him: "Take your uniform off, and when you are ready to throw for batting practice, you can put it back on. I don't care how long it takes." The next day, his uniform was not in his locker, and he came to me and said he was ready to go again.

If I had let him get by with his refusal to pitch batting practice, the next time he might have refused to do something else, and I would be in trouble. A coach has to have a stopper somewhere. Today, Don respects me more because I did get a little rough with him at that time, rather than let him get away with it.

Enthusiasm

The coach has to be alive along with his players. He has to show enthusiasm. I know there are some hitters, like our own Billy Grabarkewitz, who can hardly wait to get to the plate. He is so anxious to get there and he really shows enthusiasm. This is good for himself, the team, the fans and everyone else.

Then, there are other players who just mope along, almost dragging the bat up to the plate. I wonder whether or not they really want to hit. Well, the coach gives out the same impressions to his own club.

The energetic, enthusiastic ballplayer will accomplish more with his spare time and come nearer to his capacity than the lazy nonchalant athlete who mopes around, taking his practice halfheartedly. This type of player is not likely to improve too much. He has one thing in his favor, however. It is difficult to get him excited. In a key situation, he may be more relaxed than the fiery individual. Still, I will always take the energetic fellow who really wants to go out after them.

Concentration

By concentrating on the task at hand, the coach can often override his emotions (Fig. 11–7). At least, the experienced coach is able to do this.

I remember only too well the final game of the 1955 World Series, when the Dodgers had their first chance to win the World Championship. Southpaw Johnny Podres beat the Yankees 2–0 in a very tight game. At the time, I was surprised, as the game progressed, at the extent of my concentration. Going over in my mind were such questions as: "How is Podres pitching now? Where do we move the outfield on this hitter? Whom do I have in the bullpen? What will they do in the next situation?" When the game ended, it was almost like another game, with a little something extra, and about an hour after the game, I felt a great letdown.

If a manager or coach is concentrating and thinking about what he should do, the emotional aspects of the game are more or less secondary. An hour or so after the game, though, he will likely feel that he has been run over by a truck.

Imagination

One of the enjoyable aspects of managing or coaching is doing something a little better than the other fellow and having it pay off.

The imaginative, creative type of coach is constantly on the lookout for new ideas, ideas that can be revised and improved upon to fit his own situation. He fills his mind with new information obtained from coaching clinics, the books and magazines he reads and the many games he sees.

Sense of humor

Having a sense of humor and being able to joke with the players on occasion can be a very important quality. Even ballplayers can often be criticized in a joking sort of way. I have had ballplayers whom I could kid, ride or needle a little bit, in a joking manner. I have also had a couple of fellows who did not exactly know if I was kidding them or if I was serious.

With certain individuals, this is a good procedure, because they know they are getting the needle—and that *I* know they did not hustle on a particular play, or did not do something right. Yet, I am giving it to them in a joking, kidding or needling sort of way. I think this is better sometimes than getting the "red ass" and really pouring it on.

Certainly, an occasional laugh or funny moment can break the tension, particularly before an important contest. "I tell my kids a few jokes and funny stories before we play an important game," said Winkles. "Baseball is not a game where you want your kids all tensed up. Baseball is a loose game. You may want football or basketball players tensed up but baseball is a game of looseness. You have to be loosy-goosy when you are playing this game."

Show them how

If the coach can show a boy by demonstrating how to do it, this is better than talking (Fig. 11–2). In my case, I did not have that advantage. I had to get respect through years of managing and handling men.

In cases when I could not demonstrate, I would try to get a great hitter or base runner to demonstrate for me. I was never a great base runner so I have had Maury Wills instruct on the fine points of base running. So, I think it is good to pick out a player who can do something well and who has the ability to instruct, and let him demonstrate for you.

Actually, many of the great coaches were not great athletes. A good example is Paul Brown, one of football's truly great mentors. I believe that one reason why these coaches have been so successful is that, more than likely, they made a little more effort in learning and studying the fundamentals than the star who had all the natural ability who just went out and performed.

Composure under stress

Every coach, during his career, will experience situations of emotional stress and despair in which he must try to hold his composure in a dignified manner. We were in the final play of the play-offs in 1962, and we had a fairly good lead going into the ninth inning. Then the Giants broke loose to beat us. Possibly, this was my most trying moment in regard to holding composure.

The season was over for us, and there was nothing we could do. We tried to take this crushing defeat the best we could, and take it like men. Every coach must realize that this is going to happen to him, and be prepared if and when it happens. Then, he will know how to handle the situation and do his best to go through with it.

Relationship with umpires

In dealing with the officials, the manager or coach must be respectful to them, yet show them that he knows when they have made a mis-

Fig. 11–8. TEAM UNITY AND MORALE is extremely important to the success of any ball team. Above, manager Walter Alston compliments two of his Dodgers, pitcher Sandy Koufax, left, and infielder Jim LeFebvre, for their all-out effort. When a team wins, everybody should feel that they won, and not "I pitched a heck of a game!" or "My home run won the game!" What should be important is that the *team* won.

take. I like to restrain myself from going out there and arguing on every close play. There will be close plays, some of which will go against us and some for us.

When a manager does go out, however, he should have a legitimate gripe. However, he should make it as short as he can and then get out of there. Some umpires will take a bit more than others, without abusing their personalities.

Every ball club expects its manager to fight for its team. Therefore, he should argue for his team as much as he can, within reason.

An understanding wife   A wife who is understanding and considerate can be an important asset to a professional ballplayer. Wives sometimes have to put up with more abuse than the manager. She sits up in the stands and listens to all the second guesses and criticisms. The manager is more or less away from it; at least, he is in the dugout, and all the shouts and comments are mumbled together.

The fans will often boo a manager as he goes on the field or comes off. This does not mean as much to me as it does to my wife, who sits and listens to such statements as: "Why doesn't he take this pitcher out?" "Why doesn't he use a pinch hitter?" and other accusations.

Team Morale

Morale and team unity are extremely important to the success of any ball team, particularly with a club such as the Dodgers, where we have no big stars. In a way, we are lucky because everyone feels he is part of this club. I think the fellows on the bench feel the same way because, when somebody gets in a little slump, we put the other fellow in.

The more a coach can make the twenty-fifth ballplayer on his club feel that he is a part of the team—that he is playing an important role in the team effort—the better off he will be.

Following a great catch by Manny Mota, for instance, Wes Parker came up to him and complimented him for his all-out effort. It is good to have one ballplayer complimenting another on his fine play. As I sit on the bench, I like to see our fellows patting each other on the back, saying, "Nice going!" This is important to the success of a team.

The coach can promote morale and team unity by talking about it and praising the guys who show this type of spirit. I like the fellow who hustles when he is not hitting, or the player who does the little things for the good of the ball club.

The skipper can bring this out during squad meetings by saying: "This guy may be in a slump, but at least, he is showing me something by hustling." I will also mention in the meeting the fellows on the bench who have not played for a week but who are making more noise than anybody else.

The coach has to talk about the importance of a strong team effort and bring it out. He has to praise those players who show good morale, spirit and pride. We always want a player to have pride in himself and the Dodger uniform. Otherwise, we do not want him on the ball club.

I like our players to help and encourage each other. Sometimes, though, I do not like it when they take to instructing each other how to hit. I draw the line there. I do not want one hitter telling the other how to hit. I would rather have Dixie Walker, our batting coach, handle it. I am not saying they do not mean well, but what usually happens is that one hitter will tell the fellow one thing and another will tell him something else. Before you know it, he is listening to everybody, and he does not know *what* he is doing. So, encourage the team to help each other in spirit and encouragement, but leave the instruction to the professional.

Loyalty works both ways

On a major league squad, the manager likes to have his entire squad loyal to him, and he has to be loyal to them, too. Team loyalty is just

The coach should preach constantly that "This is a team effort."

as important on the lower levels of play. *It is essential to a winning baseball team.*

All my life, I have tried very hard not to criticize any ballplayer publicly. I will on occasion make excuses for him by saying: "This is possibly the only thing that could have happened," or, "He was playing it this way." Sometimes, you have to dig pretty deeply to find an excuse. But I much prefer to give an excuse publicly than to say: "Well, he made a mistake. He was a bonehead player," or something like that. The coach has to protect his players this way.

The player who continually criticizes the coach with his fellow teammates is looking for his individual glories. He is more interested in having a good year than he is in worrying about the team. Of course, this will happen occasionally, but the more the coach can keep it down the better off he is. We try to discourage arguments and hard feelings between team members. Our prime objective is to develop a feeling of pride and respect for each other.

Perhaps the best thing a coach can do, when confronted with this problem, is to call a meeting of the entire squad and say: "Jimmy, you are the shortstop on this team and are responsible to play shortstop and hit as much as you can and hustle all the way. This is your job. Dan, you are a pitcher and it is your job to pitch. My responsibility is managing and it is my job as manager to decide when you bunt, hit and run, and when I change pitchers; this is *my* responsibility. If it turns out wrong, *I* get the blame, not you as a pitcher. This is *my* job, and I will do it as best as I can. You should do *your* job as best as you can."

Fig. 11–9. CHANGING PITCHERS. A big decision has to be made by the manager when he goes out to the mound. Should he take his pitcher out, or should he leave him in? One of the most important qualities of a good manager is knowing when to and when not to take his pitcher out. Here, manager Alston has just signaled his bullpen for a new pitcher.

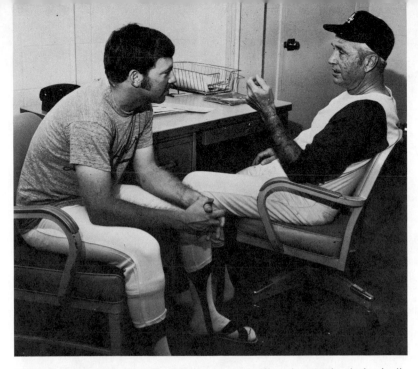

Fig. 11–10. TALKING OVER A PROBLEM is more effectively handled behind a closed door than in front of the entire squad. When a player comes to him with a problem, the manager or coach can be helpful sometimes by just listening to his troubles.

Team Effort

To play winning baseball, a strong team effort is required. An individual cannot do it by himself. I am referring to the little things in baseball, such as advancing or protecting a runner. These are the things that will win ball games. Every player must work together as a team and try to say, "We can do it!"

In his early meetings, the coach should preach constantly that "THIS is a team effort." He should tell his squad that he will recognize the individual who can advance the man from second to third, or sacrifice himself and do the little things that are good for the club. He will tell them that he expects everyone to hustle and give 100 per cent effort whenever he is on the playing field.

These are the qualities I look for in each of my players. Even though he may not hit as much as somebody else, he will do these "little things" for the good of the team. If he is sitting on the bench, he will be pulling for the *team,* not the individual.

The game of baseball requires a lot of individual ability, but sometimes a player will forget about team spirit and winning as a team. I can mention an example when a pitcher almost refused to leave the game. I went out to the mound to take him out, and he wanted to stay in, mostly for his own personal good. He was getting knocked around pretty hard, but he still wanted to get his innings in. Well, I had someone in the bullpen who was rested and could do a better job.

Now, as manager, I have to take this pitcher in and say to him: "Look, this Dodger team is not for you as an individual. For your own good, it probably would be good for you to pitch five innings and get some work on the mound. But, when it is all said and done, we are not going for Mr. X on the mound as an individual. We are going for the team as a whole. And when you are getting whacked, you have got to take your loss and go down to the bullpen and throw as much as you need. We will not sacrifice the whole team for your benefit."

Fig. 11–11. COACHABILITY. The coachable athlete who can accept constructive criticism and instruction is most likely to improve. Before the coach offers instruction or criticism, he must be sure the player is properly motivated. Here, Coach John McNamara offers encouragement to the A's young outfielder, Reggie Jackson.

Handling Men

The manager or coach should live the life that he expects his players to lead. He should treat them as he would like to be treated if he were a player. Above all, he must treat them as *men;* he should joke and work with them and be as close to them as he can, without being "buddy-buddy."

The manager is more or less the "lonely guy." He cannot afford to get "buddy-buddy" with his players. True, he wants to be respectful to them but must treat them all alike.

I do not feel that a manager can show partiality, such as going to the movies with one or two of his players or playing pool or golf with them.

The worst thing that can happen is to have little cliques here and there, in which the manager associates with some players and not others.

Criticize a player privately

Generally, if I want to talk to a player about his performance, I will talk to him individually, rather than in front of the entire squad (Fig. 11–10). Of course, there are certain times when it will be necessary to criticize a player in front of everybody for the good of the team, but mostly this sort of thing should be private.

Do not use two sets of rules

No coach should make a set of rules for one player and another set for 25 other players. *He cannot show favoritism to anyone.* All personnel have to abide by the same rules. Sometimes, when a coach is critical of his team, he should criticize the star rather than the rookie who has made two or three mistakes.

The star should not receive preferential treatment from the coach. Sometimes, the coach has to find fault with the star in order to justify getting on other players who possess less talent.

Fig. 11–12. A LITTLE MORAL SUPPORT. The fear of failure is the biggest hurdle of all for an athlete. Most young players want and need a little affection from their coach or manager. They like to have the feeling of an arm around them. Here, manager Alston finds particular delight in offering a vote of confidence to his grandson, Rob Ogle.

If he handles his players fairly, I believe every coach can get respect out of the players on the bench. One point he has to get across to his entire squad is that, "It has to be a *team* effort even if there is a lot of individual talent."

When a player comes to him with a personal problem, the coach can be helpful sometimes by just listening to his troubles. However, as a rule, a coach should not interfere with a player's private life too much.

Know each individual

In order to impart the right instruction to his players, the coach must know the individual. The first time he tries to correct some players, they will take it as finding fault with them, rather than as constructive criticism. That is, use *constructive* criticism, rather than merely finding fault. Some athletes are very touchy. The coach has to be sure that the athlete realizes he is trying to help him, and not simply find fault with him.

Keep the door open

Private interviews with the players are better than any other method. Players prefer to come into the coach's office and discuss their individual problems privately.

Players who are not playing, naturally, have more problems than those who are in the starting lineup. This is to be expected. A player sitting on the bench would not be a very good athlete if he did not feel he should be playing. He feels that he is better than the fellow playing, and this is the attitude the coach wants.

The problem is: "Why isn't he playing?" Well, the only thing the coach can tell this fellow is that he has no grudge against him. He likes him personally as well as anybody else on the club. However, in his own estimation, the other player has the edge. He might say:

"You wouldn't want me to play you just because I liked you a little better than the other fellow."

Pep up a ball club   Personally, I prefer to have too few pep meetings than too many. Of course, in football, when a team plays only once a week, most coaches give some type of inspirational message.

On occasion, I believe it is necessary to pep up a ball club, but a coach should not try to do it too often. We have a lot of meetings, at which time we go over the hitters to determine how we want to throw to them. But as far as trying to pep up a club, there are simply too many games to do it very often. The first thing a coach knows, his pep talks are bouncing off their backs "like water off a duck."

In basketball and football, when a team plays only one game a week, the coach can start two or three days in advance and mentally build up his club. In baseball, though, a coach cannot handle his team in the same manner.

The players know whom they are playing anyway. When we play the Giants, for instance, it is rather silly to have a pep talk because our players are already keyed up and ready to beat that team. In the World Series, the same thing holds true. It is not usually necessary for a manager to key up his club. In fact, he might be doing more harm than good.

Baseball is a game in which a team of players has to bear down and be aggressive, but at the same time, keep as relaxed and loose as possible. Surely, a coach does not want his pep talk to put his players into a nervous state. More than anything else, he has to *relax them.*

Getting the players themselves to instill spirit into the team is even more important than the manager saying such things as, "Let's go out and get them!" Spirited messages mean more coming from the players themselves.

Keep cool under pressure   I have always felt that the attitude of the coach in regard to the game will brush off and carry over to his players. If he is a nervous individual, jumping up and down at every little thing, his players may become jumpy, too.

A player has to be *relaxed,* whether it be hitting the baseball, fielding or throwing. Of course, we would like everybody keyed up, hustling and bearing down at all times, but at the same time, under pressure, the athlete has to be relaxed.

If he wants his players to show a "desire to win" and a "never-give-up" spirit, the coach has to get this in his own mind. Then, it has a good chance of carrying over into the players themselves.

It would be silly for me to say that I do not feel the emotions and excitement of a ball game. To me, the best way of all to lessen the emotional aspects is to concentrate on the game situation. What can you do in this situation, or what is the best route to take? What might

Concentration and relaxation go together, whether it is throwing strikes or fielding ground balls.

Fig. 11–13. A LITTLE HUMOR IS GOOD. An occasional laugh or funny moment can be good for a ball team in breaking the tension prior to an important game. Along with humor, a little agitating and needling can be good for a ball club. It keeps everybody alive and on their toes. Here, Tito Francona loosens things up with a little comedy before a ball game.

they do if I change pitchers? Whom will they counteract with? Will this guy hit and run? What do we do now?

Help the over-stimulated player

Every athlete should be a little excited and keyed up prior to a ball game, but when this brings on excessive feelings of tension and anxiety, his performance can be affected. Any way the coach can divert this player's attention away from the game to something else is usually effective. A little recreation is often helpful. Before a game, some of our fellows like to play cards, such as hearts. This helps to take their minds off the upcoming game, and sometimes this is good. However, we do not tolerate any gambling in the clubhouse.

Encourage the squad wit

It is good to have a ballplayer on the club who can be an outlet, the funny guy to provide a few laughs now and then (Fig. 11–12). A squad clown can be particularly helpful when the work begins to become tiresome.

Jim Brewer, on our club, is one of the quiet, easygoing funny guys. He says funny things at just the right time and makes everybody laugh. Len Gabrielson is pretty much the same way. He is a witty character, although he is not playing too much. Nobody thinks of Gil Hodges as a funny guy, but the dry wit that he possesses is very pleasing to a ball club.

Of course, if a team does not have a wit, the manager or coach himself has to provide a little humor. I can remember a real tough time last year, when we lost four or five games in a row. The Padres had just beaten us four in a row, and more or less knocked us out of the pennant race. There was really no one we could put the blame on. We were all in a slump, and it was everybody's fault.

Someone sent us one of those laughing dolls, the kind which is pushed on its belly and says, "Ha-ha!" I listened to it and almost laughed myself. Well, instead of having a meeting and raising hell, I could not find anything to rave about, so I walked into the clubhouse and said to Ted Sizemore (he had gotten a couple of hits): "Here, you are the only one who can laugh," and I punched the thing and it started laughing. I said: "Size, when you have finished, pass it around."

That's all we did in the meeting. And, luckily enough, we went on to win a few ball games. Sometimes, just taking the pressure off can be very beneficial.

Baseball players are probably more agitators and needlers on the ball field than in many other professions. To a certain extent, this is good, unless it reaches a point where the fellows are sore at each other. But a little agitating and needling is all right.

Be impartial   The coach has to be fair to everybody and treat them all as much alike as he possibly can. There are always going to be some fellows on the team whom he personally likes better than others, but this is something he cannot show.

The better he knows his players personally, the better he will be able to get the best out of them. There will be some he will have to pat on the back, while others, he will have to kick a little.

When a coach shows favoritism or lets one player get away with little extra things here and there, he not only spoils this fellow but gains the resentment of the entire team. The first thing he knows, he is in trouble, because just one player can cause resentment. It would not be so bad if it involved only this one individual, but it could involve the whole team. One bad apple can make the whole barrel bad!

On occasion, suggestions from the players are good for a team. Sometimes, after a player has given me a suggestion, I will say: "You have told *me* what is wrong, now I am going to tell *you* what is wrong."

Or, I might ask for their suggestions by saying: "We are doing this too much. Does anybody else have any suggestions how we can do better?"

If there is a team problem, it is often good to get it out into the open so the entire team can discuss the situation. It helps to get them all talking. If a team has a leader, this is often the man who stands up and talks for the welfare of the team.

Some subjects can be dangerous, however. If a player steps on one of his teammates, now the coach has a situation that he has to handle himself.

The coach should be careful not to let a player talk him into something. In other words, he must not let a player talk him into playing him if the coach has someone else in mind. The coach should not let players change his original idea or opinion.

For instance, a pitcher on the mound might not want to be taken out. He will say: "Let me pitch to one more hitter. I can get him out." Well, this is a good attitude for him to have. A player *has* to believe in himself.

Admit your mistakes

Every coach will make mistakes occasionally. I think it does the players good sometimes, when things go wrong, if he will say: "Well, I blew this one myself," or, "I made this mistake." Anyone hates to admit that he is wrong, but sometimes it is necessary for him to say to his team that, "I made an error in judgment."

Use a personal approach when cutting the squad

The toughest part of the manager's life is cutting a player. Usually, the young kids are the ones who are so energetic and so willing to listen. They probably work harder than some of the veterans. Yet, there comes a time when there is room for only 25 men on the ball club, and the manager has to send out this kid who has worked so hard through spring training. The boy did everything he was asked to do, and then the manager has to tell him, "We are going to send you back."

Now, the manager should be honest with him and explain to him by saying, "Look, you are just not ready." He should not make the player believe something that he does not believe himself. He has to be as honest as he possibly can, and tell the player: "We want you to go back, and this is the reason we want you to go back. Here is a plan or schedule we would like you to work on."

In addition to tacking the names of the squad on the board, I want to talk to each and every one of the individuals whom I had to cut off. By following this procedure, I think the coach will have a better relationship with these players later on. Who knows, some of my starters may get hurt, and I might want to recall some of the boys I dropped.

The more personal attention a coach can give his players whom he cut off, the better. I am sure they will respect a coach more if he has at least enough time to talk to them.

Discipline

For various reasons, some athletes need to be guided a little more than others in order to get the best out of them. I do feel, however, that a coach or manager would be better off to try to get his players to *want* to do things for the good of their own future in baseball, or for the welfare of the team.

I would much rather have them do the right things on their own than to try to be a detective and always be checking everybody. When he is the detective, the coach may catch two or three players, but there might be four or five others doing the same thing. Sure, he may find two or three, but what will happen is that they will become sore because the others were not caught. This can become a continuous thing, with the players playing "Cat and Mouse" with the coach. The coach might check them in one night; then, the next night, they will go out again after he has left.

A coach will be better off to get his players to do these things for the good of the team, rather than to make such rules as the exact minute or hour they have to be in at night. He should not have to tell them to do *this* and not do *that*.

If he has a "bad actor" on the club, there is no way that he can correct the situation by fines. He may fine him a time or two, but this will not likely change him. He will still cheat and do things the coach does not want him to do. It is much better if the coach can get the player to act on his own. If he cannot, then he will be better off with somebody else anyway.

A player has to learn that he cannot run the show. No coach should ever let a player run him. Somebody has to be boss, and the sooner the player knows that, the better off he is.

"We think that our program at Arizona State has been successful because of the discipline that we have," said Winkles. "Discipline is set down in our set of 18 rules.

"I firmly believe that a coach cannot discipline eight of his players and not discipline the others. I had a kid one time from San Diego that I had to kick off the squad. He was a catcher, and a good one. We have a rule at A.S.U. that each player takes five cuts. This means that, if he is hitting .800, he takes five cuts, and if he is hitting .069, he still takes five cuts.

"Well, every time he took hitting practice, he had a habit of staying a couple times extra. So, I went up to him and said: 'Son, can't you count to five? It is not too difficult, you know, and that's how many cuts you get. You then put the bat down and the next guy comes up and hits.' He said, 'Well, when I was in high school, I hit .481, and I hit until I felt I had the proper mental perspective for the game.' I asked him, 'What happened to the other guys?' He said, 'Hell, they all hit after I finished.'

"Well, that is not quite the way to run a program. I do not care whether a guy is hitting .900, he *still* takes the same number of cuts that the other guys do."

If they have enough desire to win, I have found that players respect and want discipline. I do feel that you have to treat them like men, not boys. Possibly, a younger team needs a little more discipline than the older ones.

"Kids nowadays are getting so little discipline at home that they are looking for it somewhere else," Winkles said, "if a coach or teacher will just give it to them. They are looking for discipline. Of course, you do not do it in a way where you beat 'em to death all the time and never give them compliments."

The coach should want to get a player started off on the right foot. He is like the kid growing up. The sooner he is disciplined, the better. Once he gets out of hand, it will be very tough to win him back.

Again, the best approach is to get him to do as much as he possibly can on his own. Then, if he does not do it, the manager can resort to fines and the coach can sit him on the bench or ask for his uniform. This alternative, though, should come only as the last resort.

"You should put your arm around them once in a while," continued Bobby. "They like to have the feeling of an arm around them (Fig. 11–12). They may not be getting that at home. They want and need a little affection. Hell, they are *kids.* Even my guys in college are that way."

In disciplining a ball club, everybody should be treated alike. True, everyone is a different individual, and when he talks to his players, the coach does not talk to everyone the same way. However, as far as rules are concerned, each and every player must abide by the *same* set of rules.

Meeting a problem head-on

Whenever a problem arises, the coach must meet it head-on. He cannot back up. The players will try to test him by trying little things, but once he has made a decision, he should not back down one iota. Take a fine; if he decides to fine a player, he must go ahead and take the money and not give it back.

On occasion, though, I have given a fine back, near the end of the season, if the offense did not happen again. I might say: "Well, if it does not happen again, you will get it back. You'd better prove to me that you want to do what is right, or the money stays where it is."

When a coach has to resort to disciplinary action, or when upset over the conduct of a player, it might be advisable to wait until the next day. Of course, the particular situation will often dictate how he handles the troublemaker. It might have been a tough ball game, everybody is disgusted and the player himself had a bad day. If they get together at that time, with the coach sore, he will likely say more than what he should say. The player, being upset, is liable to sass him more than he should.

By the next day, both the coach and player have cooled off, and now they can sit down and talk rationally about the problem and come to a better agreement. There are times when the coach has to handle the situation right at that moment, but 99 per cent of the time, he should wait until the next day.

Missing practices

When a player misses too many practices, the first thing I do is start looking for somebody else in his place. Very likely, he has not enough desire to play the game to improve to the point where he will be a winning ballplayer. This is often the player who has all the ability, and the coach does not want to lose him, so he coaxes him along. However, when the season is over, the coach may be better off to get a player who is not quite so good but who does not miss practice. The dependable player probably has more desire to improve, and by the end of the season, may be a better ballplayer than the one who has to be continually coaxed.

If a coach has to keep coaxing his players to do something, it does not help too much. The more he coaxes them, the more of it they expect and the more independent they are going to be. The sooner he lets them know that the world will go on without them—that there will still be the game of baseball, whether they play or not—the better off it will be for everyone concerned.

Late for practice As for the player who keeps coming in late for practice, I would recommend that the coach put him on the bench and leave him there. Or, he might take his uniform away for a day or so, and see if he is interested enough to come back with the knowledge that he will get to practice when everyone else gets there.

Here, we are sometimes concerned with the star performer who knows he is good and wants to have a few extra privileges. Frankly, I do not think you can have very good team morale when you have special privileges for certain players. As a team, everybody is supposed to have the same privileges. *This* is the ballplayer I do not particularly admire.

Missing curfew Laying down curfew rules for college and high school athletes is a little different from big league rules, because they play mostly day games. Here, again, I would rather employ the honor system and not be the detective. I do not believe in checking in closets and under beds and knocking on people's doors at night, except as a last resort.

I would prefer them to want to keep in shape and do good for themselves and the team. Then, if they are not willing to sacrifice here and there and stay in condition, they are not the ballplayers I need on my club. They should realize that, in order to be pennant-winning ballplayers, they must be in top condition.

However, in professional ball, in which we play mostly night games, much of the time it is midnight before we leave the ball park. The players usually eat their big meal after the game, which can then bring it to one or two o'clock. The average fan walks down the street and sees a player, and he thinks he is out past curfew, which is a little absurd.

"When we go on the road, I give the kids a fairly liberal curfew," said Coach Winkles, "like twelve o'clock, and I go to each room and pick up their key. They never know if I want to use those keys in an hour or two hours later. I can go back later and see if they left or are still there.

"However, I do not check very often with curfew," confided Winkles. "I merely tell them, 'Get your rest tonight!' or, 'I might be calling your house to see if you are in tonight around 11 o'clock.' I never call, but I tell them I might, and they do not know if I will or not."

According to Winkles, parents should be encouraged to help the baseball coach with curfew at the high school level. "If you set down a curfew, a parent should make sure that the kid is home," said Bobby. "I would put an obligation on the parent to call me if the kid is not in at a particular time."

Some athletic teams experience the situation in which the senior feels he has the club "made." As a result, he does not put out quite so hard. He is late for practice a time or two, and it is evident he does not have the old desire and zeal for the game. As to how a coach can handle this situation, I feel there is nothing better than for a junior or sophomore to take his place a time or two to get him back in line.

The problem of "senioritis"

Some ball clubs, after winning a championship, have a tendency to become complacent. In high school and college, it depends on how easy the championship was won and the individual players themselves. In professional ball, very seldom do the players become complacent. Playing against pros, they know how tough they are.

Major league clubs play over 160 regular league games. Anytime a team wins the pennant, the play-offs and the World Series, they know what they had to go through and how much effort they had to put forth. Every player should realize that what they did this year is not going to help them next year. In order to win another championship, they will have to work just as hard or even a little harder.

Actually, though, the word "complacent" is sometimes overrated. Very few players become complacent, at least the good athletes. *As soon as an athlete is satisfied with his performance, that is when he stops improving.*

Post-championship complacency

Several years back, I sent up a pinch-hitter for a light-hitting third baseman, who then showed his indignation by staging a temper tantrum in the dugout in front of the entire team.

There are, of course, two sides to this type of situation. From the player's standpoint, he *should* want to hit in a tight situation and feel that he can drive in the run. However, when he outwardly shows his disgust at the decision by the manager or coach to take him out, this becomes a situation no manager can tolerate. He is indicating in a way that *he* wants the glory, and he is not the team man that the manager wants. After a brief confrontation with the player to settle him down, it might be good to call a meeting of the entire team to prevent a similar situation.

Handling a player's temper tantrum

The proper attitude for a hitter who is replaced is to come back and offer some encouragement to the player who takes his place. Only by this type of team spirit can a ball club win the extra games. *It has to be a team unit.*

Dropping a player from the squad

Dropping a boy from the squad for training rule violations should be the last resort in disciplinary action. As manager of the Dodgers, I have had to do this only once, but if the situation again warranted it, I would do it again.

Sometimes, the coach will drop the player permanently, while at other times, he may suspend him for a week or ten days and hope he has cured the individual.

When a coach has to deal that severely with disciplinary problems, he has a player who does not really want to excel enough to be worth his trouble. Unfortunately, this may be the individual who has the natural ability. If he wanted to play badly enough, he could be outstanding.

Proper Mental Attitude

Mental attitude plays a tremendous role in the success of a baseball player. An athlete can have great natural ability but will never reach his potential unless he can develop a proper mental attitude. The ballplayer with the right frame of mind will make his natural ability work.

If a team *thinks* it can win, it will have a much better chance to win. This is the attitude we try to instill in our players. To achieve our objective, we use as much encouragement and suggestive power as we can.

Positive thinking on the part of the player is so important. To be a good hitter, he must feel he can hit, and to be a successful base runner, he has to have the confidence that he can steal a base. There is no other way.

When he takes the field, a ballplayer's thoughts should be strictly *baseball.* He can groove his mind and body to perform a skill only by concentration. He must be alert and thinking *every minute.*

When a pitcher is in a jam, rather than getting excited, we want him to look for a way to get out of it—such as using a pick-off play. We try to get our players to think out there, and think positive. This is why we drill on pick-off plays and all the other fundamental plays. Then, they repeat them over and over again until they become conditioned to the various moves and actions.

Relaxation is essential in acquiring skill and perfection. Actually, concentration and relaxation go together, whether it be throwing strikes or fielding ground balls. By concentrating on what he is doing, an athlete can remove tension and fear from his mind, and replace them with a confident mind and relaxed body.

Six Qualities of a Good Athlete

There are six basic qualities in a good athlete. They are:

1. Willingness to take coaching and study baseball
2. A spirit of competition in practice and in games
3. An intense desire to win, and to accept nothing less than victory
4. Willingness to practice hard at all times
5. Willingness to make sacrifices for the team
6. A desire to improve himself on and off the field.

The real competitor

Every coach would like to have the athlete who has the ability to concentrate when he must bear down a little extra hard. He is the competitor who will punish himself when he has to give that 100 per cent. He is willing to put in a lot of work, not only on his strong points but on his weaknesses as well. Very few athletes have been able to get to the top without punishing themselves to a certain extent.

If he wants to excel, an athlete has to do the extra things that the average fellow will not do. It is easy to hustle when a player is hitting .300 or so. The player I look for is the fellow who is willing and able to kick himself and put forth with more hustle when things go bad. *This* is the test of a winning ballplayer—not when he is a front-runner. When a player is not hitting, he should hustle even more.

The true caliber of a ballplayer is recognized when he plays under stress and strain. This is one of the qualities of a great athlete like Maury Wills. I have seen Maury play with his leg black and blue, and when he would slide, I knew he was hurting and tired. I would even offer him a day off, but he would say: "No, I'm all right." I knew he had to push himself to go into this game.

Tough in the clutch

There are certain ballplayers who seem to be better hitters in the clutch. The more intense the situation, the better they are. Others just seem to be born losers. I believe this all gets back to the mental aspect of believing that they can win and wanting to win, and putting forth that 110 per cent of extra effort.

The other fellow is more or less defeated before he goes up to bat, and thinks: "This is a tough situation, and the pitcher will likely get me out," and he usually does.

Every manager or coach wants the winning type of ballplayer. He wants the athlete who is at his best when the chips are down, or the fellow who does not tighten-up in a tight situation.

Quite often, the chief difference between the winner and the also-ran is the willingness of the winner to punish himself. We like the player who can put forth that little extra and still be relaxed during the crucial moments of the ball game. Sometimes I believe the game is as much mental as it is physical.

Courage

One of the great qualities of an outstanding athlete is being able to give his very best when he is in a slump or has lost some tough games. Instead of giving up and saying: "Well, they are too good for us," a ball club has this "bulldog" in the lineup who will not quit. This is the type of player a manager or coach is looking for. He is the fellow who will pull the team out of its slump.

Having the capability to come from behind is a tremendous attribute in an athlete. These are the players the coach needs when he is in trouble.

In addition to the coaches and manager, certain team leaders can play key roles in getting their team to bounce back. They can do it on the bench by saying: "We will get this guy, just keep pecking away at him." The first thing they know, they are back in the game. Now, if they can get a break or two, they have a chance.

Whether they won the game or not, the important thing is that they did not quit when the score was 9 to 1. They went ahead and got four or five more runs, which indicated they did not quit.

Pride

The great athletes, like Henry Aaron and Brooks Robinson, have a tremendous desire to excel, the urge to be the best. They take pride in their play. They hurt when they lose. Too many athletes are satisfied with fair or good performances, when they could do better with more effort.

An athlete should always be striving for perfection. He must never be content with mediocrity. When a coach has players who take real pride in being champions, his team will always be tough to beat!

Competition

A good baseball player welcomes competition. Most people do not compete enough—they give up too easily. They never press on. If a player is to play to his true potential, he must be willing to put out just a little more. This willingness to put out a little more than the opponents often makes the difference.

Profanity should never be tolerated

Cussing, the use of profane words, has no place on an athletic field, and the coach must not permit abusive language of any type. Actually, swearing is a sign of weakness, an admission that the individual cannot control his emotions, and shows a lack of vocabulary in expressing himself in a socially acceptable manner.

Self-discipline

If he wants to win and play his best, a baseball player must discipline his life—he must lay off smoking, drinking, overeating or anything that keeps him from doing his best.

To be mentally tough, an athlete must show a tremendous amount of self-discipline. He must *never* break the discipline of his mind. There have been athletes with great physical qualities, but who could not control their temper.

Intelligence

Baseball today requires a considerable amount of intelligence— game smartness, the ability to learn offensive and defensive plays well and then apply that knowledge to the proper situation.

Therefore, a player must study hard, not only on the field but in the school classrooms as well. He must keep up his grades, and remember that his primary interest is education and baseball is secondary. Besides, a college scholarship or a lucrative professional contract might be at stake. Players who let down in their studies are usually the ones who will let down in a game.

A hard worker

Occasionally, a manager or coach will come in contact with a player with just ordinary ability who literally "works his tail off." I can remember Bobby Lillis, who finally made it to the big leagues after a lengthy stint in the minor leagues. Here is a fellow who did everything as hard as he could. He worked and hustled all the time. He worked on everything that he possibly could work on. He lived cleanly and obeyed all training rules. Although he was never able to be an outstanding ballplayer, he did make the major leagues and stayed around for a number of years.

The most disgusting thing is to observe a player with a lot of natural ability who is not willing to work hard enough and is not willing to apply himself to the job. As a result, the coach ends up with another good athlete with just mediocre ability who continues to get into trouble. Sometimes, he would be better off without this player.

The superstitious athlete

As long as there are athletic events, I imagine there will always be some silly little superstitions. Frankly, I do not see any harm in this, unless it gets out of hand.

We all agree that acts of superstition will not help anyone, but as long as a player wants to engage in them and believes they will help him, we will let him go ahead and "do his thing." If nothing else, he will display a positive approach. For instance, if a player feels he has made so many base hits wearing a certain sweatshirt, he usually will wear it out before changing to another one.

Perhaps the most famous of superstitious acts occurs when Willie Mays touches the bag at first base on his way to center field. Some pitchers will either step or not step on the foul line. Others will lay their glove on the bench in a certain way. These are the little acts of superstition which draw the interest of the fans.

How to take a defeat   A ballplayer should feel the same way the manager does after a loss. *He should hate to lose!* It is not good for anybody to take a loss lightly. However, when he loses and he feels he has done the very best he can, he should not let it carry over into tomorrow's game. The other club has just outplayed his team. In other words, a ballplayer should forget about the defeat and start fresh. When he plays again, he should be even more determined to correct his mistakes and concentrate on winning this next one.

This does not mean that there should be any joking and laughter in the locker room following a defeat. This sometimes occurs in amateur ball, when an individual or two mistakingly take a defeat too lightly. In pro ball, we do not run into this very often. If we do, the coach should just go up to the players and ask, "What was the score of the ball game?" This can cut them down a little bit. Each situation, of course, demands a different approach.

After 17 years, has defeat come any easier? No, it is about the same—you *always* hate to lose. In some respects, though, it is tougher to lose with a good team than it is with a bad one. If a manager or coach has a poor team, he cannot expect to win as much.

Perhaps the worst thing for a losing manager to do is try to second-guess himself. He will say, "I should have bunted here rather than going for the hit and run." This is the kind of thing that hurts. Or, perhaps somebody has made a mental mistake and has cost him the ball game. These losses hurt more than those in which the other club outhits or outpitches his team.

These situations are bound to occur, but as long as he has done the very best that he possibly can and his team has played as well as it possibly can, fretting and stewing will not help the situation one bit. Even though these moments can be severe, they should not carry on into the night and into the following day or week.

Team Offense /12/

The best offense in baseball is an aggressive attack, which is capable of exerting continual pressure on the defense. This has been the trademark of some of the most successful major league teams in history, including our championship Dodger clubs. There is no question that we like our offense to be aggressive.

Types of Offense

The type of offense used depends entirely on the type of club the manager or coach has, whether it is a power or a speed club. The type of pitching that he has is another determining factor. If I have a real fine pitching staff, for example, four or five outstanding pitchers the likes of Sandy Koufax and Don Drysdale, then I know the opponent is not going to score too many runs.

If I have a club that lacks good power, I am inclined to sacrifice or play for one run earlier in the game than I would if I had a weaker pitching staff. Therefore, the offense is more or less determined not only by the type of hitters but also by whom the coach has pitching for him.

The manager or coach often tries to estimate how many runs his opponent is going to get. If someone like Koufax is pitching, I will say: "OK, let's bunt in the first inning or steal the base, try to get one run, and hope that we can hold it."

Now, if there is somebody else pitching, and we are playing a team that scores a lot of runs, I might say: "Well, they are going to score three or four runs, so we have to go for a bigger inning." Therefore, I would play my offense differently.

An aggressive attack, capable of exerting continual pressure on the defense, is the best offense in baseball.

A team that lacks the home run hitters should have players who are able to bunt, drag and push, and all sorts of ways to bring the infield in. With the infield in, the offense has a better chance to hit the ball past the infielders for a base hit.

The home run is a great weapon. I wish we had a few more. But, if the manager does not have this type of hitter, he has to go the other way. In fact, good pitching generally can handle most good home run hitters because they are free swingers. They either hit the ball out of the park, or they hit into a double play or strike out. With the infield back, they are not as much of a threat as the hitter who slaps the ball around and can bunt, drag and run.

Hitting away is not the only way to score runs. Bunting, the steal, hit and run, run and hit, and the squeeze play can all advance runners to scoring position or score them. In a close game, when one run can mean victory, the advancement of a base runner can be a significant factor in the outcome.

The Dodgers like to hit the ball to the opposite field as much as we possibly can. However, this is a technique that must be practiced over and over until it becomes a habit.

An aggressive offense

Basically, the more aggressive a team can be, the more successful it will be (Fig. 12–2). This starts with the hitter himself. The hitter has to be aggressive and believe that every pitch is going to be a strike. He should start after every pitch and be able to hold back if the pitch is a ball.

Then, he must run hard from the moment he hits the ball until he rounds first base or second and is stopped by the play. His own judgment may force him to stop, or the coach may hold him up.

Fig. 12–2. AN AGGRESSIVE OFFENSE. The speed and aggressive base running of Bill Russell have given the Dodgers a go-ahead run. By exerting continual pressure, the offense will force the defense into making mistakes.

An aggressive offense has many advantages over the team which plays conservative, safe baseball.

As soon as he is on first base, the base runner immediately has to "Think Positive" that he might be able to steal second. When he gets the sign, he must be ready with his lead and break quickly with the proper cross-over step. If the hitter gets a hit behind him, he should not be satisfied in stopping at second but should go to third or as far as he can go within reason. *He must be aggressive all the way.*

The offense must exert continual pressure on the defense, and in doing so, they force mistakes. When a top base stealing threat such as Maury Wills or Lou Brock gets on first base, he can exert considerable pressure on the pitcher. The pitcher will say to himself: "I've got to throw over there three or four times. I've got to rush my delivery." He becomes so concerned about the man on first stealing second that he gets behind the hitter. In addition, this concern takes a little concentration away from the pitcher, which is very helpful.

When the base runner gets on first base, the outfielders are thinking: "With this man on first, the chances are that he will be going to third. If the ball is hit to me, I have really got to charge this ground ball and hurry up my throw." And so, this type of aggressiveness and pressure rushes the defense into misplays and errors.

An aggressive hitter goes after the ball. He really wants to go after it, and if it is in the strike zone, he will swing at it. If it is not in the strike zone, it is like seeing the red light on the street. Everything is green and his foot is on the gas until he sees the red light. Then he has to stop. With practice, this will become a reflex action, but the importance in being an aggressive hitter is that he starts after every pitch and really wants to hit it. This is the attitude a hitter should have.

Pressure on the defense

An effective running game, sparked by well-executed bunts, the steal, hit and run, and highlighted occasionally by the exciting squeeze play, can place considerable pressure on the defense. The drag bunt, clever and daring base running, and skillful sliding are methods and techniques that develop fast-moving situations which cause mechanical and mental errors by the defense.

Indeed, an aggressive offense has many advantages over the team which plays conservative, safe baseball. The threat of a steal will often cause pitchers to lose their concentration on the hitter, while the threat of a bunt will bring in the infield, decreasing their fielding coverage. Thus, the element of threats can be effective in keeping the defense off-balance and unsettled.

There is nothing nicer to see than a player getting a base hit and rounding the base at full speed. When he decides to stop, he almost slides his wheels and goes back. If he rounds the base properly and the outfielder just juggles the ball, he may keep going right into second base. These are the things that can get that one or two extra runs a team needs to win.

True, there will be times when runners will be thrown out. It looks bad in these instances but, percentagewise, over the season, this aggressive style of play will pay off. Certainly, the coach will find it easier to slow his runners down and make them a little more cautious than he will in making them more aggressive. The timid base runner is more difficult to make more daring.

An early lead

One of the pleasant aspects of baseball is that, if a team can get out in front early in the game, the coach can do so many things. He can hit and run, steal or sacrifice if he is a run or two in front. But as soon as he gets behind three or four runs, he cannot do so many things. He cannot take wild chances, nor can he keep the pressure on the defense. So, he has to sit around and wait until his team collects three or four hits in a row.

Importance of speed

Although it is sometimes underrated, speed is extremely valuable offensively. The player with speed has a greater advantage in beating out the infield hit. He will go from first to third on 90 per cent of the base hits, more so than the slow-footed fellow who has to stop at second. The runner at second base with good speed is difficult to throw out at home plate.

Some of baseball's best teams have achieved success largely on exceptional speed. The Dodgers and the St. Louis Cardinals have taken advantage of players like Maury Wills and Lou Brock. The Dodgers have played, and still often play, for one run, using the hit and run, the steal and the bunting game. The runner at second may steal third and score on an infield ground ball. Actually, a team may go this route the entire game and be able to pick up three or four runs from these tactics. However, it has to be a team that has speed, can bunt and is able to move the ball around, such as with the hit and run play and hitting to the opposite field.

Fast, intelligent base runners such as Brock and Wills can place tremendous pressure on a pitcher. A veteran pitcher might not be affected but an inexperienced young pitcher often becomes rattled to such an extent that he will throw the ball too soon. He will lose his concentration on the hitter and might lose the little extra on his fast ball. He tries to throw it too hard and too quickly, resulting in a wild pitch.

Aggressive attitude

Building an aggressive attitude, offensively and defensively, should be the prime concern of the coach or manager. An aggressive offense is particularly demoralizing to a high school team. Quite frequently, the team that scores first will break the opponent's spirit.

A high school team cannot rely consistently on the hitting prowess of their top hitters in a scoring situation. Instead, the coach must develop techniques and plays, such as the steal, to compensate for his team's uncertain hitting and to support scoring potential.

The aggressive, positive type of coach who takes the initiative and employs the elements of surprise and deception in his offense can achieve considerable advantage.

The Batting Order

The forming of a batting order is not as simple as it seems. The manager or coach must arrange his batting order according to the players he has available. He should try to balance his lineup so that the attack is as strong as possible from the lead-off man through the ninth hitter.

The lead-off man should have a good "on base" average; he should be a fairly good hitter, although not necessarily a long ball hitter. He is the Jim Gilliam or Pee Wee Reese type, who has a good eye and does not swing at bad balls. Possessing good speed, he should have two or three ways to get on base.

The number two man should have the bat control to hit and run and go behind the runner. He must be a man who can lay the ball down if the sacrifice is needed. He should be able to pull the ball if he has to, or go the other way when the occasion calls for it. Some managers feel there is an advantage in having a left-handed swinger in the number two spot. If he is a left-handed hitter, he can hit the ball through the hole. The right-handed swinger should be encouraged to go to right field.

The number three and four men, of course, are the power hitters. If these players have equal ability, I would prefer my left-handed batter to hit third, feeling that if either of my first two men got on base, he would have the hole at first base to hit through. Ideally, the number three man should be a left-handed hitter who can pull the ball and have the power to drive in a few runs.

Generally, the number three man is faster than the number four hitter. I like to have my speed up in front. The number four hitter would be the RBI man who has the most power. He should be the hitter who occasionally can hit one out of the park. There is not a great deal of difference between the four and five hitters. The number six man is the next power hitter, although not as good as the three, four or five men.

The seventh, eighth and ninth positions are filled with the three weakest hitters playing. As a rule, the pitcher will bat in the ninth position, but the catcher is not always necessarily the eighth man in the lineup. Roy Campanella was never an eighth-place hitter, although he did hit eighth for me a time or two and didn't like it a bit.

If I had a choice of speed, I would prefer my eighth-place hitter to have the speed if possible.

In high school, and sometimes in college play, the pitcher may be one of the better hitters on the team.

Offensive Tactics

Hit and run

The hit and run is one of the greatest plays in baseball, but it requires a hitter with good bat control to hit the ball through the hole. He should be told to hit the ball on the ground. If he cannot get a piece of the ball, the runner will likely be thrown out by the catcher. This is because, on the hit and run, the base runner does not get the daring lead that he would if he were stealing.

When the hit and run is on, the manager will say: "I need a run, so I am going to sacrifice a little of my hitter's power in order to get the runner to second or third base."

There have been some fine right-handed hitters who could go to the opposite field, men like Alvin Dark, Billy Herman and our own Jim Gilliam, who had the bat control to go to the spot the fielder was leaving.

If the coach does not have this type of hitter at the plate, he should tell him to just be sure to get a piece of the ball and hit it on the ground. If he hits it in the air, everything is lost.

While the runner at first can be bunted over, the right type of hitter can accomplish more by hitting the ball into right field, thereby ending up with men on first and third. Besides, defenses against the bunt have become so formidable that many big league managers are employing the hit and run more than usual.

The purpose of the hit-and-run play is to advance the runner an extra base and to protect him from the double play. It is often used in the middle or late stages of the game. It is a good play when the pitcher is behind the batter, especially on the three-and-one pitch. With a runner on first base, the right-handed hitter will often try to hit the ball behind the runner, thinking the second baseman will cover. The batter must swing at the ball wherever it is pitched, even if he has to throw the bat at it.

"Executing the hit and run takes a certain knack on the part of the hitter," said Bobby Hofman. "You must work on it. You have to wait until the ball gets to the plate. Bill Rigney taught me just to keep my right elbow into my side so I cannot get the bat out in front of my body. You lead with your hands. The hands are out in front and you just try to hit the ball to right field."

If the catcher guesses and calls for a pitchout, the offense, of course, is in trouble. If a wild pitcher is on the mound, a manager is a little reluctant to put the hit and run on.

Run and hit

Instead of hitting behind the runner, the hitter simply tries to hit the ball, which for young, inexperienced players, is an easier skill to execute. The run and hit can cause many problems for the defense, such as breaking up a double play with a slow runner at first.

A good time to call for a run and hit is when the pitcher is behind in the count (2 and 2, 2 and 0, 3 and 1 or 3 and 2), because he must come in with the pitch. The runner should be on the move, and the hitter is instructed to go for the ball if it is in the strike zone. The run and hit is used more with a fast runner on base. If the pitch is out of the strike zone, the runner has a chance to steal a base.

The hitter should know that the runner is going, and if it is in the strike zone, "I am going to be cutting." The worst thing that can happen on a run and hit is for the runner to go and then have the hitter take the pitch right down the middle.

Hitting behind the runner

When the situation is right, some managers prefer hitting behind the runner rather than employing the bunt or a hit-and-run play. This offensive tactic is usually attempted only when first base is occupied and there are less than two out. Gilliam could hit the ball on either side of the field, or he could go to the opposite field.

In an effort to advance the runner on first to second base, the hitter tries to hit the ball on the ground between the first and second basemen. The runner will break for second. Many times, there is a lot of space in there to hit the ball behind the runner. The batter should attempt just to meet the ball. Right-handed hitters find it effective to go after an outside pitch.

With a man on second base, the manager will usually try to advance him to third base. With the bunt play proving not as successful as it used to be, many teams will have the batter go to the opposite field, particularly with a hitter like Manny Mota. The batter should try to hit the ball on the ground.

"Sometimes a young player will say, 'Well, I tried to hit it to right field,'" said Rigney. "Well, that is not good enough for me. Trying is not going to get it done, because you really have to work at it. I know what it means to single to right field with a man on first base. It gets the bullpen hot, that is what it does. It is rather difficult to beat a first-and-third situation, nobody out, with the third, fourth and fifth hitters coming up."

Hit the ball to the opposite field

The batter who has the short, quick stroke and quick wrists is the fellow who will likely have the bat control necessary to hit the ball consistently to the opposite field. Whether this is hand-and-eye coordination or what, some hitters have it and some do not.

The double play is a great morale booster for the defensive team. That is why I want my players to find a way to hit the ball to the opposite field. By doing so, the batter is hitting *away* from the double play, and more important, we have runners on first and third with only one out.

Getting a run with an out

One of baseball's unsung heroes is the hitter who is capable of getting a run with an out. With a man on first or second base, he can hit the ball consistently to right field, moving the runner around.

When that one run is so important, the hitter should actually sacrifice himself in order to score the run. All he has to do is hit the ball on the ground.

Therefore, a hitter should know how to make himself be put out. He must be able to ground the ball to the second baseman, especially when the infield is not in. He has to concentrate all the time to "Get the run! Get the run!"

If the first man doubles, the next man should ground the ball to second base, moving the runner to third.

If a left-handed hitter comes up with a man on first base, he should not even dare to think of hitting the ball to left field. For two reasons, he has to think about driving the ball through that hole. If he singles to right field, we are on first and third. If he singles to left field, we are on first and second, and still in jeopardy. But, if we have a man on third base, then *they* are in jeopardy because, now, I can get a run with an out.

Run-and-bunt play

This play is a variation of the sacrifice bunt, in which the base runner attempts a steal of the next base. To protect the runner, the hitter must bunt the ball regardless of where it is pitched.

On occasion, the run-and-bunt play is used more or less as a surprise tactic. With the bunt in order, the first baseman charges in, and as he moves in quickly, it is difficult for him to know whether or not the runner has left. Under ordinary circumstances, he will make the force play at second, but the man at first is already running and will often beat the throw. This play can be dangerous, however. If the hitter pops the ball up, misses it completely or it is a bad pitch, the runner might get thrown out.

We feel it is a good play, though. I am disappointed that we have failed to employ this play often enough. To combat the defense that teams are putting up against the bunt today, I believe it is a play that will be seen more and more.

The skilled bunter and speedy runner at first can put the run-and-bunt play on with amazing results. The bunter will bunt the ball to third and make the third baseman field the ball. The runner will just keep on going, and if the third baseman is not alert, or the catcher is slow in covering third, he has an occasional chance to go to third base with one out. This was Pepper Martin's favorite play—but the bunter has to make the *third baseman* field the ball.

A good time to execute this play is when the pitcher is behind in the count, and therefore more likely to make the next pitch a strike. The best game situation is with none out and a runner on first base.

Squeeze Play

The safety and suicide squeeze plays are usually tried in the late innings with a runner on third base, one out and the team at bat ahead, tied or no more than one run behind.

Suicide squeeze

I like the suicide better than the safety squeeze. If a team is going to squeeze, they should go ahead and squeeze. One of the dangers of the suicide squeeze is that, if the runner leaves too soon or gives the play away in any way, the first thing the pitcher will do is knock the hitter down. The hitter, of course, does not have a chance to bunt the ball, and the runner will very likely be tagged out at the plate.

Instead, the runner should wait until the pitcher's front foot hits the dirt, or until his arm starts coming through. Then, he cannot change the direction of his pitch. Now, it is up to the hitter to bunt the ball on the ground. It does not have to be a good bunt, merely on the ground, not too hard but toward the pitcher.

Many bunters, in this situation, try to lay down a perfect bunt. The ball rolls foul and it defeats their purpose. If the runner starts at the proper time, all that is necessary is for the ball to be bunted on the ground.

A quick start is essential. The runner at third has to be leaning in the direction of the plate, a walking lead, taking a step or two up the line and having his weight going forward. As soon as the pitcher releases the ball, he will change gears and go into a run.

To make sure nobody fouls up on this play, a "hold" sign is often given to the hitter, to be sure he gets it. He might answer by picking up dirt and tossing it, pulling his belt or using any other simple signal.

Safety squeeze

The runner at third base should make his move *only* if the ball is bunted on the ground. If the ball is popped up or missed, the runner does not go.

A speedy runner should be on third when the safety squeeze is employed. This is because he must not start too soon. He waits to see where the ball is bunted, and then takes off.

The ball is not bunted unless the pitch is a good one. The runner will try to score only if he thinks he can make it. A quick start is essential for the runner on third base.

As I said earlier, I do not like the safety squeeze as well as the suicide. It involves "negative" thinking: "I am not *sure,* but I will give it a try." The first thing the manager knows, his runner is bluffed back to third, or is thrown out. If he is going to squeeze, he should go ahead: "You either do it or you don't!"

Bunting

The bunting game is still an important part of a team's offensive strategy. Normally, the bunt is not used in the early innings of a game. In these innings, most teams play for a big inning and do not sacrifice

A varied array of bunts, if used skillfully, can exert the type of pressure that has an unsettling effect on the defense.

an out. Of course, a bunt has more chance of working when the play is unexpected.

In addition to being an effective weapon to move runners around, the bunt can be a surprise tactic to cross up the defense. Players today are getting better each day at faking the bunt and then swinging the bat. This tends to keep the third baseman and the first baseman back just a little, and it helps.

The ideal time for a squeeze play is with one out. If a manager has a good base runner on third and a pitcher is at the plate, he might try to squeeze him in. If he lets the pitcher hit, he will more than likely strike out or hit into a double play. So, he has the pitcher lay one down.

Or, if the winning or tying run is on first base, the coach might want to get his runner down to second base and, in addition, score the man from third. So, he tries to bunt him over. He will tell his pitcher to bunt the ball down the third base line, with the idea of getting this runner to second base. As the third baseman comes in to field the ball, the runner at third should follow him in just a step or two behind him. If he throws to first base, a fast runner might have a good chance to score. Actually, this is not a squeeze play. The offense is just trying to get the man to second and not hit into a double play. This is one of the tricky plays a coach might try, although it probably will work better in high school and college. I would not want to try it against a Brooks Robinson or a Clete Boyer.

Sacrifice bunt

The key rule in executing the sacrifice bunt is for the hitter to *give himself up.* On the straight sacrifice bunt, the batter attempts to bunt the ball only if the pitch is a strike.

Late in a ball game, with the score tied or the team one run behind, the manager will probably want to move over his runner on first base. He will tell his hitter to bunt the ball down the first base line, because the first baseman has to hold the man on. Besides, the third baseman very likely will be right on top of the bunter.

To have the best chance at all to get the man over, the bunter has to bunt the ball down the first base line. Of course, first basemen today often cheat a little and start running in before the pitcher releases the ball, so unless the base runner can take an extra step or two to counteract this, he will be in trouble.

Bunt for a hit

Since the sacrifice style of bunting would alert the infielders, a hitter should not square around toward the pitcher until the very last instant. The drag bunt and push bunt are both attempts at a base hit.

In bunting for a base hit, the hitter must know where the first baseman and third baseman are playing—if they are playing deep or shallow, and whether they are expecting the play. Some pitchers fall off the mound, so if a right-hander falls off toward first, the bunt should be directed toward third base. If a left-hander keeps falling off to the left, the drag bunt could be aimed at the first baseman, in hopes that the bunter can beat the pitcher to first base.

Push bunt

I can recall a ball game against the Giants in which the push bunt was a key factor in our victory. Jim Gilliam was at bat with a man on third, two men out and the infield back. Seeing that the second baseman was a little too deep, Gilliam bunted the ball and beat the play.

Fake bunt

In the hope that the first and third basemen will charge in toward the plate, the hitter assumes a bunting position. Then, if the infielders charge, the batter will try to slap the ball past them.

We call it a "hard bunt" or "slap bunt," in which the hitter squares around to bunt but, instead, just slaps the ball. This is a pretty good challenge against the charging bunt defenses being used now.

Base Running

Base running is controlled by the game situation. The number of outs, the score, the ability of the base runner and the fielder's arm are factors which determine whether or not the runner attempts to advance. The batter and base runner must be alert to react quickly to passed balls, overthrows and errors.

Some pitchers will have a good move to first base but a slow delivery. In this case, the runner cannot take as big a lead but he can still steal because he steals on the delivery. Other pitchers will have a quicker delivery but a poor move to first base. Here, he should try to take a bigger lead because, when he throws to the plate, there won't be as much time.

A pitcher who varies his tactics can be tough to steal on. He may quick-pitch occasionally. Next, he will come to a set and then wait a long time before his pitch. On the next pitch, he will come in quickly.

Home to first

Base running begins at home plate. The ability to start quickly and get into running stride often spells the difference between a "safe" and an "out" call. No matter what side of the plate he swings from, the hitter should try to take his first step with the rear foot. He must go hard for first, looking only at the bag, unless the coach signals or calls that the ball is through and for him to take his turn.

There is nothing more disgusting than to see the batter hit the ball to the outfield or infield, and then watch the ball and not put out full effort in going to first base. The infielder fumbles the ball, picks it up and throws the hitter out by half a step. Whereas, if he had run the

A fast, intelligent base runner can place tremendous pressure on a pitcher.

moment he hit the ball to first base, he would have been safe by a full step.

There is no excuse for a player not to run to first base. The only exception would be a pitcher at bat, on a hot day, in the seventh or eighth inning, after a tough inning of pitching. I would excuse him sometimes, *but no one else.*

The steal
If a team can use the steal successfully, they can eliminate the sacrifice. By stealing the base, the coach is much better off because, now, he does not have to sacrifice to *get* him there.

The steal itself is not only a great asset to the offensive club, but it rattles the pitcher and the fielders. The pitcher is so worried about the runner that he gets behind the hitter or makes a bad pitch. The second baseman or shortstop often has to "cheat" a little toward second base, so as to be there for the throw. Consequently, there is a wider gap to hit through.

The manager or coach, of course, has to decide whether to steal or not to steal. My "steal" sign simply tells the runner: "We want you to steal if you can get your lead." However, it does not necessarily mean he has to go on that pitch. If the manager gives a "steal" sign, and insists that his runner must go on that particular pitch, on that pitch the pitcher may quick-pitch him. Therefore, we do not want a base runner to steal unless he can get a good jump.

The good base runner has to be aware of the pitchout. Usually, if a pitchout is executed properly, even runners as fast as Maury Wills and Willie Davis will have trouble stealing the base, unless the pitcher's delivery is particularly slow. The count has to be right. Quite often, Maury will guess for a curve ball because it is better to steal on an off-speed pitch than on a fast ball.

An aggressive stolen-base philosophy has proven successful for many teams, particularly at the high school and college levels. Young pitchers may not have a good move to first or a quick delivery to the plate. In addition, young catchers may not have a quick and accurate throwing arm.

The single steal
The single steal is usually tried when a team is ahead, tied or no more than one run behind. When the "steal" sign is put on with a 3-and-1 or 3-and-2 count on the batter, the runner should be instructed to go on that pitch, although the hitter does not have to swing at the pitch. However, on any other count, the runner should steal only if he gets a good jump on the pitcher.

Basically, a team should not run when more than two runs behind, but when an outstanding runner is on base, early in the game, the coach might say: "Well, I am going to go ahead and gamble. If I get this man on second base, maybe I can pick up the one run."

The "steal" sign might be given the runner when he is on second or even third, but the runner goes only if he gets a good jump.

Double steal

There are various types of double steals with runners on first and third. Some coaches start with the straight single steal from first base, while others use the break before the pitch, delayed or long-lead types. Here again, it depends on the pitcher.

If successful, this play can result in one run scored and a runner on second base. For example, the runner on first will break for second on the pitch, and if the throw goes through to the base, he will pull up short and become involved in a run-down situation. The man on third, meanwhile, will wait until the thrown ball is over the pitcher's head before making his break for the plate.

Actually, the Dodgers do not use this type of double steal, in which we send a man from first and try to score the runner from third base. It often works at the high school level, but the major league defenses are too good for that. What happens, is that the catcher will "look" the runner back to third and then throw on to second base. If the runner starts too soon at third, he will be caught in a run-down play.

In executing the double steal, the runner at first should start toward second with a straight steal. Now, as soon as the catcher releases his throw to second base, the runner at third base has to have as good a lead as he can and then take off quickly.

Sometimes, the defense will try to trick the runners by throwing directly back to the pitcher, and the offense will likely be in trouble. However, it is a gamble play, so the runner at third base will say to himself: "I will get as good a lead as I can. I will stand still, and wait until I see that the catcher has actually thrown the ball to second base."

There are times when the catcher will fake a throw to second, and the runner at third will be in a trap between third and home. Again, I believe the double steal can be defended against quite well.

Delayed steal

The player with good speed who selects an opportunity to run should have a good chance of pulling off a delayed steal. The base runner should exploit any carelessness by the keystone combination, the pitcher or the catcher. The delayed steal is often tried with two outs, when the catcher has been lobbing the ball back to the pitcher and the second baseman and shortstop are playing deep. Or, it is sometimes tried when the second baseman has a habit of looking down after the pitch is past the hitter.

The runner should break for second base the moment the catcher starts his throw to the pitcher. The pitcher has to catch the ball, pivot and throw, while the infielder who covers must come in from his deep position to make the play.

One type of delayed double steal might be used against a rookie pitcher, especially a left-hander. As he comes down and gets set, the man on first base should start to run. I do not want him simply to jog, because if he starts jogging, it will look too much like a trap. I want him to break as though he were actually going to steal.

Although the pitcher knows there is a man on third base, if he is not concentrating at that particular moment, his first impulse is to back off, and he will likely throw to second base. The runner on third base knows this play is on, too, so he is creeping off; then, as soon as the pitcher backs off, he starts to go. Many times, if the pitcher makes only a motion toward second, the runner on third has a good chance to score before the pitcher can recover and throw to home.

The delayed steal should work particularly well at the college and high school levels. I do not think it should be used against a veteran pitcher, though, because he will step off the rubber and look to third before he commits himself to second base.

The natural impulse of many pitchers is to follow the runner. "There goes that runner!" Because he wants to do something about it, he will step off the slab and start his motion to second or throw to get the runner in a run-down. Before the defense knows it, it is too late to stop the runner going home. If the pitcher does not step off, he will very likely balk.

In fact, we have worked the delayed double steal a half dozen times in the major leagues, and it has proven to be a daring, tricky play that works. We have been caught only two or three times. However, a manager has to know how to pick his spots and situations.

Signals

The secret language of baseball is signals, and no team gets very far without them. If a team is to win, a simple but effective system of communications must be set up. Flashing his signals from the bench or from the coaching lines, the manager or head coach can coordinate individual efforts into team action.

Signs, in the case of young players, can be quite simple and few in number, while signs with older and more experienced players can cover more situations and plays. Whatever the system, each member of the squad should know the signs perfectly.

Too many signs on a team can be worse than none at all. A baseball player may have enough trouble keeping his mind on the game situation, without having to worry about a long, complicated series of signals. As Yogi Berra once said, "How can you *hit* and *think* at the same time?" Yogi, of course, was exaggerating the situation, but it is true that a player must concentrate on the task at hand, whether it be hitting or fielding.

Signals that take too much mental effort to comprehend should not be used. They should be simple. Unquestionably, the effective-

A. On deck, checking the pitcher and game situation.

B. Stepping in, receiving the signal.

Fig. 12–3. OFFENSIVE ROUTINE (Cesar Tovar).

ness of signals depends upon their execution. A simple set of signs, combined with an indicator or key, plus some decoy motions for camouflage, can be most difficult for the opposition to intercept (Fig. 12–4). Any natural movement of the cap, hands or arms, mixed in with other natural actions, will do the trick.

Actually, the causes of missed signals are quite simple. The player did not look at the coach, he did not look at the right time or the manager did not give the signal properly. There is no excuse for a player not to know the signs, even If they are complicated to a certain extent. He has all his free time to learn the signals.

After the signals are used awhile, there should be no missed signs. That is the trouble with the "flash" sign. If the manager gives a "flash" sign and the player does not happen to be looking at the right time, he does have an excuse. However, the first time the hitter turns around and looks at the coach, the coach should give a "yes" or "no." "Yes—I'm going to give you a sign," or, "No—I won't."

For instance, if the coach rubs down below the belt, it means, "No, there is not a sign." If he rubs anything above the belt, the player has to be alert, because a sign will be given. As soon as the coach hits the key with one hand, he will give the sign with the other hand.

A simpler set of signs should be given high school players—more holding signs, such as hands on the knees or belt, or keeping them there a little longer. The coach should either face him, walk toward

A. The key (touching #24 with left hand).

B. Both hands to letters (indicates he will use second signal after key).

Fig. 12–4. MANAGER'S KEY METHOD TO SIGNAL COACH. The key to start the signals is #24, using the hit and run as an example. The first sign touched after touching the key is the signal, unless otherwise indicated by using both hands to touch the same spot. Then it will be the second signal after the key is touched. Using the key method, a set of signals can be as follows: Take (touching the cap); Bunt (touching the opposite leg); Hit and run (touching the letters) and Steal (touching the opposite sleeve).

him or walk away from him. It is more important to have the players sure that they get the sign, rather than be too concerned about the opposing club stealing them.

Coaches should be pretty good actors. They have to make some kind of movement or signal-giving motion on practically every pitch. They should do a lot of faking constantly, so that, when they *do* give a sign, it is not obvious.

Practice The manager or coach should not be satisfied just to go over the signs with his team and let it go at that. Sufficient practice time should be devoted to executing them until they are well understood. They should be used in all intrasquad games, with the coaches performing their duties on the baselines under typical game conditions.

Major league players have a chance to practice their signs all through spring training. The signs are basically the same as those used the previous year, but there might be a change in the key or in the "yes" and "no" part of it.

In a meeting, we will go through them quite thoroughly. Then, we have a coach stand up and give the men a sign. I will pick out some-

| C. Going to sleeve (first signal after key). | D. Back to letters for hit-and-run signal (second sign after key). |

Fig. 12–4. (Continued) MANAGER'S KEY METHOD (Walter Alston).

body and ask, "What sign is *that?*" We will go through them until we have them down quite well.

Types of Signals

The most common types of signals given by a coach or manager are: flash signals, holding signals, block signals, combination signals, pump signals and word signals.

"Flash" signals

Flashing signs is a common method used to make them harder to detect. Actually, they are just what the name implies. They are *flashed* to the players through a particular act. While they are fine for the more experienced player, they are not recommended for players in the junior circuits.

The value of "flash" signals is that they can be given quickly. By mixing them in with other movements, the coach can camouflage his signals. However, the player may miss the signals, since the coach has to give them quickly. He can give the "flash" sign in one quick motion. He may touch his face for a "bunt," flick a hand across his uniform chest for the "take" or touch his leg for a "hit and run."

As shown in Figure 12–7, Danny Ozark, the Dodgers' third base coach, demonstrates some typical "flash" signals; however, without the indicator, they would be meaningless. Suppose the indicator sign is touching the belt buckle; the next signal is *it*, the sign that counts. If it is the "steal," he will rub the left thigh with his left hand.

After flashing the actual sign, he will continue signaling in order to avoid detection. The batter can do his part by continuing to look at the coach briefly after receiving his orders.

Holding signals

"Holding" signals are those which are held for several seconds, and are ideal for younger players. The clenched fist, the bent elbow or the hands on the knees are all examples of the "holding" type of signal. If the coach took off his cap for a few moments, he would be giving a "holding" sign.

The third base coach might assume a natural, relaxed position of his hands on the knees, which could be his "bunt" sign of the day. However, he had better give decoys before and after. He can make the hands-on-knees sign even more difficult to intercept by instructing his players to ignore the sign unless his thumbs are widely extended from the fingers.

The "holding" sign is the simplest for the player to get because it is held long enough for the message to sink in. A player can look more than once if he is in doubt about the signal.

The disadvantage of such a signal is that the sign is held for so long that the opposition may catch on to it. If the coach feels he is being closely watched by the opposition, he may have the player next to him send the signals to the players.

Fig. 12–5. GIVING THE STEAL SIGNAL. In picture A, the manager moves both hands to his cap, to indicate that the second signal after the key will be the steal sign. After giving the key and his first signal, he flashes the "real" steal sign (as shown in picture D).

A. Indicates second signal after key will be used.

B. Going to key #24 (tells coach to start taking signs now).

Signals that use different parts of the coach's body, or divide his body into blocks or sections, are called "block" signals. The coach can go from the head down to his shirt or arm. He can go clockwise, dividing his body into four parts. Or, he can go up and down.

Block signals

The bunt could be touching the face; hit and run, the letters of the shirt; the steal, the belt, etc. Or, the coach could give the hitting signs on one side of his body, and the running signs on the other side.

Touching the cap, head or face could be used for the first three hitters in the lineup, rubbing the shirt could be used for the next three hitters, while rubbing the pants could affect the last three.

The signal is sometimes determined by the number of rubs. For instance, the take sign could be one rub, and the bunt, two rubs. If he rubs his shirt once or twice while the first three batters are up, this would mean nothing, since the shirt signals apply only to the fourth, fifth and sixth hitters.

Regardless of the age level or the experience of the players, block signals are good to use. This system does have a disadvantage, in that occasionally the coach has trouble remembering the numerical position of the players in the lineup.

A combination sign is two or more motions tied together to represent a single sign (Fig. 12–5). Quite often, one of these motions or acts is the key sign. The key signal, for example, is covering the belt buckle with the hand. This by itself means nothing. The "steal," which is

Combination signals

Fig. 12–5. GIVING THE STEAL SIGNAL. (Continued) (Walter Alston)

C. Going to leg for first signal after key.

D. Completing steal signal by touching opposite sleeve.

touching the cap, also means nothing by itself. However, when the cap is touched and the belt buckle is covered, the "steal" is on.

The coach could have a set of signs starting with the cap, face, shirt and pants, which can be one, two, three and four. He will tell his players: "I am going to give you a certain number of rubs, and anytime I hit one of those spots, it counts."

Combination signals can also be used for the hit and run, bunt and squeeze play. Although a different sign is used for each, the same key sign can be used.

Rub-off signals A "rub-off" signal is a last-instant order used by the manager to cancel previous signs. Every team should have a "rub-off" sign which, when flashed, takes everything off. As an example, I have given the "hit-and-run" signal. However, I might reconsider because I feel a pitchout could be coming up. Changing my mind, I will give a "rub-off" signal, which takes the play off.

Removing the cap is commonly used as a "rub-off" signal, since it is easy for the players to catch.

Word signals Although word signals have some merit, they have a disadvantage in that the noise of the crowd will sometimes prevent the third base coach from hearing them distinctly. Word signals can be associated with the action desired. They are sometimes used for the base runner on third when the squeeze is on.

Giving Signals

Baseball signals are taken either directly from the head coach or from the manager on the bench, or relayed to the coach on the coaching lines. While high school rules prohibit the head coach from going on the base lines, one college coach is now allowed to coach on the line. Most major league managers prefer to stay in the dugout (Fig. 12–6), while their lieutenants handle the duties on the coaching lines (Fig. 12–7).

Whatever arrangement is used, the system should not be awkward to the hitter at the plate. With the head coach in the dugout on the third base side, the right-handed hitters will have to turn around constantly to look for the signs, unless they are relayed to a coach on the base lines.

If the team at bat is occupying the dugout on the first base side of the diamond, and the head coach is on the bench, right-handed hitters might take their signals directly from him. The hitter can take an occasional glance at the coach as he approaches the batter's box or as he steps into the box.

Left-handed batters can take their signs from the coach in the third base coaching box. The head coach should give this coach the signal in plenty of time so he can relay it on to the hitter. When the team occupies the third base dugout, left-handed batters get their signals directly from this coach, and right-handed batters from the first base coach.

Major league teams place considerable emphasis on the indicator system, using combination signs. In simpler terms, a specific key sign determines whether the signal is off or on. A coach may give any signal he wishes, but it does not mean a thing unless he has given an indicator sign first (Fig. 12–5).

I like the indicator because we can do a lot of faking. If I do not give the indicator, nothing happens. If I give the indicator, the first thing I touch is usually the sign I want to give.

Let us assume the indicator is a clap of the hands. The coach can touch any part of his body but he is not giving a signal. However, if he claps his hands and then adjusts the peak of his cap, the sign (the "take") is on.

The position of the coach in the coach's box may also be used as an indicator. If the coach is standing at the far end of the box, the signs are off, but if he is standing at the end nearest the hitter, the signs are on. This procedure can also be used in reverse, of course.

Indicator system

Receiving Signals

The correct execution of signals demands that the player look at the coach or manager at the right time. The proper times for the batter to look for the signals are when he is approaching the plate before entering the batter's box, and just after each pitch thrown to him while he is at bat (Fig. 12–3A).

After he receives the signal, the batter should continue looking at the coach so the coach can decoy the opposing team with additional motions and gestures. The hitter can take the signals either in the box or out of it. However, base runners should take the signals while standing on the base.

Pee Wee Reese probably was the best player I have seen at receiving signals. After I gave him a sign, he would just keep looking and looking. The first couple of times, I was not sure whether he got the sign or not, but in his own way, he was decoying to keep the other club from knowing the sign was given. All good sign-takers react the same way, in a nonchalant manner, and go ahead and execute it.

If the batter is doubtful about a sign, he should ask the umpire for time, step out of the batter's box and take another look. I would rather have my hitter sure that he has not missed the sign. He can act as though he is tying his shoelaces. Then he can take another look at his coach, who will either give the sign again or give him the "rub-off."

On the squeeze play, which is a surprise tactic, the coach might take the play off if he thinks the hitter has tipped off the play.

To prevent the other team from stealing the signals, we have added a "release" sign. If I give a player a signal, I will tell him it will be the first or second sign after the key, but he must keep looking until I release him. This is what we call a *release sign*. The batter will also know that he has not missed anything. Besides, it prevents a player from looking away as soon as he gets the signal.

Signals for the Batter

The signals that are given to the batter are: 1) the "take," 2) "hit" sign, 3) "hit and run," 4) "run and hit," 5) "sacrifice bunt" and 6) "squeeze bunt" (suicide or safety).

When explaining signs to the players, the coach should tell them: "You are always hitting, unless I give you a sign to do something else. The sign I give you stays on until I take it off or give you a different sign."

The "take"

The "take" sign is one of the most used signals in baseball. When the hitter looks down at the third base coach and he gives the "take" sign, the batter must not swing at the next pitch. The team may be several runs behind, and the coach wants the hitter to wait out the pitcher in hopes of getting a walk.

Managers, however, should not put on the take so often they make the players feel "he is taking the bat out of my hands." The "take" is used mainly to control the ball and strike on the count of three balls and one strike, two balls and no strike, three and nothing or the first pitch following a base on balls.

To signal the batter to "take," the manager might touch the peak of the cap, which means the batter should keep right on taking pitches until the manager rubs the sign off or gives another sign.

"Hit" sign

We like to have definite "hit" signs. Normally, when the manager wants his hitter to hit a 3-and-0 pitch, it is already understood that, "Anytime I don't give you a 'take' sign, you are hitting." Too often, however, the hitter will look around, and if his manager does not give him a "take," he may in his own mind wonder, "Well, I wonder if he gave me the 'take,' and I didn't see it."

Consequently, in certain situations, I will give the hitter a definite "hit" sign. He is in a much better frame of mind when I give him a definite "hit" sign, than if he worries about whether he missed the "take" sign.

"Hit and run"

The "hit and run" is employed to protect the base runner. The batter swings or throws his bat at the ball, regardless of where the pitch is thrown. The coach might place his hand on his nose, and it is important for him to know that both the hitter and runner have the sign. The runner might answer by putting either hand to his belt buckle. The hitter can answer by putting either hand to his face. On this play, the hitter must try to protect the runner and endeavor to hit the ball on the ground.

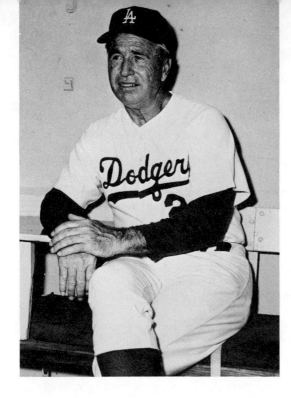

Fig. 12–6. SET OF SIGNALS FROM SITTING POSITION. All signals can be given with only a slight difference in position. The manager or coach simply crosses over with his hands, using a vertical division of his body. The hit and run can be signaled by crossing the letters with the right hand. The bunt (shown here) can be signaled by the left hand crossing over.

When the count is 3 and 1 or 2 and 0, the "run-and-hit" sign will go to both the runner and the hitter, which actually means that, "I want the runner to go on this pitch, regardless, and the hitter should swing at the pitch if it is in the strike zone."

"Run and hit"

On this play, the batter must protect the runner who is breaking for second with the pitch. He must bunt at the pitch, whether it is a strike or not. Putting the right hand on the left wrist could be the sign for the "bunt and run."

Like the "hit and run," the runner should answer the sign by placing either hand to his left buckle. The hitter can answer by putting either hand to his face.

"Bunt and run"

The "sacrifice bunt" is given to the batter when the coach wants to advance a runner or runners. In the sacrifice, the hitter should bunt only if the pitch is a strike. The runner on first base does not break for second until he is sure the ball is bunted on the ground.

Actually, I have about six ways to give the "bunt" sign. When I am sitting on the bench, I often cross one leg over the other. Anytime I take my left hand and place it on my right leg, the "bunt" sign is on (Fig. 12–6). Lately, I have gone to the open hand. The third base coach will then relay these signs to the hitter.

"Sacrifice"

There are two types of squeeze bunts: the suicide, and the safety squeeze. The success of the squeeze play, of course, depends upon the bunting ability of the batter.

"Squeeze bunt"

1. Suicide Squeeze

This play requires the greatest precaution to make certain nobody fouls up. As a result, a "holding" sign is often used to be sure the batter gets it. In turn, the batter can use a set "flash" reply, like picking up dirt and tossing it.

When the third base coach feels the hitter has the sign, he will give a signal to the runner on third base, a word message such as, "Be alive," or a remark giving the runner's first name.

The runner can acknowledge the signal by touching a part of his uniform.

2. Safety Squeeze

On this play, the batter should bunt only if the pitch is a strike. Actually, the same sign for the sacrifice can be used for the safety squeeze because the batter bunts only if the pitch is a strike.

Signals for the Base Runner

The signals that are given to the base runner are: 1) the "steal," 2) "double steal," 3) "delayed steal" and 4) "suit yourself." These signals are given directly to the base runner.

The "steal"

The "steal" is a holding or combination sign which is relayed to the runner on first base by the third base coach. The "single steal" sign could be pulling up the belt or placing the left hand on the right elbow.

On any count, the runner should go *only* if he gets a good jump on the pitcher. If the runner does not go down on this pitch and his coach does not rub the sign off, the "steal" sign is still on.

"Double steal"

There are various types of double steals with runners on first and third. Many coaches start with the straight single steal from first, while others use the break before the pitch, the delayed and the long-lead types.

The signal for the "double steal" might be placing the left hand on the right wrist, or clasping both hands. To signal the runner on third base, the straight "double steal" sign should be given, followed by another sign to tell him the type he wants to use. Many teams employ an entirely different sign for each type of double steal.

If the pitch is fouled off by the hitter, the sign stays on unless the coach rubs it off. If the coach does not want the runner on third base to try to score, he will put on the "single steal" sign.

"Delayed steal"

Only a fast runner should attempt the delayed steal. A signal such as touching the neck could be used, and the runner will break for second base the moment the catcher starts his throw to the pitcher.

"Suit yourself"

On this sign, the base runner has the prerogative of stealing any time he can get a good jump on the pitcher, not necessarily on the next pitch.

A. Indicator (sign to follow)   B. Bunt sign

Fig. 12–7. SIGNALS FROM THIRD BASE COACH. After receiving a signal from the manager on the bench, the base line coach has the responsibility of relaying it to the hitter and base runners (Danny Ozark).

Typical Set of Signals from the Base Coach

Indicator (sign to follow)—Right hand to belt buckle.
Take—Right hand rubs letters of shirt.
Hit and run—Right hand rubbing right thigh.
Take-off—Rub down on right arm.
Steal—Rubbing left hand on left thigh.
Bunt—Moving right hand to cap.
Release (hitter may look away and hit)—Rubbing down on left arm.

Stealing Signals

Some coaches and managers often tip-off their signals. They never seem to acquire the knack of giving them properly. Perhaps they are not good enough actors, which really is what topnotch signal callers are: good actors. Many coaches have the habit of being too deliberate when they give a sign. Although their decoying tactics are nonchalant, when they flash the actual signal, they overemphasize it. Consequently, they give most of their signals away.

Primarily, the "hit-and-run" and "steal" signals are the ones to look for. They can help a team, especially a hit and run. If we can pitchout on a hit-and-run play, we have a good chance to throw a man out.

Opposing managers and coaches, along with keen infielders and catchers, are always watching for tip-offs of this type. In picking up signals of the opposing team, a coach and player on the bench might

Fig. 12–8. MAKING THE TURN. On all base hits, the first base coach keeps encouraging the runner to make the turn by waving his arm in a circle and yelling, "Make your turn!" On errors through the infield, the coach is important in advising the man to go to second base by saying, "Go for two!" (Jim Gilliam).

combine to decode the play. One man will sit there and watch the coach to observe what he is doing, or what he touched, while the other man will watch the hitter. He will say, "He's looking, he's looking, he looked away!" Quite often, the last thing the coach did before he looked away might be the signal. This goes on for a couple of innings, and before long, they will come up with the signal.

After receiving a signal, many players will immediately stop looking at the coach. This often enables the defensive team to steal the signal. When a weak-hitting pitcher comes to bat with a teammate on first base and fewer than two out, the "bunt" sign can often be picked up.

I like to believe our signs are pretty foolproof; at least, I hope so. In addition to having many sets of signs, we have signs that are easily switched from a fast ball to a curve ball, and vice versa. We can switch them by just a little extra rub here and there. Basically, the signs remain the same but, once in a while, I will add a "switch" sign which reverses the set. Now, they are getting fast balls instead of curve balls.

Stealing signals from the catcher is a calculated risk that a lot of hitters are willing to take. Most hitters will take signs if they are relatively sure they are 75–85 per cent correct. Most of them are stolen from second base, with the runner watching the catcher giving the signals. If he happens to recognize a set of these signals, he may start immediately relaying signals to the hitter.

Fig. 12-9. "STOP! STAY AT THIRD BASE!" signals the third base coach. This type of guidance is effective when the runner is coming from second and it is a question whether or not he can score. Here, Coach Danny Ozark goes down the line where the runner can see him better. In addition, it gives him more time to make up his mind.

Fig. 12-10. THE RUNNER AT THIRD BASE. Coach Danny Ozark instructs the base runner, Bill Russell, not to use a cross-over step in coming down the line. Notice that the runner stays in foul territory in the event of being hit by a batted ball.

Fig. 12–11. "STAY UP!" yells the on-deck hitter as he holds his hands high above his head. Assisting the base runner is one of the duties of the on-deck hitter (Dick Green).

Through the years, baseball signals have provided players and spectators with many serious and dramatic moments, and some humorous ones as well. One day, "Preacher" Roe, the former stylish southpaw of the Brooklyn Dodgers, was pitching to a Pittsburgh rookie who nervously backed out, stepped in, backed out again and, a third time, looked at the third base coach, unable to interpret the signal. Finally, Roe, in his Arkansas drawl, exclaimed: "He wants you to bunt, son, B–U–N–T!"

Duties of Base Coaches

The coaches at first and third bases can play an important role in the success of any team. Essentially, their primary duties are giving signals and assisting base runners. Therefore, they must be constantly alert and be the type of individuals who can remain calm and make the right decisions even when the action gets hectic.

The base line coaches must be proficient at relaying signs from the bench coach to the hitters (Fig. 12–7). The head coach or manager on the bench gives the base coach the sign as quickly as possible after every pitch. Then, the base coach relays it to the hitter as he steps back into the batter's box.

First base coach

The coach at first base gives encouragement to the hitter, and once the ball is hit, he helps the batter-runner any way he can. If there is an error on the throw, the coach will instruct the runner to go to second or stop. If the ball is hit to the outfield, he will move to the front of the box and point toward second and yell, "Make your turn!" or, "Go for two!" (Fig. 12–8). He might wave his arm in a circle in addition to yelling for the runner to go to second. If he is sure the runner cannot advance, he should yell, "Hold up!"

The coach should tell the base runner how many outs there are and remind him to be alert for signs. He might cup his hands around his mouth so his voice will be better directed at the runner. He can advise him whether this is the tying or winning run, especially if the team is two or three runs down in the eighth or ninth inning. If he is the first man on, he might say, "Your run doesn't mean anything—do not take any chances!"

If the first baseman is playing behind the runner, the coach has to face the first baseman and let his runner know when to get back. He should warn the runner to be careful if the pitcher has a good move. If a fly ball is deep but will likely be caught, the coach should tell the runner to tag up, or if it is shallow, to go halfway. A constant chatter will help the runner become more familiar with his voice, such as, "All right, all right," "Get back" or, "Look out."

Third base coach

The coach at third base takes over the guiding of a base runner after he passes first base, particularly when the ball is behind the runner (Fig. 12–9). Actually, the only guidance from the coach is on the ball hit down the right field line. If the ball is hit in front of him, we want the runner himself to make the decision.

When the ball is hit down the right field line, the ball is behind the runner, and we do not like our runners to turn around and look at that ball while running. Rather, he should look over to the third base coach to see whether he should come to third or stay at second. Some coaches instruct the base runner to look at the coach when he is about 20 feet from second base.

If he wants the runner to round third base, the coach should move down the line toward home plate 15 feet or more. If he wants to stop him at third, the coach has to be in front of the runner where the runner can see him (Fig. 12–9). He can motion by signs: "Stay," "Hold up" or, "Stay on the base."

If the runner is coming from second base and it is a question of whether or not he can score, the coach should go down the line where the runner can definitely see him. In this situation, we instruct our runners, "You run until the coach stops you." Now, we would not have the coach down the line if we did not want him to round the bag. Therefore, it is necessary for the runner to keep running until he is stopped. This gives the coach a little more time to make up his mind whether this man can score or not. As he rounds third base, the runner can see the coach and hear him say either "Get back!" or, "Come on!" Most of this is by waving the hand or by arm motion, rather than by mouth.

When a runner is on third base, the coach should give him the same type of information as that given the runner at first base, such as outs, game situation and the location of the ball. He should be reminded how the infield is playing, or to tag up on all fly balls. The coach might tell the runner to go home only if the ball goes through the infield, or to try and score on an infield ground ball.

Offensive Drills

No time should be lost while practicing drills. Anytime a team runs any type of drill, the coach must insist that no time be wasted. He must line his players up and get them going quickly. Unless the coach keeps his drill nice and snappy, sure enough, the players will die on him. So, do not give them any time to rest. *Keep them moving!*

Game situation drill

A base runner is placed at first base, with nobody out, and the batter is told to hit the ball anywhere he pleases. We instruct our pitcher not to throw the ball hard. Rather, it should be nice and easy so the batter will hit the ball somewhere. We encourage him to practice going to the opposite field and hitting behind the runner. When three outs are made, we clear the bases and bring the runner back to first base and start again. We never start without a runner on base.

We never permit an outfielder to lob the ball back in. He must throw it hard every time he fields the ball. We want him to fire the ball and hit the relay man.

Most base runners do not take the extra base the majority of the time when they could. The best way to teach a boy to take the extra base and not get caught is to have him make up his mind when he rounds his base. On a single to right field, with a runner on first and the throw going to third base, the runner must look for the ball immediately as the relay goes into the cutoff man. The only time he goes on to second base is when he knows the ball is going to be over the head of the cutoff man. Therefore, he must look at the height of the ball when it comes in.

We do this drill for about 30 minutes, since there are so many different situations involved in it. Then, we change and put the other players in the field, and the regulars come in and get some good base running experience.

When we do this drill, we make sure we have coaches at third and first base, so that it presents a regular game situation.

Base running drill

Lining up at home plate, the players run down to first and practice rounding the base. We want them to tag the inside of the bag, making their pivot properly, and continuing to second base. The runners should practice proper running form.

We will then have our players line up at first base to practice their leads and breaks. After taking a lead of about 12 feet from the bag, he breaks for second base on a signal from the coach. The first step should be a cross-over step.

The coach will call out the normal lead, the steal lead, the one-way lead, the regular steal, the delayed steal and the hit and run. The runner will make the proper start as the pitcher delivers the ball to an imaginary hitter.

In another routine, a coach will hit a ground ball to the outfield to be handled by an outfielder. We have the batter-runner round first base and see how far he can go toward second and still get back before the relay. A player can find out by experience how far he can go. These types of setups are all excellent gamelike drills, very similar to the various game situations.

Double steal drill

The infielders and the battery combination take their positions, with runners on first and third. This drill not only provides offensive work but the coach can establish his defense setup at the same time. The drill begins when the pitcher starts his delivery. The runner on first starts for second in a straight steal attempt, and the man on third waits until he is fairly sure the catcher is throwing through, then he breaks for the plate.

This drill can be performed in two parts:

1) The catcher makes all his throws to second base so that runners learn the technique of the play.
2) The catcher tries to outmaneuver the runners. The runner at first base should purposely get caught in a run-down occasionally.

Squeeze play drill

With the coach observing the action, the batter and base runner at third execute the squeeze play. The runner practices his timing on when to leave, while the batter turns around and bunts the ball. A line of runners is at third base, while another line could be at first or second base, or both.

Getting a good lead at third base, the runner breaks for the plate as the pitcher is about to release the ball. It is advisable to work this drill with signals so that the batter and runners learn to execute this play under game conditions as realistic as possible.

During our base running drills, instead of squeezing the runner in from third, we will instruct him to score on a ground ball. We have him wait at third base and, when a ball is hit on the ground, he practices his walking lead and timing on a ground ball. If the ball is hit on a fly to the outfield, he has to go back and tag up.

Sliding drill

Every team should have a sliding pit where this phase of the game can be practiced. The team lines up about 40 feet away, and one-by-one, the players run and slide in the pit. The infield can also be used, or the players can take their spikes off and practice on the grass.

The player should be taught to slide on either side, and later, he can learn to slide away from the tag, with an infielder covering the base.

Hit-and-run drill

While we are taking batting practice, we place a runner on first base and a half-dozen hitters take turns executing the hit and run. On the first pitch, the hitter must hit the ball where it is pitched and the runner must go.

The pitcher receives good practice holding a runner on, and the runner practices taking his lead and moving to second base on the hlt-and-run play. If the batter misses the ball or fouls it off, the runner stays at second base. Now, the same hitter takes the next pitch with a runner on second base, with nobody out, and tries to move the runner to third.

We encourage the batter to hit the ball to right field. If the runner can be advanced, he goes on to third, and we put on the squeeze play.

Bunting drill The bunters form a line near home plate, while the runners line up at first base. The pitcher and catcher, along with the infielders, assume their defensive positions. Using proper bunting procedure, the batter lays the ball down. Later, runners are placed at first and second base, and the defense tries to make the force play at third base.

Speed development The manager or coach should have some idea of the speed of each player, and the most scientific way to ascertain it is by using a stop watch. Each player should be timed *individually*.

Perhaps the best way to have the players run is from a cross-over start for a distance of 60 yards. The average young player takes between 7.4 and 7.3 seconds to run this distance.

In addition to finding out the speed of his player, this drill will give the coach an opportunity to provide some suggestions on running technique and form.

Team Defense /13/

While pitching has been said to be at least 70 per cent of baseball, even the finest pitchers in the game need the support of a sound defense. Indeed, good pitching and a sound defense will prove a winning combination for any baseball team.

The Primary Needs

The pitching staff must keep the ball in the park and prevent the hitters from hitting it too hard and too often. Then, it is up to the fielders to convert a high percentage of their fielding chances into outs.

The Dodgers have always tried to emphasize defensive excellence and tightness. I believe it reverts back to the speed that we have prided ourselves with all through the years.

The defense must be heads-up and alert. Every player must be "in the ball game" at all times. People have said that our Dodger teams "make errors but not mistakes," which, to me, is quite a tribute to our defensive record. Certainly, the many hours we spend on relays, cutoffs and other defensive tactics during spring training pay off with victories in league play.

Defense is the key to a sound and solid baseball team. The team that makes the fewer number of errors or mistakes in fielding and throwing will normally be the team that wins the game. Basically, the reasons for failure in defense are that players hurry their throws, throw off balance, are out of position or actually do not know what to do. Beyond the pitching, the ingredients of a sound defense are speed and good ground coverage. The center fielder who can cover ground, get the good jump on the ball and employ a strong and accurate arm,

---

Defense is the key to a sound and solid baseball team.

---

will prove a great asset to his team. The shortstop and second baseman, with their quick and sure hands, alertness and knowledge of the hitters, will cover the ground and make the plays necessary to championship ball.

In addition, it is essential to have a top receiver. The catcher who can handle the pitcher can be an extremely valuable man. He should be the "quarterback" of the ball club—a good, solid aggressive receiver.

The New York Mets, 1969 World Champions of baseball, are a good example of a team which few people figured had a chance for the pennant. They started out by winning a few games, then started to roll along. Soon, they found out that they could win, and the more they won the more confident they got, giving them more team spirit. Before long, they *believed* that they could do it.

Their morale was great! Everybody was hustling and diving after catches. Team spirit and a confident attitude are so important. If a team is fortunate enough to win a few games, they find out that they can do things. Then, they go ahead and *do* them. This is the team spirit, morale or momentum that carries a team over the rough spots and gives it the little "extra" that it needs.

The top defensive teams have the ability to execute effectively the basic fundamentals of defense. They have the players who possess the quickness and agility to get to the ball and field it properly.

"Strong down the middle" The secret of defense is to be "strong straight down the middle" (Fig. 13–2). A sound defense consists of a good defensive catcher who can throw, a consistent double play combination and a fast, dependable center fielder who can throw and keep the runners from going from first to third.

The double play is the greatest defensive weapon in baseball. The double play can get a team out of a tough inning better than anything else. Therefore, the shortstop and second baseman must be able to make this play when the situation requires it. It should be the first thing on their minds whenever there is a man on base. On many occasions, the double play is missed by just a fraction of a second. It is such a close play at first base that the well-executed and perfect pivot on the double play can make a great many of the close ones succeed. Surely, if a team lacks a Sandy Koufax to strike men out, then the double play ball is the factor that will take the heart out of the big inning.

Good Pitching An old baseball adage states that, "Good pitching stops good hitting." If the defense keeps the other team from scoring, it has been said, "You cannot lose." This means that, if a team can hold their

The double play is the greatest defensive weapon in baseball.

opponents to one or two runs, it does not have to have the greatest hitters in the world to score a couple of runs themselves.

The best pitcher in baseball is still the pitcher who has a little something extra on the fast ball. The off-speed pitches, of course, complement the fast ball, but a staff of hard-throwing pitchers will always command the respect of opposing hitters.

With a staff of pitchers who can throw strikes, a well-drilled, alert defensive team will prove hard to beat.

A Sound Defense

The best teams in baseball, year-in and year-out, are blessed with outstanding mound work and a solid defense. Interestingly enough, the top clubs achieved their success because they applied successfully the following old-fashioned virtues of baseball defense:

1. The ability and concentration to make all the routine plays consistently and correctly
2. Ability to convert the difficult, tricky-hop ground balls into outs
3. Ability to make the double plays consistently
4. Relay and cutoff men at the right place and time
5. Hitting the relay and cutoff men with good outfield throws
6. Backing up efficiently on overthrows
7. Keeping opposing base runners close
8. Pitchers keeping their pitches down
9. Not making any unnecessary throws
10. A fast, dependable center fielder who can throw
11. A catcher who is capable of handling the low ball, and who can throw
12. A catcher who can handle the pitchers, and be the team "quarterback"
13. Players in the field who can run and throw
14. Using two hands in fielding whenever possible
15. Every player heads-up, alert and ready to hustle
16. Knowing what to do with the ball before it arrives—*thinking all the time!*
17. Team spirit—thinking more about the *team's* needs than about individual accomplishments.

Hard Work and Team Spirit

Certainly, these virtues of defensive excellence do not come by themselves. They are the result of practice and concentration, with the players becoming familiar with each other—and, above all, a

The secret of defense is to be strong straight down the middle.

great amount of hard work and *pulling together as a team.* The manager and his coaching staff must continually strive to stimulate a kind of dedicated concentration on the part of each player, to be able to make all the routine plays consistently and correctly.

Every player must have a strong belief in the total success of the team. Instead of being removed from the game and brooding about not playing, a player should accept pitching and lineup changes with a spirit that it is best for the *team.*

Hours of practice can help make a fielder fundamentally correct. One of the basic things each outfielder and infielder has to do during a ball game is to anticipate that the ball is going to be hit to *him.* He is more or less thinking: "If the ball is hit to me, what should I do with it? What play do I make?"

Team play

Victory can come if a group of players will really go to work together, as a team. This is particularly true when the team is in the field. Each player must have the same purpose and goal, and it is this kind of group feeling or team spirit that wins games.

I like to see the little "pepper," the talking back and forth, but unfortunately, this has gone out of style. The old-time ballplayers had a little more chatter and pep than the modern-day clubs. I do not know whether this is because of the big parks with the large crowds, and the players having difficulty hearing each other.

I think it is important for an infielder to chatter back and forth to his pitcher. Once an out is made and they pass the ball around the infield, they should do it with some enthusiasm and pep, rather than in a dead, lackadaisical manner.

Every manager and coach looks for the born leader to direct his team in the field, the Pee Wee Reese or Maury Wills type. The shortstop or second sacker who can turn around and talk to his teammates, such as, "One out" or, "Two outs," can be a great asset to a ball team. He tells them where to throw the ball or to hit the cutoff man—everything the manager wants to say himself.

According to Paul Richards, "No defensive strategy can be successful unless every player on the field will practice the basic rule of the game: *think and hustle.*" The player's preliminary thought in the field is: "What should I do if the ball is hit to *me?*" If he does not have every play planned *before the ball is hit,* he simply will not have enough time to think. The more thinking he can do, the more alert and aggressive he can be. And, of course, there is no substitute for hustle.

Defensive Alignment

The defensive positions of the infielders and outfielders, to a large extent, are determined by the stage of the game and the ability of

Good pitching stops good hitting.

the hitter. The score, inning and speed of the base runner are all factors to be considered in establishing the correct alignment and depth of the fielders (Fig. 13–2).

Early in the game, or when they are more than two runs ahead, a team might play deep and give up a run. With runners on first and third bases and less than two outs, many teams will play at double play depth, unless the winning run is at third.

When a run cannot be given, the infield should be played tight, such as late in the game when a runner is on third with the tying or winning run. Otherwise, it is best to play at normal depth.

When one team is leading by a large score, the team in front will be conceding a run or two and looking always for the double play, or even one out, to break the back of the inning.

The third baseman should play even with the bag for speedy players, especially good bunters and left-handed hitters. When a bunt situation is in order, the third baseman should move in on the grass. He should be moving toward the plate just as soon as the bat drops.

The third and first basemen must protect the lines against two-base hits, more so with two outs than with no outs. Late in the game, guarding against a two-base hit is considered fundamental strategy.

The alignment of the outfielders is determined by the type of hitter at the plate. Is he a left- or right-handed hitter? Can he pull the ball? Is he a line drive hitter? They must also be ready to execute assignments of covering and backing up the bases.

Fig. 13–2. DEFENSIVE EXCELLENCE. Defense is the key to a sound baseball team, of which speed and good ground coverage are perhaps the prime essentials. Below, with a runner on third and two outs, the Dodger infield has been moved back to "just play the hitter."

Fig. 13.3. HITTING THE RELAY MAN. Relays and cutoffs are team plays which are the glue in the defense. During spring training, major league teams practice these plays by the hour. Above, Pat Kelly, after fielding a long drive off the fence, hits the relay man with a good throw, quick and on a line.

Relays and Cutoffs

Relays and cutoffs are team plays which require a great deal of practice and teamwork to be executed properly. Too often, missed cutoffs and relay plays have given opponents the extra base which led to the run that decided the game. During the early spring training season, major league teams work on these plays by the hour. They are the "glue" in the defense (Fig. 13–4).

If the outfielder can hit the cutoff man, he can keep the hitter from going to second on the throw-in. This is important, because now the base runner cannot score on a single and is still set up for a possible double play.

A team that shows poise and confidence is one that has practiced these plays over and over until there is no hesitation or uncertainty in their execution. Poor execution of fundamentals and lack of self-assurance are nothing more than the lack of practice. I am sure that many teams on the lower levels of play do not devote enough drill time to this phase of defense.

Relays

Most teams use a double cutoff. They will send out the shortstop or the second baseman. They will put either one behind the other player, in case there is a bad throw. The outfielder has to hit the first man who comes out for the throw. It must be a good throw, quick and on a line.

On a base hit to right center field, for example, the second baseman will go out to take the relay throw (Fig. 13–4). Use of the voice is important in this defensive situation. The shortstop is the backup man, about 30 feet or so behind. He should tell the relay man where the ball should be thrown. He should call out: "Home," "Second base" or, "No play," depending on where the play should be made.

The relay man should raise his hands and yell, "Here!" In order to catch the ball on his throwing side, he should step forward with his

Fig. 13–4. THE RELAY MAN moves out to take the throw from the outfielder. In order to catch the ball on his throwing side, he steps forward with his right foot in the direction of the throw. Holding his hands letter-high, he provides a good target (Bernie Allen).

right foot in the direction of the throw. This maneuver turns his body slightly toward the infield, to his left, enabling him to make his throw more quickly.

Cutoffs

The purpose of the cutoff is to keep the hitter from taking an extra base, if no play occurs at home. On a base hit to center field, with a man on first base, the first baseman is the cutoff man. The third baseman is often the cutoff man for the left fielder.

The cutoff man should assume a position about 40 feet in front of the catcher and in a direct line with the throw from the outfielder. He listens for the catcher's call of "Cut it" or, "Let it go." He should be ready to throw to second base to catch the runner.

The outfielder stands out there and thinks: "Now, I've got Lou Brock running at second base. I have very little chance of throwing him out at home, unless I get that terrific line drive with the one-hop catch. Therefore, I must be sure to throw the ball low so that the cutoff man can cut it off and make a play on the hitter going to second base."

Even on routine fly balls to the outfield with no one on base, the outfielders should get into the habit of making *good, low, hard* throws into second base.

We like to have as many free men as possible get in a line so that, if the cutoff is missed, one of them has a chance to recover the ball quickly and hold the opposition down to the least advanced base.

Even major league teams miss some cutoffs, and the result is often the ball game. If the outfielder can hit the cutoff man, he will prevent the runner going to second on the throw.

Run-down play

Whenever a player is trapped between two bases, he should be run back toward the base he left. Ideally, it should take no more than two throws to retire the runner (Fig. 13–5).

A   B

Fig. 13–5. THE RUN–DOWN PLAY. A man caught in a run-down situation should never be allowed to escape. Above, the runner has been run back to third base, rather than toward home. In picture A, the catcher has thrown the ball to the third baseman, who should be moving toward the runner for a quick tag. In picture B, the catcher has moved out of the base line to avoid possible interference.

The important point in a run-down play is to make the runner *commit himself*. If a runner has been caught off first base, the first baseman has to get the runner started toward second a little and then give the ball to the second baseman. The second baseman should get him running as hard as he can and then throw the ball to the first baseman, who makes the tag.

The player with the ball must run at full speed toward the runner, while holding the ball in a throwing position. One good fake with a full-arm motion will often fool the runner and make him change direction and run into the tag.

When this play fails to work, the infielders involved probably did not get the runner going at full speed. They also may have tried to throw the ball too many times; before they knew it, they were running into each other.

Defensive Play Situations

With runners on first or first and second, quick thinking by the defense is necessary. The pitcher and the first baseman should break in. The third baseman should position himself almost on top of the bunter, forcing him to bunt to the first baseman, who has a chance of getting the man at second. Of course, the second baseman must cover first base (Fig. 13–6).

The most effective way to defense the sacrifice bunt is to throw the batter high, fast balls in the strike zone.

With runners on first and second, if the ball is bunted on the third base side, the pitcher should break quickly toward the third base line. If he can handle it quickly enough, he should make the play at

Fig. 13-6. DEFENDING AGAINST THE SACRIFICE BUNT. Moving quickly off the mound, the pitcher makes his throw to second base to force the runner and spoil the sacrifice attempt. Otherwise, he will go to first base, with the second baseman coming over for the throw.

third base. In fact, if he is alert, a good fielding pitcher can make this play most of the time, but it requires a significant amount of practice time to perfect. However, if the ball is bunted hard enough and the pitcher cannot get to it, the third baseman must be sure to go after it instead of going to the base. This is a tough play for the third baseman.

Defending against the steal

The pitcher must keep the runners tight. If the base runner gets a running start, he has a good chance of stealing a base. Therefore, the pitcher should always remember to *make the runner stop.*

The pitcher must hold the ball long enough to make the runner stop, before he throws it to home plate. However, if the runner has a big lead or starts his break, the pitcher should step back, off the rubber.

The second baseman and shortstop must communicate with each other in order to know who is covering. As soon as the runner at first breaks, the shortstop or second baseman, whoever is covering, must break with him. He should not wait until the ball gets by the hitter; he must be there *on time.*

Defending against the double steal

With runners on first and third, the shortstop and second baseman must determine who will cover second. Normally, the shortstop is the cutoff man with a left-hander at the plate, while the second baseman handles this role with a right-handed batter.

With men on first and third and the runner on first trying to steal, the catcher must first give the runner at third a quick look. If the runner at third has too big a lead, he may attempt to pick him off. Merely looking at the runner will very likely start him back toward third, and then the throw can be made to second base to get the runner going into second.

The four basic ways to stop the double steal are:

1. Look the runner back to third, then make the throw to second base
2. Have the catcher throw directly back to the pitcher and then trap the runner off third
3. Throw directly to the shortstop, who moves in about ten feet in front of second base
4. Have the catcher throw directly to third.

The last three plays must be made on prearranged signals.

Defending against the squeeze play

There is no defense unless the pitcher knows the exact pitch the squeeze is to occur on. If the runner has tipped-off the play by breaking too soon, or the bunter has squared around too soon, the pitcher can defense the play by knocking down the hitter. Otherwise, the only defense in a squeeze situation is to come to a set position, and use high fast balls that are hard to bunt. The runner should not be allowed to get too much of a lead.

Defending against the hit and run and run and hit

Actually, it becomes a guessing game, with the catcher trying to guess when these plays will be attempted. A pitchout, however, will break up these offensive tactics. Since the hitter is told to hit the ball no matter where it is pitched, the pitch should be thrown high and away, or impossible to hit. Then, the catcher's job is to throw the runner out at second.

Pick-off play

On the play at second base, many teams like to use the "count" play. The "daylight" play has also been used successfully. Whether it is executed at first or second, the pick-off play requires an alert pitcher who is aggressive at throwing the ball. A pitcher who is not aggressive, or one who is slow in his actions, will have a difficult time making this play.

On the "count" play at second base, the pitcher takes the sign and goes into a stretch position. The moment he comes to this position, he should turn his head toward second base. As he turns his back toward the plate, he should say, "One thousand one and . . ." This time span is usually about two seconds, depending upon how fast the pitcher is executing the pivot and throw. Then, he should whirl and make his throw. The second baseman or shortstop will break at that precise moment.

When the runner at first base takes too long a lead, the first baseman and pitcher can team up to pick him off. When the pitcher looks over to check the runner before his delivery to the plate, the first baseman gives his sign, such as hitching up his pants. Then the first baseman should dash behind the runner, and the pitcher throws the ball over the base.

We prefer that the shortstop go in and take the throw at the bag and have the second baseman back him up. We feel this is more effective than having the shortstop go out a few feet, with the second baseman coming in and backing him up.

If a speedster like Willie Davis or Lou Brock hits a single to left, for example, he should round first base running at full speed. Now, if the outfielder should get a little nonchalant and lob the ball into the shortstop, who is out in front of the bag 15 or 20 feet, the base runner might very well keep on running. By the time another relay is made, the runner has slid safely into the base.

The reason we do this is to protect against the exceptional base runner who might try to outhustle the play in which the shortstop moves out to short left field. If it is an ordinary base hit and not too deep, we want our outfielders to throw directly to second base. If the ball gets by either man, the first baseman is also in a good backup position. The catcher and right fielder are going down to the first base area, too.

This procedure also applies on a single to right field. On a routine ball, the right fielder throws directly to the second baseman, rather than hitting the cutoff man some 15 feet in front of the bag. However, the batter-runner is not as likely to outhustle the throw in from right field as he would on one from the left field side.

Defensive Situations

Situation #1: Single to left field, no one on base.

Diagram 13–1.

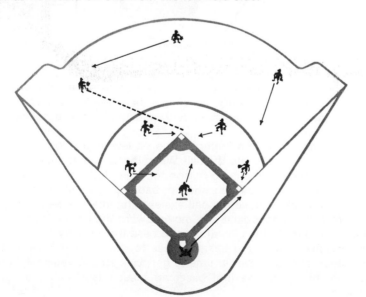

Situation #2: Single to left field, man on first.

This is a routine play, nothing special, but one that must be executed properly. The shortstop has to move out to the cutoff position, in line with the left fielder's throw to third base. If the third baseman calls, "Cut it off," he should cut it off. If the runner keeps on going into third, the shortstop should let it go through.

The pitcher backs up third base because of the likelihood that the play will be made there. The catcher remains at home plate, while the first and second basemen cover their respective bases.

Diagram 13–2.

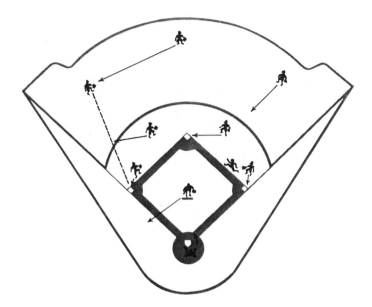

Situation #3: Single to left field, man on second, first and second or bases loaded.

This is a basic cutoff play in which the third baseman serves as the cutoff man. We like the third baseman to handle this play because he can get into the cutoff position very quickly; the first baseman has much farther to go.

The cutoff man is in a better position a few steps closer to home plate, so he can move into the ball. When the ball comes in all the way from the outfield, there is no reason for the cutoff man to just stand there and take the throw on a short or bad hop. Instead, he can either move in or back to make the ball easier to handle. So, we prefer him to be closer to home plate and move toward the ball, so as to be in a position to make the play at second base if necessary.

Occasionally, the third baseman has to dive after the ball in the hole, and cannot recover in time to get back and serve as the cutoff man. In this case, the first baseman must hustle into the cutoff position.

Diagram 13–3.

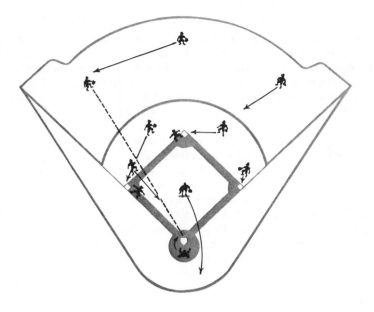

The shortstop goes out to a spot in left center to become the relay man. Instead of going to second base, the second baseman comes over and backs up. He is the "trailer" man, about 30 feet behind the shortstop in line with third base.

Situation #4: Double, possible triple to left center, no one on base, or man on third or second, or men on third and second bases.

Diagram 13–4.

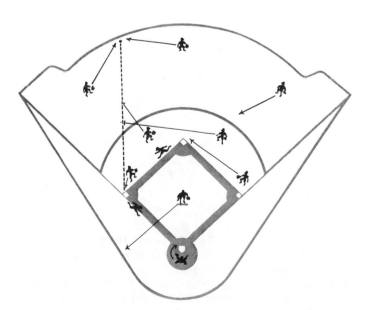

This play demands a double-cutoff man, a "trailer." If a hurried throw does miss the mark, the defense still has a chance for a play at third or home. If the hit is a sure double and the first baseman has nothing to do at first base, he should go over and cover second base.

Since he may not be sure which base he should back up, he should go halfway between home and third and then back up the base where the throw is going. If the play develops at third base, he will go there.

Situation #5: Single to center field, man on first.

This is a simple cutoff play in which the shortstop is the cutoff man on the throw from center field to third base. He lines himself up with the throw. It is up to him or the third baseman to call, "Cut it off" or, "Let it go."

Actually, in a big league game, where there is a lot of noise made, the shortstop usually makes up his own mind, depending on whether the throw is on the line or not. He also knows who is running and whether he has a chance to throw out the man at third, or if he should cut the ball off and make the cutoff play at second base.

Here, again, it depends on the score. Sometimes, if the winning run is going in to third, he may have more of a tendency to let the throw go through.

Diagram 13–5.

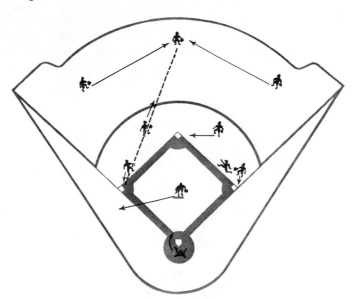

Situation #6: Single to center field, men on first and second, or men on first, second and third.

This situation involves two different throws. The pitcher breaks halfway between second and third, not knowing whether the throw is going to third base or directly home.

If the throw is to home plate, of course, the first baseman has to be in a cutoff position, a spot 45 feet from home plate in line with the throw. If the throw goes to third base, he must hustle back to first base to cover that bag.

The shortstop should be the cutoff man for a possible throw to third base. The second and third basemen cover their respective bases.

Diagram 13-6.

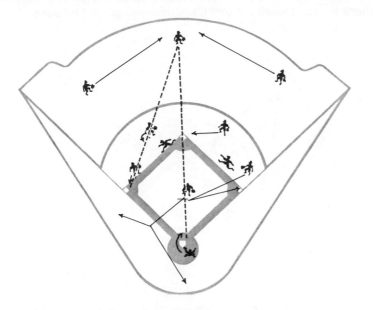

This is a routine play which involves the runner attempting to go to third on a base hit to right field. The shortstop stations himself about 45 feet from third base, on a direct line from third base to the outfielder fielding the ball.

The pitcher moves over and backs up third base in line with the throw, and the second and third basemen cover their bases. The left fielder should move in toward third base as quickly as he possibly can. By the time the runner goes from first to third, he has a chance to get in quite close and be of some assistance.

Situation #7: Single to right field, man on first base, or men on third and first.

This is also a routine play, where the first baseman takes a cutoff position about 45 feet from home plate. The second baseman has to cover first base for this reason: if the throw is late or the catcher yells, "Cut it off," the first baseman will cut it off and throw it to the second baseman.

If the second baseman is not behind him at first base, this runner can go two-thirds of the way down and still come back if the ball is cut off. But if the second baseman comes in behind him, we will have him in a trap. Thus, the second baseman is the key to the play; he must come over to first base.

Situation #8: Single to right field, man on second base, or men on second and third bases.

If the first baseman dives after the ground ball and prevents him from acting as the cutoff man, the third baseman has to come in quickly for the cutoff play. We will just have the first and second basemen criss-cross. After attempting to field the ball, the first baseman continues on and covers second, while the second baseman, after his unsuccessful attempt, continues to cover first base.

Diagram 13–7.

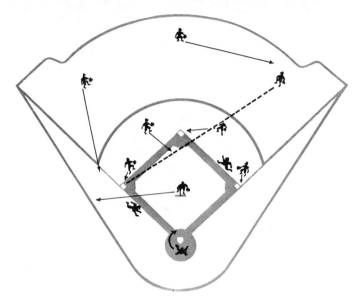

Diagram 13–8.

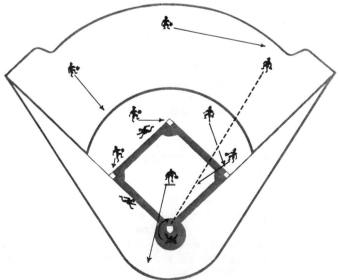

Diagram 13–9.

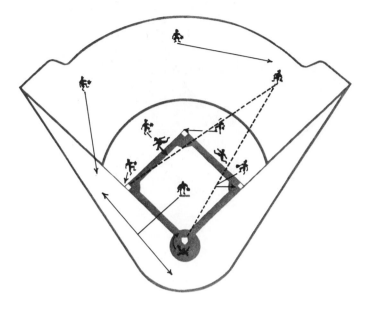

Situation #9: Single to right field, men on first and second, or men on first, second and third.

The shortstop comes over and acts as the cutoff man for the throw to third base. The second baseman has to go to second base.

The first baseman becomes a cutoff man in case the throw is made to the plate, but if the throw goes to third, he must return and cover first base. The pitcher goes halfway between third and home to see where the throw goes.

The right fielder makes a low throw to the shortstop to keep the tying or winning run from going to third base. The left fielder moves into a point near the line and backs up third base.

The important thing in this situation is always to keep the tying or winning run from going to third with less than two out. Therefore, the right fielder should never make a foolish throw to the plate.

Occasionally, the pitcher has to become the cutoff man in this situation. If the first baseman cannot get the ball in the hole, he keeps moving toward second, and the pitcher covers first in case the first baseman fields the ball. Since he is out of position, he just stops and comes back into the cutoff position.

Situation #10: Double, possible triple, to right center field.

The second baseman goes out to a spot in short center field, in line with third base, to become the relay man. The shortstop trails behind him about 30 feet, in line with third base.

The first baseman trails the runner to second base, where he covers the bag, ready for a play at that base. In backing up third base, the pitcher plays as deep as possible. With the catcher protecting home plate, the left fielder moves in toward the area of third base.

Diagram 13–10.

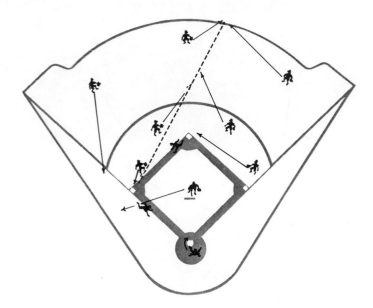

If the play is at the plate, the second baseman again is the relay man, with the shortstop trailing behind. The first baseman is the cutoff man, with the pitcher backing up home plate.

Situation #11: Double, possible triple, down right field line, no one on base.

The second baseman becomes the first relay man on the play to third base, with the shortstop becoming the "trailer" relay man. The first

Diagram 13–11.

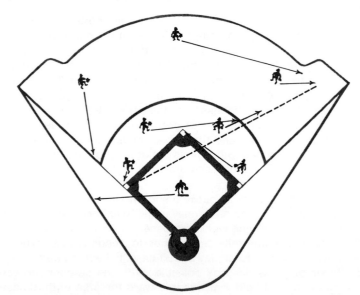

baseman trails the runner into second base, and the pitcher backs up third base. The left fielder moves into an area behind third base.

With a runner on first base and the play at the plate, the second baseman goes to a spot in right field along the foul line in line with the right fielder and home. This is the rare situation when the first baseman goes out as a "trailer," while the shortstop covers second base.

The pitcher goes to a spot halfway between third and home to see where the throw is going.

When anticipating a bunt, the third and first basemen should charge in when the pitcher throws the ball. The pitcher then breaks toward the plate.

Situation #12: Bunt situation in order, with a runner on first base.

Generally, if the ball is bunted hard, the play should go to second base. However, if the play at second is doubtful, the fielder should make sure he gets one out by throwing to first base.

The catcher fields all bunts possible, but when the third baseman fields the ball in close to home plate, he moves down and covers third base. The second baseman, in covering first base, "cheats" by shortening his position and his distance from the bag.

Diagram 13–12.

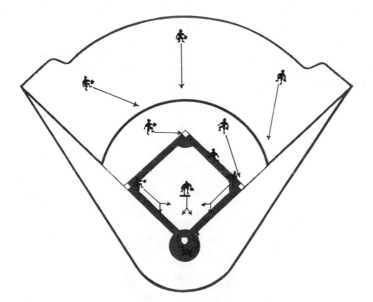

The third baseman's judgment is the key to this play, and he is in full charge. The first objective is to retire the runner at third, but at least one runner *must* be retired.

The third baseman takes a position on the edge of the grass, just inside the line and four steps in front of the bag, and stationary. Upon

Situation #13: Bunt situation in order, with runners on first and second.

Diagram 13–13.

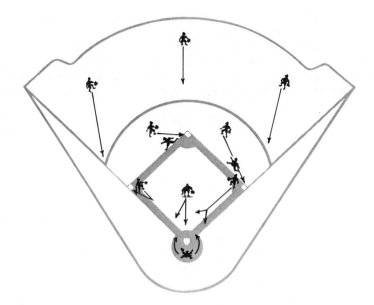

delivering the ball, the pitcher breaks toward the third base foul line and strives to field the ball. On a ball that the pitcher can handle, the third baseman moves back and covers the base.

On balls bunted down the line, if he feels he has a better play, the third baseman should run the pitcher off. The play to first base is much easier for him in this situation.

Diagram 13–14.

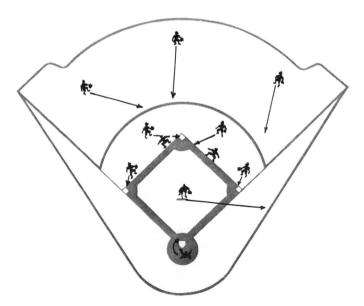

The key rule is: *Run the runner back to the bag from which he came.* The ball should be given to the forward man, in this case the second baseman, and he should run hard at the runner, but not with a faking motion of the arm.

The tagger, the first baseman, should stay in front of his bag, and inside the base line. This will give him the proper angle of the throw. When the runner is about fifteen feet from the tagger, the tagger should make a break toward the runner. This is the sign to the thrower to give the tagger the ball on his first step. The thrower makes an easy, chest-high toss, not a quick, hard throw.

When the run-down play is worked correctly, one throw is all that is needed to get the runner at any base. The man without the ball must avoid interfering with the runner.

Situation #14: The run-down play, with men on first and second, man on first picked off.

Diagram 13–15.

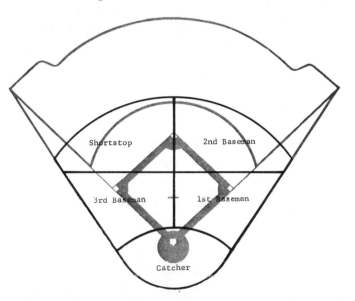

An infield pop fly will be the responsibility of all infielders, and they must try for the ball until one fielder takes charge by calling for the play. As designated in the diagram, each infielder has his area, but occasionally he may take the play out of his area if he takes charge of the play. The play should not be called too soon, especially on windy days.

On questionable pop flies around the mound area and after one or more infielders have called for the play, the pitcher should call the last name of the fielder he thinks is in the best position to make the play.

All pop flies hit directly behind the first and third basemen will be the responsibility of the second baseman and the shortstop. The

Situation #15: Pop flies to the infield.

first and third basemen, rather than the catcher, should take all balls between home and first and third bases, because the cut or slice of the ball is moving it back toward the infield.

Defensive Signals

From his dugout position, the manager should watch his infielders and outfielders to be sure they shift according to the hitter and the game situation.

When we want to move somebody over in the infield, we will use hand signals. For instance, if we want our second baseman to move over, we will hold up two fingers on the left hand and point to the direction he should move with the right hand. Now, if we want to move the outfield over, we use the towel. Anytime we use the towel, the outfielders know they have to move over (Fig. 13–8).

Infield deep

The signal commonly used for the infield deep or normal position is both hands raised chest-high or above, with the palms of the hands turned toward the fielders.

Infield halfway

The hands are crossed in front of the chest.

Infield close

For the short position, the hands are both waved in short circles toward the chest.

Pitchout

Another defensive signal is the call for the pitchout. The pitchout sign is given to the catcher if the coach anticipates a steal or a hit-and-run play. The clenched fist is often used as the pitchout signal.

Fig. 13–7. COMMUNICATION. On fly balls between infielders and outfielders, the outfielder has the right-of-way, since he is moving in. Here, Willie Mays has called for the ball and infielder Tito Fuentes moves quickly out of the way.

Fig. 13–8. POSITION SIGNALS. Anytime the manager uses the towel, the outfielders know they have to move over. Here, manager Alston effectively moves his outfielder toward the right field line. He uses hand and finger signals to move an infielder over.

Double steal defense

When there are runners on first and third and a double steal is anticipated, I have signals which I will give to my catcher. We have three different ways in which we defense this play:

1) Throw through to second
2) Throw back to the pitcher
3) Throw directly to third base.

There is the question of whether I want him to throw through or not, although 90 per cent of the time we will have him throw through. I will tell my catcher: "If I don't do anything, you go ahead and throw through or throw to the shortstop. Now, if I want you to throw directly back to the pitcher, I will rub across my shirt, which will mean, 'Throw it back to the pitcher or make the bluff play.'"

We also have a signal to throw directly to third base, without even a bluff. This play will often catch a runner who has a double steal in mind. When a weak hitter is coming up, we do not want to take a chance of throwing the ball to second base, so the catcher just turns and fires directly to third base. On occasion, we will catch the over-aggressive base runner.

If the catcher is throwing to second, he might signal the pitcher by adjusting the side of his mask with his gloved hand. If he wants the pitcher to cut off the throw, the catcher should clench his fist before giving his sign. The pitcher might reply by removing his glove and tucking it under his right arm.

Some coaches signal their catchers to use one of the following moves:

Signal	Action
1. Throw through to second base	Rubbing shirt and pants downward

2. Throw back to the pitcher   Rubbing across the shirt

3. Full bluff throw   Folding both arms

Intentional pass

In giving a batter an intentional pass, we will whistle, and when the catcher looks up, we hold up four fingers, or point to first base, meaning, "Put him on."

Defensive Drills

Along with hitting and base running practice, the practice program should be built around the use of sound, effective defensive drills. While game experiences are extremely important, no other coaching technique is more beneficial to the defense than well-supervised drills in which the coach serves in the role of instructor.

The following defensive drills can serve as the nucleus of a well-rounded training program. The coach must use his judgment as to the length of each drill. Every drill should be executed in a spirited and enthusiastic manner, rather than in a dull, listless atmosphere. Hustle and enthusiasm will do much to make a practice period productive and enjoyable.

Game situation drill

This drill is designed to give a team practice in all types of game situations. One team plays its regular normal defensive positions, while another team acts as base runners lined up behind home plate. Along with many other objectives, this drill provides the outfielders with valuable practice in backing up bases.

The coach, standing by the batter's box, hits all types of balls with a fungo bat to any position in the field. Before each ball is hit, the coach calls out the number of outs, inning and score. The runners will run until they are thrown out or forced, or until they score or three outs are made.

Bunt defense

The defense must drill against all possible bunt situations. The bunt defense drill will also provide valuable practice in bunting. The offense is divided into two groups: the bunters and the base runners.

A runner is put on first base, with the first baseman playing on the bag. After taking his set position, the pitcher throws the ball to the plate and the bunter lays the ball down. The play is made at first or second base.

The defense tries to make the play at second base, if possible. The second baseman covers first base and the shortstop moves over to second base.

Coverage on steals

This drill gives the defense practice at keeping the base runner close to first base and throwing him out at second base. The pitcher, catcher and infielders all get good defensive work, while the base runners get experience at taking a good lead and getting a good start.

The pitchers form a line behind the mound, and the base runners form a line near first base. The pitcher tries to prevent the runner from getting too big a lead, and if the runner thinks he has a large enough lead, he will try to steal second base. The catcher gets practice at throwing to second base, and the infielders receive experience at covering the base and taking the throw.

The coach should watch the pitcher closely to detect any balk motion. He should acquaint every pitcher with the correct rules pertaining to proper delivery to home and motion to the bases.

Double steal coverage

To drill the team in this defensive setup, the infielders and the catcher should assume their regular positions. The runners are divided into two groups: one group at first base, and the other at third. The pitchers form a line near the mound.

After the ball is thrown to the catcher, the runner on first tries to steal second. The catcher must make one of three choices: throwing to second base, throwing to the pitcher, or faking a throw to second and throwing to third.

If a runner is going to be thrown out, he is encouraged to stop and get caught in a run-down play.

Relays and cutoffs

During spring training, we spend many hours on defensive drills, when relays and cutoffs are practiced over and over. We use all our extra men as base runners and simulate game conditions by fungoing base hits all over the outfield. The pitcher pitches to the catcher, just as in a real game. The fielders execute their particular assignments according to the various situations.

In another drill, we line up all our outfielders in center field. Each one takes four turns fielding and throwing the ball. We make sure the players are deep enough so that they must throw to the relay man. The relay man should be the second baseman or the shortstop.

Run-down play

The run-down play should be practiced often, with the drill involving the entire team, either as fielders or runners. The pitchers form a line at the mound, and the catcher and infielders assume their proper positions. The runners line up close to first base.

The runner at first base permits himself to be picked off by breaking for second, and it is the responsibility of the defense to put him out. Later, the runners will form a line at second base and the same situation will occur there. Finally, the runners move down to third base and permit themselves to be picked off.

Pick-off play drill

The pitcher, along with his catcher and infielders, needs practice in executing the pick-off play. The pitchers form a line off to the first base side of the mound, while one pitcher takes his set position on the rubber. The base runners form a line near second base. The second baseman and shortstop assume their normal positions.

Conditioning /14/

The game of baseball, as a conditioner, does not provide enough physical activity to develop a player physically to meet the special emergencies which often arise during a game. Too often, the player who has to dash from first to third comes up with a pulled leg muscle. He simply is not conditioned to go 100 per cent on plays which demand a great deal of stamina and endurance. An all-out effort leaves him exhausted and unable to perform at maximum efficiency.

"Actually, much of the running in baseball is really of the short variety, mostly quick starts over a short distance," said Bill Buhler, the Dodgers' team trainer. "Therefore, if a player has to go from first to third or sprint a long way to retrieve a ball, usually, he is so winded he is lucky to make it."

There is a noticeable trend among baseball coaches and managers to supplement actual game experience with special conditioning exercises.

The successful teams in baseball today are giving their players vigorous and steady doses of stretching and strengthening exercises and considerable running. In many instances, they are employing the conditioning techniques of other sports such as track and football, all designed to get players into top condition.

Where the problem arises, however, is during the season itself. The majority of baseball teams, at all levels of play, are *not* continuing an adequate program of conditioning through the season. Consequently, the fitness level of many baseball players actually goes down as the season progresses, unless a concentrated form of conditioning work is offered.

An individual will be a better ballplayer if he will stay in condition.

"More and more, we are finding out that we have to work the players harder and more often," stated Professor Calvin Boyes, Head Baseball Coach at Sacramento State College. "Like the track coach has discovered, we are finding that athletes, when conditioned extensively, will come out in better condition than if they were given too much rest. Coaches today are finding the best results by giving their athletes a steady and oftentimes heavy amount of conditioning and training throughout the season."

For a long time, baseball coaches and players assumed that heavy conditioning exercises would have an adverse effect on player performance. Exercises for the development of strength, it was thought, would interfere with coordination, or athletes would become muscle-bound.

Because of this inadequate emphasis on fitness, baseball has often been criticized by fitness authorities, who have felt the player could be more effective if he developed better stamina and endurance, increased vigor and strength.

During the past decade, a growing number of major league teams have done a great deal to overcome this criticism. The St. Louis Cardinals are among the teams who have proven that exercise and conditioning are essential for baseball success. The Cardinals began their present fitness program during the winter of 1959 at St. Louis University. Dr. Robert Bauman, their trainer, and Dr. W. C. Eberhardt, Director of Physical Education at St. Louis University, combined their scientific know-how to set up the Cardinals' present program of exercises and running. It was their rejuvenation of aging Stan Musial which started the Cardinal players exercising.

Musial, one of the all-time greats of baseball, who some thought was finished as a player, worked very hard that winter. Stan continued heavy conditioning work all spring, and bounced back to have one of his best seasons.

Baseball coaches are becoming increasingly interested in off-season conditioning programs for their players. These programs are beneficial to the coach and the player because more time can then be devoted to the fundamentals of the game and less on in-season conditioning. Furthermore, the player will have a greater opportunity to make the team as well as lessen his chances of injury.

Need for Extra Fitness

Does the baseball player need a high level of body fitness? "He definitely does!," declare both Buhler and Bauman. "We often find that batting, fielding and throwing work are not sufficient to gain proper

---

A more effective conditioning program must be followed by the player throughout the season.

---

conditioning," explained Bauman. "When greater demands are made, a player needs additional strength, power and endurance for peak performance."

If two players have the same degree of ability, skill and natural talent, the stronger athlete will have a better chance of succeeding. He will have more power and speed, and very important, he will have more stamina to practice. In addition, good conditioning builds confidence and assurance. Players can extend themselves physically much sooner without fear of muscle pulls and strains.

"We are convinced that the exercise program has been an integral factor in our team success during the past decade," asserted Bauman. "The players are conditioned both physically and mentally with an exercise program which begins in spring training and is carried through the regular season. We try to sell our players on the idea that 'Your body is your best friend.'"

Generally, the amount of pregame conditioning work performed by baseball players has been relatively little. This has been just as true on the lower levels of play as on the professional level. I am inclined to agree that the baseball player, as a rule, would be more effective if he devoted more time to daily conditioning exercises. The additional strength, flexibility and endurance will enable him to be a more efficient player.

A more effective conditioning program must be followed by the player *throughout the season.* Conditioning should not be merely a spring training program which ceases once the league season gets underway. What is needed is a daily pregame program, which must be closely adhered to from opening day to the close of the season.

In my judgment, every player on the team should take the time and effort to follow a sound form of daily pregame conditioning, and develop the mental discipline to make it work for him. Later in the chapter, we have presented an example of a daily program which I firmly believe will prove a big asset to any baseball player. Activities include much needed running work, warm-up and stretching exercises, throwing, batting and fielding.

Plenty of running

Running is the greatest conditioner. Therefore, baseball players, like the athletes in other sports, should do a lot of running. There is no better activity than running to get in shape and to develop much needed speed and stamina (Fig. 14–2).

If he is not getting enough running, a player should stay after practice and run on his own.

We want our players to get as much running as they possibly can.

Objectives of a Good Conditioning Program
1. A stronger, more powerful body
2. Increased speed and quickness
3. More agility, flexibility and coordination
4. Increased resistance to injury
5. Greater stamina and endurance for a stronger finish.

Coach's message to his players

The coach must sell the idea to his athletes that an individual will be a better ballplayer if he will stay in condition. I believe that a coach can often talk his players into doing something, rather than forcing them into it. I doubt if a coach can ever force a player to do anything if he really does not want to do it.

There are so many good ballplayers around that a coach should not have to fool with the individual who does not want to take care of himself. This player will soon eliminate himself because, when there are two athletes with equal ability, the one who takes care of himself

Fig. 14–2. PLENTY OF RUNNING. There is no better activity than running to get in shape and to develop much needed speed and stamina. Below, Jimmy Lefebvre, left, does his daily jogging, which should be a part of every player's off-season conditioning program.

We, as baseball coaches, must give our players proper conditioning throughout the season, and not just during spring training.

CALVIN BOYES, Head Baseball Coach
Sacramento State College

---

will be the one who is going to last. The fellow who is always going out and getting drunk will soon be finished.

If a boy really wants to play, he will take it on himself to get the most out of himself. I really do not worry too much about the player who does not want to play badly enough to stay in condition. If he does not want to stay in condition to play this game, he should do something else.

We try to set up a year-round conditioning program for our players. **Off-season program**
The off-season provides a good time to work on the weights, or any other type of body conditioning program (Fig. 14–3). Even before the players go home, we emphasize the stretching phase of our program. Buhler will alert and brief them on what to do during the

Fig. 14–3. OFF–SEASON TRAINING ROUTINES. These pieces of conditioning equipment comprise two of the favorite off-season training routines among professional ballplayers. On the left, John Vukovich of the Phillies swings his own bat and donut weight hundreds of times each day. Picture B shows Vukovich strengthening his hands and wrists by rolling the rope and weight onto the bar he is holding.

A. Swinging the weighted bat

B. The wrist roll weight

Following a good conditioning program during the off-season and keeping his weight down can be the most sensible things a baseball player can do.

winter. Following a good conditioning program during the off-season and keeping his weight down can be the most sensible things a base-ball player can do.

When he reports to spring training, he should be in fairly good shape. If he does this, the training program will not only be easier for him but he will have more time to devote to the skills of hitting and fielding.

Typical Off-Season Conditioning Program

1. Warm-up calisthenics
2. Strengthening and stretching exercises
3. Weight training and isometric-isotonic programs
4. Swinging weighted bat (or player's own bat with donut)
5. Running (wind sprints and jogging)
6. Sports activities (handball, bicycling, golf, tennis, etc.).

Before he begins a conditioning program for baseball, the player should have a thorough physical examination by a physician. If he should have any organic or functional disturbance, it will be discovered at this time.

Endurance and stamina

The purpose of our off-season conditioning program is to develop circular-respiratory endurance through activities that place progressively greater demands on the heart and lungs.

Good stamina is a major factor in any activity that involves fairly prolonged movement of the entire body, such as in running, swimming, bicycling, rope jumping, handball, squash and basketball.

Once he begins his workout program, the player should do some running each day. He must have good legs to stay in the game. However, before he begins his daily run, he must remember to *always warm-up properly.* By doing twice as much warm-up work as he thinks is necessary, he will not bring a pulled muscle to the training camp.

"We recommend jogging and wind sprints to our players," said Buhler. "We suggest a daily jog of two or three miles. Tennis, handball, basketball, bicycling and swimming are also very good. We also have a few exercises for general stretching to stay in shape for the spring training program ahead. Most of the hitters like to swing a weighted bat during the off-season. The wrists are so important in this game."

Some players stay in good physical condition by playing basketball regularly, little scrimmage games, which is all right if they do not get

---

The successful teams in baseball today are giving their players vigorous and steady doses of stretching and strengthening exercises and considerable running.

---

hurt. Generally speaking, though, I do not recommend basketball for the average player.

Handball is one of the best off-season forms of exercise to improve agility. It conditions the entire body. No wonder so many baseball players get out on the handball courts in the off-season. In addition to having fun, they develop the quickness and agility which are so much a part of the game of baseball.

Some players play golf, which is better than nothing. At least, they are getting their legs in shape. Some like to hunt, which is all right if they can keep from shooting themselves or being shot. Any physical exercise that keeps the body in good and agile condition is commendable.

Weight training and isometric training programs have been used effectively by college and high school teams during the off-season, although they have not been as prevalent on the professional level. Bar bells, weighted bats, dumbbells and the metal ball are examples of weights being used by ballplayers, while the Exer-Genie exercises

Weights and isometrics

Fig. 14–4. USE OF WEIGHTS. The pros like to strengthen their hitting muscles by swinging dumbbells and weighted bats, and tossing the metal ball. Here, a St. Louis player performs his daily routines with the dumbbell under the close supervision of Dr. Robert Bauman, the Cardinals' veteran trainer.

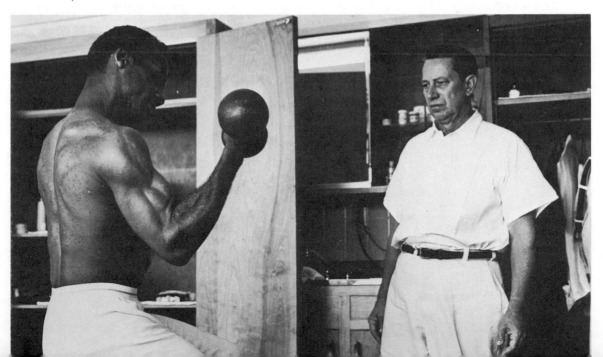

have proven the most popular isometric-isotonic program of conditioning.

The use of weights has not been as widespread on the professional level. As a general rule, players in the major leagues do not use bar bells as extensively as high school and college athletes. However, the pros do like to strengthen their hitting muscles by swinging the dumbbells (Fig. 14–4) and weighted bat (50 to 80 ounces), and tossing the Medi-Exercise ball ($3^1/_8$ pounds).

I have not been in favor of a weight lifting type of conditioning program because I have felt that athletes tend to develop heavy muscles through the use of weights. The more flexible the muscle can be, the better.

There are, however, a number of outstanding major league players who have found weight programs to be beneficial. Sam McDowell, one of baseball's hardest throwing pitchers with the Cleveland Indians, credits much of his success to hard conditioning, both during the season and the off-season. Reggie Jackson, Rusty Staub and Carl Yastrzemski are three power hitters who have trained with weights. McDowell mixes a heavy schedule of running with his work with the weights and the Exer-Genie. He devotes much of his strength work to flipping around his weighted Medi-ball and handling the dumbbells. Interestingly enough, he fastens a baseball to the end of the Exer-Genie ropes to resemble actual pitching motion.

Sam's heavy conditioning work begins January first, and during the next six or seven weeks until spring training time, he does a great deal of running. He prefers running in the outfield from foul line to foul line.

The Cardinals' winter program

A program of running, special conditioning exercises and workouts with a metal ball helped extend Musial's career for five years. Having achieved remarkable results with Stan, the Cardinals' management made sure that every player on the team received the same treatment. All St. Louis players were directed to go through the same running, twisting and bending routine. The results indicated that the program developed strength, speed, suppleness, agility and endurance.

All the program involves is some running and jogging, 15 minutes of stretching exercises and a brief workout with a metal ball.

Emphasis on running

We always begin with running because it is all in the legs. When the legs are in shape, there is no strain on the arm. When the legs get tired, a pitcher will start forcing his arm, and that is when he is susceptible to pulled muscles.

We tell our players to get out there and run. That is the first thing they do in the morning. Usually, they start by jogging a quarter to a half mile on the first day, and then gradually work up to a mile.

Then, we progress to coordinated running which involves cross-over steps, skips and hops, striding, and then running laterally. These are things that keep the player agile.

This routine is followed throughout our winter program, every day and all through spring training. Then, when the players are out on the field, they continue their activity. Whenever a fly ball is hit, this routine is continued.

When they are not scheduled to work, our pitchers run for 25 to 30 minutes daily. They use the wind sprint method, running hard for 50 yards and walking back briskly.

Following the running program, they progress to 15 minutes of exercises, including arm and leg stretching and a great deal of twisting, bending and suppling work. We want our players to be stretched out before they begin their regular drills. The remainder of the exercise routine is built around two to four games of handball each day.

Suppleness

Suppling work can be done either by cutting down on the size of the weight or by not using any weights at all. For example, if an athlete does some exercises to strengthen his leg muscles, he had better do some running, too. If he does some lifting with his arm muscles, he should also do some throwing.

Exercises and running both go together. If a player goes into one and not the other, the pendulum will swing more to one side, and he will build up muscles which will be of no advantage to his sport.

A supple muscle is one that is loose and not tied up. There is no contraction when a player gets a flowing of the muscles in coordination with the opposite group of muscles. He must have this coordination for throwing.

The following stretching exercises, performed each day, will help a player remain supple during the off-season:

1. *Trunk twister* Placing the hands on the hips, twist the entire torso to the right side for ten counts. Then twist to the left for ten counts.

2. *Hamstring stretch* While standing erect, cross one foot over the other, with the heel of the crossed foot up. This keeps the pelvis straight as you reach down toward the ground. Touch the ground with the back leg straight, for ten counts. Then, cross the other leg and repeat for ten counts.

3. *Groin stretch* The feet are spread as far apart as possible (about four to five feet), with hands on hips. On the count of ONE, push the hips forward while keeping the shoulders back. On the count of TWO, return to start, 15 counts. Do it slowly—stretch and relax at intervals, rather than in rhythm.

4. *Grapevine* Stand with both heels tightly together. Bend

Fig. 14–5. SPEED IMPROVEMENT. A highly competitive program in sprinting is designed to improve a player's starting and sprinting ability. By using the stop watch, the competitive factor is added. Here, Merv Rettenmund sprints up to 15 yards, after executing a good cross-over step.

down, extend both arms down between your knees, around behind your ankles, and hold the fingers together in front of your ankles without losing balance. Hold for a FIVE count. Repeat five times.

5. *Rope skipping* Alternate one minute of skipping and one minute of rest, then repeat (the pace should be 75 steps per minute). After two weeks at that pace, increase to one-and-a-half-minute skipping and a half-minute rest, and repeat.

Speed Improvement

Many baseball players fail to realize their maximum running potential. While speed cannot be created beyond a player's potential, a highly competitive program in sprinting can be followed (Fig. 14–5). Since much of the running in baseball deals with quick starts over a short distance, the sprinting distances should range from ten up to forty yards.

The prime objective is to get the player's running muscles and wind in shape and to improve his starting and sprinting ability. By using a stop watch in the running program, the competitive factor is added. Besides achieving good conditioning, the player will be running for the sake of "beating" the stop watch.

The sprinting program should start from four to six weeks before the opening practice, and should continue on a three-workouts-per-week basis. It is essential to keep a chart each day, as well as a file of the daily charts for reference use.

The proper sprint technique includes four components: the stance, the start, the run and the finish. An ideal location to start from is the batter's box. After taking a hitting swing, the player "explodes" from a good follow-through and sprints 90 feet down to first base. Reaching the bag should be comparable to hitting the tape in a sprint. Or, a player might move laterally with a good cross-over step and sprint up to ten or fifteen yards.

Spring Training

Basically, our spring training program consists of stretching exercises to increase coordination, flexibility and endurance. The players will stretch their arms to the sky, stretch their legs, bend and twist their trunks and bend their knees.

Our warm-up exercises are designed for the gradual stretching of the muscles, which causes the muscle fibers to become more extensible and elastic. The adhesions have to be stretched out. The greater the extensibility of a muscle, the more forceful the contraction.

We like our players to loosen up their muscles by running. They jog just about every day, except when they pitch. They also do their regular hard running and wind sprints.

"We want our players to run a mile in around six and one-half minutes," said Buhler. "Of course, we do not always get everybody to do it, but that's our primary goal. We have our players run on the six-tenth-mile track which we have at Dodgertown."

Typical day

During the first part of spring training, a major league team will arrive at the ball park between 8:00 and 8:30 A.M. After a "skull session," during which time some of the plays are gone over, all players go out for the exercise session.

During the first week, they begin with twelve minutes of work, but later on, they work up to thirty minutes on calisthenics. Sometimes they finish up with a game or two, just to vary the routine so they will have some laughs and fun.

Our calisthenic program is not boring because the exercises are varied. We mix them up each day, and try never to give the same thing twice. Repetition of the same exercises becomes tiresome. We have enough exercise routines so the players do not have to repeat the same thing.

When the squad finishes the calisthenics, they come in and change sweat shirts, take off their sneakers and put on baseball shoes. Then, they go out and loosen up for batting practice. The squad splits up. One group takes hitting, and another group goes down to another field. The pitchers work on covering first base, while others practice bunting in the cage. This practice lasts for one and one-half to two hours.

Then, the players come in and take regular infield and outfield practice. Those who need it take extra hitting in the cage. The entire workout is finished about 2:30 P.M.

We have one workout a day, which is enough to get a squad into shape. If anything more is done, the players will become tired and bored.

Fig. 14–6. SIDE STRADDLE HOP. These stride-jumping warm-up exercises serve to supple the ankles, knees and hip joints (Nelson Briles).

Group Calisthenics

During the training and exhibition seasons, most big league teams perform calisthenics as a group. By having the entire squad work together, we find that the players become more involved and interested in the program. The older players, in particular, can set a good example for the rest of the team. Soon, everybody is working hard.

As for the Dodgers' policy on calisthenics, we insist that everyone on our squad take daily calisthenics with the team. Calisthenics is like everything else—a player can get out of it only what he puts into it. He can go out on the field and go through the motions and spend the entire 15–20 minutes, and not get much out of it. On the other hand, if he does it correctly, I feel he will derive some real good from it.

Cardinals' Conditioning Exercises

A special group of conditioning exercises was prepared for the Cardinals by Dr. W. C. Eberhardt. These exercises are classified in eleven categories, with six movements in each area. They are arranged progressively according to difficulty, and can easily be performed in less than ten minutes.

Baseball players should continue with these movements, even after the season gets underway, and perform them throughout the season.

1. *Springing movements* (Fig. 14–6)   These stride-jumping warm-up exercises serve to supple the ankles, knees and hip joints. Stride-jumping can be followed by jumping sideward, forward and backward, and also cross-stride jumping.

2. *Shoulder suppling*   To stretch all the tight ligaments and muscles in the shoulder area, the throwing arm should be swung in a circle

Fig. 14–7. TRUNK TWISTING. These bending and circling exercises strengthen the region of the trunk (Nelson Briles).

movement, forward and backward, upward and downward. Swinging movements constitute an excellent loosening-up exercise for pitchers.

3. _Leg suppling_ These kicking and jumping movements stretch the ligaments and muscles in the hips, knees and ankle joints. From a standing position, the legs should be kicked forward, backward and sideward. The player should jump to a straddle stand from a squat stand, later jumping to the push-up position.

4. _General trunk exercises_ (Fig. 14–7) These trunk-bending and circling exercises strengthen the anterior, posterior and lateral trunk.

Fig. 14–8. LEG STRETCHING. This exercise keeps the hamstring muscles loose and properly stretched before beginning strenuous running (Nelson Briles).

427

From a straddle stand, the player should bend down to touch his feet. The routine continues to a lying position in which the legs are raised upward and downward, as well as sideward.

5. *Hip joint suppling* From the hurdle seat position, the player should reach forward to touch his toes and then return to the starting position. These exercises loosen up the large muscles of the hip, assuring greater ease of running movements and striding. Leg swinging and hip suppling should also be done from lying and sitting positions.

6. *Lateral trunk* These trunk-bending exercises increase the lateral flexibility of the spinal column and strengthen the large muscles of the waist. From a straddle stand, arms overhead, the player should bend his trunk slowly to the side and back. Later, he should dip his trunk toward the straight leg.

7. *Leg stretching* (Fig. 14–8) This is an exercise which keeps the hamstring leg muscles loose and properly stretched before beginning strenuous running. In addition to leg stretching, it serves the trunk and back. The player bends his trunk forward and down, keeping his knees straight and touching the ground with the palms of his hands.

8. *Leg strengthening* These knee-bending movements strengthen the muscles in the upper and lower legs, thighs and calves. With the feet together, hands behind the head, the player should bend his knees slowly to a sitting-on-heels position, then straighten the knees slowly. Later, he can do the duck waddle, with walking steps interposed between.

9. *Abdominal exercises* These sit-ups and knee bends from a lying position strengthen the upper and lower abdominal muscles, and also stretch the muscles of the lower back. The sit-ups should be done from a lying position, with the hands overhead. Later, the knees should be bent and then straightened.

10. *Arm strengthening* To develop the wrists, upper and lower arms, chest and shoulders, the player should do push-ups, along with fist-clenching and hand-shaking movements. From a straddle stand, arms at the sides, he should bend his hips and then place, first, his left hand to the ground, then his right hand, to a push-up position, walking forward and backward on his hands.

11. *Neck exercises* Head-turning exercises loosen and relieve tension and tend to strengthen the neck muscles. From a sitting position, with his hands on his lap, the player should turn his head to the left,

Fig. 14–9. DAILY WIND SPRINTS during pregame practice can be beneficial in protecting the athlete when he is called upon to make a long run during the game. Outfielders, particularly, should get in some light pregame running.

right, upward and downward. From a lying position, on his back, with the arms sideward, he should raise his hands and back off the ground, while his head remains on the ground.

Other calisthenics are:

1. Jumping jack
2. Windmill
3. Trunk twister
4. Knee bends
5. Alternate toe-touches
6. Stomach rocker
7. Sit-ups
8. Abdominal curls
9. Bicycle

Pickups

This is one of the best conditioning drills available to the ballplayer. It is excellent not only for the legs but for the entire body as well. Two players are about nine feet away from each other, and one rolls a ball to the other—first to one side, then the other. Each player works in an arc of about ten feet.

The ball must be picked up with two hands and returned with an underhand toss. The players might begin with 25 pickups and increase until 50 is reached. Along with running, this drill should be performed daily throughout the season by the pitchers.

Common problems

Care of the players' feet is the chief concern of our trainers during the first part of spring training. With all the running that takes place, the feet become very tender, and there are quite a few blisters early in training. But after about two weeks, the feet toughen up quite well. In addition, foot vibrators help in conditioning the feet.

We have had very little back trouble, due to the emphasis placed on back exercises. As soon as a player develops a weak back, he is given back stretching and strengthening exercises.

Stretching is one of the best ways to prevent bursitis, according to Bauman. "Every morning on arising, an athlete should raise his arms to the sky twenty times," said Bauman, "and he will never have bursitis. He should reach and stretch, and when he thinks he has stretched high enough, he should stretch some more.

"Very little work is done with the players after spring training," said Bauman. "Our pitchers receive little attention after the season begins. Sure, they may have something warm placed on their arms on cold days before the game, but they do all of the stretching routines by themselves after June. After June, they are in good enough shape to take care of themselves."

During the Season

During the season, the player has to maintain the good level of conditioning and fitness he achieved during the off-season, preseason and early season.

The type of exercise used by ballplayers during the season is more for flexibility than for strength. Before a game, we want our players to stretch their muscles as much as they can and loosen them up, but not overbuild them. I am concerned, though, over any exercise that really builds up the muscle to where it becomes heavy, and not as flexible as the loose muscles.

Running is a great conditioner

We want our players to get as much running as they possibly can. We want them to run daily sprints and do a certain amount of jogging. This is the only way to build up endurance, which is so important in this game.

Wind sprints can be very beneficial in protecting the athlete when he has to extend himself occasionally for the extra distance (Fig. 14–9). Outfielders often fail to get enough running because their pregame work is not as strenuous as that of the infielders. They catch a few fly balls and do a little shagging, but that is the extent of it.

Most catchers will run to first base on ground balls to the infield so they get some running in carrying out this fielding chore. The pitchers, of course, are required to run 20 to 30 minutes daily, except

Fig. 14–10. PREGAME WARM–UP EXERCISES. Every player should devote the time and effort to a regular schedule of daily pregame stretching exercises, such as this leg stretching exercise for the groin. By combining stretching exercises with four to six wind sprints of 60 to 75 yards, he will be properly prepared for all-out competition (John Vukovich).

Fig. 14–11. PEPPER. This is a favorite activity of all ballplayers. Here, Maury Wills joins two other Dodgers in a brisk game of pepper. The fielders throw the ball to the hitter, whose responsibility is hitting accurate grounders and line drives. The game must be kept moving.

when pitching. This usually involves 12 to 15 one-hundred-yard sprints to develop power and stretch out the muscles.

During the season, I am not in favor of jogging over an extended period. The ideal program would be to have everyone on the team run a number of wind sprints during pregame practice to build up their legs, so they can take care of themselves in situations which call for lengthy sprints or runs. Otherwise, muscle pulls and strains will likely occur, which can sideline a player for a good portion of the season.

"The Cardinals have been successful in giving our players both strengthening and stretching exercises," according to Bauman, their trainer. "Every day, our players can be seen around the clubhouse and on the field exercising before the game by doing stretching work and using a metal baseball, a weighted ball and performing other resistance exercises."

A player will get on the table and do leg stretching to get his hamstrings stretched out, just before he goes out on the field to run and loosen-up. Many players like to do a great deal of abdominal and trunk work. An individual will get on the table, and with someone holding his legs, he will get his body all the way over the edge of the table from the belt up to his head. If he should have a weakness in his back, he will strengthen his back muscles every day. These exercises can be performed out on the field as well.

"Some of the other players will take the weighted balls and exercise the upper torso and stretch it good," explained Bauman. "Each one seems to have a different routine for the various parts of his body. Lou Brock works on his legs and stretches them constantly. This is necessary in order for him to get those quick starts in stealing bases."

Pregame Conditioning Program

Every player on the team should follow an effective form of daily conditioning, before or after each game. While the conditioning work of a ballplayer is normally done before a game, he may wish to do his heavy running following the game. This is particularly true if he feels it takes something out of him when done before a contest.

1. *Stretching exercises:*
   a. Touching toes
   b. Leg stretching for the groin (Fig. 14–10)
   c. Hurdler's stretch (hip joint suppling)
   d. Reaching back through legs
   e. Hanging on bar (for pitchers)
2. *Running* (before or after game):
   a. Wind sprints (starting slowly, picking up good speed, then slowing down at finish) (60–75 yards; 4–6 times)
   b. Jogging around field (1–3 times)
3. *Throwing:*
   a. Warm-up catch (10 minutes)
   b. Pepper (Fig. 14–11)
   c. Fielding practice (during batting practice)
   d. Infield and outfield drill
4. *Batting:*
   a. Swinging weighted bat (or using donut)
   b. Batting practice (as many cuts as possible)

Group or individual exercises

Should the group exercises performed in spring training be continued during the regular season? The great majority of teams, on all levels of play, do not exercise as a group before a game. Not only has this been a tradition, but there is always the situation in which some players would rather do calisthenics by themselves. The general feeling has been that each individual has certain areas of his body which need stretching more than other areas, so players would rather do the calisthenics individually or in pairs.

In the past, most managers have not insisted that the team perform pregame exercises together. Unless the majority of the team is in favor of group exercises, most managers or coaches have felt they should not insist upon the entire team performing calisthenics as a group. The general thinking is that this can create more harm morale-wise than the good which can come through conditioning the body physically.

"We would prefer having the team exercise as a group," said Bauman, "but permit the players to perform the exercises by themselves." In either case, members of a baseball team should go through the routine of exercises daily. I think it is becoming increasingly clear that there is a tendency for even those who play regularly to lose some of their strength and stamina over the course of the season. In many instances, this can be corrected by pregame running and conditioning exercises. Whether this work is done individually or as a group is not the key issue. The important thing is that daily conditioning be practiced by every ballplayer.

Pitcher's pregame massage

While the massage is effective in relaxing the upper torso of the pitcher, before a game, trainer Buhler tries to get him to think about something else for about five or ten minutes before he goes out and warms-up. "We start from the waist up, and go over the entire back," said Buhler. "We will stretch the arm out, then we will turn him over on the side and work on the shoulder and try to get the capsule loose.

"We will do a few slow and easy arm stretches," continued Bill. "We will crank the shoulder slowly and pat him on the back. We try to keep the arm stretched out as much as we can so we will not have his elbow shortening up."

The ice pack treatment

Following a ball game, the pitcher's arm has a tendency to become sore. It is our belief that the soreness comes from some type of bleeding. More than likely, it is strictly capillary bleeding, since there is no pooling of the blood. There is no sign of black or blue marks from it.

According to our theory, we make the pitcher sit for half an hour with the elbow immersed in ice water and an ice bag on the shoulder (Fig. 14–12). We feel this tends to cut down on the bleeding and helps to eliminate most of the soreness. As a result, the pitcher is ready to pitch one day sooner.

"We have had quite a bit of success with this method," said Buhler, "and that is one reason why we are staying with it. Normally, we

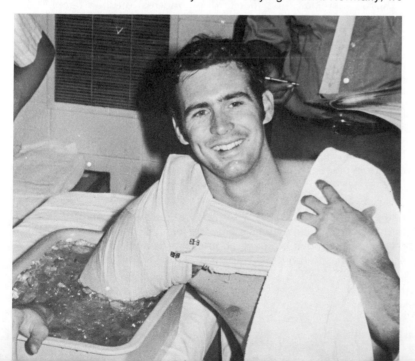

Fig. 14–12. THE ICE PACK TREATMENT. Using the technique made famous by Sandy Koufax, the Dodgers' Bill Singer, following a pitching performance, sits for half an hour with his elbow immersed in ice water and an ice bag on his shoulder. The treatment tends to cut down the bleeding and helps to eliminate most of the soreness.

have the pitcher sit for 30 minutes, although with Koufax, there were times he went 45 minutes. The ice is in a fiberglass basin or tub, immersed with ice water, with the temperature always around 35 degrees. The ice bag is a rather large plastic ice bag that we use. We place it on the shoulder and wrap it with an Ace bandage.

"We have no complaints from our pitchers. As soon as the game is over, they know that they must come in and sit down. In fact, the sportswriters come in with them, and they are interviewed at the same time."

Typical College Program of Calisthenics

"We are firm believers in calisthenics because they can compress into a short length of time a considerable amount of body conditioning," explained Cal Boyes, head baseball coach at Sacramento State College. "The first thing we do is take a big lap around the field, and then we do approximately ten minutes of calisthenics."

The Hornets do about ten repetitions of each of the following exercises:

1. Windmill
2. Side straddle hop
3. Squat benders
4. Trunk twister
5. Arm circler
6. Burpee
7. Leg scissors
8. Leg lift
9. Hurdler's stretching
10. Grass drill (or running drill)

Grass drill

This excellent conditioning drill begins with the players running in place. When the coach hollers, "FRONT!" they just kick their legs out from under them and go down on their front. On the command, "BACK!" they kick their feet through and rest on their back. Then, the coach yells, "UP!" and they come up and continue to run in place. Then, he says, "DOWN!" and they flop down again.

Running drill

If the grass is wet, the team can run-in-place, rather than go down to the ground. They should imagine they are running the bases. The coach will say, "You have hit a slow roller, now dig for first!" He tells them to bring up their feet quickly, and imagine they are "running on a hot stove."

After five or ten seconds, the coach will say, "Now, you are going to steal, dig for second!" and they will dig like that. The same procedure is practiced for second and third, finishing with an imaginary fly ball.

Running relays

Rather than finish practice with wind sprints, which can be drudgery for the players, many teams divide the team up into four- or five-man relay teams. A glove is placed about 25 yards away, and a player from each team has to run down and around the glove and come back and touch the next man. To provide some variety, the coach should make his players run backward, or even hop down on one foot and then on all fours.

"Then, when they are puffing pretty well and have a good sweat up," explained Coach Boyes, "I have them jog all the way into the clubhouse. However, I try to poop them out at the end with some good running. We do this throughout the season, every day."

Warming-Up

No athlete should ever begin competition without a period of preliminary warm-up activity. Before he starts going at full speed, the player must get blood flowing into his muscles at a faster rate. An athlete should warm-up until the muscles in his arms and legs feel loose, and have begun to perspire a little. Otherwise, he is asking for pulled and strained muscles.

Staleness

The common causes of staleness are overwork, worry, monotony and, occasionally, dietary deficiencies. Rest or change of activity and a revised diet is the surest cure for staleness. However, prevention is better than the cure.

Players should not be overworked. The daily practice sessions should be made interesting, and the practice routine should vary somewhat from day to day.

Weight Training

Weight training, if designed to improve muscle tone and not develop bulging muscles, can be an effective conditioning method for players who could use more strength and stamina (Fig. 14–13). Weights have been used by high school and college baseball coaches to help strengthen and lengthen muscles and increase their range of movement. The weights should never be heavy ones, but rather, small light ones that can be easily used with many of the exercises related to baseball movements.

Ideally, a player should begin his weight program from four to six weeks before organized workouts begin. Those who need more strength and muscle tone often begin early in the fall.

"During the fall, we lift the weights Monday, Wednesday and Friday," said Coach Winkles of A.S.U. "It takes them about 45 minutes to do the routines. The freshmen have the weight room Tuesday, Thursday and Saturday.

"If a boy will work well enough on the weights during the off-season, that strength will carry him through the baseball season. Then, he can start again after the season is over."

Bar bells, weighted bats, dumbbells and the metal ball are all light weights that vary from the three-pound Medi-Exercise ball on up to the 20- or 30-pound bar bell. When spring practice gets underway, most coaches confine their weight work to the weighted bat (donut) and the metal ball. However, if a player has an injury, working with such weights as the dumbbell or the weighted shoe can be helpful in the rehabilitation of the injured muscle, ligaments or tendons. In this situation, the weights should be used continuously during the season.

The weighted bat is highly recommended by coaches and hitters alike. Ted Williams believes the weighted bat was responsible for his increased strength. As a young hitter, during the off-season, he often swung the weighted bat 400 times a day. Ted was able to isolate all his swinging muscles with his weighted bat.

The donut, which can be fastened to the player's bat, is being used with growing popularity (Fig. 14–3A). The big advantage of the donut over the weighted bat is that the player can swing his own bat.

"If a ballplayer continues with a weight program and also goes on with his regular activities, such as throwing and swinging the bat," said Buhler, "I do not think he will become muscle-bound, as long as it is controlled. However, I do not think an athlete should work with weights on his own. Generally, he is not able to control what he is doing, and he often does too much."

Since the forward and reverse curl exercises tend to build up the biceps muscle, adding bulk, they should not be given emphasis in a weight program.

The Dodgers, for the most part, do not use weights. We do not feel we gain that much strength from their use. Bulk is not that important in baseball. Of course, when a player is injured, we will have him do rehabilitation resistor exercises. We have a weight room next to the clubhouse which includes a lat machine, a leg press, a knee machine and some slant boards.

During his first year with the Dodgers, Wes Parker worked quite extensively with weights, but he has stopped using them now. He was successful in putting on the weight that he needed, particularly in the region of the chest.

An off-season weight training program can be very beneficial to pitchers, provided they do *not* follow the "overload" theory. We are strongly opposed to the development of heavy muscles in the pitching shoulder. Baseball players should rely on the "repetition" idea, starting with five repetitions per exercise, and working up to the maximum number.

Bench press   The starting position is lying on the back on the bench, with both knees raised, with arms extended and elbows locked. Using a wide grip on the bar bell, his palms face toward his feet. The bar is slowly lowered to the chest, and pressed back to the starting position. He keeps both feet flat on the floor.

Military press   Using a pronated grip, the bar is slowly pushed overhead from chest-level, until both arms are fully extended. The athlete should

Fig. 14–13. LIGHT WEIGHTS. The weights should be light enough to be performed easily. The exercises should be related to baseball movements such as those above. Since the triceps muscle is normally weak, the triceps-extension can strengthen the throwing arm, as well as provide more power to the front arm in the batting swing (Donn Johnson).

maintain an erect neck and back, and extended, locked knees. He should avoid jerky movements or a lean.

Triceps extension

Since the triceps is normally a weak muscle, this exercise can strengthen the throwing arm significantly. From a standing position, the individual holds the bar bell behind the head, in the shoulder-rest position (Fig. 14–13). He then presses slowly overhead until both arms are fully extended. The hands should be placed nine to twelve inches apart.

Lat pull

This exercise is good for the triceps muscle and the shoulder. It can be performed from a standing or sitting position. Extending his arms straight out and keeping his elbows locked, he pulls down on the bar to the region of his legs. His palms are down.

Wrist curl

From a sitting position, he grabs the bar bell in his fingers, *not his palms.* His forearms rest on his thighs; his palms are facing up. As he does his curl, he rolls the bar right up his fingers. Then, he lets it back down. Both palms are brought toward the body as far as possible, and returned to the starting position.

Leg press

Sitting in the chair of a Universal machine, the individual's legs are in a bent position. His feet are on the pedals, the pressure on the balls of his feet. His hands grip the side of the chair. On the count of "ONE," he straightens his legs out, and on "TWO," he returns to his bent position.

Fig. 14–14. THE METAL BALL is used in the clubhouse by many big league pitchers to stretch and strengthen the muscles in the shoulders and arm. The chrome-plated ball weighs $3\frac{1}{8}$ pounds. Ray Washburn, left, has found the ball to be of tremendous value in his successful recovery from an arm injury.

The squat

If a Universal machine is not available, the squat exercise should be used with the bar bell and weights. From a standing position, the athlete holds onto the bar with his palms facing forward. His feet are approximately shoulder-width apart. To prevent deep knee bends, he squats down no farther than the chair or bench.

The bar is in the shoulder-rest position. The body is lowered to a sitting position by flexing the legs until the buttocks contact the bench. The athlete must avoid bending his back.

A dedicated effort

For a weight program to be successful, the athlete must be dedicated. He must *want* to get stronger because it will improve his game. The player who does not want to improve his game will receive little value from the program simply because he will not work hard enough at it.

Metal ball exercises

The Medi-Exercise ball was developed by Dr. Bauman and is manufactured by the Van Sickel Company of St. Louis, Missouri. It is used in the clubhouse to stretch and strengthen the muscles in the shoulders and arms (Fig. 14–14). The chrome-plated ball, weighing $3\frac{1}{8}$ pounds, is the same size as a baseball.

"We use the ball for psychological reasons as well as strengthening," explained Bauman. We have also found the ball to be of tremendous value in the rehabilitation of players who are recovering from surgery or injuries.

"We start with a pendulum swing, with the ball down low and the player's body bent," continued Bauman. "Then, we have the player raise his arm up high and stretch. When he thinks he has stretched high enough with his arms, he should stretch a little higher."

Next is the fundamental position of pitching. The player's elbow should be bent at a right angle, his shoulder level, and then he should rotate all the shoulder muscles. All players should do this exercise at least once a day, just to keep the muscles supple, strong and loose.

The Exer-Genie Program

The Exer-Genie exercises offer perhaps the newest and most successful program of physical conditioning in sports. By starting each exercise isometrically, the athlete obtains significant strength benefits, and by combining it with isotonic movement, he derives the further benefits of endurance and flexibility. "Iso-kinetic exercise" is the newly-applied theory involving a constant speed with a constant resistance through a complete range of motion.

The Exer-Genie unit consists of an engineered cylinder and a nylon rope that can be pulled back and forth through the cylinder with equal resistance in either direction. Because the exercise is started isometrically, tired muscles are produced and needless repetitions are eliminated. The isometric phase produces the tired muscle or muscle group in just ten seconds, and then the tired muscle is worked to move through a range of motion working against a preset resistance.

When using the Exer-Genie exerciser for a specific exercise, however, through a throwing or hitting range of motion, the isometric hold should not be used. "If the athlete were to apply the isometric hold at the point in the range where he begins the pitch, an injury to the joint structures of his arm could result due to the poor mechanical advantage," explained Professor Gene A. Logan, Professor of Physical Education at Southwest Missouri State College, who has done extensive study on the Exer-Genie program.

Still, some coaches are not completely sold on the fact that the Exer-Genie program develops the baseball player in the way he needs to be developed. "True, most players can use additional strength and endurance," said Coach Boyes; "however, I would not want them to work on weights or any form of resistive program that would add bulk or tie up muscles in any way, particularly the biceps muscle, which is so important in throwing."

"Of course, there are those players who are slender and not overmuscled," said Boyes, "who can use some improvement in strength and muscle tone. In these cases, we do suggest an off-season weight training program. Otherwise, I like our players to work on things that they actually will do in a ball game, combined with a great deal of running and stretching exercises."

Control is perhaps the key to how extensive the Exer-Genie exerciser program will be employed in the future by baseball players. If adequate control measures can be set up, there is no reason why properly applied specifics cannot be used as an important training procedure. Scientifically valid results indicate, for instance, that velocity of baseball throwing can be increased significantly by means of moderately light resistance. Like other conditioning programs, harm can come to those poorly-guided athletes who choose the heavy resistance route and fail to use good sense.

There is, of course, a right way and a wrong way to use the Exer-Genie exerciser. Close supervision is important to see that the player is using it correctly. Players should work in pairs, with one player exercising, and his partner handling the trailing rope and controlling the amount of resistance needed to make him work at his capacity. *Caution should be taken not to work with excessive weight.*

Good preseason conditioner

A number of college and high school coaches and professional players have advocated a weight program in the fall, from October first through December fifteenth, then changing to Exer-Genie exercisers for a six-week preseason conditioning program. The preseason program should be a period of *total conditioning,* in which the players go through almost the entire ten-station circuit.

New baseball circuit

A new ten-station circuit has been designed to meet the unique fitness needs of baseball players. Two outstanding baseball coaches, Vernon Law, the former pitching ace of the Pittsburgh Pirates, and Glenn Tuckett, coach at Brigham Young University, served as consultants on the program, which required extensive research and study (Fig. 14–15).

A workout on the circuit takes from ten to thirty minutes, and requires twelve Exer-Genie exercisers. According to Law and Tuckett, the ten-station circuit period should precede each practice session and should be continued throughout the season as well as during the off-season and preseason. However, many coaches have questioned the advisability of using the entire circuit during the season, choosing, rather, to use only the specifics or none of them. The exact merit of the Exer-Genie program during the season must await further use and study.

Players should always begin each exercise period with easy bending and stretching. They should exercise correctly with as much resistance as possible, while maintaining proper form. As strength increases, the intensity of the workout should also increase.

For strength exercises, high school athletes should use a starting resistance of ten pounds, while twenty pounds is recommended for college and professional players. The athlete simply dials the desired resistance. To increase resistance, pressure should be applied to the trail line. A partner controls the resistance, while feeding the trail line toward the unit.

The athlete should exercise in one smooth, continuous movement, without hesitation or relaxation. He should breathe as normally as possible while exercising.

The ten-station circuit with the Exer-Genie exerciser includes the following (Fig. 14–15):

1. Batting swing
2. Lats pull (22 secs.)
3. Baseball throw
4. Triceps pull (22 secs.)

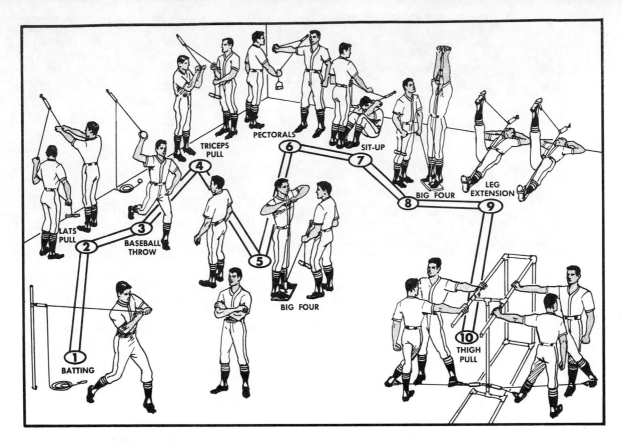

Fig. 14–15. TEN–STATION CIRCUIT FOR BASEBALL PLAYERS, using the EXER-GENIE exerciser. The above circuit requires 12 EXER-GENIE exercisers.

5. "Big Four" (24 secs.)   8. "Big Four" (24 secs.)

6. Pectorals (22 secs.)   9. Leg extension (22 secs.)

7. Sit-up (22 secs.)   10. Thigh pull (22 secs.)

The specifics

When spring practice begins, many coaches will stop using the circuit training and confine their weight resistance work to just the specifics. The "specifics" refer to the simulation of a specific motion of an activity, such as throwing and hitting a baseball. They allow the athlete to concentrate on his form while he is simultaneously attempting to increase strength and flexibility. They utilize those muscles that are involved in the actual motion of the fundamental skill or technique, and a slight degree of resistance is applied.

A baseball player should refrain from using too heavy a weight, and an increase in weight should be made slowly.

The specifics include the following exercises:

1. Baseball throw   4. Hip rotator

2. Triceps pull   5. Leg extension

3. Hitting swing   6. Running lines

Training Rules

Training rules are set up for a purpose. In addition to being guide-lines to help players stay in tiptop physical and mental condition,

Fig. 14–16. BATTING SWING. In performing this specific exercise, the player follows the basic technique of hitting. The rope to the Exer-Genie exerciser is fastened onto the handle of the bat, between the hands (Wayne Hironaka).

they contribute to a sense of team unity, toward the ultimate end of attaining the goals we want to reach. Observing a curfew, wearing coats and ties on the road, abstaining from smoking and drinking are practices which require the discipline of the mind.

Rules of training will help a player play to the best of his ability. If a team has the proper mental attitude to begin with, training rules will take care of themselves.

Fig. 14–17. BASEBALL THROW. Having the ball fastened to the rope of the exerciser, the player can execute a complete throwing motion. Resistance is set at $2\frac{1}{2}$ pounds but can be increased slightly if the athlete can handle the extra weight without sacrificing form for strength. The isometric hold should not be used at any point through the range of motion because of the disadvantage to the levers (Wayne Hironaka).

I like to think the Dodgers have fair training rules, but at the same time, they are as strict as necessary. I feel that the best way is to sell the players on the idea that it is for their own good, as well as the team, for them to take care of themselves. I prefer to stay out of their private lives as much as I possibly can.

We do not check them in, and we do not run a checkup very often. If a fellow is staying out too late, or doing this and that, the coach or manager will soon hear about it. If we are suspicious that someone is overdoing it, we might check up. Then, we will let him know we *mean* it.

Frankly, I do not like our players to be out late. After a night game, 1:30 A.M. is reasonable, while 12 midnight is proper after a day game.

Basically, a coach has to treat *everyone* alike. Even the stars have to obey and report at the same time as the reserves. If the coach resorts to preferential treatment, it can easily spoil the morale and spirit of the team.

Players like to be treated like men, and the coach has the right to expect them to treat him the same way. Actually, I have not had much of a problem along this line, and I am probably more lenient than a lot of managers. Whether this is right or wrong, I feel I can get more out of them by letting them have a little more freedom and putting a little more responsibility on *them,* rather than making me actually enforce the rules.

Members of the Arizona State University baseball team follow 18 basic rules. Coach Bobby Winkles gives the list of rules to every player before he ever comes to A.S.U. Their impressive record indicates

Baseball—"the A.S.U. way"

Fig. 14–18. TRICEPS PULL. Since many hitters have weak triceps muscles, this exercise can be valuable. After exerting maximum isometric contraction for ten seconds, the athlete moves through a range of motion down toward his thighs (Wayne Hironaka)

that these rules have been good for the team. The Sun Devils have won many NCAA and conference championships.

"When we, as coaches, make rules," said Bobby Winkles, "we must make rules that can be abided by. And they should apply to the star players as well as the 20th player on the squad. They do not just apply to the lower half of the squad, but the regulars must abide by them as well.

"Before any player reports to a practice," said Winkles, "he knows *exactly* what we are going to do. They know what to expect from me as their coach, and they know what I expect of them as players. So, we get started off on the right foot."

Following is the list of rules which members of the A.S.U. baseball team abide by:

1. "Huh," "Uh-huh," "Naw" and "Yeah" will be replaced by "Yes," "Yes, sir," "No" and "No, sir."
2. Do not lose your composure.
3. Drinking of *any* amount will be dealt with severely.
4. Smoking will result in suspension.
5. Go to class—we will *not* pay for tutors for anyone who misses a class.
6. Run everywhere you go.
7. Do not sulk—see the coach if you have a complaint or problem.
8. Do not ever argue with a teammate.
9. No swearing on the field.
10. No arguing with the umpire.
11. No throwing bat or helmet.
12. Always practice good manners in dorm, cafeteria and everywhere on or around the campus.
13. Anyone being evicted from dorm or apartment or kicked out of cafeteria will lose that part of his scholarship.
14. Report to practice and to the classroom on time.
15. Pitchers run to and from the mound.
16. There will be no long hair or sideburns.
17. Wear socks at all times—dress neatly—no thongs.
18. This program is considered the best in the country. It was made that way by hard work and good players who have pride. You have to be good to be a SUN DEVIL. *Be proud of it!!*

Social life   An athlete has to sacrifice a lot of things to stay in top condition, particularly the extra time that he must put in to become an outstanding player. However, athletes should be allowed to date just as well as nonathletes. In fact, girls are often a good influence on athletes. Unless his girl friend consistently keeps him out past curfew, I see nothing wrong with dating. If he wants to play this game badly enough, the player will get his date home before curfew time.

Personal appearance

All athletes should try to be neat. I have always urged my men to dress well, with clean shoes, conservative haircuts, shirttails in and socks on.

Most of the Dodgers eat in the hotel restaurants, and we like them to have a coat and tie on. However, the mode of dressing has changed considerably, and we want our players to feel free to dress as they want.

The nicest thing the Dodgers have done the past year is to provide blue blazers and gray trousers for those on the club. On all of our plane trips, we all wear the same uniform, which I think is fine. Here again, it shows a certain amount of pride in the Dodgers. Other than that, we just like the players to be well dressed, casual if they prefer, because times have changed a little.

While the appearance and grooming of athletes on other teams and in other sports have changed somewhat drastically, our boys have not gone overboard. I think our boys are very respectable, as far as their appearance and dress go. Fortunately, we do not have any long hair, although some of the players wear their sideburns longer.

If necessary, I would insist they keep both at a reasonable length. I think I can do it jokingly, teasing and needling them. However, if it got to a crucial point, rather than see the mustache and beard, I would insist on removing it. I would cross that bridge when I got to it, but fortunately, I have never had to do so.

If a player insisted on having a mustache or goatee, what should the coach do? I believe it is entirely up to the respective coach. If a coach is willing to allow it, all right, but in my case, frankly, I would *not.*

I like to think that I am as open-minded as anyone. I have accepted the longer sideburns, and I have not said anything about them. However, just because *I* feel that way does not mean that everyone has to feel the same way.

"At Arizona State, we make quite an impression on the local community, particularly with little kids who are growing up," said Coach Winkles, "and to me, it is important that no boy should want to look like a girl. Sideburns are not bad, but here is what you find out. If you let them go with long sideburns, the next thing they want to do is grow their hair long. So, I do not let either get started."

High school athletes in the San Juan Unified School District of Sacramento have had to conform to a newly-established grooming code. The district board adopted a set of three grooming rules for athletes in its nine high schools:

1. No facial hair of any kind (beard or mustache).
2. Skin must show around the ears and must also show between the collar (not T-shirt) and the hairline.
3. Sideburns must be neat and not lower than the bottom of the ear.

Proper playing weight

Most players are assigned a weight that the manager and trainer feel would be their best playing weight. Nothing destroys conditioning or causes an athlete to become ineffective more quickly than being overweight. Since fat is of little help, only muscle tissue is considered beneficial to his play.

Perhaps the greatest problem with professional ballplayers is putting on too much weight after the season is over. By disciplining himself during the off-season, an athlete will not have to punish himself to lose that ten, twenty or thirty pounds in January and February.

Despite the latest fad diets, reducing is still a matter of calories. To lose weight safely, he must burn up more calories through physical activity than he gains through the food he eats.

Here are a few hints to athletes who might be getting too heavy:

1. Watch the carbohydrates. They are usually the most fattening—pies, bread, pastries, cakes, soft drinks, pizza, candy, potatoes, rice, noodles, etc. They supply plenty of calories.
2. No alcohol and beer.
3. No between-meal snacks. (This means TV snacks, too.)
4. Schedule your eating so that you never exceed your needs.

Common sense will tell an athlete to eat less when he is trying to lose weight. If he has a special weight problem, he should contact his trainer, who will consult with the team physician about the problem. It is important for the coach to check regularly to see if his athletes are keeping their proper weight.

Proper diet

A well-rounded diet plays a vital role in the physical fitness of an athlete. A person today has the benefit of good food, and good food supplements, and he should take advantage of them. Three meals a day, with as little eating as possible between meals (especially after the evening meal), is the best plan.

The last regular meal should be eaten at least three to four hours before game time. Physiologists recommend such nongreasy, nongasforming foods as bread, honey, broiled steak, baked potato, green peas, ice cream and either fruit juice, vegetable juice or tea.

I think that steak is ideal as a pregame meal. I have always been a steak and potatoes man, but it should be left up to the individual, just so it is a sound, well-rounded meal (Fig. 14–19).

The following is a daily menu for a player playing a game under the arc lights:

Fig. 14–19. THE PREGAME MEAL. Steak is a favorite meal among athletes on all levels of play. A sound, well-rounded meal includes a baked potato, vegetables, salad, toast, iced tea and fruit or ice cream (John Vukovich).

Breakfast
    Orange juice
    Bowl of cereal
    Two eggs and bacon
    Short stack of
       toast and jam
    Milk, coffee or tea

Afternoon Pregame Meal
    Green tossed salad with dressing
    Steak (medium)
    Baked potato
    Toast
    Iced tea or lemonade
    Fruit salad

Postgame Meal
    Fruit juice
    Green salad
    Cheeseburger or similar sandwich
    Milk or hot chocolate
    Pie and/or ice cream

More important than the menu is *not to eat too late.* A player should have at least three hours, preferably four, before the game actually starts.

Most professional ballplayers, who play mostly at night, eat their big meal after the game. They eat a snack around 3:30 P.M., and then report to the ball park between 4 and 4:30 P.M.

Proper sleep and rest

It is best to have a regular pattern of sleep. An athlete should try to get *eight hours or more each night,* not four tonight and twelve tomorrow. When they perform at night under the lights, some players find that a short nap in the early afternoon is beneficial to their performance in the evening. They feel sharper after a short nap. Personally, I am not in favor of too much rest during the day. True, a ballplayer should try to keep off his feet and more or less relax during the day until he comes to the ball park, but I would not recommend too much rest. The important thing is to get eight or nine hours of good sleep each night.

I do not like our players to play golf after the season starts. I think a ballplayer has to take it easy, stay off his feet and save his energy for the game.

Drinking and smoking
Drinking alcoholic beverages is something we try to guard against because we feel it is harmful and very detrimental to the physical fitness and performance of an athlete. Rules about drinking alcoholic beverages should be stricter among young athletes. I do not mind professional players having a cocktail, but when it comes to excessive drinking, there is no question but that it cuts down on the individual's athletic ability. We do not want it, so we frown upon it.

Smoking is not only detrimental to athletic performance but studies indicate quite conclusively that tobacco smoking is considered a crucial factor in the causation of lung cancer and cardiovascular disease. For those adult players who insist on smoking, medical authorities urge them to use moderation.

In counseling his players not to smoke, the high school or college coach should stress the financial expense as well as the health hazard.

Drug Abuse
During the past twenty years, drugs of all kinds have been used in increasing numbers in America. Tranquilizers and barbiturates such as sleeping pills and "mood control" pills have become a concern of those in athletics. Another type, amphetamines, has the opposite effect, giving a feeling of stimulation. "Greenies" are perhaps the most widely-used of the amphetamines that give an "up" or a "high" sensation. In past years, athletes have been introduced to these drugs through their trainers and doctors, before the danger of their use was recognized.

Physicians of major league baseball clubs are *unanimously opposed* to the use of stimulants such as "greenies" and all other forms of pep pills. "The use of amphetamines could have harmful effects on an athlete," they contend, "and should not be prescribed."

As for the use of "hard drugs" (heroin, opium, cocaine), the physicians feel these could become a problem if the national trend of increased usage among young people continues. But it is generally felt that hard drugs will not likely be a major problem in athletics, for the basic reason that addiction to such drugs soon destroys a man's ability to compete.

Marijuana, however, is a different situation. Statistics show that young people in rapidly increasing numbers are using this drug. Yet, a number of physicians and psychiatrists who were in favor of legalizing marijuana before are changing their minds because of what they have observed happening to young people who habitually use this drug.

Dr. D. Harvey Powelson, director of the student psychiatric clinic at the University of California Berkeley campus, once advocated the legalization of marijuana, but no more. Over the last five years, he has treated 500 students, and he now believes there is a deadly cumulative effect on the minds of those engaging in prolonged use of this drug. He has seen, in those using marijuana daily for a long period (six months to a year), symptoms similar to those observed in organic brain diseases.

Young people tempted to experiment with marijuana would do well to consider carefully Powelson's finding. It is a deceptive argument that there is as yet no scientific proof of marijuana's harmful effects. Scientific proof often is years in the coming. Marijuana hasn't been proven harmful, *but it certainly hasn't been proven harmless either.*

The effects of marijuana, socially as well as mentally, seem to be closer to those of alcohol than to those of harder drugs. To be successful, therefore, an antimarijuana campaign must be tied strongly to an antialcohol campaign. Many young people believe that the use of marijuana is equivalent to that of alcohol, contending that a society that approves of one cannot legitimately condemn the other.

Perhaps the least understood drugs used presently by athletes are androgen hormones and anabolic steroids. "While they have some effect on physique and weight gain, there is always the risk of liver damage and other health dangers," according to Dr. Thomas E. Shaffer, pediatrician at Ohio State University. "In young athletes who have not completed their growth, the hormones may decrease the height which the athlete would ultimately attain." In effect, these drugs are doing the exact *opposite* of what the athlete intended. If an athlete is to attempt hormone therapy in hopes of improving his athletic performance, he certainly should do so only under the strict care of a physician.

Baseball, under the direction of Commissioner Bowie Kuhn, has initiated a drug education and prevention program. The main points of the program are:

Education program

1. Drugs have definite, harmful physiological side effects
2. Drugs do not really improve a man's ability to perform, but only make him *feel* he is doing better
3. Drugs tend to be habit-forming, with damaging long-range consequences.

"We feel the growing use of drugs by young people in this country will sooner or later present a serious problem for baseball unless we educate," said Commissioner Kuhn. "Therefore, we intend to increase our participation in community action programs designed to combat drug problems among the young."

Professional athletes, in increasing numbers, have been getting involved in trying to combat the drug problem among the young. Wes Parker and Jim Lefebvre of the Dodgers, for example, have spoken on the subject of drugs to more than 25,000 junior high school students in the Los Angeles area. In addition to citing the harmful effects of drugs, they have tried to motivate the kids into doing something constructive, like planning a new youth center or trying to help somebody who is handicapped.

"I don't take any kind of pills," said Lefebvre, "and I don't think they could help anyone in any way, even temporarily, and especially an athlete. A baseball player has to be relaxed and calm under pressure. Pills might relax him temporarily, but if he came to rely on them, they would put him on edge. If he were nervous or jittery or had the shakes, he could hardly hit a fast-breaking curve ball or pick up a sharp grounder smoothly."

Injuries and Their Treatment

Many baseball injuries could be prevented by more effective conditioning and by observing various precautionary measures. Injury prevention and good health habits should be constantly stressed by the trainer and coach. All injuries must be promptly recognized and reported, and proper treatment must follow.

Common minor injuries can be treated quite effectively by a trainer or coach (Fig. 14–20). In the case of serious injuries, of course, or when an ailment persists, the team physician should be consulted.

Fig. 14–20. TRAINING ROOM. Injuries should be reported immediately to the team trainer. The training room should be a place of business, and not a lounge (Bill Buhler).

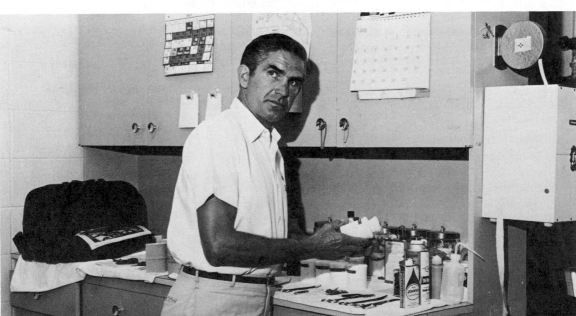

Heat and rest is perhaps the best remedy for a sore arm. As explained earlier, the ice-pack treatment used immediately after a game can help eliminate soreness. Rotation of the arm while under a hot shower is often beneficial, while massage is very helpful, although it should be done only by an experienced trainer.

Where are the locations of most of the serious arm injuries? There are four basic spots:

1. "Little League elbow" is one of the most common, located inside the elbow, and is sometimes called "epicondylitis."
2. Overextension of the arm, an area just behind the elbow.
3. The long head of the triceps becomes overextended.
4. The biceps tendon.

Pitchers who suffer shoulder injuries are often placed on a program of stretching, working with the weighted ball and therapy, including ultrasound, diathermy and whirlpool (Fig. 14–21). Treatment should be under the supervision of an M.D.

Arm injuries

When a youngster suffers from a "Little League elbow," the bone is not really formed as tightly as it should be. As a result, it pulls away, freeing the bone. In some cases, a physician will splint it, in the hope that it will adhere and grow back to where it was before. Otherwise, he will perform surgery on it.

"Little League elbow"

X-ray therapy, under medical direction, is often used to rejuvenate tired throwing arms. When an injury does not respond to other treatment, or when fast treatment is needed, quite a few trainers are employing this type of treatment.

"We used it with Curt Flood when he had his bad shoulder," stated Bauman. "He received a series of X-ray treatments which helped him

X-ray therapy

Fig. 14–21. THE WHIRLPOOL BATH. Players who suffer arm injuries are often given whirlpool treatments. Here, Manny Mota bathes his injured elbow in the training room at Dodger Stadium.

considerably. The X rays bounce off the bone where there are attachments to the muscle tissue, and the inflammation in that area is relieved.''

Muscle bruises ("Charley horse")

Ice should be applied at once. Then, after 24 hours, moist heat applications should be administered, followed by massage and light exercise. A stone bruise should be protected with a sponge rubber pad.

In the case of a pulled thigh muscle, a band of tape should be applied, one inch above the injury and one inch below it.

The hamstring pull

As soon as a player pulls a hamstring muscle, trainer Buhler will start him on oral enzymes to cut down on local bleeding and to eliminate pooling of the blood.

"We will 'ice down' the area and leave the ice bag on for an hour on the leg," explained Buhler. "Then, we will start the wrap. We prefer to wait for 24 hours before we will make a decision. If he experiences considerable pain or swelling in the area, very likely we will not do anything for 72 hours. Then, we start with our whirlpool and the general modalities we have, and go through the gamut of exercises again.

"Normally, with hamstring injuries, we have to figure on almost four weeks without reinjury and almost six weeks for a complete heal-up. It depends on how severe it is."

Knee injuries

An athlete with an injured knee should begin his rehabilitation program as soon as his physician permits it. Ice or ice water should be applied immediately, and a pressure bandage should be used. Normal movements should be resumed as soon as possible, although the athlete should stay off the leg as much as he can.

The recovery of Orlando Cepeda's bad knee is a good example of the Cardinals' exercise program (Fig. 14–22). When Cepeda came to the Cardinals, he had an ailing knee and was on almost complete rest. His knee was filling up with fluid, which necessitated a postcartilage operation.

"We put him on a program of isometric and isotonic exercise," declared Dr. Bauman. "The area that was swelling was treated and coagulated, and while he was with our ball club, not once did he have to have his knee aspirated, which is remarkable. When aspiration is used, we draw fluid out of the joint by means of the hypodermic needle."

Cepeda did strengthening exercises with heavy shoes, both extension and flexion work. Within six weeks, his flexion of the knee joint had increased by at least five per cent. Orlando's big bat soon became a powerful force in the Cardinals' drive to a series of championships.

The weighted shoes weigh 22 pounds apiece, and Cepeda uses from 30 to 40 repetitions daily for both legs with those shoes. "Ac-

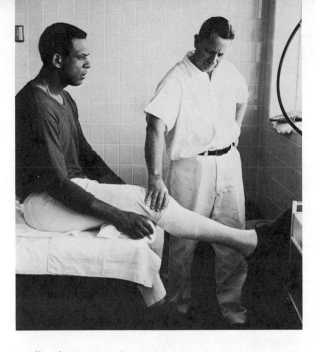

Fig. 14–22. REHABILITATING THE KNEE. The weighted shoe can be helpful in the rehabilitation of the injured muscle, ligaments or tendons. To keep his previously injured knee strong, Orlando Cepeda does his weight work daily throughout the season. His trainer carefully supervises his conditioning program.

tually, therapy such as ultrasound and whirlpool helps only in returning normal circulation to the area," said Dr. Bauman. "The exercises really do the work in rehabilitating the muscles."

If the knee is only sprained and swelling is not evident, the joint might be treated with rest, and cold compresses should be applied. The player can resume play as soon as symptoms allow. However, if extensive swelling occurs ("water on the knee") and the patient is unable to extend the joint, he should be examined by the physician and X-rays taken.

The injury might be the result of a tearing of the capsule of the joint, or ligament or cartilage damage. Treatment may consist of traction, application of cold packs, a plaster shell or adhesive strapping. In some cases, surgery may be necessary.

Knee bends

Many people today believe knee bends are not good, and that athletes should avoid them. Dr. Bauman does not agree. "Catchers are doing knee bends all the time," he explained, "and they have some of the strongest knees among all athletes."

Where the problem has arisen, some coaches have overdone knee bends. They would have a player "duck-walk," with his knees bent, the entire length of the field. This is nonsense, but a controlled number of knee bends is essential to strengthen the muscles of the knees. Knee bends should be done in moderation, just as push-ups or anything else.

Sliding burns

The "strawberry" type of abrasion is actually quite easy to treat nowadays. After scrubbing the area with a mild soap, the trainer will dry it and put on a mild antibiotic cream. A talcum pad will prevent it from sticking, and then he will tape it over. The pad will be changed every day.

Healing can be hurried by cleanliness and by protecting the wound from repeated injury. In severe cases, an ultraviolet lamp will sometimes be used.

Spike cuts   Such cuts are often deeper than they appear to be on the surface. Occasionally, tendons or major blood vessels may be injured.

Soap and water is the best cleansing agent. The player should be immediately examined by a doctor to see if stitches are necessary, and to determine whether or not an injection should be administered.

Blisters   Blisters should *not* be opened, unless they become large or infected. The irritation of the skin by friction actually is the cause of a blister. Quite often, blisters occur on the palms or fingers of the hand, either by throwing or gripping the bat. They can be prevented by toughening the hands during the preseason training program.

If the blister is going to be exposed to further friction, it should be covered with adhesive tape. If the blister opens and the outer skin is destroyed, the wound should be treated like a sliding burn.

Athlete's foot   Athlete's foot is caused by a fungus infection in the skin. For prevention, the individual should dry his feet thoroughly after each shower, and should apply a light dusting of Desenex or Sopronol powder to the feet once a day. If the Desenex powder is used in the morning, the Sopronol powder or ointment should be used at night, or vice versa.

Jock itch   Jock itch usually is the result of chafing in the groin between the legs. It is a fungus infection which has been transferred to the groin region by the jock strap.

The troublesome chafing can be prevented by drying the groin area thoroughly and applying a good dusting powder. Using a clean supporter, and even inserting soft pads, are good measures. Many athletes put their jockey underwear shorts on first, then put on their supporters.

Sprained ankles   The treatment of a sprained ankle depends on its severity. Quite often, tendons around the joint are torn and an X ray is necessary. The team physician should see all such injuries.

Immediately after the accident, the ankle should be surrounded with ice packs and the injured player should be taken to a physician. In the case of a severe sprain, and when considerable swelling takes place, strapping should be applied. The foot should be elevated and surrounded by ice for a period of 24 to 48 hours. The patient should be under constant supervision.

Fingers are occasionally injured when struck by a thrown ball, particularly those of a catcher. A simple sprain can be treated with ice or cold soaks and light exercise. If the tendon which extends the finger is torn from the bone (baseball finger), the player may be unable to extend the finger. This injury should be examined by a doctor and treated with splints or by surgery.

Sprained thumb and finger joints

The training room is for taping, first aid and the treatment of injuries. *Absolutely no horseplay should be tolerated in the training facilities.*

Training Room

Players are told: "Do not throw old tape, soiled white goods, equipment or any other articles on the floor." We want our players to use the disposal containers for refuse, and keep this area clean and sanitary.

Treatments are given before and after practice, and it is the responsibility of each player to report injuries *immediately.* "Never miss a treatment period!" the players are told.

The training room facilities of Buhler, the Dodgers' trainer, consist of:

1. Diathermy machine (2)
2. Ultrasonic machine
3. Whirlpool baths (3)
4. Heat lamp (infrared, etc.)
5. Vascuclimactic machine
6. X-ray unit (30-mil unit)
7. Hydroculator (makes hot mud packs)

A well-equipped medicine kit should include:

Training kit

Band-aids
Ace bandages
Liniment
Dusting powder
Smelling salts
Doughnuts (rubber)
Antacid tablets
Ethyl chloride (with physician's approval)
Tape
Sponge pads
Rubbing alcohol

Fungicide
Tincture of green soap
Bunion plasters
Salt tablets
Gauze
Disinfectant
Cotton
Aspirin
Vanishing cream
Sulfathiazole
Vitamin C pills

Professional Organization /15/

Good organization, along with capable personnel, is the surest way for a big league baseball club to achieve success. Careful attention to the details of organization is a *must,* both on the playing field and in the front office. Only through effective team management can maximum utilization of time, coaching effort and player participation be achieved.

We go out on the field to accomplish basic objectives, and we will give as much time as is necessary to their fulfillment (Fig. 15–2). We do not go out just to have a two-and-a-half or three-hour practice. A carefully planned schedule is necessary if the practice program is to be successfully adapted to the needs of the squad. Intelligent planning can pay off with victories later on. We like our players to be punctual, even early, for all practices, games and departures. We urge them to use the time after practice to improve themselves.

The Dodgers' practice sessions at Vero Beach are always busy. The players move quickly from drill to drill, and from area to area. They are always moving. We believe a team plays like it practices, and if the players are allowed to practice sloppily, they are going to play a sloppy game.

The secret of good performance at critical moments is found in *drill.* It is through drill, *and drill only,* that the manager or coach can be reasonably sure of good performance under game pressure. Individuality or initiative, however, should not be drilled out of the players.

The main thing in managing is getting along with 25 grown men. You've got to keep everybody happy and up for 162 games.

Team Management

No other responsibility of a manager is more essential than providing his team with leadership. *He must make his players want to play!* To accomplish this task, he must possess three basic qualities of leadership:

1. The respect of his players
2. The ability to teach
3. The ability to inspire his players to put out a little extra.

The able manager can assert his leadership by his own enthusiasm, by shouting encouragement to his men on the field. He is constantly urging his players in the dugout to talk it up.

Before each game, the manager has to decide who is going to play. He makes out the lineup and posts it on the dugout wall early enough to inform his team who is scheduled to play that day.

Another responsibility of the manager is establishing an effective set of signals, and giving them during a game. A typical set includes signals for a batter to hit or take a pitch, bunt, sacrifice, hit and run, squeeze play or steal. When the third base coach receives a signal from the bench, he will flash it to the batter.

Handling pitchers is perhaps the most important responsibility a manager has during a ball game. He has to watch for those little signs that will tell him his pitcher is losing some of his stuff.

In watching his players on the field, the manager must make certain they are playing each hitter properly. Occasionally, he has to tell a player to shift his position on the field.

Another prime responsibility of the manager is maintaining discipline, and seeing that players are staying in proper physical condition. If necessary, the manager may have to fine a player for breaking the club rules.

While a no-nonsense attitude on the bench is necessary, the capable manager knows when to break up the tension with some timely humor.

Spring Training

The primary concern of the manager is to organize the training program in such a way that everyone gets in good physical condition before the league season begins. He has to keep in mind that some players have played winter ball, while others have come out of the cold country and their arms are not as strong.

Planning the daily workouts is extremely important in using the time to the best advantage. With such a large squad of players, it

I realize that if we don't win, I will be blamed, but if I have the best club, there is no reason why we shouldn't win.

is essential that everyone be kept busy, rather than have anyone standing around. A workout in which everybody is kept moving for three or four hours is far better than keeping them out on the field for six or seven hours, with other players standing around the batting cage. As a result, we have made it a practice to divide up the squad.

Some baseball people maintain that spring training is too long, which may be true if the sole concern is getting the players in condition to play ball. However, spring training is not too long in respect to the number of young ballplayers that the manager and his aides want to see and to give a chance to play in exhibition games.

Nor is it too long for the majority of pitchers, who take a little longer to get in top condition. We generally have 15 to 20 pitchers in spring training, therefore it is hard to give them enough innings unless we play enough exhibition games. A good spring training program enables pitchers to get their control and become fairly sharp with their command.

In spring training, there are a lot of young players coming in to fill up the roster, new faces whom the manager has never seen play. With such a large squad, the manager has the problem of setting up

Fig. 15–2. THE DODGERS' PRACTICE PROGRAM is set up to accomplish basic objectives. Below, with manager Alston looking on, the team goes through a spirited session in sliding, with outfielder Willie Davis taking his turn.

A manager or coach should not criticize his players publicly any more than he has to.

a program that will take care of everyone. He particularly wants to take a good look at his young talent.

Role of the manager

Essentially, the prime responsibility of the manager is to see that all of his sessions and drills are organized and that everyone is kept busy throughout the practice. Generally, I spend most of my time with the rookies, finding out the little things which are so vital in this game. I want to see if they can hit and run and lay down a bunt, or what they need to work on most.

Making out the training schedule, of course, is a very important responsibility. He has to make his practice sessions interesting and challenging, and cover all the essential areas of the game, with the emphasis on conditioning, both physical and mental.

Generally, I turn the direction of the practice sessions over to my coaches, although I will make suggestions here and there. I believe this is what the major league manager should do, particularly if he has qualified coaches available. He should give his coaches the authority to make suggestions and corrections. This is why a manager should have meetings with his coaches—to see that they all agree, for example, "This is how the cutoff should be made." It is much better when his coaches have the authority to say: "Look, you did this wrong!" The players, in turn, must realize that the coaches have this authority.

As a rule, I have made it a practice to praise my players. I will even try to find some excuses for them occasionally. For example, when somebody "pulls a rock," I might say, "At least, he did this part right," or, "He didn't have a lot of time to think about it. There was a split-second decision to make, and he made it wrong."

I am convinced that a manager or coach should not criticize his players publicly any more than he has to. In my judgment, 90 per cent of a manager's criticism should be given privately, in his own office. Once in a while, if a case is severe, he may need to get on some individual in front of his teammates. Of course, that is the severest thing he can do. Once in a while, this may be warranted, but not too often.

Opening meeting

The first thing we do in spring training at Dodgertown is get the players together in a meeting and talk to them. I try to explain to them what I expect of them and what they can expect of me. The sooner we get acquainted and understand each other, the better we can achieve our objectives.

We believe a team plays like it practices, and if the players are allowed to practice sloppily, they are going to play a sloppy game.

Daily practice

We have a squad meeting every morning at 9:00 A.M. In the meeting, besides talking about fundamentals and tactics, I will discuss the day's practice schedule (Fig. 15–3).

Actually, a typical daily schedule of ours consists mostly of batting practice. Perhaps more than 80 to 90 per cent of our practice time is spent on hitting. This shows how much stress we place on "the hitting game." However, while hitting is going on, everyone on our squad is busy doing many other things. For example, the infielders handle numerous ground balls during batting practice. This is also a good time for individual instruction. I might say to Coach Hartsfield, "Hartsfield, you take this fellow and stay with him for a few days, and see if you can help him."

Quite often, during batting practice, we will make it look like a real game situation. We will have base runners carry out their responsibilities, while those on defense take their respective positions.

After a meeting of approximately 30 minutes, we will go out on the field and do our calisthenics and loosening-up exercises.

Loosening-up

The first thing we do in the morning is to run the entire squad around the field. After jogging once or twice, the squad goes through about 15 to 20 minutes of group calisthenics. Bill Buhler, our trainer, supervises the exercises, which are *not the strenuous type*. We do not try to develop large muscles. They consist more of loosening and stretching exercises. Everyone on the team does these together. Meanwhile, the manager and coaches more or less stand around, and just observe if everybody is putting forth. Quite often, they will join in, too.

"Pepper"

After the calisthenics, the balls and bats are brought out, and we have the players divide up into "pepper" groups. This is an easy conditioning and loosening-up session, approximately 30 minutes in length. In these "pepper" games, we insist on no more than two fielders and one hitter. We feel they get more work this way. We like to spread them out so they have plenty of room.

Later on, we have another man join the fielders, so now we have three fielders and one hitter. Then, we spread them out so that the hitter will get a little work hitting the ball to the player on the far right, and then pulling the ball to the left. All the throws now come from the pitcher. It is like having a pitcher, shortstop and second baseman, and the hitter has an opportunity to hit both ways. We want him to learn to hit the ball to either fielder he wants to. When we feel there has been enough of that, we break it up and go on to our next drill.

Fundamental drills   We gather the infielders in the infield, and one of our coaches takes a position around the mound area. Half the fielders are at short, half at second and two or three first basemen handle the throws at first base.

First, the coach tosses the ball on the ground to the shortstop side, and the fielders make the double play. After a fielder has worked from the second base side, he moves over and becomes a shortstop. We criss-cross back and forth to make the double plays.

This drill can be rather fun; the players see how many plays they can handle successfully in a row without a miscue. At times, we have gotten up to 100 without an error. When one fielder fumbles or makes a bad throw, we start all over. This provides a little competition, and it becomes fun making the double play. Early in the season, we do not want the hard throw—it is just ball handling and footwork practice.

Sometimes, we even do this drill with outfielders. We will have left-handers and everything else out there. Here again, it is exercise, plus footwork and ball handling practice. Once in a while, we will find an outfielder who can make a double play for us. This is one of the ways we find extra infielders, outfielders who might become infielders when needed.

After that drill, we move over to third base and practice fielding one-handed bunt plays. We like all of our infielders to learn how to come in and field the bunted ball. At times, we will bunt the ball hard to them and have them go to second base. We want them to get in the habit of knowing what they should do and where to throw the ball.

When somebody fields the ball improperly, one of our coaches is instructed to correct him immediately. He will take the player aside and work with him individually.

Another competitive drill we do in spring training is the old basketball "Figure 8." We will practice this in the outfield when we want to do a little more than jog around the track. From this drill, we are able to pick out those players who can cut and go, running behind a man just like they did in basketball years ago. Here again, this type of drill is better than simply jogging or running around the track. The players like to do it more, and they will put forth a little more effort this way.

We will divide the pitchers into three-man groups and then play "pepper," one thrower and two hitters. We will then place a pitcher at the same distance as second base. The pitcher throws the ball to the batter, and the batter hits the ball back to him. After catching the ball, he turns and throws as though he were throwing to second base. However, there is another hitter there who is hitting the ball back to him. So, this time, he catches the ball, turns and throws to the other hitter. This is just another little simple drill to get the pitchers accustomed to throwing the ball to second base.

We sometimes give the catchers extra throwing. They will throw from home to second base, for example. The outfielders will work at the same distance from which they would normally throw to the cutoff man. All of these little drills, for the most part, are loosening-up exercises.

Our ball club does a lot of running, not so much for strength, but to build up and maintain stamina. The pitchers probably run a lot more than anyone on the ball club. I am not too much for the really hard running, but I do feel that daily running before or after the game will prove beneficial to outfielders and infielders, as well as to pitchers.

A coach should start the players out easy, back and forth across the outfield. He can actually throw them a ball, or use the fungo if he can handle it skillfully. Whatever type of running, it should begin rather slow and easy, gradually building up. If the players are to do any sprinting, they should do it in the *middle* of the run, after they are completely warmed-up. Then, they can slow down or taper off a little toward the end. Toward the end of a sprint, when the muscle is tired, an athlete is more likely to pull it than he would when warmed-up and not too tired.

Outfielders often have to be forced to run a little more than they would like. They are more inclined to get by than anybody else. Generally, the infielders are always doing something, so we do not worry about them as much as we do the outfielders. This type of running can be more of the sprint type, where they have to go from first to third or first to second, and get their legs in the proper condition.

For a while, we jogged a mile at the end of a workout, which is good to build up stamina. However, I do not like the long type of running, especially in the spring when the grass and sand is loose, because players can come up with badly pulled muscles.

Normally, we will divide the squad up into three different groups. During our staff meeting, our coaches will be told what groups they will supervise (Fig. 15–3). For example, I will give Danny Ozark the veteran players, with maybe a dozen batting practice pitchers. I will turn Danny loose with a group and say, "You go to the stadium and practice."

Then, I will give Roy Hartsfield most of the rookies, and he will have the assignment of batting practice on another field. Red Adams, our pitching coach, will take the pitchers, and he will go to the batting cages where the pitching machines are located. Coach Jim Gilliam may go with Red to serve as the instructor on bunting, which is so important to pitchers. If I have three groups, two will be hitting at the same time on different fields, while the pitchers will be in the batting cages.

During batting practice, we urge our hitters to do a certain amount of hitting to the opposite field. Quite often, we will place a runner on

Fig. 15–3. MANAGER AND HIS STAFF. During the staff meeting, the coaches are told by manager Walter Alston what group each man will supervise. Seated, left to right, are Dixie Walker, Roy Hartsfield, Alston, Danny Ozark and Carroll Beringer. Standing are Jim Gilliam and Red Adams.

first base, with a hitter at bat, and we will use the regular infield at their positions. On the first pitch, we will instruct the hitter to pretend the hit and run is on. Therefore, the pitcher will work on holding the runner on, and the runner will take his appropriate lead.

When the first pitch is made, he will go to second base, and the hitter tries to hit the ball toward right field, from a line drive down. Whether the hitter is successful or not, we will still keep the runner on second base. Now, we will pretend he is on second base, with nobody out, and try to advance him to third base.

On the next pitch, the hitter will try to squeeze him in. We will have a coach over at third base to tell the runner when to go. If he runs too soon, he will tip-off the play and get our hitter knocked down. So, we will instruct him in how not to tip-off the play. We tell him to go just as the pitcher releases the ball, or when his foot hits the ground. If everything goes well, he will squeeze the runner in on the next pitch.

Following this play-situation routine, we will give each batter five or six swings, in which he must try just to meet the ball or hit the ball where it is pitched.

After he takes his last swing, the batter goes to first base, where he becomes the runner for the next hitter. He will do the same thing as I have described earlier. Sometimes, if the hitter executes the hit and run successfully, advances the man to third and performs the squeeze play, we will give him an extra swing or two as a bonus.

We try to make batting practice as much of a gamelike situation as we can. That is why I do not like our pitchers shagging in the outfield.

I would rather have my pitching coach take the pitchers and work on the skills they employ in a ball game.

In spring training, we have several extra coaches in camp, including those who will be handling our top farm clubs. They are all instructed as to where to go and what to do. When we find a player is having trouble at the plate, uppercutting or overstriding, we will turn him over to Dixie Walker, our batting coach, who will take him to one of the cages where the pitching machines are located. Dixie will give him individual instruction and work him on the machine first, then have a couple of pitchers available to throw batting practice. We have seven pitching machines located in netting cages, plus a couple that can be placed on different fields.

After batting practice, we have the squad get their arms in condition and go into a 10- to 15-minute infield practice, while the outfielders chase fly balls and work on their throwing.

The infielders are able to get into condition long before the outfielders, because all during batting practice someone is hitting ground balls to the infielders. However, outfielders have always had trouble getting enough throwing and fly-shagging work. We try to make our outfielders field ground balls and charge them. Frankly, I have not come up yet with a really good drill for outfielders.

Special sessions

We will pick a day when we will hold a special practice session on cutoffs and relays, run-down plays and other basic fundamentals. Instead of hitting, we will have everyone get their arms loosened-up and spend an entire morning working on cutoff plays and the like. The regulars will take their positions in the field, while the rookies become the base runners. We will have one of our coaches act as the hitter.

We will go through just about every possible situation in a ball game. For instance, there is a man on second base and a base hit is going to right center field. We will want the defense to perform exactly the way they would in a ball game. The pitcher will even have a pitcher to back him up on these regular setup plays. If something is not done correctly, we will try it again.

Of course, the cutoffs and relays lead right into base running. The coaches will be on the coaching lines, telling the base runners where to go and what to do. Another coach will be out on the field, helping the defense.

Length of practice session

I have found that I get better results from *one* practice session, than if the players know they have to be on the field for two hours in the morning, come in for a sandwich and then go back for another two hours. I have found that they begin pacing themselves when they know they have another session in the afternoon. On the other hand,

We try to have a peppy, energetic practice, one which is short but gets the job done.

if they know they are going to be out there for five or six hours, the coach does not get good results either.

If the players are not at practice on time or do not put out, we will go into a longer practice session. We have so much work to do, that we stay out on the field until we do it. This is one "whip" the manager has at his disposal—he can keep the players out there as long as necessary.

Frankly, we try to conduct a peppy, energetic practice, one which is short but gets the job done. A manager often has to vary his sessions so that they do not become monotonous. Sometimes, he has to yell at a few of his players to keep things active and get the most out of them. Most ball clubs, though, have a couple of good leaders who can keep up the tempo of the practice by their spirited chatter and hustle. This means more than all the yelling that the manager or coach might do.

As long as they will give me four good hours, I am satisfied. Of course, if we did not have the facilities to divide the squad, we would have to stay out there much longer. I definitely feel we will get better results when everyone gives 100 per cent and our practice is not so long.

I do not have any set time when we finish a practice session. If we have a lot of work to do, we may finish as late as three o'clock. If we finish at two o'clock, that is all right, too. We will go through the work, and once the work is over, that is it. Of course, if the manager can vary his practices, and make them more interesting, the players will respond with greater enthusiasm and spirit.

Then, by the time practice starts getting a little dull, the squad is ready to play an intrasquad game or a game off the pitching machine. This phase of the practice program can be quite competitive, and this is what the players prefer, rather than merely going out and working hard.

Off-the-field activity

After work, I allow those players interested in playing golf to do so. I figure that if they are still able to play golf after *we* are finished with them, that is well and good. But we insist that they *walk*. I would rather have them on the golf course than playing cards, downtown or on the beach.

We have a swimming pool at Dodgertown but very few ever go in. I do not think a lot of swimming will do them any good. As long as it is within reason, a quick dip is all right, but we do not want them to get waterlogged or sunbaked.

Fig. 15–4. THE GRAPEFRUIT CIRCUIT. A good schedule of exhibition games during spring training serves an important role. They provide an organization with a greater opportunity to see more of their young players in game action.

Selecting the team

In making up his squad, the manager has to decide who is going to play and where, which rookies he will keep and the veterans he has to let go. In selecting the team, he has to consider their past records and what they have done. He cannot always go only by what he sees in spring training.

This is why the manager has to work closely with the director in charge of minor league farm clubs: in our case, Al Campanis (Fig. 15–13). Actually, Al is more familiar with the past records of our young players than I am. We constantly meet and talk over the personnel and what might happen.

Some kids who have compiled great records in the minors have a little trouble when they first arrive in the major league. Obviously, they are a little nervous at the beginning, and they start pressing and trying too hard. Then, there are those players who will play even better than their past record indicates.

The manager has to look at each of these young players, and be able to judge what he can do against major league pitching, day-in and day-out (Fig. 15–4). Can he play defensively? Where can the manager play him? How many positions might he play? Then, the manager has to look at the rest of the squad and determine where this player will best fit in.

Every morning, before we get dressed for practice, I will meet with the coaches. We talk over the day's schedule and the different players. At least twice a week, we have a staff meeting with Mr. Campanis, at which time all our coaches, even the head scouts, are present. We will discuss the needs of the team, how we might fill them, whom we might keep and who has to go back for another year. Both Al and myself are in constant communication with our club president, Peter O'Malley, and other members of the Dodgers' front office (Fig. 15–5).

The toughest time for any manager is cut-down time, when he has to go up and tell a player: "You have to go back down," or, "We have

467

Fig. 15–5. DISCUSSING TRAINING PROGRESS with manager Alston is Peter O'Malley, president of the Los Angeles Dodgers. A major league spring training operation entails far more than what takes place on the playing field. As a result, there have to be close ties between the manager and the administrative staff.

to let you go." Some of these kids have busted their fannies all through spring training, hustled and done everything that the manager has asked them to do. However, we are allowed to carry only so many players on the squad, so we do not have any alternative at cut-down time.

In picking his team, the manager has to be impartial, objective and deliberate. Personally, there may be players whom he likes better than the fellow who can play a little better. However, he has to keep personalities completely out of his mind, and select the player who will fill the greatest need.

Squad selection, of course, depends on the club needs. For instance, in an effort to bolster our hitting attack, we keep an eye open for those who swing the bat. The Dodgers have always been partial to speed. I think it is a great quality. However, if a player cannot run too well, we want to be sure he can swing the bat to make up for his lack of speed.

We are constantly looking for the "team players": those who are more interested in the success of the *team* than in their own individual success. We are proud of the fact that, over the years, we have worked together as a team. This is something the manager has to create. We make it a practice to praise a player when he does something for the team, like sacrificing himself to advance a man or playing the game as it should be played. By talking about it and praising him this way, much can be done to develop the proper team attitude.

True, we like to have our best defensive players at positions through the middle of the diamond, that is, pitching, catching, shortstop and second base, and in center field. However, it does not always work this way; for example, right now, the Dodgers' best defensive man—Wes Parker—is at first base.

During the Season

As opening day approaches, the manager has to decide on his starting lineup and opening day pitcher. Basically, he should also have a reasonably good idea who his regular starting pitchers will be and what his bullpen will consist of. He should have at least three good starters, ideally four, with at least one of them a southpaw.

An effective bullpen has at least two relievers, one a right-hander and the other a left-hander, who can be effective for two or three innings. In addition, two "long relievers" should be available, who can come in early in the game and go to the seventh or eighth inning.

Many managers in baseball today are using the "platoon" system. They use left-handed hitters against right-handed pitchers, and vice versa. I have found that right-handed hitters hit right-handed pitchers better than lefties hit lefties, and that left-handers hit right-handers better than right-handers hit left-handers. This is because the hitters see so many more right-handed pitchers in the league.

Game preparation

Since we play mostly night games, we get to the ball park at 4 P.M., approximately four hours before game time. First, we will check to see if everyone is healthy and able to play. Buhler, our trainer, has a fairly good record of the physical status of our club. He knows when they are hurt, for instance, who might have a sprained ankle. Every day, he gives me a good report on our personnel. Then, I go ahead and make up the lineup and post it in the dugout.

The pitchers usually are the first players to arrive on the field, and we allow our pitchers about 20 minutes to hit, mostly bunts and short-stroke swings. We urge our pitchers to slap the ball and keep from striking out. We urge them to hit the ball to the opposite field.

Our batting instructor, Dixie Walker, takes over with bunting practice. This is live and off the regular field. When the pitchers are finished, we like to take them down to the pitching machine and give them another "going over" down there.

The reserve, or extra players, who are not in the lineup, are the next group to hit. They take about a half-hour of batting practice. With the best pitching available, they are urged to hit balls to the opposite field and take their own free swings. While the extra men are hitting, we have the pitchers shag balls hit to the outfield.

Since the regulars hit last, they do not have to be at the park until maybe an hour later. Since they are playing regularly, we feel they should have the privilege of coming in a little later. While the regulars are hitting, the extra men have to shag the balls. During this time, the pitchers are running in the outfield.

Pitching machines are available throughout pregame practice, and the men are kept pretty busy with special instructions from Dixie Walker. If we have a couple of players who want extra hitting, such as those fellows in a slump, this work has to take place before the pitchers hit. Generally, each day, we will have two or three hitters who come out on the field before the pitchers hit. They will take 20 minutes or so, and we try to give them special batting practice pitchers. We have as many as a half-dozen pitchers to throw batting practice.

While at home, all of this hitting takes close to two hours of time. As a result, we can get a considerable amount of hitting work accomplished, which is not the case when the club is on the road.

The batting practice that hitters normally get is not always the answer to their problems, since it is not enough like the type of hitting and pitching they get during a game. It is often mediocre pitching, since hitters get in the habit of wanting straight balls right down the middle and not too much on it. After the hitters have had time to get adjusted at the plate and the season is well underway, batting practice should be as much like game conditions as possible. The pitcher should be instructed to put a little stuff on the ball and take a little off the fast ball.

Managers often have a hard time convincing their hitters to want this kind of batting practice. They like everything down the middle. They say, "I want to get my timing," but it is not very good practice when they are timing the half-speed fast ball. In a game, they will hardly ever get one of those!

Following batting practice, the visitors and then the home club take infield drill, at which time the outfielders are able to make long throws to the bases. Then, they are hit fungos by our coaches (Fig. 15–6).

Squad meetings The majority of our squad meetings consist of defensive strategy talks about how to pitch to the hitters, how the defense should play

Fig. 15–6. PREGAME INFIELD DRILL should feature a great deal of hustle and enthusiasm. The players should sound off and keep up a steady stream of chatter. While the infielders are kept busy, the coaches hit fungoes to the outfielders, with the pitchers assisting on the relays.

them and what to expect from their pitchers. On occasion, we will review the basic fundamentals.

Early in the season, or anytime we feel the team has made some mental errors or thrown the ball to the wrong bases, we will go over cutoff and pick-off plays, bunt situations, the various bunt defenses and things of that kind. When we change our signs, we will usually review the new set at a meeting.

I like to point out specific plays that a certain player made, so that everyone remembers precisely what we mean. I might say: "This ball should not have been thrown to third. It should have been thrown to second."

The coach should not want to place too much blame on one player for making a mistake. He is only picking out this individual as an example. If he wants to be critical, he had better cite other mistakes made by everybody else. This takes some of the pressure off the one player, yet everyone knows what player he is talking about.

Relations with the news media

Once the season starts at home, the writers and radio-TV people start coming in from the time we start to hit. I have a responsibility to be available to the news media both before and after the game (Fig. 15–7). Of course, when we win, it is very easy.

I have found that the best way to handle the press is to be as honest as I possibly can with them. When there are some things I cannot answer, I simply say, "I cannot answer that." Occasionally, I have said: "Off the record, I'll tell you this . . .," and I have never yet found anyone to break the rule. I really appreciate that. I feel that I can talk to them more freely this way. For instance, when I do not want something in print, I will say: "Off the record . . .," and they will honor that.

The team captain

When a team captain is appointed, the first thing the coach must do with this individual is instruct him as to what his duties are and what

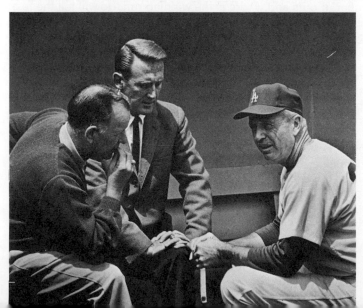

Fig. 15–7. RELATIONS WITH NEWS MEDIA. Before and after each game, the manager has a responsibility to be available to the radio-TV people and baseball writers. Here, manager Alston talks about his team's chances with the popular play-by-play announcers of the Dodgers, Jerry Doggett and Vin Scully, *right.*

Fig. 15–8. "YOUR ATTENTION, PLEASE!" are the familiar words of the Dodgers' public address announcer, John Ramsey, in giving the starting lineups of the day's game. "Leading off for the Dodgers . . . at shortstop, number 30 . . . Maury WILLS!" After giving the game lineups, Ramsey hurries up to the press box, where he performs his PA duties.

is expected of him. Precaution should be taken that he does not override his authority and reach the point where he wants to criticize one of his own teammates.

On the field, I like my captain to more or less direct traffic around the infield. He also takes the lineup to the plate and talks to the umpires just prior to game time. I feel it gives him a little more leeway in talking to the umpires.

The word "captain" itself is not so important. If a team has a leader, the leader on the infield is going to take over anyway. A good example is young Bobby Valentine, up from our Spokane farm club. This fellow is a born leader. He is always out there yelling such things as the number of outs and where is the winning run. He will tell the rest of the infielders and outfielders the same things the coach would want to tell them. He is the leader of the infield, and this is more important than the term "captain."

Planning for trips I am glad I do not have to worry about the planning of road trips. Lee Scott, the Dodgers' very capable traveling secretary, takes care of this important responsibility. It is quite a job in itself, informing our pilot as to when we are leaving. He has such problems as obtaining service for the entire group, securing service at the airport and arranging for personnel to service our big jet plane which is owned by the Dodgers. Lee checks the traveling list to make sure all our players are available. In addition, he has to take care of the hotel reservations for the players, the coaching staff, writers, radio-TV, trainer and clubhouse men. He also gives out the meal money to members of the team. No wonder Lee has a fulltime job!

Fig. 15–9. ENJOYING A VICTORY. Following a hard-earned victory, Walter and Lela Alston relax and enjoy themselves. "If we lose," said Walt, "Lela will not bring up the subject unless I want to talk about it. Otherwise, we talk about the kids at home or something else."

By the time he arrives on the major league scene, the big-leaguer has learned how to dress. If he does not want to be called "bush," he adopts a standard of dress that is used by professional ballplayers everywhere. There is a correct way to wear a baseball uniform, just

How the major leaguer dresses

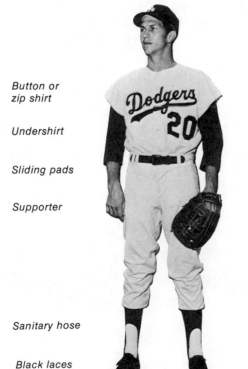

Snug-fitting cap

Button or zip shirt

Undershirt

Sliding pads

Supporter

Shirt tucked in pants

Correct pant length

Sanitary hose

Outer stockings

Black laces

Proper shoes

Looking the Part

Fig. 15–10. WEARING THE UNIFORM. There is a correct way to wear a baseball uniform, as demonstrated by Don Sutton.

473

Fig. 15-11. A MAJOR LEAGUE OPERATION, such as this capacity crowd of 56,000 at Dodger Stadium in Los Angeles, requires a combined front office staff of many people. Supporting the manager and his team on the playing field are such important areas of management as ticket sales, field maintenance, group sales, public relations and promotion, concessions, radio-TV, advertising, ushers and traffic controllers, medical staff, minor league operations, player personnel and scouting. Under the direction of the board of directors and the control of the administrative staff, they are a coordinated team.

as there is a proper way to wear a suit of clothes. When people remark that, "He looks like a ballplayer," they are referring to the fact that this player wears his uniform like a major leaguer. Figure 15-10 describes the ballplayer's dress when ready to play ball.

Fig. 15-12. THE CHIEF EXECUTIVE. The man most responsible for the development of the Los Angeles Dodgers into one of baseball's most successful franchises is Walter O'Malley, chairman of the board of directors. Through his keen vision, planning and administrative prowess, the Dodgers' organization has been a model which other major league clubs have tried to emulate.

474

Fig. 15–13. PLAYER PERSONNEL. Acquiring the best possible players is the prime responsibility of the director of player personnel, Al Campanis. The farm system is the lifeblood of any major league baseball club, which depends on its minor league teams to furnish it with promising young talent each year.

Player personnel

Acquiring the best possible players is the prime responsibility of Al Campanis, our director of player personnel (Fig. 15–13). Each year, we try to select the 40 best players in the organization and have them report to Dodgertown for spring training. Campanis often has to make decisions on whom to keep and whom not to keep, whether to trade a player or not to trade him. He has to depend on the advice of the manager, the coaches and scouts, but in the end, *he* will have to make the decision. Therefore, he has to be a judge of talent, often having to decide between two players. Many times, players are of similar ability, and it is not always the player who looks good right now who becomes the star.

There are several ways in which we acquire new players:

1. The annual player draft
2. Player development in minor leagues
3. Acquisition by trade
4. Signing men as free agents.

When young players arrive in the big leagues, it should be realized that they are not finished players by any means. They still have to develop and be taught the finer points of the game. "Baseball is perhaps the most overcoached and yet undertaught game that is played today," according to Campanis. "There are so many refine-

---

We are constantly looking for the "team players": those who are more interested in the success of the team than in their own individual success.

---

ments in baseball, as compared to football. For example, a player can graduate from four years of college football and go right into pro football and get a regular big league assignment. But in baseball, it is a rarity when a player can come off the college campus and move right into major league play."

Temperament and mental attitude have a lot to do with the speed of one's development. Some players are what we call "plotters." They need some acceleration, whereas other players can skip a classification and make very rapid advancement. As in education, there are quick learners and slow learners. The same is true as far as ability is concerned.

The only substitute for experience is outstanding natural ability. For instance, Sandy Koufax, who had never pitched professionally, started right out in the big leagues, and never did get sent to the minors. However, he had exceptional ability. Tom Seaver is another example of a young pitcher who made it to the big leagues in a very short time. Yet, Bill Singer served his regular apprenticeship of five years in the minor leagues. Singer, though, started his professional career at the age of 17.

"In going out and seeing our farm clubs play," asserted Campanis, "we will often see the early potential of a Bill Singer or a Willie Davis, and we will come back and pass this along to Walt. This information is also supplied by our scouts. Walter relies on our judgment, so we must pass him an objective report."

Each year, we have a number of players who are eligible for the player draft because of the amount of time they have spent in the minor leagues. The player selection is done numerically, depending on the position in which each team finished the previous year. Since these players become eligible for the draft, we have to protect them.

Fielding a balanced club, of course, is a prime objective. Therefore, we have to consider the number of pitchers, catchers, infielders and outfielders on our squad.

Through our extensive scouting system, we have scouts stationed throughout the country looking for players with major league potential.

During the off-season, I am in contact with the front office almost weekly. We have minor league and major league meetings, in which we talk about whom we might draft and whom we might lose in the annual draft. In addition, we are constantly considering for whom we might make a deal. These things go on all through the winter months.

Making player trades

Basically, the reason a big league team makes a trade is not merely for the sake of trading, but to satisfy a need. For example, if we should need a relief pitcher, we will begin to scan another club which might have a surplus of relief pitchers. Should this club need a right-handed hitting outfielder and we have a surplus of those, we might very well make a deal.

So, when a team wants to trade, what they are saying, in effect, is that they are trying to satisfy a definite need. Occasionally, some clubs will trade a very good ballplayer. A prime example was the Frank Robinson deal between Cincinnati and Baltimore. Robinson was traded for Milt Pappas, a pitcher whom Cincinnati needed very much, and since the Baltimore club needed a hitter, they made the trade. The ideal situation, of course, is for a club to develop their own players so that they are not in need of a trade.

Through the years, I have observed that, in many of the trades in baseball, both ball clubs quite often get what they want. Sometimes is appears that one club has gotten the better of the deal the first year. But it takes more than one year for a trade to really indicate whether it has been more beneficial for one club or the other.

Fig. 15–16. THE NUMBERING SYSTEM for each position—the basis of scoring.

Fig. 15–17. A PAGE FROM A WORLD SERIES SCOREBOOK, showing a detailed record of the Baltimore Orioles' half of the first game of the 1970 World Series with the Cincinnati Reds at Riverfront Stadium in Cincinnati, Ohio, October 9, 1970.

Team *BALTIMORE, A.L.* Date *OCT. 9*

PO	A	E	Player	Pos	1	2	3	4	5	6	7	8	9	10	11	12	AB	R	H	RBI	SB
1	0	0	BUFORD	7	F2			9		S-9 6-4		F7					4	0	1	0	0
7	0	0	BLAIR	8	8			S-8		K2		5-3					4	1	1	0	0
6	0	0	POWELL	3	K2			HR-LF		DP 4-3		BB					3	1	1	2	0
2	0	0	F. ROBINSON	9		9		7			F2	Kc					4	0	0	0	0
3	3	1	B. ROBINSON	5		5-3		6-3		HR-LF		Kc					4	1	1	1	0
4	1	1	HENDRICKS	2		F2		HR-RF		K2		K2					4	1	1	1	0
2	0	0	D. JOHNSON	4			6	Kc		BB		D-RF					3	0	1	0	0
2	3	0	BELANGER	6			Kc	K2		S-8		1BB					3	0	1	0	0
0	0	0	PALMER	1			4-3	K2		Kc		9					4	0	0	0	0
0	0	0	RICHERT (9)	1													0	0	0	0	0
7	7	2	Attendance 51,531		0/0	0/0	0/0	2/2	1/1	1/1	2/0	0/0	0/1				33	4	7	4	0

Is a great deal of trading good or bad for baseball? I think, if a player is an outstanding one, it is best to keep him and develop him. Having become quite popular, he often has strong appeal to the fans and possesses good drawing power. On the other hand, a change of scenery might do him some good. For instance, if a player has a mental block, he may feel he cannot play well in a certain park. Then, the change will probably help him.

A new park might be more conducive to his style of pitching or hitting. A player might feel that he has not had the opportunity to play as often as he thinks he should. Playing for another manager might help him. Therefore, the player's psychological approach can play an important role.

Overall, though, we are always striving to build the type of ball club for which we do not have to make many deals. To a large extent, then, this means that we are quite satisfied with our group of players.

Keeping Score

Keeping score provides the coach or manager with valuable game records and statistics, and can also add to a fan's enjoyment of a baseball game. The play-by-play record tells what each player has done in the field and at bat. Scoring a game is actually very simple, when using a system such as the one devised by The Sporting News Publishing Company, 1212 N. Lindbergh Blvd., St. Louis, Missouri 63166 (Figs. 15–16 and 15–17). A copy of their detailed "How to Score" manual, including the official rules of scoring, can be obtained for only fifty cents by writing The Sporting News.

Signs and Numbers Used in Keeping Score

S–LF	Single to left field	F9	Fouled to right fielder
D–LC	Double to left-center	5–3	Grounded out, third baseman to first baseman
T–CF	Triple to center field		
HR–RF	Home run to right field		
B–S–3B	Bunt single to third base	DP (with 4–3 beneath it)	Hit into double play and was out, second baseman to first baseman (6–4 in space of runner who was retired, if ball was hit to shortstop)
S–SS	Infield single to shortstop		
BB	Base on balls		
IBB	Intentional base on balls		
H by P	Hit by pitcher	DP (with 3 beneath it)	Lined to first baseman for double play. A.S. 2–6—out on attempted steal, catcher to shortstop
FC	Fielder's choice		
E–2B	Error by second baseman		
ET–1B	Throwing error by first baseman		
Sac.	Sacrifice bunt		
SF	Sacrifice fly		
SB	Stolen base	K_2	Struck out swinging
T	Advanced on throw	K_c	Called out on strikes
PB	Passed ball	K_{2-3}	Struck out but had to be thrown out, catcher to first baseman
WP	Wild pitch		
7	Flied to left fielder		
L8	Lined to center fielder	K	Foul tip third strike

Fig. 15–18. THE OFFICIAL SCORER has an important responsibility in the conduct of a baseball game. He must make vital decisions such as determining a hit or an error, a wild pitch or a passed ball. Here, Bob Hunter, one of baseball's most distinguished writers, handles the official scorer's duties for the day.

This system also records each runner's advancement around the bases. Immediately beneath the symbols showing how the batter got on base, the scorer can show his advancement by completing the parts of a square equivalent to the number of bases he advances, in a counterclockwise pattern.

Determining Averages

Batting Average Divide the total base hits by the total times at bat.

Slugging Average Divide the total bases of all safe hits by the total times at bat.

On-Base Average Divide the total number of times a player reaches base (hits, hit by pitcher, fielder's choice, errors and walks) by the total times at bat.

Fielding Average Divide the total of the put-outs and assists of the fielder by the total number of put-outs, assists and errors.

Earned Run Average Divide the total earned runs allowed by the total innings pitched, and multiply by nine.

Team Percentage of Games Won and Lost Divide the number of games won by the total games played (both won and lost).

A full point is added to the average in cases where the remaining fraction is one-half or over.

Scouting

The scout must be a good judge of baseball talent. From the physical standpoint, he must look for players who have a good arm, good hands and can run. Some boys do not possess all of these attributes, therefore a scout has to make allowances for them.

The shortstop who can run very well and has a good arm is an excellent example of this. If he is not a good hitter but hits from the left side, the player might be the type who can get on base by bunting or slapping the ball around. He does not have power, so the manager has to make allowances for this lack because the shortstop position is not as demanding for power. The position itself is basically defensive in nature, but probably no team can win a championship without an outstanding shortstop.

Basically, scouts look for a young man who has a quick bat, correct form and takes a good stroke at the ball. Does he have power? Does he make contact? Actually, hitters are hard to scout. Pitchers are somewhat easier to judge, since it is not difficult to see whether or not a pitcher can throw hard.

When scouting an outfielder, the scout looks for more power than he would in a shortstop. From a physical standpoint, he looks for a strong arm, speed and the ability to hit for power.

The mental aspects are also very important. The temperament and character of a player will prove a key factor in his success in baseball. How does he take adversity? Can he survive a batting slump? This is why we like our players to be able to react positively during moments of adversity. This will determine, to a large extent, whether or not they can bounce back.

There is the young prospect who does not care for school, and the only thing on his mind is playing baseball. This is the boy who normally should sign if he has the potential talent.

On the other hand, if a boy is scholastically fit, loves school and does very well academically, he is likely the type who should pursue his education immediately and delay his professional baseball career. To a great extent, it depends upon the temperament of the ballplayer, whether or not he has the ability and desire to study.

Some of the young men who go into professional ball upon graduation from high school come back during the off-season and work toward their degree during the fall semester. Occasionally, a ball club will give a boy a scholarship, and he will take advantage of it.

Personally, I am pleased when I see a young professional player return to school during the off-season. He can be the greatest ball-

Fig. 15–19. BIG LEAGUE SCOUTS are usually on the scene whenever top amateur and semipro games are played. Generally, a scout will look at a boy's size and physical build, arm strength, speed afoot and fielding ability.

482 / PROFESSIONAL ORGANIZATION

player in the world, but there is always the possibility that he will come up with a bad arm or suffer a serious injury.

The following are the main qualities a major league scout looks for in a young prospect:

1. Desire (Does he *want* to play?)
2. Speed (Can he run?)
3. Good arm (Can he throw?)
4. Good instincts and reflexes
5. Quick bat (Can he swing a bat?)
6. Aggressiveness (Does he hustle?)
7. Aptitude (Does he learn quickly?)
8. Character and habits
9. Physical qualifications (build, size, etc.).

A ballplayer should not be judged on his performance during one game. A boy can have a great day and go five for five because the opposing pitcher was "made for him." The first impulse of a scout is: "That is the boy I am going to draft!" However, this could be a mistake because that boy was fortunate enough to hit against a certain type of pitcher. He might not be as effective against pitchers with different stuff. Therefore, a scout must make sure he watches a boy during *at least* five or six ball games.

How attractive is scouting financially? The salaries vary according to the scout's experience and background, particularly whom he has signed before. If he is fortunate enough to sign a superstar, his status and security can be strengthened considerably. Some scouts make from $10,000 to $15,000 a year, while others are in the $20,000 bracket. It depends on the organization and on the scout himself.

"A scout has to practically live with the boy," said Bill Avila, scout for the Philadelphia Phillies. "He has to meet his parents and see what the boy does off the field. Occasionally, a good prospect will look good on the field, that is, good glove, fine swing and a strong arm. Then, word gets out that he is participating in this wild party until two o'clock in the morning, or he is on a marijuana bend with a certain crowd. Well, the scout has no other alternative than to walk away from that boy, even though he knows this young man is a fine ballplayer. He has to forget him, and when another scout signs him, he can say to himself, 'He is making a big mistake!' "

Scouting opponents

We have a scout who is given the assignment of scouting our next opponent. For example, before San Francisco comes into town, we obtain a full, detailed report on the Giants' personnel. Of course, it is not necessary for our scout to give me another report on Willie Mays or Willie McCovey. The only thing that I am interested in is a

Fig. 15–20. PROFESSIONAL BASEBALL has been good for Mr. and Mrs. Emmett Alston and son, Walter, of Darrtown, Ohio (population: 250), fitting testimony that major league baseball beckons young athletes in every town and city in America, large or small.

new ballplayer whom I have not seen, or to know the fellows who have been hot in the last few days. I want to know how other clubs pitch to him and how to get him out. I want to know whether he is a high ball or low ball hitter, an inside or outside hitter, or if he is a fast ball or breaking ball hitter.

Should a graduating high school senior, one who has outstanding potential, go to college and play collegiate ball, or begin his professional career as an eighteen-year-old? This is a common question confronting many young athletes, one which major league scouts have to deal with constantly. We asked Campanis this very difficult question, and Al answered it this way: "It would depend on his ability. If he has the ability of a Sandy Koufax, Mickey Mantle or Willie Mays, I would say, 'Go into professional baseball.' If there is a questionable ability involved, then I would say, 'Go to college.' However, we should

A professional career?

A. A swing. . . . Bye, bye, baby!

B. Another round-tripper for Willie

Fig. 15-21. WILLIE MAYS, A BASEBALL INSTITUTION with the San Francisco Giants, has been a prolific producer of home runs, challenging the immortal Babe Ruth.

keep in mind that many of these players can do both. He can sign a contract and still receive a college scholarship or enough money to provide for a college education. He has an opportunity to attend college during the fall semester. True, it will take him longer to complete his education, but this player will not need this education until he is through playing baseball. So, actually, you might say that he can have his cake and eat it too.''

Professional baseball is one of the most lucrative sports in America. Salaries in the big leagues range from the minimum of $12,000 on up to the super contracts of $100,000 or even up to $150,000 which stars like Willie Mays (Fig. 15-21), Hank Aaron, Pete Rose, Bob Gibson and Harmon Killebrew have received. The average big league salary today ranges from $25,000 to $30,000. Along with this income, the players receive meal and hotel expenses when on the road. Furthermore, the majority of major league players have their names connected with advertising promotions and make a countless number of public appearances.

With the lucrative bonuses and salaries that major league clubs pay, plus the large World Series checks, no wonder so many youngsters want to become big league ballplayers!

College and High School Organization /16/

There is no easy formula for developing a winning baseball program. Indeed, the task of fielding a championship team involves many factors, over some of which the coach has little or no control. However, no factor is more important to team success than a dedicated coach who gives and demands 100 per cent effort and leaves *nothing* undone in setting up a sound organization of conditioning and training.

Building a successful baseball program on the college or high school level is a cooperative effort and includes the school administration, faculty, community and the news media. If the coaching staff does not have the support and cooperation of both the school and the community, the task of producing a top caliber baseball program is very slim, indeed.

Fielding a team that is well conditioned, fundamentally sound in basic techniques and well disciplined in offensive and defensive team strategy and play should be the primary objective of every organizational plan. However, a number of major problems often make the job more difficult.

Weather conditions are unpredictable, particularly in the northern regions of the country. For instance, in Connecticut, the practice program starts on the first Monday of March, so the first concern of coaches in that region of inclement weather is to practice indoors. Then, too, the length of the daily practice session is sometimes limited by school districts. Another problem can be a meager budget,

Baseball needs more coaches and managers who can teach and are capable of communicating.

which forces the team to play with poor equipment and inadequate facilities. In this area, the tiled infield, which can drain effectively, indoor facilities and batting cage can be of inestimable value to a baseball program.

Getting along with competing spring sports in the school can at times be a difficult problem. In a small school, especially, it may be necessary to adopt written policies governing sports, in order to assure cooperation from all concerned. The agreement should list the number of sports in which a boy may participate in the spring, and on what levels.

Getting more coaches with professional backgrounds will do much to help the situation, but it is important that they be able to teach, too. Just because a man was a professional baseball player does not necessarily mean he would qualify as a teacher.

Baseball needs more coaches and managers who can teach and are capable of communicating, men with the ability to impart knowledge, for instance, of "how to make the double play." I know of a major league coach who told a player, "Here is the way you make the double play . . ." That was all there was to it. He failed to break down this basic fundamental as to the approach to second base, getting under body control, the four or five ways of making the double play, how to react if the ball is thrown to infielder's right, etc.

Baseball coaches are unanimous in declaring that the quality of officiating is one of the key factors in a successful baseball program. Unquestionably, an umpire who lacks the consistency, judgment and necessary knowledge of the rules can spoil the game. Therefore, every athletic director and baseball coach should give just as much care to the selection of their baseball umpires as they do to basketball and football officials.

We hope the time will soon come when the college will give us more of a finished product. We would then be able to give him less time in his minor league apprenticeship. We have players who have either graduated from college or finished at least three years of college; still, they have to go to the rookie leagues and the class A leagues. They simply are not ready to play in a higher classification.

"Of course, the climate is a big factor," said Al Campanis, director of player personnel for the Dodgers. "In the Eastern or Northern colleges, they are not able to play too many ball games. When I was at New York University, for example, we played a total of 20 intercollegiate games, and some practice games. Well, you are not going to develop a player by having him play 20 or 25 games. Now, here on the West Coast, the University of Southern California plays about

When two teams get together, the team that makes the fewest mistakes is going to win the ball game.

BOBBY WINKLES

55 games, plus some practice games. This is the type of program that will develop ballplayers and will enable them to move into a higher classification of baseball."

Increasing schedules, rather than decreasing them, would improve the play. What we need are more summer programs to develop college and amateur players. Through the Amateur Study Commission, we have expanded the number of college summer leagues to five. A special fund of $125,000, administered through the Commissioner of Baseball, provides for the development of college players in the following programs: Atlantic League, Basin League, Central Illinois League, Valley League and California College League.

Team Management

The organization of a baseball program involves many aspects which the coach should be concerned with year-round. Indeed, the job of a head baseball coach is often a twelve-month assignment on the college level.

The management of a baseball team includes the following areas:

1. Conditioning and training
   a. Off-season
   b. Preseason
   c. During season
2. Team selection
3. Game preparation
4. Facilities and equipment
5. Maintenance of the playing field
6. Public relations
7. Player recruitment
8. The budget and its use
9. Making the schedule
10. Planning for trips
11. Selecting umpires
12. Scouting needs

A Coach's Code of Ethics *

1. It is the duty of the coach to be in control of his players at all times in order to prevent any unsportsmanlike act toward opponents, officials or spectators.
2. Coaches are expected to comply wholeheartedly with the intent and spirit of the rules. The deliberate teaching of players to violate the rules is indefensible.
3. Coaches should teach their players to respect the dignity of the game, officials, opponents and the institutions which they represent.

* As compiled by the American Association of College Baseball Coaches.

Fig. 16–2. A GOOD BRAND OF BASEBALL. This exciting play, showing a Washington State University Cougar sliding aggressively across home plate, is the type of action that can stimulate any baseball program.

4. Coaches should confine their discussion with the game officials to the interpretations of the rules, and not constantly challenge umpire decisions involving judgment.

5. Whereas friendly banter between players is not to be prohibited, cursing, obscene language, malicious or personal remarks to opponents or spectators should not be tolerated at any time. Rather, the players should spend their energies toward encouraging their teammates to better efforts.

6. Coaches should emphasize the fact that their base coaches must confine their remarks to their own teammates, and not "ride" the opposing pitcher.

7. Coaches, themselves, should refrain from any personal action that might arouse players or spectators to unsportsmanlike behavior.

8. Coaches should expect from the umpires a courteous and dignified attitude toward players and themselves.

9. Coaches should seek help from school administrators in controlling unruly students and spectators.

The Training Program

During spring training, when a team has to go through some tough conditioning programs and countless fundamental drills, the manager has to convince his players that this is the basis for a winning ball club. In order to execute the skills properly, they must perform the fundamental techniques correctly. Therefore, a team must constantly practice and drill on the basic fundamentals (Fig. 16–3). It must drill and drill over and over again, until the techniques become habitual.

Fig. 16–3. FUNDAMENTAL DRILLS are the basis of a winning ball club. A team must practice and drill on the basic fundamentals until the techniques become habits.

Fig. 16–4. GOOD COMMUNICATION is essential to successful coaching. Messages to the squad given at the opening or close of a practice are more effective when delivered before a group which is seated and gives their undivided attention.

Preseason

The preseason phase of the practice season consists of conditioning and training. The emphasis should be on mastering individual offensive and defensive fundamentals, in which the coach devotes considerable time to individual and small-group supervision. As a rule, most coaches like to take the pitchers and catchers by themselves

Fig. 16-5. BATTING PRACTICE. During early practices, the batting cages should be alive with activity, as every hitter gets in his quota of swings. When the pitchers need work, they should replace the machines, as the situation indicates in this picture. Pitchers should be instructed to throw the ball "down the pipe, with a little something on it."

for the first week, and then work with the infielders and outfielders the second week.

During the first week of practice, the pitchers should be given a conditioning routine of calisthenics, wind sprints, jogging, pepper and fly ball chasing, along with intensive instruction and supervision in the fundamentals of pitching. While the pitchers are doing their conditioning work, the catchers are receiving instruction in the fundamentals of their position.

On Monday of the second week, when the remainder of the squad reports, the coach must divide his supervision between four different groups: pitchers, catchers, infielders and outfielders. During the practice session, one or more of these groups will be largely on their own, making it necessary for them to be engaged in set drills and activities. However, the coach is always close by to offer necessary direction and guidance.

Teams in the northern areas of the country have to confine a good portion of their preseason work to indoor activity. Because of time and space limitations, indoor gym workouts generally are limited to returning members of the varsity, jayvee and freshmen teams of the previous year. A general call for all other candidates is issued as soon as the squad can get outdoors. For indoor batting practice, pitching machines are used inside of nets. A batting tee is used, in which the batter hits the ball into the wall or net (a whiffle ball, rubber ball or tennis ball). To improve his wrists, the hitter should swing fast and hit the balls quickly. The tee should be placed out in front of the plate so he can meet the ball out in front. Infielders can get fielding practice with the off-the-wall drill. They are instructed to throw a rubber ball against the wall and field it.

During the early practices, the coach should tell his hitters not to try to hit the ball too hard. Like a pitcher, a coach does not want his hitters to pull their back or arm muscles. He must insist that everybody just make contact.

"We do a lot of opposite field hitting, pretending the hit and run is on, advancing a man from second to third," stated Winkles. "We do this a lot in the batting cages, where every pitch is pretty much the same speed and over the plate. We work on the little things, such as getting our players to hit the ball to the opposite field.

Fig. 16–6. PORTABLE BATTING CAGE. This piece of equipment is a top-priority item, designed to be pulled out to the home plate area for pregame hitting practice. It can also be placed in the left field or right field corners, while work is being accomplished on the infield part of the diamond.

Fig. 16–7. THE AUTOMATIC PITCHING MACHINE has proved a valuable training aid to a baseball program, particularly this Curvemaster machine, which hurls curve balls and fast balls with strike zone precision.

"With our club, we have to insist on a lot of these little fundamentals," continued Coach Winkles. "I talk about hitting the ball to the opposite field and hitting the ball where it is pitched. If a fellow has trouble with the inside pitch, we make him stand close to the plate, and using the pitching machine, we get him to rotate his hips. And if he has trouble with the outside pitch, we move him away from the plate and make him hit a lot of outside pitches."

The next phase of the training program starts with preparation for the league games, and continues until about two weeks before the season ends. During this period, the daily practice sessions are geared to the development of team defense and the correction of

The league season

individual flaws and weaknesses. Conditioning activities must be closely adhered to each day, not only by the pitchers but by the rest of the squad as well. The coach should make sure each player performs his stretching and loosening-up exercises and does his running daily.

Whenever necessary, players are assigned to individual activities or placed in remedial groups where they may work on individual weaknesses, such as a catcher needing extra practice on his footwork, or a pitcher who has a poor pick-off move to first base.

With proper organization, the coach may run many of the team defensive and offensive drills simultaneously during these practice sessions. Base running drills can be made a part of the defensive situation drills, and bunting practice will prove more realistic with a defensive infield at their respective positions to practice bunt defense. Furthermore, various members of the squad can work on various aspects of team offense and defense while others are working on individual weaknesses.

Late season   During the final weeks of the season, the coach must do everything within his means to make the practice sessions as interesting as possible. As the season approaches its end, practice can often become boring, due mainly to a lack of interest among the players. Consequently, practices should be shortened considerably, and emphasis on fundamentals, conditioning and corrective work eliminated. Quite often, the best solution is to schedule a few practice games or substitute newer and more appealing forms of drills and activities.

To add variety to late-season practice sessions, fun activities should be offered along with the more serious activities. An entire practice could be devoted to an amusing hour of fun activities. The squad might engage in a baseball track meet, utilizing baseball skills in the manner of a track meet. Or, an intrasquad game could be scheduled, with each player playing a different position each inning.

To spice up a baseball practice, the session can be shortened, and the teams can play an intrasquad game with the count advanced on a hitter to a two-ball, one-strike count. A variation of advancing the count is to play one-strike or two-strike ball.

To speed up an intrasquad game, one team can stay on the field for six, nine or twelve outs, with the bases cleared after each three outs.

Another interesting game that can be played is "Tee Ball," in which a batting tee is placed on home plate and a regular game is played, with the batter hitting the ball off the tee.

If a team is doing poorly and getting a little stale, the coach might give them a few days off and not let them come to the ball park. "Sometimes I will not let them pick up a ball or bat for three days," said Winkles, "because they are probably suffering from staleness."

Daily Practice

I have found it necessary to have a set pattern for our practice sessions so the players will know what they are supposed to be doing every minute. Players must not only be in top physical condition, but prepared mentally as well. It is recommended that daily schedules be mimeographed in detail for all squad members, complete with the activity each player is to participate in and the time for participation. In fact, we feel the coach should keep an eye on his watch in order to devote the proper amount of time to each phase of the practice session.

Generally, players will report on the field ten or fifteen minutes before the coach begins the practice session.

They begin loosening-up by either playing catch or getting into a pepper game. Some of the players will use this time to do a few stretching routines by themselves. Teams using the Exer-Genie program at this time will have their players go through the specific exercises (described in the Conditioning chapter).

Then, at a set time, such as 3:00 or 3:30 P.M., the entire squad will go to a designated area for group calisthenics, consisting mainly of stretching and loosening-up exercises. A pitcher and catcher will begin warming-up for batting practice work.

After the loosening-up period, batting practice gets underway, with most of the squad taking part in this hour-long period. While the hitters are taking their cuts in the batting cage, the infielders are kept busy all the time fielding ground balls. Besides fielding the ball off the bat at the plate, they receive additional grounders from the fungos hit by the coach or extra pitchers. It is essential that the player hitting the fungos learn to time his hits so they are made *between* pitches to the plate.

The batting phase of the practice should be divided into groups, with never more than five players to a group. This time can also be used for drills and instruction.

An eighteen-man squad could be deployed in the following manner: seven fielders; one catcher; one pitcher; a shagger for the pitcher; two fungo hitters; one pitcher warming up; one bullpen catcher and four hitters.

Following batting practice, the infielders receive ten minutes of ground balls in rapid succession. The coach is close by to make any corrections necessary, occasionally demonstrating the proper procedure. While this fielding work is taking place, pitchers and catchers can be hitting fungos to the outfielders. The extra catchers can be working along the sidelines on such fundamental techniques as shifting and throwing, blocking the low ball and handling pop flies. The pitchers can work on their moves to the bases.

After completing this phase of the practice, the entire squad should be called into the infield to participate in 20 minutes of general fundamentals. Among the areas covered in this important team session are base running, pick-off and cutoff plays, the defense and offense of the delayed and double steals, bunt situations and handling pop-ups to the infield and outfield. Work on pop-ups should not be taken too lightly. Many games have been lost because of poor execution in fielding pop flies, which can be corrected through greater emphasis during practice time.

Regular infield practice is the next phase of the session, starting with the outfielders making their throws to the bases and the infielders throwing the ball "around the horn."

Infield practice normally consists of eight rounds. The first three rounds are designed to execute the put-out at first base, and the second three rounds to execute the double play. The remaining two rounds are designed to give the infielder practice at fielding the slow roller, throwing to first base and fielding and throwing to the plate.

During infield practice, the ball is hit directly at the infielder on the first round, to his right for the long throw, and then to his left. This gives the player a chance to practice moves in all directions.

Hitting the ball too hard can be a major fault that should be avoided in infield practice. Infield practice is basically a warm-up period, and should be conducted to instill confidence in the players prior to the game.

Even though the practice is on the homeward stretch, the coach must insist on plenty of pep and enthusiasm in this drill. Fungo hitters, meanwhile, are hitting fly balls to outfielders, making sure they get practice moving in all directions.

Before they leave the field, all players must complete their daily running work. Not only should the pitchers get their running in, but the outfielders, infielders and catchers should wind up their practice by running wind sprints. The players assume a lead-off stance, and using the initial step, run a distance of 60 yards, then walk back. Other running drills that may be used include circling the bases and relays.

The workout I have just discussed should be used daily until the team is ready to play a game, in about two weeks. Then, three days—such as Monday, Wednesday and Friday of each week—can be devoted to practice, while Tuesday, Thursday and Saturday can be reserved for full-scale intrasquad games. These games should be nine full innings in length, running for a period of two hours.

I would like to point out that the practice workout outlined should be subject to change in any manner the coach sees fit. As the training season moves along, the coach will be able to observe where his team is weak, and can arrange his practice schedules to correct these weaknesses.

To save precious time and encourage hustle, players should be urged to run to their new areas each time there is a change.

```
┌─────────────────────────────────────────────┐
│          Daily Practice Periods              │
│                                              │
│     Prepractice loosening-up      15 min.    │
│     Group warm-up                 15 min.    │
│     Fundamental drills            15 min.    │
│     Batting practice              60 min.    │
│     Bunting practice              15 min.    │
│     Infielder's throwing          10 min.    │
│     Pitcher's fielding drills     15 min.    │
│     Infield, outfield drill       15 min.    │
│     Running drills and relays     10 min.    │
└─────────────────────────────────────────────┘
```

First Week (Pitchers and Catchers)

Practice Schedule

First Day

1. Play catch upon arrival on field
2. Warm-up
   a. Run around field
   b. Group stretching exercises (10 min.)
3. Pepper game (15 min.)
4. Pitchers throw to catchers (15–20 min.)
5. Fielding drills (30 min.)
6. Covering first base (15 min.)
7. Hanging from bar (three to five seconds, two or three times)
8. Bench step-up drill (15 seconds, 10 times with each leg)
9. Running
   a. 50-yard wind sprints, or
   b. Run two complete laps (half-mile track)
10. Catchers throwing
    a. Short throws from squat position (10 throws)
    b. Long throws to second base (127 feet)

Second Day

1. Play catch
2. Warm-up
   a. Light running
   b. Group stretching exercises (10 min.)
3. Pepper game
4. Throwing to catchers
5. Fielding drills
6. Covering first base

7. Hanging from bar
8. Bench step-up drill
9. Running
10. Catchers throwing to first and third base

Third Day

1. Play catch
2. Warm-up
   a. Light running
   b. Group stretching exercises
3. Pepper
4. Throwing to catcher
5. Fielding drills (20 min.)
6. Work on pick-off plays at second base (20 min.)
7. Hanging from bar
8. Bench step-up drill
9. Running
10. Catchers throwing to first and third base

Fourth Day

1. Play catch
2. Warm-up
   a. Light running
   b. Group stretching exercises
3. Pepper
4. Fielding drills (30 min.)
5. Fielding bunts down third base line
6. Covering first base
7. Pick-off play at first and second base (20 min.)
8. Throwing to catcher (25 min.)
9. Hanging from bar
10. Bench step-up drill
11. Running
12. Catchers throwing to bases

Fifth Day

1. Play catch
2. Warm-up
   a. Light running
   b. Group exercises
3. Pepper
4. Fielding drills (30 min.)

5. Work on covering first base (20 min.)
6. Review pick-off plays at first and second (25 min.)
7. Throwing to catchers
8. Hanging from bar
9. Bench step-up drill
10. Running

Sixth Day

1. Play catch
2. Warm-up
   a. Light running
   b. Group exercises
3. Pepper
4. Review fielding drills (30 min.)
5. Work on covering first (20 min.)
6. Throwing to catchers (20–25 min.)
7. Review pick-offs at first base (15 min.)
8. Review pick-offs at second base (15 min.)
9. Hanging from bar
10. Bench step-up drill
11. Running

Second Week (Entire Squad)

First Day

1. Opening squad meeting
2. Loosening-up (playing catch and pepper) (15 min.)
3. Group warm-up
   a. Run around field
   b. Group stretching exercises (10 min.)
4. Fundamental drills: fielding ground balls (all infielders)
5. Pitchers throw hitting practice in two batting cages
6. Pitchers' (groups 3 and 4) work on pitches and control
7. Infielders' work on throwing to bases (20 min.)
8. Pitchers' work (30 min.)
   a. Pick-off play at first base
   b. Covering first base
9. Batting practice during entire practice session: infielders, outfielders and catchers in two cages (two bunts and eight cuts)
10. Infield drill (pregame routine)
    a. Get one twice
    b. Get DP twice

    c. Slow rollers
    d. Throw to home plate
11. Base running drills
12. Wind sprints (start off easily, pick up speed, then taper off)

Second Day
1. Loosening-up (play catch and pepper)
2. Group warm-up
    a. Run around field
    b. Group exercises (10 min.)
3. Fundamental drills: infielders' ground ball practice
    a. Pitchers fungo grounders to infielders (one hitter and catcher for each infield position)
    b. Infielders work on getting away throws
    c. Work on making double play (pivots and throws)
4. Bunting demonstration
5. Pitchers throw hitting practice in two batting cages (stress good bunting technique)
6. Pitchers (groups 1 and 2) work on pitches and control
7. Pitchers' work
    a. Pick-off play at first base
    b. Covering first base
8. Batting practice in two cages during entire practice session
9. Infield drill (pregame routine)
10. Running drills

Third Day
1. Loosening-up
2. Group warm-up
    a. Running
    b. Group exercises (10 min.)
3. Fundamental drills: infielders work on fielding ground balls
4. Pitchers throw batting practice (40 pitches each)
5. Pitchers' (groups 3 and 4) work on fundamentals
    a. Pick-off play at second base
    b. Fielding bunts (throwing to all bases)
    c. Covering first base
6. Sliding demonstration and practice (bent leg technique)
7. Batting practice in two cages during entire practice session
8. Infield drill (pregame routine)
9. Base running drills

Fourth Day
1. Loosening-up
2. Group warm-up
   a. Running
   b. Group exercises
3. Fundamental drills: infielders' ground ball practice
4. Batting practice
5. Pitchers' work:
   a. Review pick-off plays
   b. Covering first base
   c. Fielding bunts
   d. Work on squeeze play (with runner on third base)
6. Teach proper base running techniques
7. Batting practice during entire practice session (in two cages)
8. Infield drill (pregame routine)
9. Running drills

Fifth Day
1. Loosening-up
2. Group warm-up
   a. Light running
   b. Group exercises
3. Fundamental drills: infielders practice on grounders and double play execution
4. Instructional session on hitting to opposite field and hit and run
5. Batting practice (stress opposite field hitting)
6. Pitchers' work:
   a. Review the squeeze play (offense and defense)
   b. Defensive work on breaking up the sacrifice play at third base (runners on first and second, and no outs)
7. All players work on base running situations, i.e., double steal, bunt defense, etc. (offense and defense)
8. Infield drill
9. Base running drills
10. Wind sprints

Sixth Day
1. Loosening-up
2. Group warm-up
   a. Group exercises

3. Infield drill
4. Batting practice
5. Base running situations:
   a. Breaks and leads
   b. Double steal defense (first and third)
6. Batting tee baseball game
7. Running relays

Finance

In the great majority of schools and colleges, the baseball program must depend on financial sources other than gate receipts. While gate receipts are significant enough to assist programs at the larger schools, most contests on these levels do not charge admission. Instead, students are assessed an activity fee at the beginning of the school year, with a portion being placed in the athletic fund for baseball. Or, students may purchase an athletic card which permits them to attend all athletic contests. In other cases, the gate receipts of all sports are placed in a general athletic fund, from which a portion is allocated to baseball. Ideally, though, funds could be allocated to baseball from the regular school or P.E. budget.

Due to the meager amount of gate receipts, small schools often have to use other means to raise money. Concessions, school dances, the sale and advertising revenue derived from game programs and many other projects are all common and can work effectively.

The budget

Each year, the baseball coach prepares a budget, or a statement of the anticipated expenditures and receipts for the coming season. A budget is an estimate of costs in regard to the purchase, care and repair of equipment and uniforms; home game expense, travel, scheduling of games, medical expense, care and maintenance of the field, awards and all other expenses involved in maintaining a team.

Home games involve the expense of officials, policing and advertising expense, which must be planned so as to conform to the budget as closely as possible.

The budget is largely based on past expenditures and receipts, but changing conditions, from year to year, may require careful planning and control.

SACRAMENTO STATE COLLEGE
VARSITY BASEBALL BUDGET
Proposal #2   1970–1971

Miscellaneous Expenses	Total
Awards	$400.00
Cleaning	400.00

Publications	21.00	
Recruiting	30.00	
Scouting	20.00	
Telephone	25.00	
Oranges/cokes	50.00	
Baseball Writers' lunch	30.00	
Total Misc. Expenses		$ 976.00

Home Games

Umpires—Single games	$350.00	
Doubleheaders	630.00	
Police	320.00	
Rental—Renfree field	25.00	
Total Home Games		$1,325.00

Equipment and Uniforms

Shoes (24)	$360.00	
Caps (60)	210.00	
Batters' gloves (12)	48.00	
Catchers' leg guards (2)	30.00	
Batters' rosin bags (1 Doz.)	7.50	
Pitchers' rosin bags (1 Doz.)	2.00	
Catchers' body protectors (2)	26.00	
Undershirts (12)	72.00	
Sun glasses (4)	8.00	
Batters' rungs-donuts (4)	12.00	
Catchers' masks (2)	30.00	
Catcher's mitt, Rawlings (1)	25.00	
Catcher's mitt, Wilson (1)	25.00	
Inner hose (10 Doz.)	40.00	
Jackets, nylon (5)	75.00	
Batters' helmets (21) (7 reg., 7 left flap, 7 right flap)	192.00	
Uniforms, grey (6)	150.00	
Shirts, green sleeve (24)	144.00	
Pants, white (6)	60.00	
Baseballs (40 Doz.)	840.00	
Bats (20)	820.00	
Hose, 9″ pro-stirrup, green (60)	120.00	
Hose, striped (50)	150.00	
Home plate (1)	12.00	
Pitcher's rubber (4-sided) (1)	25.00	
Scorebooks (3)	10.50	
Bases, Hollywood (1 set)	75.00	
Total Equipment and Uniforms		$3,569.00

Games Away

Fresno State	$259.00	
University of Nevada	224.00	
University of San Francisco	196.00	
Chico State College	436.00	
University of Pacific	134.00	
Humboldt State College	988.00	
U.C. Davis	134.00	
San Jose State College	214.00	
San Francisco State	196.00	
Santa Clara	214.00	
Total Games Away		$2,995.00

TOTAL MISCELLANEOUS EXPENSES	$ 976.00
TOTAL HOME GAME EXPENSES	1,325.00
TOTAL EQUIPMENT AND UNIFORMS	3,569.00
TOTAL GAMES AWAY EXPENSES	2,995.00
	$8,865.00
TOTAL GUARANTEES PAYABLE	200.00
TOTAL REQUESTED	$9,065.00

Facilities and equipment

The type and extent of the facilities and equipment should be based on the size of the budget. However, funds for good equipment and uniforms is one of the most important factors in building a successful baseball program. There are no substitutes for top quality uniforms and equipment, but unfortunately, some school administrations limit baseball expenses by buying inferior goods, on the grounds that the sport does not pay its way.

As a rule, equipment should be purchased from representative jobbers of sporting goods from well-known manufacturers. Buying is usually made through several concerns, since no one manufacturer makes all the best equipment to fit a team's needs.

The following list of equipment and supplies has become standard for baseball programs throughout the country:

Backstop	Bats (including fungo bat)
Bat bag	Gloves
Bleachers	Rosin bags
Training room	Lockerroom (and showers)
Batting cage (portable)	Pitching machine
Catching paraphernalia	Scoreboard
Batting tee	Baseball bag
Bulletin board	Bases and home plate
Public address system	Sliding pit
Protective screens (pitcher, first base and behind second base)	Baseballs
Batters' helmets (protective)	Drinking fountain
Players' dugouts (benches)	Pitching control target
Training kit	Motion picture projector
Pitcher's plate	Indoor batting practice net

All schools and colleges should have an equipment room where equipment can be stored when not in use. The storage space should be well ventilated, dry and cool. During the playing season, an attendant takes care of the repair and laundering of equipment. Clean socks, undershirts and supporters should be available each day. Shoes should be treated with a good leather oil, while gloves and mitts should be cleaned with a good cleaner such as tetrachloride and oiled with a leather oil such as Rawlings Glovolium. Uniforms, jackets and caps should be dry-cleaned and mothproofed for storage.

Inexpensive uniforms and equipment represent a policy of false economy. Good uniforms will cost $25 to $40 each but will last for four or five years. To the contrary, cheap uniforms must be replaced about every two years and are more expensive on a cost-per-year basis. Most schools will have the players provide the most expensive single items, gloves and shoes. Items of personal equipment should include:

Personal equipment

Uniforms (and stockings)	Belt	Supporters (and cups)
Sweat shirts	T-shirts	Sliding pads
Inner hose	Jackets (warm-up)	Traveling bag
Glove	Shoes	
	Caps	

During recent years, there have been countless training aids and equipment, as well as gimmicks, made available to baseball coaches and their programs. The purpose of these aids is exactly what the word implies—to assist and aid the training and instruction of the athlete. Of course, the extent of their individual value varies with the product.

Training aids

A select number of training aids have been fortunate to receive widespread approval and use by the baseball programs, from the big leagues down through the youth leagues. The following is a list of aids which can be of value in the development and training of a baseball player:

1. Automatic pitching machines (Curvemaster, Fig. 16–7), Dudley "Olympia" and "Professional," Port-O-Pitch
2. Batting tee
3. Weighted donuts for the bat (Elston Howard)
4. Pitching spinner (Johnny Sain, Walnut Ridge, Arkansas)
5. Power-stride (Harmon Killebrew, Salt Lake City, Utah 84101)
6. Bat grips (Flexi-Grip)
7. Swing-Rite hitting net (Kenny Myers)
8. Megaphone (Fedtro); bull horn (Posey)
9. Motion picture camera (8 mm-Bolex)
10. Stop watch (Hanhart)
11. Playmaster chalkboard (Program Aids Co.)
12. Instant replay equipment (Video Logic Corp., Mountain View, Calif.)

Excellent instructional training films are available free on a loan basis from various sources throughout the country. Perhaps the largest library of 16-mm baseball films, including many World Series and All-Star game films, is the Major League Baseball Film Division,

Training films

1650 Broadway, New York, N.Y. 10019. There is a service and mailing charge of $2.00 per film for educational and charitable groups.

In addition, many major league clubs have "how-to-play" films available for community use. *Batting with Ted Williams,* rated by many as the best film on batting ever produced, can be obtained through Sears, Roebuck and Company, 7401 Skokie Blvd., Skokie, Ill. 60076.

If a movie camera (8-mm) and funds for film are available, motion pictures taken of players can be very helpful in eliminating flaws in hitting, pitching and other basic fundamentals.

Loop films are particularly effective in enabling the players to view the correct technique from start to finish. The Athletic Institute (805 Merchandise Mart, Chicago, Ill. 60654) has produced a set of 20 cartridge units of full-color 8-mm loop films which are excellent for Little League through high-school-age players.

Other Responsibilities

Scheduling of games

Most schools are in some conference or league, and games are usually scheduled at a meeting attended by representatives of all schools well before the start of the season. The respective coaches, through their athletic directors, will fill out their schedules with non-conference contests. There has been a recent trend toward more pre-season tournaments on both the college and high school levels. In addition to stimulating interest and appeal of the baseball program, they can furnish a significant means of revenue.

Agreement as to dates of the games is perhaps the major problem of such scheduling. Each team in the league will play an equal number of games at home and away. Games away from home involve travel expense, and school teams must consider time taken away from classroom work.

Most teams are able to play an average of two to four games each week throughout the season. The number of games played often depends on the material on hand, particularly the number of pitchers.

Travel policies

When traveling to out-of-town games, members of the baseball squad should keep in mind that they represent not only themselves but their school and community as well. Therefore, their standard of dress and appearance should be taken very seriously.

Among the policies adopted by many school teams when traveling are:

1. Report ahead of scheduled time. The bus will not wait.
2. No gambling whatsoever!
3. Do not take candy or food with you.
4. Wear a shirt and tie. Be neat and well-dressed.
5. Coaches will sit with their players on the bus.

6. Arrange in advance the meals at restaurants.
7. Members of the squad must eat and stay together.
8. Each player must take care of his own gear.
9. Be well-behaved on the bus going to the game.
10. Players must return with the team, unless excused by the head coach.

Study and grades

Off-season preparation by the coach also involves checking on grades, making sure his players are hitting the books and making certain that prospects are eligible for participation. Most low and failing grades are due to one or more of the following reasons:

1. Failure to study
2. Careless, sloppy, incomplete or late homework assignments
3. Goofing off, inattention in class
4. Failure to grasp or understand class material.

"A sloppy student will make a sloppy ballplayer," according to Coach Winkles. "This is why I have made it a rule never to intercede with the faculty for reinstatement of a player chopped from the squad for scholastic deficiencies."

Player notebook

The team notebook, if prepared properly, can be a very effective training aid, particularly in the coverage of areas which call for outside study and viewing. Play diagrams of the team's offensive and defensive situations are a good example of the instructional material and data which players can take home to study.

Individual coaching points on the various positions, defensive and offensive signals, team rules and regulations, tips on the prevention of illnesses, dressing room requirements and other pertinent information can appear in the notebook.

Public relations

The news media provide the principal link between the baseball coach and the public. Therefore, it is in the best interest of the coach and his program to cooperate to the fullest extent when dealing with the press and with radio and television.

Team support is directly related to the coverage of the team by the news media. Keeping the public informed and interested is the surest way to bring them out to the stadium.

In dealing with the press and radio-TV people, the baseball coach should:

1. Be honest, cooperative and fair
2. Refrain from playing favorites with reporters
3. Provide fair treatment to all media

4. Request the availability of a sports information man who can coordinate the distribution of all news
5. Never use the news media as a propaganda or psychological tool
6. Admit newsmen to the dressing room just as soon as possible after the game
7. Never expect a reporter to be a cheerleader
8. Invite reporters to attend practice sessions and meet with them after practice
9. Reserve the press box and camera locations for the working press.

Promoting the baseball program

Baseball organization, whether on the college or high school level, involves "selling" the values of baseball to the athlete, his parents, the faculty, the administration, the student body and the community. The idea that "baseball is a very worthwhile endeavor" must be promoted to the fullest.

A baseball coach has to be a salesman. He must sell not only himself but the sport as well. Therefore, he should welcome the opportunity to speak to almost any group on his program.

The following techniques should be considered by the baseball coach in promoting his program:

1. Send out weekly news releases containing information on the progress of the team.
2. Distribute information brochures to the news media and to opposing schools.
3. Inform the parents about what their sons are doing. Write to the prospects and parents. Arrange home visitations.
4. Hold an annual awards banquet, highlighted by the presentation of letters to deserving players.
5. Hold baseball clinics in the community, assisted by various players.
6. Encourage the players to watch professional contests, either in person or on TV.

Season report

A friendly relationship should exist between the baseball coach and his program with the administration and the faculty. Therefore, the administration should be provided with a complete report on the previous baseball season.

The report should include:

1. Participation
2. Success of the program
3. Failure of the program
4. Grades and attendance
5. Equipment and facilities
6. Records

7. Physical condition
8. Needs

9. Comments
10. Outlook

Building a farm system

Winning college and high school teams, typically, are blessed with a successful feeder or farm system. To be successful, the high school program must have an organized feeder system.

The foundation of a winning high school team, to a large extent, can be built years before through organized community baseball leagues such as Little League, Babe Ruth, Pony and Colt, Connie Mack and Legion ball.

Another good feeding source is the junior varsity program, which will maintain the development chain which begins in the youth programs. A jayvee schedule of 16 games against the best possible opposition will prove extremely beneficial to the varsity program.

In many instances, the success of a team in the spring depends directly upon how much baseball its members played during the previous summer.

In guiding coaches of youth programs in the community, the high school coach might emphasize the importance of the fast ball pitcher and encourage future pitching prospects to reduce the number of breaking pitches.

Stress should be given in the youth leagues to the development of a good catcher. The effectiveness of a pitching staff can diminish rapidly with the presence of an incompetent receiver. Of the remaining positions, the shortstop and the center fielder are well worth developing to the fullest.

Scouting Opponents

The more information a baseball team has about the opponent, the greater chance there is for victory. However, there is a minimum of scouting in college and high school baseball. The travel cost is perhaps the main reason, plus the fact that not too many players on the lower levels of play are capable of putting scouting information into practice. However, it can be beneficial to know the tactics of opposing teams and the various abilities of the individual players.

A "book" can be compiled on opposing hitters, listing their types and habits. For example, is he a good high ball hitter? Can he hit the breaking pitch? Is he adept at bunting?

Defense, too, can be scouted. Can the pitcher or catcher be run against? What weak links do they have in various defense situations?

When scouting a team, the individual scout must:

1. Take away the most important material he can obtain
2. Exploit the weaknesses of the team scouted
3. Above all, *never guess.*

Construction of the Diamond

The best kind of baseball can be played only on good ball fields. A well-constructed and maintained ball diamond pays off in many ways—a better brand of baseball, higher player morale and, from the crowd standpoint, greater attendance (Fig. 16–9).

Three major features are common to all good playing areas:

1. Good construction
2. Good soil structure
3. Dedicated maintenance.

Fig. 16–8. BIG LEAGUE DUGOUT. This well-constructed dugout at Arizona State University is an example of the high caliber approach which the Sun Devils have taken toward their baseball program. Right, Coach Bobby Winkles directs his team during one of their many night games at home.

Fig. 16–9. A MODEL BASEBALL FIELD. A well-constructed and maintained playing field like Harry Renfree Field in Sacramento can be a major asset to any college or high school program. Equipped with lights, the field is operated and maintained by the Sacramento Recreation and Park Department. Observe the facilities behind the backstop, which include the press box, concessions and rest rooms.

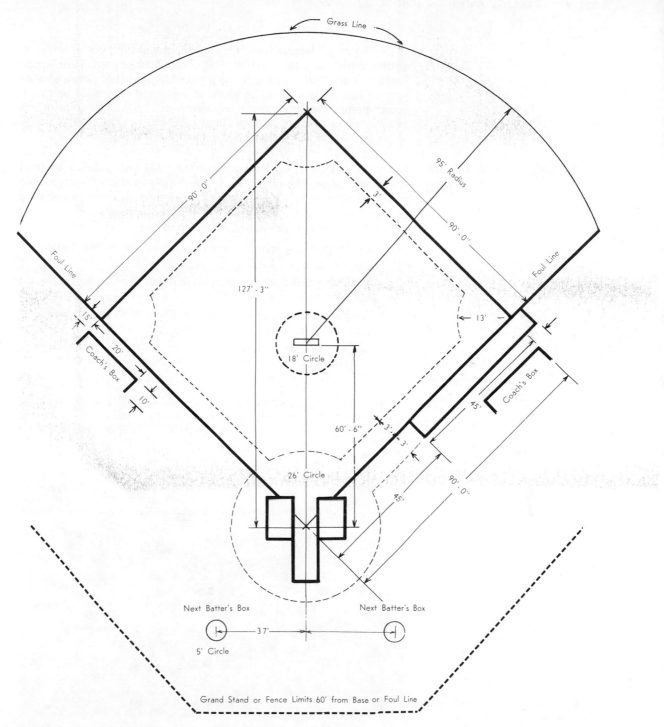

Grass Line

95' Radius

90' - 0"

90' - 0"

Foul Line

Foul Line

3'

127' - 3"

18' Circle

Coach's Box

15'

20'

10'

13'

Coach's Box

45'

60' - 6"

3'

3'

90' - 0"

26' Circle

45'

Next Batter's Box

Next Batter's Box

5' Circle

37'

Grand Stand or Fence Limits 60' from Base or Foul Line

Diagram 16–1. DIMENSIONS OF A REGULATION–SIZE DIAMOND.

On the major league level, the trend is toward the use of artificial, synthetic turf manufactured by such companies as Astro Turf, Tartan Turf and Poly-Turf. Of course, the present high cost of such a playing surface has limited its use to those schools and recreation and park departments who can afford it. However, this type of playing surface has considerable merit, and very likely in the future, the great majority of playing fields will be surfaced with artificial turf.

Maintenance of the Field

A well-maintained field for ballplayers to play and practice on is of vital importance. Nothing is more damaging to the self-confidence and development of players than to make them attempt to learn the game on a poor playing field with inferior equipment.

The qualities of a well-kept ball diamond are:

1. A field that has firm but spongy turf on which the ball will take "good hops."
2. A pitcher's box built and shaped to hold up under the pounding a pitcher gives it.
3. A batter's and catcher's area with firm footing for hitters, without the presence of deep holes.
4. Well-constructed base paths to allow for the maximum speed of runners, without leaving large divots.

Fig. 16–10. GRASS MOWERS. Pulling five mowing units, this tractor-mower is ideal for large turf areas such as a ball field, and will maintain a fast mowing schedule. The infield grass should be cut closer to the ground than the outfield grass.

Fig. 16–11. DRAGGING THE FIELD. After each practice or game, this cocoa fiber mat is effective in brushing the skinned portion of the infield, which smooths out the top soil. An occasional wetting and dragging should keep it firm but not too hard.

Fig. 16–12. LINING THE FIELD. After the home plate area has been raked, the base lines and batting boxes are lined. The wooden frame is excellent for marking the 4' x 6' boxes. The coaching boxes and on-deck batting circles are also lined, unless they are of a permanent nature.

Fig. 16–13. WATERING AND RAKING. After filling in the holes and cutting the grass, the infield area is given a good watering (20 minutes), using a spray nozzle. The pitching mound and home plate areas are then raked, resulting in a smooth and well-cushioned playing surface.

RECOMMENDED FIELD DIMENSIONS

CLASSIFICATION	Base Distance	Pitcher's Distance	LF & RF Line	Center Field	Area Size (in acres)
Little League	60 ft.	46 ft.	180 ft.	200 ft.	1¼
Pony League	75 ft.	54 ft.	250 ft.	300 ft.	2
Babe Ruth (or Senior Little League)	90 ft.	60 ft., 6 in.	300 ft.	335 ft.	3
High School, Legion or Connie Mack	90 ft.	60 ft., 6 in.	310 ft.	360 ft.	3½
College or Nonpro	90 ft.	60 ft., 6 in.	335 ft.	400 ft.	4
Professional	90 ft.	60 ft., 6 in.	335 ft.	400 ft.	4

Maintenance Equipment The following tools and equipment are recommended for proper care of the playing field:

1. Rakes (Fig. 16–13)
2. Shovels
3. Mat (cocoa-fiber, steel, rubber, etc., for dragging) (Fig. 16–11)
4. Tamper
5. Wheelbarrow
6. Tarpaulins for mound, plate and base areas
7. Drags (nail drag, etc.)
8. Float (wooden, rakelike)
9. Mowers (five-gang) (Fig. 16–10)
10. Roller (heavy)
11. Line marker (Fig. 16–12)
12. Line trough
13. Watering equipment (hose, spray nozzle, etc.)
14. Batter's box marker (wooden frame) (Fig. 16–12)
15. Chalk line
16. Edge cutter
17. Brooms
18. Tractor
19. Spreader
20. Aerifier
21. Roto-tiller
22. Verticutter
23. Sprayer with boom
24. Flame thrower (portable)

Umpiring The game of baseball demands the highest qualities of good officiating. Since he must make a decision on every single play, an umpire must be constantly alert in making repeat decisions which require consistency of judgment. The fact that he is challenged continually makes it imperative that he possess considerable endurance, mental and emotional poise.

The following qualities are considered by John W. Bunn, in his book *The Art of Officiating Sports,* to be most important in a good official:

Qualities

1. Quick reaction time
2. Confidence
3. Calmness
4. Consistency
5. Judgment
6. Cooperation
7. Integrity
8. Thorough knowledge of the rules

In addition to his familiar dark blue outfit with ample pockets for balls, an umpire needs a special protector, a mask, shin guards and special capped shoes. He should have an indicator for recording balls and strikes, and should *always* carry a rule book.

Uniform and equipment

Youth League Organization /17/

The successful operation of any youth baseball league depends largely on responsible leadership. Little League, Babe Ruth, Pony-Colt and other amateur programs have had many managers and coaches of the finest caliber, but despite the good leaders, we are all forced to admit that they have had too many poor ones. Many of them have done serious harm to their players and have given critics the opportunity to blast the programs. In my judgment, these are the people who represent the greatest threat to youth baseball programs.

Certainly, the thousands of managers, coaches, umpires, league officers and other adults who volunteer their services in youth programs deserve strong praise from the community. I would like to take this opportunity to salute the many dedicated baseball men and women who contribute their time so that youngsters can play this great game of baseball. In doing so, they are making better citizens of the boys of America.

Leadership Needs

There would be no amateur baseball without the local organization and the men who administer the local program. These gentlemen spend many hours making playing rules, raising funds, making schedules and planning for the next season.

However, without effective leadership, vision and purposeful goals, volunteer effort leaves much to be desired. Essential to good leadership is knowledge and understanding of youth. The manager or coach should have a real love for youth. He must not be the type of

When boys cease going to bed with a ball under their pillow and a bat near their bed, something will be gone forever from our American way of life.

FORD FRICK

person who must win at all costs. Rather, he should make it possible for his boys to go out on the field and have fun.

Frankly, I do not believe that a boy of Little League age should play in a national championship. It is difficult enough for him to make the adjustments needed for a city championship. As for All-Star teams, too often the right boys are not selected. Consequently, the boys who are not chosen have the feeling that they are inferior. At twelve years of age, *no* boy should be made to feel inferior. Somewhere along the line, Little League has to be changed so that young kids do not acquire a fear of inadequacy so early in life.

It is unfortunate that so many young players give up baseball as early as thirteen or fourteen years of age. These youngsters have literally been "burned out," the result of too much pressure, publicity and recognition. In many cases, the demand has been too great—from the manager, their parents and the fans.

Youth sport programs, nevertheless, are here to stay. Little League, Babe Ruth, Pony-Colt, American Legion and the other youth programs give millions of kids a chance to play baseball on organized teams, under safe conditions and under qualified leadership.

In addition to the many programs for boys, there has been a sharp increase in the number of girls playing on organized softball teams, particularly in California. Judging from the keen response, plus the fact that competitive sports for girls and women are definitely on the upswing, further growth can be expected.

Basic Attributes of a Youth Baseball Program

1. Instruction in rules
2. Basic fundamentals
3. Sportsmanship
4. Teamwork
5. Respect for others (both players and adults)
6. Promptness
7. Courtesy (obedience)
8. Fun

Play fair, win honestly, don't brag about winning or cry over losing.
BABE RUTH

Fig. 17–2. A GOOD YOUTH LEAGUE BALL FIELD takes many months of work, gifts of material and considerable labor by groups of determined people. These are the people who are willing to give their spare time and effort to realize a field of which everyone associated with the program can be proud.

A youth league manager need not be a tactical genius nor must he be an authority on child psychology, although the latter would be helpful. Managers and coaches must, however, possess leadership ability and the knowledge to work with young boys. Teamwork, good sportsmanship and discipline should be the goals of every manager and coach.

The manager must be a leader. He should be able to inspire respect. Working with youngsters requires considerable patience and understanding, above everything else. He must realize that he is entrusted with the physical, mental and emotional development of young boys (Fig. 17–3).

"The heart of Little League baseball is what happens between manager and boy," according to Dr. Arthur A. Esslinger, a distinguished physical educator and member of the Board of Directors of Little League Baseball, Inc. "It is your manager, more than any other single individual, who makes your program a success or failure. He controls the situation in which the players may be benefited or harmed.

"If Little League is to become qualitative," continued Dr. Esslinger, "then we must do something positive about improving the quality of leadership in its day-to-day operation. Just because an individual is willing to devote time to managing is not enough of a criterion upon

Qualified managers and coaches

Fig. 17-3. RESPONSIBLE LEADERSHIP. Managers and coaches must possess leadership ability and the knowledge to work with young boys. They should be able to make the boys feel at ease, that they go out on the field to have fun.

which to base his selection. Just because he knows something about baseball is likewise an inadequate basis for his selection.

"Your manager needs to know the purposes of the program, and how to evaluate progress toward attaining them. He should be acquainted with the best ways of imparting to his players what he knows about baseball. Then, there is the matter of understanding boys and how to relate to them.

"This is an age of hero worship," continued Dr. Esslinger. "If the boy chooses as a model an adult who represents the highest ideals

Fig. 17-4. THE IMPORTANCE OF WINNING should not overshadow the more important goals of Little League baseball. Teamwork, sportsmanship, discipline and having fun are program objectives which will prove far more beneficial to the boy.

Fig. 17–5. PLAY–OFF CHAMPS! While these boys stand proudly as champions, the pressure-packed road to the title did not come easily. The manner in which these youngsters coped with the pressure and emotional strain of tournament competition can very well be attributed to the leadership they had—their coaches, managers and parents.

of gentlemanly behavior and clean living, both the boy and his parents are fortunate."

When Clyde Marks took over as president of the Fruitridge Little League in Sacramento some years ago, he outlined four objectives which he wanted his players and officials to keep constantly in mind:

1. *Fundamentals*—to teach the fundamentals of baseball
2. *Sportsmanship*—to teach the boys how to win and lose
3. *Obedience*—to learn to obey their manager and coach, to respect them while under their control
4. *Fun*—to provide fun for the youngsters.

While instruction is important, coaches and managers of youth programs should also be concerned about making a player feel that he is wanted and needed. Young players should be told often that they are doing a good job. Much too often, the Little Leaguer goes to bed at night crying because he was not given the opportunity to play, or he had been bawled out for making an error.

"I can recall a district play-off when a young catcher made an error, a ball got away from him and the tying run scored," recalled Bill Avila, one of Sacramento's strongest supporters of youth baseball. "The coach got up immediately and bawled the boy out in front of 500 people. He immediately took him out of the ball game and sat him on the bench. The poor boy sat at the end of the bench, sobbing. Why couldn't he have taken the youngster out at the end of the inning? He could also have gone down and put his arm around the boy's shoulder and told him why he was taking him out.

"Another incident I can recall concerned a little boy who struck out with the bases loaded," continued Avila. "His parents shouted to him, 'Now you have to walk home!' And that boy, with tears in his eyes, walked home. This is not the type of parents or managers that we need in baseball programs involving our youth. It cannot and should not be tolerated!"

There are those who believe the umpire is the most important adult in youth baseball programs. Unquestionably, the integrity and

The umpire

We are here for the benefit of the boys, and not for the grownups' benefit.

CLYDE MARKS, *Former President*
Fruitridge Little League
Sacramento, California

stature of baseball is personified by the umpire. "His status as a volunteer, his devotion to the program and his desire to widen the scope of his own experience and knowledge has reflected creditably on Little League," stated Peter J. McGovern, President of Little League Baseball, Inc. However, finding men in the community who will accept the responsibility of umpiring is not easily accomplished.

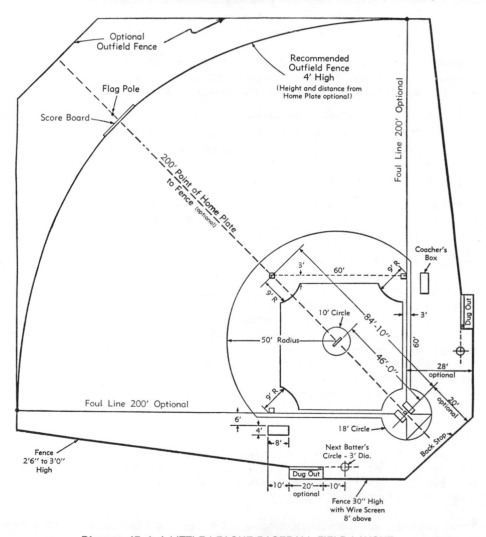

Diagram 17–1. A LITTLE LEAGUE BASEBALL FIELD LAYOUT.

The quality of leadership represents our biggest problem, and until we solve it we can never realize the full potential we have.

DR. ARTHUR A. ESSLINGER,
Member of the Board of Directors
Little League Baseball, Inc.

Fig. 17–6. THE UMPIRE is a key person in the success of any youth baseball program. Finding a capable staff of umpires should be a prime objective.

The sponsor

The sponsor is a very important man in amateur baseball. He donates the funds to purchase bats, balls and uniforms, pays entry fees and, if his team wins a local championship, it is he who donates more funds for travel and lodging when the team goes to a national or state tournament.

The objective of every youth baseball league should be to create teams of as nearly equal strength as possible. Surely, an unhealthy sign is apparent when a sponsor or manager is determined to build a "superteam," one with national championship potential. Goals of this type are not good for any young athlete, since they place too much pressure on him.

Fig. 17–7. MANY THANKS TO OUR SPONSORS. A youth baseball program could not exist without local sponsorship. Here, the Hangtown Little Leaguers of Placerville, California are treated to a preseason Ice Cream Social, at which time the many sponsors are recognized for their important contributions.

523

Role of parents

Parents, especially fathers, should take a sincere interest in the play of their boy and encourage his progress. They must not only help their boy get started in a program but, in addition, do everything within their means to make sure he derives a reasonable amount of fun and satisfaction from his participation. As long as parents, and managers, too, keep this goal in the proper perspective—that a youngster will have fun playing the game—the problems that arise will take care of themselves.

Parents should come out and enjoy the games, and not criticize their boys for their wrongdoing on the field. They should not cause any disturbance among the players or other parents.

Baseball programs for youth would be better off if parents would confine themselves to being spectators, and let the coach and manager run the team. And when his boy has a bad night, like making three errors, the father should put his arm around him and say: "Son, you just had a bad night, but even the big leaguers have bad nights. So, go to bed and forget what happened today, because, tomorrow, you might go three-for-three and make three sensational catches!"

Organizing a Local League

The impetus to start a league usually stems from a group of people who have the desire to provide a program of baseball for boys in their own neighborhood or area. By means of communication with district administrators, state directors or personnel of established leagues, prospective organizers can receive the necessary information and guidelines.

Survey the potentials

The organizing group must begin to survey its potentials. How many boys in the age bracket they have in mind reside in the area? What are the possibilities of enlisting volunteer personnel to serve as officers, managers or coaches? How about financial support? Prospective sponsors? Field facilities? If they wish to affiliate with the

Fig. 17–8. VOLUNTEER WORKERS such as this mother provide an extremely valuable service to the program. Concessions, like this one, are an excellent source of income for the local league.

national program, the rules and regulations of the national program must serve as guidelines to all future planning and procedure.

The group should make an effort to acquaint parents and the entire neighborhood or area with their intentions. By utilizing various media, they can familiarize a good number of people with the program.

League organization

The next step is organization on a firm, local basis. If enough interest was shown at the first gathering, another meeting should be called promptly, say in a week or ten days.

Naming a temporary chairman should be the first order of business at the meeting. This person should tell the group what took place at the earlier meeting, and outline the purpose of this meeting. Several committees should be formed to explore fully the total aspect of the proposed league. They will want to go into each phase of the program in detail.

The organization of a central committee should be started without delay. Membership of this committee should consist of not less than three and as many as five people. The responsibility of this committee should be to carry out the following assignments:

1. Determine the initial expense involved and the cost of field maintenance.
2. Secure the field site. Wherever possible, an entirely new field should be secured, thus adding to the recreational facilities of the community. However, existing facilities can be re-designed effectively.
3. Develop the field for play in accordance with league rules and requirements.
4. Procure field equipment—bases, home plate, pitcher's plate, etc.

To keep costs down, it is advisable for the central committee to select adult members who can perform some of the necessary work to equip the field for play.

The committee should first survey the possibility of several sites, and consider the cost of developing, maintaining and equipping them. Their findings should be reported back to a general meeting for approval or rejection. The whole group should be given an opportunity to approve or disapprove the recommendations of the committee.

Once the recommendations are approved, the committee should be authorized to negotiate for the purchase or loan of the area. Additional authorization should be given to spend the necessary amount of money that the committee decides is needed to develop the field.

Each league must have a field on which the teams can play at least for certain periods during the day. If they should join forces with another league, an agreement should be made as to sharing the labor and cost of maintaining the field.

If at all possible, the league should obtain its own field (Fig. 17–2). Certainly, the use of a diamond laid out for other age groups will work a hardship on the league. Even though it may cause some strain on league resources, every effort should be made to acquire a permanent field.

Ideally, the field should be laid out so that the setting sun is shining from first base toward third base. A grass infield, of course, is most desirable, in which the base paths are surfaced with sandy loam.

The regulation Little League diamond is complete with dugouts, bleachers, concession stand, public address system, home run barrier and a fence that completely encircles the field to protect it. The typical playing field takes many months of work, gifts of material and considerable labor.

Administration of the league

Each league should elect five officers—president, vice president, secretary, treasurer and player agent. All officers should be members of the league's board of directors.

Board of Directors

The management of the property and affairs of the local league should be vested in the board. The number of directors should be not less than five nor more than 15. The board membership shall include the officers, including a player agent, and a minimum of one manager and one volunteer umpire. The board shall have the power, by a two-thirds vote of those present at any regular or special meeting, to discipline, suspend or remove any director, officer or committee member of the league.

President

The president presides at league meetings, and assumes full responsibility for the operation of the local league.

Vice president

The vice president presides in the absence of the president, and works with other officers and committee members.

Secretary

The secretary records the minutes of meetings, and is also responsible for sending out notices of regular and special meetings.

Treasurer

The treasurer signs checks, dispenses league funds as approved by the president or vice president, reports on the status of league funds, keeps local league books and financial records and prepares budgets.

Player agent

The player agent conducts the annual player selection system, and assists the president in checking birth records and eligibility of

The major objective of a Little League is to provide fun for the young-sters.

AL ROSEN

players. The player agent or another league official should be designated as safety officer, to enforce and maintain the safety code.

League constitution

Each league should adopt a constitution to suit its own needs. The constitution should spell out such things as administration, membership, qualifications, financial policy and meetings.

One other step that should be considered is incorporation. Incorporating a local league will give it a degree of permanency and stability otherwise lacking. A corporation is a convenient means of holding title to any real or personal property which the league may own. As a general rule, incorporation relieves the officers and managers of personal liability for damages as a result of injuries to spectators or other mishaps. Those individuals who are personally and directly responsible for the injury may, however, remain liable.

Financing the League

A very important phase of planning is providing the necessary financial support for the league. Every possible source of financial assistance should be explored in order to maintain and operate the league. Needless to say, good judgment should be the guide in raising funds and making expenditures.

It takes a significant amount of money to keep a local youth league in operation. In a typical Babe Ruth League, for instance, nearly $10,000 is expended annually by some 20 teams to pay for baseballs, bats and other equipment, umpires, scorekeepers and other related expenses.

Generally, representatives of business firms, service clubs or other organizations will volunteer to sponsor teams in the league. The responsibilities of these sponsors should be explained, and after screening them, they should be recommended to the committee.

The backbone of Little League or any other youth baseball program is *local sponsorship.* Unquestionably, the program could not exist without this support. Funds for baseballs, bats, uniforms and other equipment are furnished by the sponsor. However, the sponsor does not own or govern the team he sponsors. Neither should he be an influence in the selection of team managers.

If sponsors do not volunteer at first, it is the duty of the finance committee to contact potential sponsors and offer them the privilege of sponsorship, subject to the approval of all league members. However, businesses engaged in the sale of such products as beer, liquor, tobacco and other goods considered detrimental to youth, are not acceptable as sponsors.

The bulk of the local league's funds will come from its sponsors. As a rule, the cost of sponsorship for each team is about $300 the first year and somewhat less each year after that. In return, the sponsoring business or organization has its name on 15 uniforms, plus other benefits. In addition to uniforms and equipment, the charter should include blanket accident insurance protection (about $18 per team) and public liability insurance.

There are any number of ways to raise money in the community. If necessary, the league may decide to pass the hat at all games, with the proceeds being used to improve the playing field. Charging admission, though, is against the policy of Little League and many other youth programs. It is further recommended that teams not ask their sponsors for additional funds once the season is under way.

There are two other excellent sources of income: the concessions stand at the field, and advertising on the outfield fences, in the program and score cards. Those who provide the money will receive advertising space on the fences and in the programs.

During the second year of operation, however, the league will have less equipment to buy because many items will not need to be replaced. The third year, the expense will run higher, as some uniforms and equipment will need replacing.

Public Relations

The purpose of public relations is to keep the league before the public in its best image. It should be the aim of the publicity director, therefore, to make the league known within the community.

The chief responsibility of the publicity director is to collect news and prepare it for presentation by news and sports editors of the local newspapers and on radio and television news programs. He should also strive to encourage community interest in the program by whatever means are available to him. It should be mentioned, however, that public relations is, in one sense, the responsibility of *all* league officers and personnel.

Printed statements should be released to all news media simultaneously, typewritten and double spaced. Stories must have reader interest or news value. Never should a publicity man argue with the editor about publishing a story. As his league grows, it will grow in interest to the community, thus getting better coverage by the news media.

The following are examples of news stories which may be released:

1. Listing of a complete playing schedule for each team.
2. Description of field location, facilities for parking, seating and list of game times.
3. Opening day program story, including team rosters showing the boys' names, ages, addresses, uniform numbers and positions.
4. After each game, the box scores, plus highlights of the game, should be released to all newspapers and radio stations.

Fig. 17–9. EVERYONE PLAYS! The best public relations slogan any program can have is "Participation for all." Every youngster should have the opportunity to play at least one inning, including one time at bat.

5. Events which might produce unfavorable publicity should be discussed with league officials as soon as they occur, and then any necessary facts should be given to the press.

The Tryout Plan

One of the key factors in the success of any youth baseball program is a tryout plan that provides the necessary balance of teams in the league. This plan is based on five tests, in which players are selected for teams on the basis of points. Effort should be made to divide the players so that teams are well-balanced as to players with hitting, running, fielding, pitching and throwing abilities.

Each youngster who indicates a desire to try out for the league should have an opportunity to do so. Registration dates should be announced well in advance of the tryout periods, and every effort must be made to communicate with the parents of boys in the appropriate age group.

The league should require all candidates to have physical examinations. No boy should be allowed to play on a team unless he has passed a physical examination.

Fig. 17–10. MAXIMUM SAFETY should be given a youth baseball program. The protective helmet should be worn on the base paths as well as at bat. Observe the mandatory rubber-cleated shoes worn by this Little League catcher. Little League, Inc. has its own research laboratory, under the direction of Dr. Creighton J. Hale, who has done extensive research and testing on all aspects relative to the well-being of young players.

Minor Leagues

The purpose of the Minor League program is to provide training and instruction for those boys who, by reason of age and maturity, or who lack sufficient skills, do not qualify for selection in the regular Little League.

According to Little League rules, any boy who will reach the age of eight years before August first and who will not attain the age of thirteen years before August first shall be eligible to compete. A boy whose name appears on a major league roster shall not be permitted to play with a minor league team.

The Minor League program is the responsibility of the chartered Little League. It must be restricted to the boundaries of the local league, and its players are subject to selection by draft or auction by any team of the local league.

Daily Practice

Practice sessions should be organized so that no one is standing around with nothing to do. The players should shift from one drill to another at frequent intervals. Different drills should be used from day to day to maintain the interest of the boys. The coach should encourage his players to "talk it up" during the practice, including words of encouragement. The players should not have to stand around and listen to their coach talk for long periods of time. Above all, practice should be *lively,* and it should be *fun.*

If practice has been scheduled for 9:30 A.M., it should start *exactly* at 9:30 A.M. Practice should not be held up for two or three players who are late in arriving. On the other hand, it should end approximately as scheduled.

Upon arriving at the field, the players should be encouraged to loosen-up by playing catch or engaging in a pepper game. Those who participate in the pepper game should take turns batting and fielding. The batter should choke up on the bat, and merely punch the ball.

Batting practice

Having a pitcher who can get the ball over the plate is essential to a good batting practice. The chief concern of the manager is keeping the practice moving at a brisk pace without players losing interest in what is going on. The players should hit in their regular batting order.

Generally, each player might lay down two sacrifice bunts, take three swings, and then try to beat out a bunt for a base hit. However, batters on the Little League level should not be restricted to a certain number of swings. Limiting the number of swings often places undue pressure on the poorest hitters, who need the practice the most. In fact, a youngster may need a dozen swings to hit one ball.

After running to first base, he should stay on first and break for second when the next batter bunts the ball. Once he gets to second, he should repeat this procedure until he reaches third, and finally home.

Typical Practice Schedule	
Opening message	5 minutes
Warm-up	10 minutes
Base running	10 minutes
Batting practice	10 minutes
Play situations	35 minutes
Announcements	5 minutes

Only the next two hitters should be awaiting their turn at bat, taking their practice swings. The rest of the squad should be in the field, retrieving the batted balls. The reserve players should be given numbers in the batting order. Every player should take an active part in batting practice. An extra pitcher should feed balls to the batting practice pitcher, while the players rotate as coaches.

Between pitches, an experienced coach can fungo ground balls to the infielders, while another coach might do the same thing with the outfielders. Caution should be taken never to hit a ball at the same time the batter is swinging, to prevent two balls being hit to a fielder at the same time.

Drills involving play situations can be enjoyable and helpful to the team. The coach should place a team in the field and use his extra players as base runners. He can set up any kind of situation he might encounter in a regular contest. For example, he can tell his players that the score is tied in the last half of the final inning, with a runner on second and one out. One variation of this drill is to set a batting tee in front of home plate, and the batter can hit the ball off the tee with one or more runners on base.

In conducting infield and outfield drills, the coach should try to build confidence in his players. Therefore, he should try to hit balls they can handle easily. While the infield drill is taking place, a coach should be hitting fly and ground balls from the foul territory behind third base to the outfielders. He should alternate hitting the ball to their left, right, in front of and behind them. An extra pitcher or catcher might be positioned halfway to catch the balls thrown in by the fielders.

The final five minutes of practice should be devoted to the few announcements that must be made. Before he begins, the manager should instruct his team to be seated. He will receive better attention this way. The most important announcement is the time of the next practice or ball game. He should announce the date, reporting time and playing field several times, since some inattentive youngsters have a habit of not hearing what is said.

Amateur Baseball Programs

Little League Baseball, Inc.
P.O. Box 1127
Williamsport, Pa. 17701
(9–12, 13–15, 16–18)

Babe Ruth Baseball
524½ Hamilton Ave.
Trenton, N.J. 08609
(13–15, 16–18)

Boys' Baseball, Inc.
Washington, Pa. 15301
(Bronco: 11–12; Pony: 13–14;
Colt: 15–16)

American Amateur Baseball Congress
P.O. Box 5332
Akron, Ohio 44313
(Stan Musial: unlimited age; Connie Mack: 18-under;
Mickey Mantle: 16-under; Sandy Koufax: 14-under;
Pee Wee Reese: 12-under)

American Legion Baseball
P.O. Box 1055
Indianapolis, Ind. 46206
(18-under)

Dixie Youth Baseball
P.O. Box 222
Lookout Mountain, Tenn. 37350

National Baseball Congress
Box 1420
Wichita, Kansas 67201

National Amateur Baseball Federation, Inc.
1929 Addaleen Drive
Milford, Mich. 48042
(Soph.: 17-under; Jr.: 19-under; Sr.: open)

Fig. 17–11. BOBBY–SOX PROGRAMS. With the emphasis on more competitive sports for girls and women, a sharp increase in the number of female softball programs is taking place in America. One of the most avid participants of the opposite sex is Kim Ogle, granddaughter of manager Walter Alston.

Tournament Play

Tournament play, for those teams fortunate enough to participate, provides a memorable climax to regular season play. As we stated earlier, state and national tournament action places undue emotional strain and pressure on young boys and girls. However, it does provide the players whose teams qualify with the opportunity to round out their career in the program with new experiences of travel and associations.

Much of the responsibility in postseason play rests with the adults who supervise, conduct, manage or carry out some other role. The tournament director, of course, has complete jurisdiction in the conduct of the competition. Playing rules for the tournament, however, may vary slightly from those of conventional local league competition. Responsibility for establishing league age and residence of players who comprise the tournament teams rests with the league president.

Yuma Boys Baseball

The city of Yuma, Arizona has gained the recognition of having one of the finest baseball programs for youth in America (Fig. 17–12). Interestingly enough, the program is organized at the playground level and is not associated with the national program of Little League baseball. Yuma Boys Baseball is sponsored and under the direct supervision of the City of Yuma Recreation and Park Department.

During the 1970 season, a total of 1,000 boys playing on 54 teams saw action in the four-division league, each with a major and minor league. The rapidly expanding program did not just happen. A great amount of time and hard work has gone into the organization of such a program. Behind the Yuma program is a group of men, including 108 coaches, who volunteer their time and energies to the task of organizing the leagues. Many of the most-valued volunteers have been involved in this activity for several years.

Fig. 17–12. YUMA'S BASEBALL COMPLEX provides an ideal area of operation for a baseball program. Four big league diamonds are kept busy throughout the spring and summer. This modern $500,000 playing site is also the home of the San Diego Padres for their spring training.

The final interpretation of all rules is under the direction of the Yuma Recreation and Park Department. These rules shall not be interpreted in any way as to conflict with the objectives of the Department. The objectives of the program are:

1. To develop fair play and sportsmanship
2. To develop skills in baseball
3. To develop team spirit
4. To develop health in body and mind
5. To develop an understanding of and respect for the rules
6. To develop self-control over emotions and speech
7. To develop responsibility
8. To develop democratic and American ideals
9. To encourage fun and enjoyment.

According to the Yuma officials, the most important factor in conducting a sound, wholesome baseball program is the quality of leadership to which youth are subjected. Therefore, the type of person the team coach or manager is—that is, his actions, habits, attitudes and character—may be a good or poor influence.

More than any other factor, these leaders determine whether an activity helps the players learn sportsmanship and fair play, or whether it actually contributes to unsportsmanlike attitudes and conduct. "There are no inherent good things concerning baseball," explained Brent Marchetti, director of the Yuma Recreation and Park Department. "How the game is *conducted* is what counts!"

An important feature of the Yuma Boys Baseball League is the spring training program which is conducted three days weekly, 4:30 P.M. to 6:00 P.M., from March 9 through April 17, at four city playgrounds. Supervised by experienced coaches who possess a strong knowledge of the game and of youth, the boys are taught the following basic fundamentals:

1. Throwing
2. Catching
3. Fielding
4. Fly ball catching
5. Batting
6. Sliding (only the bent leg slide).

According to Conrad Lujan, program supervisor, "The five-week training program plays an extremely valuable role in the development of our players."

Teams in the Yuma Boys program are formed in each area after spring training and tryouts. The number of teams that will be formed in each area will depend on the number of boys wishing to participate.

Officials of the program demand that teams be formed as equally as possible in all respects. Major league players are placed on teams by means of a draft conducted by the Yuma Recreation and Park Department and selected by the coaches of the various teams. Minor league players are placed on teams at the discretion of the area supervisors and the Recreation and Park Department.

Player draft

The player draft rules in the Yuma program apply only to major league teams. All coaches and managers participate in the spring training sessions so that they may become familiar with, and be able to evaluate personally, each boy who is eligible for the draft.

During spring training and prior to the draft, the player agent prepares a list of all eligible candidates to be distributed to the coaches and managers of the various teams. Players are drafted first according to age. All twelve-year-old players are drafted first, followed by the eleven- and ten-year-olds.

Each manager or coach is numbered in reverse order to the position which his team held in the final standings at the close of the preceding season. In case of a tie in the final standings, the number for the draft selection is decided by a draw, and thereafter, the teams alternate in each round.

Awards

Trophies are given to all-city championship and runner-up teams, while individual certificates are awarded to the boys who participated on each championship team. In addition, at the conclusion of the All-Star Invitational Tournament, team trophies and individual certificates are awarded to the champion, runner-up, third-place and sportsmanship winners.

Epilogue

The game of baseball, in contrast to the significant and sometimes dramatic changes in football and basketball during the past fifty years, has remained relatively much the same as when the old-timers played in the ''golden twenties.'' Interestingly enough, the playing rules and regulations of baseball have changed very little from the days of Babe Ruth, Rogers Hornsby and Lefty Grove.

True, the tactics and strategy, offensively and defensively, have varied through the years relative to emphasis and application, and the athlete himself has changed with the times and the various physiological, psychological and sociological factors that affect him.

Perhaps the biggest changes have been in the execution of the many fundamental techniques, influenced largely by individual styles, playing conditions and the type of strategy and tactics employed by the managers and coaches.

The bat and ball very definitely have experienced alterations through the years. The thick-handled, heavier bat used by the old-timers has been replaced by the modern thin-handled, whiplike bat, lighter in weight. Indications are that more hitters today are reverting to a heavier, thicker-handled bat to get more wood on the ball.

From 1920, when the lively ball was introduced, and up to the present era, there has been a variance in the liveliness of the ball. Perhaps no one but the manufacturer knows whether the balls are juiced up, deadened or the resiliency characteristics of the yarn used. At any rate, the general feeling today is that the ball is livelier than it has ever been, and will become even more so in the future.

The gloves of the players, particularly, have changed greatly in size and quality. They are much larger and provide a webbing which adds to the sureness of the catch. Furthermore, the playing fields today are much superior to those used by the old-timers, and the new artificial surfaces promise to give bounces truer than ever. Outfielders, when playing on artificial turf, very likely will have to play a little deeper due to the quickness in which ground balls skip up the alleys.

Indeed, 1921 was a memorable year, in which the lively ball and Babe Ruth created a home run craze that has influenced the game significantly ever since. Through the years, the desire to hit home runs has been universal. But even though the home run has been an exciting play, particularly when it means the ball game, it is actually over too quickly to make an ordinary inning exciting.

The main excitement of baseball, then, is in aggressive base running, fine fielding plays and extra base hits in which the speeding runner attempts to arrive ahead of the thrown ball. More base hits result in more runners on base, and therefore more action. Aggressiveness on the base paths, such as Maury Wills stealing second base or a successful theft of home by Rod Carew, has given the game the same dynamic stimulation as electrifying fielding plays by Brooks Robinson and Wes Parker.

Yet, there have been periods in baseball history, such as the 1960s, when pitching has dominated the game. Sandy Koufax, Bob Gibson and Tom Seaver are good examples of hurlers who have handcuffed opposing hitters with their overpowering stuff. With the frequent use of relief pitchers, today the batter seldom faces a tired pitcher. In fact, the domination of the hitter by the pitcher may have taken away some spectator interest because the fan likes runs.

No wonder, then, that baseball has tried to help the hitter—shorter fences, a smaller strike zone, a lower mound, even restrictions on the pitcher by preventing him from wetting his fingers. Since hitting makes baseball exciting, the game has encouraged hitting.

Batting

Desire for power by the hitters characterized the decades of the 1950s and 1960s. Hitters generally found themselves going for the long ball. Consequently, many of them hurt themselves by employing a big arc in their swing, as opposed to the shorter, compact swing which concentrated on contact.

Prior to World War II, there were quite a few hitters content with making good contact and spraying the ball to all fields. High averages from .350 to .400 were common throughout the 1920s and 1930s, as batters concentrated on hitting the line drive and just getting on base.

As baseball moved into the 1950s, however, the era of the long ball emerged, and with it came a rash of home runs. The livelier ball, a stronger athlete, thin, whiplike bats and shorter fences all were felt

Fig. E–2. BATTING (Tony Gonzales).

to be responsible for the home run derby—highlighted by Roger Maris, who belted 61 home runs in 1961.

This dramatic change from the shorter, compact swing to the long, hard arc resulted in many home runs but, unfortunately, brought with it large numbers of strikeouts. The home run craze produced a hitter who took a full rip regardless of the situation. Furthermore, it failed to meet the challenge of the better equipped pitcher who had accumulated more knowledge and new deliveries, plus the availability of the late-inning stopper doing his specialty. It is easy to see that all of these factors had their effect on the batting averages.

The hitter's never-ending desire to swing for the fences was not the only factor in enabling pitchers to dominate the game. More games under the lights, a more knowledgeable pitcher with more pitches, such as the slider, screwball and sinker, a stronger defense blessed with greater speed and superior gloves and a smoother playing field for the defense to maneuver on, all have worked to the advantage of the pitcher.

Fortunately, the hitters, with the aid of their hitting instructors (and the rulemakers), are doing something to put some punch back into the game. While the long ball will still be with us, more hitters are moving up on the bat, hitting the ball where it is pitched, and going for the opposite field. Baseball's top hitters today are concentrating more on line drives, swinging slightly down on pitches and stroking balls through the holes of the infield. More hitters are shortening up on their stroke and working for contact, punching the ball if necessary.

539

Since the early 1960s, when Maury Wills popularized the practice of swinging from both sides of the plate, switch-hitting has been playing an increasingly greater role in baseball. Players who have good running speed and are not blessed with great power, make good prospects for switch-hitting, particularly if they can make good contact with the ball consistently.

Offensive Strategy

Managers and coaches of the modern era have been more power-conscious than their predecessors. The hit-and-run and sacrifice plays have been used with less frequency, with base stealing coming to the front as an offensive move. As a rule, more teams are playing for the big inning. The bunting game and playing for one run have been used less and less.

Pinch hitters are being used with greater frequency. Left-handed swingers are sent up against right-handed pitchers, and right-handers against southpaw pitchers. Likewise, left- and right-handed hitters are being platooned with increasing regularity. By substituting frequently, managers create the opportunity to have their best players in the lineup in crucial situations.

Modern baseball's most successful teams have utilized an aggressive attack, exerting continuous pressure on the defense. Of course,

Fig. E-3. DOUBLE PLAY (Tito Fuentes throwing, Lou Brock running).

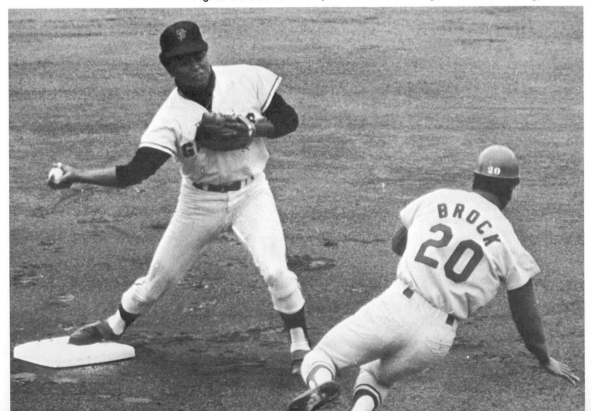

the type of offense used has been based on the type of club, whether it be power or speed.

The drag bunt, clever and daring base running, and skillful sliding are modern offensive methods and techniques that have developed fast-moving situations which cause mechanical and mental errors by the defense. The element of threats has proved to be effective in keeping the defense off-balance and unsettled.

Pitching

The best pitcher in baseball is still the pitcher who has a little something extra on the fast ball. Indeed, the king of all pitches is still the fast ball. The modern pitcher has more pitches with which to keep the batter off-balance. In general, there are more pitchers today with more pitches, and with more balls thrown at different speeds. The increased use of the slider and other breaking pitches such as the sinker, screwball and knuckleball have influenced play. The slider and the greater control of breaking pitches have made batting much tougher. The pitcher who has four different pitches and can change speeds on most of them will have the advantage over most hitters.

Relief pitchers are being used to a greater extent today. The percentage of the hitters who have to face a new pitcher and adjust to his pitches has placed the advantage in favor of the pitcher. A strong

Fig. E–4. PITCHING (Tom Seaver, N. Y. Mets).

Fig. E–5. AGGRESSIVE SLIDING AT HOME PLATE (John Mayberry).

bullpen has become a prerequisite for winning.

In addition to the starters, most pitching staffs have long-relief men, short-relief men and spot-situation men. Quite often, the starter is not expected to go the distance. Therefore, he is told to go all-out until he gets tired. Then, there will be someone else to take over the mound chores.

Defensive Strategy

Defense is still the key to a sound and solid baseball team. The team that makes the fewer errors or mistakes in fielding and throwing will normally be the team that wins the game.

Beyond the pitching, the ingredients of a sound defense are speed and good ground coverage. The top defensive teams are still those teams that have the ability to execute the basic fundamentals of defense effectively. As it was years ago, the secret of defense is to be strong straight down the middle.

A more effective pitcher, more knowledgeable, with better control and possessing more types of pitches and speeds, perhaps has been the major factor in a stronger defense.

Game Conduct

The chief complaint among baseball critics is that the games are too long. When more runs are scored, which is what the majority of the fans like, the games are longer. Still, there are too many time-consuming delays which can very well be eliminated.

If our officials would enforce the rules and demand that players be ready at all times, this problem could be solved. The pitcher, for instance, need not remain in the dugout until his time to bat. He should be in the on-deck circle, like everyone else.

Since the conduct of a ball game rests to a large degree on the umpires, every effort should be made to provide the most able and qualified umpiring possible. Unquestionably, the quality of umpiring is a key factor in the success of baseball programs on all levels of play.

Training Methods

Baseball training methods are more scientific today than ever before, with more and more instruction on fundamentals. Baseball is obtaining more coaches and managers who can teach and are capable of communicating and imparting knowledge.

The widespread use of pitching machines, batting cages and nets has been a significant change through the years. This has enabled far more players to get in more hitting in a shorter period of time and in a smaller space, indoors as well as outside. In addition, the batters can be watched from different angles at a closer distance.

Baseball, in the 1930s and 1940s, was still a game taught by throwing a ball and hitting it. Then, during the late 1940s and early 1950s, pitching machines, targets and batting cages came into use; by the 1960s, every team had them. More gimmicks are being used to aid the players in their training. Batting tees, pitching targets, weights and exercisers, and spinners are just a few examples.

New video replay instructional equipment is now available to baseball teams to speed the training of the players.

Conditioning

The successful teams in baseball today are giving their players vigorous and steady doses of stretching and strengthening exercises and considerable running. They are following a more effective conditioning program throughout the season, from spring training until the World Series.

Increased emphasis on conditioning has given the game of baseball a much needed "shot in the arm," particularly at a time when demands are being made to speed up the game, to add more aggressiveness, speed and hustle. There is a noticeable trend among coaches and managers to supplement actual game experience with special conditioning exercises.

The Modern Athlete

Baseball is better today because athletes are bigger, stronger and faster than their counterparts of two and three decades ago. This can be attributed largely to a better diet from birth, superior coaching and improved training methods. The typical young professional athlete very likely has had considerably more competitive game experience than the old-timers.

While size and strength are important essentials in baseball performance, speed, agility and quick reflexes are of greater importance today. Speed has proven to be extremely valuable, both offensively and defensively. Some of baseball's best teams have achieved success largely through exceptional speed.

Equipment

The overall quality of fielding today has become better because of larger and improved gloves. More plays are executed with one hand, particularly at first base and at home plate. The one-handed catch is now accepted, although it can be overdone and result in a lazy catcher who is unwilling to shift his feet properly.

Facilities

Smoother playing fields have resulted in superior fielding to that achieved by fielders 25 years ago. The ball takes a truer hop on a smooth field and results in a more positive, confident fielder.

Playing fields with fast artificial turf have favored speed and the hitters. In fact, some observers feel artificial turf will add 20 points to a good hitter's average, since the ball gets through the infield so quickly.

Lowering the pitching mound from fifteen inches to a maximum of ten inches has favored the hitter. Normally, pitchers have been more effective when throwing from a higher mound in which the angle of the pitched ball is more difficult to follow.

Forecasting the Future

Since the spectators like a run-scoring game, there will very likely be more high-scoring games in baseball. The average spectator would prefer to see more base hits, not necessarily home runs, because the result is more runners on base and therefore more action. The general opinion is that the game is too slow, with some games taking as long as three and four hours. Therefore, the prime concern should be to speed up the tempo of the game and still provide plenty of thrills and action.

Fig. E-6. RUN–DOWN PLAY (Wes Parker throwing).

An aggressive offense will be the goal of every team, as managers and coaches strive to take advantage of all the speed and power they can secure. A multiple attack will be used—the power swing and the short compact stroke, daring base running and skillful use of the bunt—all designed to exert continuous pressure on the defense.

Hitters will be going after the average and concentrating more on singles and doubles. Instead of the uppercut swing, they will be trying to develop a more level swing or even swinging slightly down on pitches above the waist. Good contact on the ball will be the prime concern of the hitter.

The arts of base running and bunting will be improved. Players who possess speed and quickness will use an occasional drag or push bunt to get on base. More running and hustle will be demanded of the players, even when going out and coming in from their positions. On the intentional pass, the hitter will move immediately down to first base without the traditional four wide pitches.

Baseball will become even more specialized. In the big leagues, and on down through the youth leagues, there will be more platooning and lineup changes during the game. In fact, a substitute batter will be allowed to hit for the pitcher, without the pitcher having to leave the game. A warm-up cage will be available for the pinch hitter, similar to the bullpen for the relief pitcher.

Coaches and managers will continue to use relief pitchers frequently. Pitching staffs will continue to have relievers for long, short and spot-situation assignments. However, pitchers will be directed to make their pitches with less time between pitches, and a clock will be available to enforce this rule. Bullpens will be closer to the infield, or a motor scooter will be used to transport relief pitchers to the mound.

A strong defense will still have its strength down the middle, with speed and range being the key essentials. A smooth double play combination will continue to be the dream of every coach.

Coaches will offer, in their training programs, greater repetition of fundamentals through a more organized practice schedule. As in football, more drills will operate throughout the practice session, but in addition to the competitive element, fun and enjoyment must always be a part of the game.

While many coaches have indicated a need for changes in baseball, there are those who still like the game as it is, explaining that, ''It's the main reason it holds its tradition as the national pastime.''

Index

C